AF654494

Empowerment of Rural Women in Developing Countries

About the Editor

T. Haque is a well known Agricultural Economist. He obtained his Ph.D. degree from Patna University (India) and Post Doctoral training from Iowa State University, Ames, U.S.A. Dr. Haque is currently Director, Council for Social Development, New Delhi and Senior Adviser, LANDESA (formerly Rural Development Institute), New Delhi. Earlier he served as Chairman, Commission for Agricultural Costs and Prices, Govt. of India, ICAR National Fellow at the National Centre for Agricultural Economics and Policy, New Delhi and Director, Centre for Agrarian Studies, NIRD, Hyderabad. He also served as consultant to several international organizations, including FAO, ILO and The World Bank. Dr. Haque is author of six books and about 100 research papers and reports. His areas of specialization are land reform, food security and sustainable agriculture and rural development.

EMPOWERMENT OF RURAL WOMEN IN DEVELOPING COUNTRIES

Challenges and Pathways

Edited by

T. Haque

Published for

All India Women's Conference

&

Council for Social Development

CONCEPT PUBLISHING COMPANY PVT. LTD.
NEW DELHI-110059

© Editor

All rights reserved. No part of this work may be reproduced, stored, adapted, or transmitted in any form or by any means, electronic, mechanical, photocopying, micro-filming recording or otherwise, or translated in any language, without the prior written permission of the copyright owner and the publisher. The book is sold subject to the condition that it shall not, by way of trade or otherwise, be lent, resold, hired out, or otherwise circulated without the prior publisher's written consent in any form of binding or cover other than that in which it is published.

The views and opinions expressed in this book are author(s) own and the facts reported by them/her have been verified to the extent possible, and the publishers are not in any way liable for the same.

ISBN-13: 978-93-5125-109-5

First Published 2015

Published and Printed by

Concept Publishing Company Pvt. Ltd.
A/15-16, Commercial Block, Mohan Garden
New Delhi-110059 (India)
T: 25351460, 25351794, *F*: 091-11-25357109
E: publishing@conceptpub.com, W: www.conceptpub.com
Editorial Office: H-13, Bali Nagar, New Delhi-110 015, India.

Cataloging in Publication Data--*Courtesy:* D.K. Agencies (P) Ltd. <docinfo@dkagencies.com>

International Summit on Empowerment of Rural Women (2013 : New Delhi, India)
Empowerment of rural women in developing countries : challenges and pathways / edited by T. Haque.
p. cm.
Includes bibliographical references and index.
ISBN 9789351251095

1. Women in rural development--India--Congresses. 2. Women in rural development--Developing countries--Congresses. 3. Women in rural development--Government policy--India--Congresses. 4. Women in rural development--Government policy--Developing countries--Congresses. 5. Women's rights--India--Congresses. I. Haque, T. (Tajamul), 1947- II. Title.

DDC 305.420954 23

Foreword

Although gender disparity has affected the lives of women both from the urban and rural sectors yet the impact is visible more on rural women in view of the circumstances, conditions and difficulties in accessing resources and services and decision-making opportunities.

Empowering rural women economically is an essential part of realizing their rights. Economic empowerment goes hand in hand with social and political empowerment. In most of the rural areas, the primary symbol of wealth and respect is owning cultivable land and/or cattle. When a woman earns and saves enough to buy either one on her own, or starts earning through other means, she automatically gains immense respect and voice in her family and within the community.

However, often when a woman earns, control over her earnings rests with the male members of the family. She has no freedom to spend her earnings as she wishes.

Several policies and programmes of the Government have aimed at women's advancement in different spheres; still there is a wide gap between the policies and their implementation. There is a need for a balanced approach on achieving gender equality and empowering women.

The Beijing Platform for Action commits to ensure women's equal access to economic resources, including land, credit, science and technology, vocational training, information, communication and market, as a means to further the advancement and empowerment of women and girls.

AIWC, continuing its mission of empowering women, specially focusing on rural women, is striving for a better quality of life through sustainable livelihood, providing skills and opportunities to rural women to become economically self-sufficient.

The priority theme of the 56th session of the Commission on the Status of Women (CSW) in March 2012 was "Empowerment of Rural Women and Their Role in Poverty and Hunger Eradication". AIWC conducted a side event on "Empowerment of Rural Women in South Asia – an NGO Experience" on 29th February, 2012 during the CSW56 Meeting in New York.

All India Women's Conference (AIWC) collaborated with Council for Social Development (CSD) and organized an International Summit on Empowerment of Rural Women to elaborate on the challenges and threats to economic empowerment of rural women and to identify practical actions for accelerating rural women's economic empowerment, narrowing down the gap between urban and rural women.

The report narrates the views expressed by eminent experts from national and international organizations and puts forth some recommendations for consideration by the policy-makers, social activists and NGOs.

Bina Jain
Patron, AIWC

Acknowledgements

I am extremely grateful to Mrs. Bina Jain, Former President, All India Women's Conference and Prof. Muchkund Dubey, President, Council for Social Development for their initiative and support for organising the International Summit on Empowerment of Rural Women, in New Delhi on September 2-3, 2013 where most of the papers included in this volume were presented and discussed. Besides, the help received from staff of All India Women's Conference and the Council for Social Development especially, Jaya Nair, Gitesh Sinha, Rita Khurana and Sheela Sabu of CSD and Sheela Kakde, Usha Nair. Vijaya Bhasin and Sheela Sathyanarayanan of AIWC is gratefully acknowledged.

T. Haque
Editor

Acknowledgements

[illegible]

Contents

List of Tables

List of Figures

Profile of the Contributors

Abul Hossain is the Project Director of Multi-Sectoral Programme on Violence Against Women of the Ministry of Women and Children Affairs. Dr. Hossain is a career bureaucrat with excellent educational and research background on issues of national and international importance. He has facilitated consultation for drafting and approval of Women Development Policy 2011, National Child Policy 2011 and Domestic Violence (Prevention and Protection) Act 2010 of Bangladesh. Prior to that, He worked as Chief Executive at Regional Public Administration Training Centre (RPATC) under the Ministry of Public Administration during September 2003-January 2006. Dr. Hossain's fields of interest include governance, human resource management, local resource mobilization, anti-corruption, poverty alleviation, feminization of poverty, promoting right based approach, access to justice and gender based violence.

Anamika Priyadarshini is Senior Research Associate at the Council for Social Development, New Delhi. She did her Masters in International Development from Cornell University and is currently pursuing PhD from the Department of Global Gender Studies, State University of New York at Buffalo. She is associated with home-based workers' international network HomeWorkers Worldwide and has been working to underscore these workers' issues since 2001. She has taught undergraduate students of SUNY Buffalo and masters students of the Centre for Development Studies, Central University of Bihar. Furthermore, she has worked with national and international non-governmental organizations as a development professional, researcher and trainer for over seven years.

Anjali Godyal is Programme Leader, Capacity Building Center, holds a Post Graduation in rural management from the Institute of Rural Management, Anand, Gujarat. She has over 7 years of experience working with rural communities in the areas of health, education and governance.

Anjali Makhija is the Group Leader, Capacity Building, at Institute of Rural Research and Development (IRRAD) holds Master's Degree in social work from Delhi School of Social Work, Delhi University and a bachelors' in Economics (Hons). She has 20 years of experience in leading grassroots teams and building capacities on themes related to education, reproductive and child health and governance. Currently she is the chairperson of the Gender Committee at IRRAD, co–chairs Panchayat Advisory Group at IRRAD, and is a member of the management team. She was earlier member of Training Committee of UN Global Compact.

Ann Turinayo is a knowledge management and communications specialist with skills and experience in strategy formulation and implementation, as well as in Monitoring and Evaluation. She worked with international development organisations such as the International Fund for Agricultural Development (IFAD) and the Netherlands Development Organisation (SNV). In addition to the knowledge management and communications role, Ann currently serves as a gender focal point for the IFAD Uganda Country Office, where she has organised a gender working group for the IFAD-supported projects. Ann holds a Masters Degree in Language and Literature and has over ten years experience in analytical and technical writing, editing, as well as capacity building and training.

Becca Asaki, AIDS Campaign Coordinator, Huaioru Commission (New York, USA) currently coordinates the AIDS Campaign of the Huaioru Commission and GROOTS International working to enhance the organizing, leadership development and network-building of grassroots women's groups and NGO partners in Africa working in the context of HIV/AIDS care giving, livelihoods, and food security. She has co-authored articles documenting grassroots women's community-driven social protection practices and caregivers' analysis of shifting health policies published in *Gender and Development* and the *Journal of Health and Human Services* Administration. She spent over three years studying and working with women's and community-based organizations in Costa Rica, Japan, Turkey, India, Thailand, Taiwan, Croatia, Serbia, Bosnia, and South Africa.

Bidyut Mohanty, is at present serving as the Head, Women's Studies Unit, Institute of Social Sciences (ISS), New Delhi. For last five years she had been teaching as a Visiting Professor in the Global and International Studies, University of California, Santa Barbara in the Spring Quarter. She has been coordinating several projects on HIV and AIDS and role of Panchayats, Trafficking and local government's new role as well as the Total Sanitation Scenario—A Reality Check.

Connie Magomu Masaba is the Project Manager of the Vegetable Oil Development Project Phase Two (VODP II), in the Ministry of Agriculture,

Animal Industry and Fisheries, in Uganda. The Project is funded by the International Fund for Agricultural Development (IFAD), Government of Uganda and a private sector partner. She holds a Master's Degree in Business Administration, a Master's Degree in Agricultural Economics and a Bachelor's Degree in Agriculture. Prior to the current position, she worked with the Ministry of Agriculture as the Project Coordinator of the Vegetable Oil Development Project phase one and with the Faculty of Agriculture and Forestry in Makerere University Kampala. Her area of research has been small holder agriculture, women and agriculture, etc.

T. Haque, Director, Council for Social Development is a well known Agricultural Economist. He obtained his Ph.D. Degree from Patna University (India) and Post Doctoral training from Iowa State University, Ames, U.S.A. Dr. Haque is currently Director, Council for Social Development, New Delhi and Senior Adviser, LANDESA (Rural Development Institute), New Delhi. Earlier he served as Chairman, Commission for Agricultural Costs and Prices, Government of India, ICAR National Fellow at the National Centre for Agricultural Economics and Policy, New Delhi and Director, Centre for Agrarian Studies, NIRD, Hyderabad. He also served as consultant to several international organizations, including FAO, ILO and The World Bank. Dr. Haque is author of six books and about 100 research papers and reports. His areas of specialization are land reform, food security and sustainable agriculture and rural development

D. Hein Tran is an attorney and leads Landesa's efforts to elevate, through a variety of policy avenues, the issue of secure land rights for the poor as a key tool to help alleviate poverty and hunger in the developing world. Tran was previously counsel at a law firm in Washington, D.C., where she focused on appellate and government/regulatory cases raising novel issues of constitutional law, criminal procedure, and statutory interpretation. She previously clerked for Justice Ruth Bader Ginsburg on the U.S. Supreme Court and Judge David S. Tatel on the U.S. Court of Appeals for the D.C. Circuit. Ms. Tran received her J.D., magna cum laude, from Harvard Law School, M.P.A. from Princeton University Woodrow Wilson School of Public and International Affairs, and B.A., magna cum laude, from Yale University.

Jaya Lekshmi Nair is Senior Research Associate with Council for Social Development. She has completed her Master's in Physics from the University of Kerala. Her main role in the organization is research coordination and policy advocacy. Prior to joining CSD, she worked with RDI/Landesa as a research coordinator. She has been actively involved in field research on women's land tenure issues.

Mayra Gomez is the Co-Executive Director of the Global Initiative for

Economic, Social and Cultural Rights, a non-governmental organization which seeks to combat global poverty by strengthening the international human rights framework through creative standard setting and by forging new collaborations with development and environment sector allies. Focusing on women and economic, social and cultural rights, she has worked as a consultant to the mandates of the Working Group on the Elimination of Discrimination against Women in Law and Practice, the UN Special Rapporteurs on the Right to Adequate Housing and on Water and Sanitation, as well as with UN-Women and the Office of the High Commissioner for Human Rights. Prior to coming to the Global Initiative, Mayra served as the Senior Expert on Women and Housing Rights with the Geneva-based Centre on Housing Rights and Evictions (COHRE). Her research publications have been widely cited by organizations such as Amnesty International, Plan International, the United Nations Development Programme (UNDP), UN-Habitat, among others.

Mondira Bhattacharya is an Associate Fellow at the National Council of Applied Economic Research, New Delhi. She completed her PhD in Agricultural Economics from the Centre for the Study of Regional Development (CSRD), Jawaharlal Nehru University (JNU), New Delhi. Her research interests cover issues in agricultural geography and the impact of related economic policies on the concerned farmer segment. She has several research publications to her credit. Before joining NCAER she had worked at the Confederation of Indian Industry, Council for Social Development and the Institute of Economic Growth, New Delhi, in various capacities.

Monica Banerjee is Director, National Foundation for India, an indigenous and philanthropic trust set up in 1992. She obtained her Ph.D. degree from the Centre for Rural Development, IIT, New Delhi in 2004 and was Visiting fellow at the London School of Economics in 2006. Her work at the foundation comprises fostering Indian voluntary sector, particularly in rural and remote areas, to recover the spaces and agency of ordinary people for collective action. Leads NFI's programmes on Education including early childhood care, Community Health, Peace and Justice-thematic programmes that enable India's grassroots voluntary organisations build their capacities and leverage their work that are instrumental in bringing a change that strikes at the root causes of poverty and inequity.

Naseem Shaikh is the Team Leader Swayam Shikshan Prayog and Co-Facilitator–Asia GROOTS International. Naseem has two decades of experience in organizing rural grassroots women to build their economic, social and political competencies and move from the margin to the mainstream. Naseem has led missions of grassroots leaders to Kenya,

Philippines, Nepal, to grow and foster grassroots women's networks through peer exchanges and to embed long term strategies, have borne fruit. These insights from practice are centred on her long years of sustaining and scaling up a movement of self help groups that includes over 80,000 women in rural India and build their capacities to reduce vulnerabilities through access and control over land and agriculture, water and sanitation and health services and build a culture of resilience.

Nidhi Tandon is from East Africa and is based in Toronto, Canada—she is an agrarian economist, social activist, animator and writer working with women and with marginalized communities to raise their voices in a globalized world. Her company, Networked Intelligence for Development, consults on women's relationships with water, energy, natural resources, food security, climate change and related policy decisions. Nidhi has published critical pieces on the impact of the bio-fuel industry on food security and farming livelihoods; implications of land grab on peasant land rights; and on the immediate climate-related challenges that impact small farmers.

Nitya Rao is Professor of Gender and Development at the University of East Anglia, Norwich, United Kingdom. With academic specialisations in rural management and development studies, she has worked since 1985 as a researcher, teacher, trainer and social activist focusing on gender equality and women's empowerment, within broader issues of resource rights, social equity and rural development. Her research focuses on two major strands: gendered changes in land and agrarian relations, migration and livelihoods and its impact on agency, identity and material well-being, as well as equity issues in educational experience and provisioning and its implications for livelihood choices and the construction of gendered subjectivities.

Padmaja Mishra is Professor of Economics at Utkal University, Odisha. She has also worked as Director, Womens' Studies, Utkal University. She has done her Master in Economics from Utkal University, Ph.D. from The University of East Anglia, U.K. and Post Doctoral Work at the University of Maryland, U.S.A. Her specialized areas of research are Gender studies, Economics of Environment and Development. She has many research publications to her credit along with a couple of edited books. She is a member of many academic and policy making bodies all over India.

Pinaki Halder, State Director, Landesa, West Bengal is a Social Development Executive with 25 years' experience in project planning, implementation, monitoring, and evaluation (more than six years with UNICEF in West Bengal, UP and Assam) and in policy formulation at State and national level with proven skill of strategic communication, networking, advocacy and negotiation. Mr. Halder was a member of West Bengal Civil Service and possesses good exposure to human and social development, governance issues including local self-government, women and gender issues, child related issues, and National Flagship programmes.

P. Prasanthi is State Programme Director of Andhra Pradesh Mahila Sangham, for the last seven years. She has Master's Degree in Social Work from Andhra University. She is currently engaged with adolescent girls on Life Skills Education and Empowerment; Facilitating Empowerment process among women and girls by evolving suitable and contextual strategies with a focus on strategic gender interests of women; Doing training programmes for functionaries of Government and NGOs on issues of girls and women with participatory approach.

Sanjay Patnaik is currently State Director, Landesa/RDI, Odissa. He has M.Phil Degree from Jawaharlal Nehru University, New Delhi. His field of specialization is land and forest rights especially of marginalized people including *dalits*, scheduled tribes and women. He has several published papers and reports on land and forest right issues in Odisha.

Sarita Pradhan is a Post Graduate and M.Phil. in Sociology from Central University Hyderabad (India), and Post Graduate Certificate in Business Management from Xavier Institute of Management, Bhubaneswar. Presently, Sarita is working as Gender Specialist in Landesa, Odisha (India) since 2011. Her key result area is securing land rights for the marginalized women. Sarita has 14 years' of experience in development sector in various projects in Health, Disaster Management and Gender. She was associated with a study on Women and Land conducted by Landesa in Karnataka; Study on Women's Land Ownership and Food Security by IFPRI; Mid-Term study on Women's Land Ownership by Landesa.

Seema Gaikwad, Regional Advocacy Advisor, Asia and Pacific, VSO International, has 22 years in the development sector. She has provided support to grassroots and national organizations in India, Nepal, Bangladesh, Philippines, Laos, and Cambodia, Indonesia and virtual programme development and direction in Mongolia. Prior to this, she was Asia Regional Coordinator in the International Land Coalition (ILC), a global coalition of organizations addressing the issues of land rights and access to land for poor women and their families in rural areas.

Shivani Bharadwaj is Programme Director Sathi All for Partnerships (SAFP) and also coordinator of global forum 'The Consult for Women and Land Rights (CWLR)' and is an active member of Women and Habitat Network. She is a member of the steering committee of the World Urban Campaign and Gender Equality Action Plan of the UN Habitat. Currently she also coordinates research initiatives for South Asia Think Tank Initiatives and guides policy discourse on migration.

Soma Kishore Parthasarathy is a researcher/activist and consultant on issues of Gender Livelihoods and Sustainable Development and is based in Delhi. Trained as a regional and social planner from the Centre for Environmental Planning and Technology Ahmedabad, She has worked with leading NGOs-ISI, Nirantar etc. as well as briefly with the Government of India, Department of Women and Child Development. She has also served as Consultant to the Planning Commission and as Senior Advisor to UNDP on the Livelihoods Programme. Soma has over the past 10 years been engaged in enabling community based organizations and NGOs to undertake collaborative action Research on a range of issues such as Gender Citizenship and Education, on Education and Empowerment perspectives in SHGs and on the Micro credit sector and its scope and limitations for empowerment of marginalized women.

Sonali Mukherjee is affiliated with Institute of Social Sciences, New Delhi, India. She has extensively worked on Gender and Development issues. She has done her Doctoral research among the Bison-horn Maria of Bastar region of Chhattisgarh State, India, with special emphasis on the status of women. Presently she is directing an ICSSR project, "Structural roots of gender violence", a study of Haryana and West Bengal.

Soya Thomas is working as the team leader, Gender at Kudumbashree state poverty eradication mission. Coordinating and facilitating Gender Self Learning programmes and Nirbhaya activities in Kerala. She has 10 years of experience with women and child development organizations/ Institutions, facilitating programme interventions for the empowerment of women as well as action research programmes on violence against women and children.

Steven Jonckheere is an Associate Land Programme Officer at the International Fund for Agricultural Development (IFAD). He has also worked with civil society organisations and research institutes and has over 8 years of experience in working on land and natural resources issues and institutional development, mainly in Sub-Saharan Africa and Latin America.

Subhalakshmi Nandi, Programme Specialist, Women's Economic Empowerment, UN Women Office for India, Bhutan, Maldives and Sri Lanka leads the women's economic empowerment programme for UN Women in Bhutan, India, Maldives and Sri Lanka, with a focus on strengthening gendered approaches to policy and programme on rural livelihoods and employment. She has over a decade of experience working with grassroots women's organisations in India, in tribal areas of Gujarat and in the Bundelkhand region of Uttar Pradesh (UP). Her work has been on feminist organising for women's right to livelihoods, including gender perspectives in social protection, bringing attention to women's economic identities as workers and farmers, and working on women's education and literacy. Subhalakshmi has researched and published papers nationally and internationally on the issue of Self Help Groups (SHGs), microcredit and women's empowerment.

Sudha P. Rao, Advisor, Planning Commission, Government of India is an officer of Indian Economic Service (Batch of 1981). At present she is working as Adviser Women and Child Development Division in the Planning Commission since July 2007. She has also been Adviser Voluntary Action Cell and Handloom and Handicrafts Cell. During the three decades of her career she has served in various capacities in different Ministries. Among others she has worked both as Director and Adviser in the Commission for Agriculture Costs and Prices. She holds a Post Graduate Degree in Economics from JNU and M.Phil from both University of Delhi and University of Punjab. She has authored several articles which have appeared in research journals and books.

Susamma Vargheese, is the National Programme Manager of ILO/ACTRAV Norway Partnership Project on 'Trade Union for Social Justice'. Ever since she joined ILO in 1996, she has been extensively working on various 'workers' issues like empowering rural women workers and youth and strengthening bipartite initiatives between employers and workers organizations through a process of social dialogue. Together, with Dr. T. Haque, he has co-authored a book *The Path of Deliverance–Organizing and Empowering Rural Informal Economy Workers.*

Introduction

T. Haque

Women in general are powerless in both developed and developing countries. It is more so in rural areas of South Asia and sub-Saharan Africa. The gender inequality index, prepared by United Nations Development Programme (UNDP) shows that women in sub-Saharan Africa are relatively more subordinated to men, followed by those in South Asia, Arab states, Latin America and the Caribbean. The Europe and Central Asia as well as East Asia and the Pacific have relatively low gender inequality (*UNDP: Human Development Report, 2013*).

In developing countries where agriculture continues to be the main source of livelihood for either majority or a vast number of population, rural women's access to ownership and control over land, forests and other natural resources, is the first prerequisite for empowerment of rural women. Unfortunately, majority of women in the rural areas of developing countries do not have ownership and control over the land which they cultivate. In fact, majority of them work as either agricultural or non-agricultural labourers in the informal sector. In the absence of secure land right, they fail access to institutional credit and modern inputs as well as other support services in agriculture and consequently their productivity and incomes remain low. Even as labourers, they receive comparatively lower wages than men for the same or similar nature of work. Consequently, their work and living conditions remain far from decent. Secondly, it has been historically observed in most countries that women's access to quality education upto a certain level helps improve their access to organized sector employment and incomes and consequently their social status and bargaining power for a better deal in the society.

In addition, due to inadequate health care facilities and lack of safe drinking water and sanitation, rural women suffer from various diseases and ill health, having their adverse impact on productivity and incomes.

About 3.9 million women under the age of 60 years are estimated to die every year. Moreover, appropriate institutional arrangements such as women's self-help groups, co-operatives or group farming and rural women's adequate and effective participation in local self-government act as instruments of change.

It is true that in the past two decades or so, the gender disparity has significantly declined in many countries, especially in educational enrolment, life expectancy, labour force participation, etc. But still there are huge gaps. There are various policies and programmes in almost all countries to reduce or remove gender gaps in development. In almost all countries, there are several best practices for empowerment of rural women. However, rural women in the developing countries of Asia and Africa continue to remain largely marginalized and vulnerable, as victims of unequal, exploitative traditional social systems. Over and above this, there is an all-round despair because of poor governance of some otherwise affirmative schemes and programmes of government.

This volume contains papers and notes presented by eminent experts at the International Summit on 'Empowerment of Rural Women', organized by the All India Women's Conference and the Council for Social Development, New Delhi on September 2-3, 2013. Also some other invited papers have been included. The Summit was attended by several eminent scientists scholars and policy administrators namely, M.S. Swaminathan, President, M.S. Swaminathan Foundation, Peter E. Kennore, FAO Representative in India, Rebecca Tavares, Country Representative, UN Women Office for India, Sri Lanka, Bhutan and Maldives, Lise Grande, UN Residence Coordinator and UNDP Resident Representative, New Delhi, Eng. Wassfi Hassan N.EI–Sreihin, Secretary General, AARDO, New Delhi, Ratna Prabha, Additional Secretary, Ministry of Women and Child Development, Government of India and Vijayanand, Additional Secretary MoRD, Government of India and others.

The book is divided into four parts. Part I gives an introduction and overview of the book. Part II includes papers on land rights of women. Part III presents papers dealing with rural women's access to education and health. Part IV covers papers on rural women's organizations, including self-help groups, neighbourhood groups, Panchayati Raj Institution etc. Part V includes papers analyzing the trends in the employment of rural women as well as impact of migration on rural women. Part VI presents notes on some best practices for empowerment of rural women.

The chapter by **Haque** on Empowering Rural Women gives an

overview of the Challenges and Pathways for empowerment of rural women in developing countries. This chapter highlights the need for an integrated policy and institutional support system for empowering rural women, through access to secure and effective land rights, education, health care formal sector employment and organizations such as self-help groups, Panchayati Raj Institutions, etc.

Seema Gaikwad's chapter on 'Gender Inequality in Developing Countries: The Case of South Asia' points out that countries with very high level of human development show greater parity in educational attainment of women and men. The adverse sex ratio due to sex selective abortion, low labour participation, earning gaps, inequality in the ownership of land and other assets, high maternal mortality, and lower educational attainment of women in developing countries are matters of concern. Besides, women's low educational levels, unequal social status and limited decision making power negatively influence their nutritional status and that of their children.

Sudha Rao's chapter on 'addressing Gender Disparities in the Twelfth Five Year Plan, analyses the India's gender concerns raised in Twelfth Five Year Plan and also the Challenges of bridging the gender gaps in development. This chapter points out that the ending of gender based inequalities, discrimination and violence is an overriding priority in the Twelfth Plan. For economic empowerment, the Plan expects to increase women's employability in the formal sector and focus on women's work participation. The chapter emphasizes that effective participation of women in institutions of governance, especially Panchayats is an assured way of empowering rural women and integrating gender concern in development.

The chapter on 'Women's Land and Property Rights and the Post, 2015 Development Agenda' by **Mayra Gomez and Hien Tran** points out that the link between women's land and property rights and sustainable human development is evident for a wide range of issues. Strengthening Women's secure rights to land can help empower them to reach their potentials as citizens and as economic actors and enable them to take control over their own lives.

Nitya Rao's chapter on 'Gender Differentials in Access to Land', analyses the constraints, enabling factors and their impacts on women's status. According to Rao, women own and control a small share of total household assets, if at all, even though they contribute a disproportionately large share of labour to the maintenance of the household. Such inequality puts them at disadvantage across different spheres of life and work, whether in accessing other productive resources, seeking decent employment, setting up an enterprise or even just bargaining for better outcomes within the household. Also in the absence of adequate land or security of tenure, they are unable to access inputs, extension services or markets, which can help improve productivity. Assets, especially land contribute to strengthening women's voice and in household decisions. However, an enabling environment in terms of equitable laws and affirmative action policies are probably the starting point for women to make and secure their claims.

Shivani Bhardwaj, in her chapter entitled 'Land Rights for Women: Planning Gender Inclusion to Address Gender Resource Gap' highlights the point that the existence of a gender resource gap is a violation of constitutional obligation of the state. The resource gap at the basic unit of society impacts the resource gaps at all the other levels.

The chapter on 'Negotiating Gender and Land Rights in Pluralistic Terrains with Tribal Women in Southern Rajasthan' by **Soma K. Parthasarathy** brings out how property rights and issues related to property and land are generally considered the domain of men, although transitions are evident with the changing policy and socio-cultural environment. Women are themselves engaging in discussions related to land and property resources, but are not consulted in decisions related to these resources. Also there is an inverse relationship between access to forest and common property resources and women's assertion of claims. It is further observed that in areas where the livelihoods depend to a large extent on the forests and land and agricultural activities are limited, women's involvement in discussions and resolution of matters related to land is much higher and disputes are less. Parthasarathy concludes by saying that the adoption of inclusive and gender just policies that give women opportunities to enter governance spaces that would enable tribal societies to develop in an environment of equality, justice and rights is critical for empowerment of tribal women.

Becca Asaki's analysis of Huairou Commission's Land and Housing Campaign's Global strategy as a platform for women's security of tenure, reveals that globally women are making progress in securing land and housing rights through different tenure systems and yet they still represent the largest group marginalized by development policies, land policy and land administration. Huairou Commission's global initiative on women's security of tenure, is a multi-stake holder platform to advance an alternative approach on women's security of land tenure that is informed and centred in grass root women's experiences.

Pinaki Haldar's chapter on Land Rights and Women's Empowerment, is based on Landesa's practical field experiences in West Bengal, where Landesa is closely working with the government, for implementation of Nijo Griha Nijo Bhumi (NGNB) Scheme which allocates homestead plot of 5 cents in size to landless families. The women headed households from scheduled tribes, scheduled castes and minority communities are given priority, titles being given in the joint names of wife and husband. The paper shows how secure land rights for women create an extraordinary ripple effect, improving the health and nutrition status of women and children and also reducing domestic violence against women.

Nidhi Tandon's chapter entitled 'Potentials of Land Rights to Contribute to Gender Equality in Developing Countries' provides some international evidence suggesting that when women share in assets and land ownership, there are positive correlations with higher food expenditure and rural productivity. However, despite such evidence governments seem to be either unable or unwilling to invest or commit to systematic changes that would boost women's control over land and its production. The chapter suggests that within the broader framework of peasant's land rights, the voices of women need to be amplified, not only in determining what their priorities are, but in supporting their management of and decision making about production, storage and local marketing systems.

The chapter on Lease Farming as a Livelihood Option for Rural Landless Women' by **T. Haque and Jaya Lakshmi Nair** is based on a case study of Kerala. This chapter analyses how lease farming can be a viable livelihood option for landless rural poor, especially women in India. In the absence of land ownership and education, majority of landless and semi-landless rural women are engaged as agricultural labourers with low wages and remaining trapped in poverty and indebtedness. But lease farming by landless women in Kerala and shows the path way for their poverty reduction and upward social inability. Even though agricultural tenancy is banned in Kerala is providing hand holding support to JLG (Joint liability groups) women in leasing in land and improving their livelihoods. It has helped empower the poor women both socially and economically.

The chapter on 'women farmers and gender disparities by **Subhalakshmi Nandi** brings out how collective identity of farming women, is critical for their empowerment. In India and in many parts of the global South, group approach in the form of Self Help Groups (SHGs) has enabled women to access some of the entitlements like land, credit, training and market linkage. The experience of group land leasing in Kerala and Andhra Pradesh show that institutional linkages between group leasing and land development under Mahatma Gandhi National Rural Employment Guarantee Act, has gone a long way in ensuring food security and livelihood support to poor women.

Anjali Godyal and **Anjali Makhija's** chapter on 'Access to Health and Education for Women in Rural Mewat, underscores the need for improving rural women's access to quality health care and education. This chapter points out that the existing programmes for women on health and education are not able to reach the intended beneficiaries because of poor implementation. Various models of information education are required to create mass awareness and mobilize masses among women to take care of their education and health needs. Besides, a strong advocacy with men folk, especially the youth, is required for their co-operation and understanding to promote gender equity.

Naseem Shaikh's chapter on 'Driving Demand and Increasing Access to Health and Education in Maharashtra is based on the results of a field experiment by an NGO, called Swayam Shikshan Prayog in rural Maharashtra. This is a development organization whose goal is to move poor women and communities from the margin to the mainstream of development. The experiments show that rural women can more effectively access health and other services if they are part of organized women's groups. Being part of a SHG, has helped women to spot avenues for participation and capitalize on opportunities to access basic services.

The chapter on status of Rural Female Employment in India by **Mondira Bhattacharya** analyses the declining trends in work force participation rate of rural women which could be largely attributed to increased educational enrolment, income and lack of adequate formal jobs other than construction and those under unsafe or unsuitable work conditions. According to her, the goal should not merely be to increase female work force participation, but also to provide opportunities for decent work that will in turn, contribute to the economic empowerment of women.

The chapter on Socio-economic Impacts of Migration on Women–A Study in Odisha by **Padmaja Mishra** reveals that the economic benefits of male outmigration on female family members depends on the amount, frequency and mode of remittances. If the amount of remittances is high, the *de facto* female household head and other women feel empowered, as also the expenditure on food and children's health and education improve.

Besides, the women migrant in the city find themselves economically empowered if they are employed. However, heavy migration out of rural areas due to extreme poverty and lack of economic opportunities should be redressed by appropriate rural development policies and programmes.

Susamma Varghese's chapter on socio-economic impact of outmigration points out that women migrants tend to remit to their home destination more than men and migration provides an opportunity to escape caste division and restrictive social norms and increased economic opportunities in cities. In case of male migration also, women are empowered with increased interaction in society, including their participation as workers and decision makers of households and also of communities. However, due to lack of coherent policy framework, proper enforcement mechanisms and decent work conditions, migrant women and men workers live and work under inhuman conditions. Therefore, there is need for an appropriate legal and policy framework on migrant workers.

Anamika Priyadarshini in her chapter entitled 'The Invisible Workers and their Needs Politicization', reveals that liberalization of Indian economy since 1990 had an adverse impact on women home based workers and even those engaged in small scale and cottage industries. Priyadarshini points out that there is need to research the needs of women home based workers, working in extremely poor conditions and help them in accessing education and skills to find appropriate space in the global chain of production.

Prasanthi's chapter on 'Mahila Samakhya for Women's Empowerment—A Quiet Revolution towards Sustained Change' analyses the impact of Mahila Samakhya programme in Andhra Pradesh which was launched in 1988. The main focus is on recognizing the centrality of education in empowering women to achieve equality. Mahila Samakhya programme has demonstrated that sustainable process of grassroots facilitation and decentralization of leadership and power is possible. The unique process enabled the rural poor women as change agents and icons of democratic leadership. The process involved planning from grassroots, women centred interventions, capacity building and facilitating holistic perspective of empowerment–physical, social, economic, political and legal. Also women's collectives emerged as pressure groups for planning and action, evolving into a cadre of activists to address issues of violence against women and girls.

The chapter by **Soya Thomas** on Kudumbashree Experiences in Kerala shows how organization of poor rural women as Joint Liability

Groups (JLGs) with initial handholding support from Panchayati Raj institutions have helped in empowering them, socially, economically as well as politically.

Patnaik and Pradhan in their chapter on Women Support Centre in Empowering Rural Women, shows how women support centres in Ganjam district of Odisha has helped in providing land and other livelihoods and social security benefits to single women and women headed households. Landesa (formerly Rural Development Institute) oriented and built the capacities of all stakeholders at the district, Block and sector levels in this regard.

Monica Banerjee's chapter on 'Rural Women in Local Self-Governance–State and Beyond,' analyses the State's ability to alter gender relations in India. According to her, the State's laws, policies and programmes do not seem to have ushered genuine social or gender justice, especially among rural societies. Voluntary organizations within the civil society space are more capable of creating impact, as their need based and flexible constructive work amidst a community in a reasonable small area seems to be much better placed to address democratic and gender deficits on ground than the States' top down and inflexible approach at development with only partially engendered institutional arrangements.

Bidyut Mohanty in her chapter on 'Women's Empowerment in Panchayat, brings out that one-third reservation on local self-government (Panchayat) has generated a large number of grassroots women leaders throughout India, which in turn has created a social mobilization. However, women are unable to function properly in the Panchayati Raj institutions, because these institutions are devoid of real power and depend on Central and State governments for financial resources.

Connie Magomumasaba *et al.* presented a chapter on 'Ensuring Women Benefit from Inclusive Business Models: A Case Study of the Oil Palm Project in Uganda. The chapter, based on practical field experience in Uganda, points out that an effective partnership can be developed between small farmers and the private sector and that such partnerships can produce positive development outcomes for rural women and men. However, government has a critical role in building confidence and trust among the partners and in ensuring that both men and women participate in these interventions.

Abul Hossain's chapter entitled 'Reducing Gender Disparity through Empowerment of Grassroots Rural Women in Bangladesh: Issues and Strategies', points out that traditional attitudes and gender-stereotyped roles towards women often prevent society as a whole to recognize women's equal rights in both private and public sphere. However, efforts by government machineries and non-government organizations have helped in recent years to empower women by way of improvement in livelihood, reduction in poverty and maternal as well as child mortality. In addition, efforts of mobilizing the poor rural women, providing them training and credit, encouraging them to start new entrepreneurships and linking them to the marketing chains in the urban areas have created an enormous opportunity for employment of rural women.

Sonali Mukherjee's chapter on 'Strategising Livelihood Approaches: Empowering Lives' brings out that providing micro-credit to women through self-help groups can help them out of poverty provided a focused and sustained effort is made. Particularly access to formal education and training coupled with credit and marketing can augment their production as well as earning capacity.

Box-I: Required New Deal for Women in Agriculture

- Legal land titles, including allotment of surplus land and joint patta.
- Equal returns for equal work.
- Access to Kisan credit cards and other forms of institutional credit;
- Engendering of the MGNREGA (2005), PPVFR Act (2001) and BD Act (2002).
- Running Support services for women, such as crèches and day care centres, preparation of noon meals in the definition of 'work' for women.
- Nutrition supplement and support services, including temporary crèches for pregnant women, mothers, adolescent girls and infants in the 0-2 age group in the MGNREGA.
- Food Safety, trade and legal literacy movements among women through rural knowledge centres.
- Engendering the Curriculum and Agricultural and Veterinary Universities.
- A Gram Panchayat Mahila Fund in Every Panchayat for community activities for essential gender specific needs.
- A National Board for New Deal for Women in Agriculture headed by the Union Minister of Agriculture.

Source: National Commission of Farmers, Government of India, 2004, presented by M.S. Swaminathan at the International Summit on Empowerment of Rural Women, IIC, New Delhi, September 3, 2013.

In addition to the above mentioned chapters, some valuable notes and power points were presented during the summit, a brief description of which would be in order. M.S. Swaminathan, an internationally well known scientist underlined the need for a new deal for women in agriculture, as given in Box-I. Peter E. Kenmore, FAO Representative in

India discussed the importance of gender parity in accessing farm inputs and services from the points of view of productivity enhancement. Kenmore highlighted how the extension methodology, like Farmers' Field Schools in Tamil Nadu is helping both women and men to understand better the sustainable natural resource management practices. Besides, according to him, women migrants face more discrimination in labour market, housing and social safety nets. In the absence of adequate proof of residence, they are unable to get their food entitlements from the public distribution system and consequently face higher incidence of hunger and poverty. Many girl women also fall victim to trafficking.

Anne Lasimbeug's note on Land Rights of Indigenous Women in South-East Asia shows how indigenous communities right to land and natural resources are systematically violated by states and corporation in South East Asian countries. Economic development policies in these countries aim to large scale plantations, massive logging of forest, mega dams, economic corridors, national parks and poverty eradication projects, dispossessing peoples of their lands and natural resources. As a result, the survival of indigenous communities is threatened. Loss of land has impacted indigenous woman more adversely, in relation to their roles in sustainable resource management, food security, enhancement of traditional knowledge and biodiversity and keepers of culture. Also attempt to integrate and relocate communities in new settlement often result in them being socially marginalized.

Godavari Dange's note on The Sakhi Women's savings and credit Federation that has 80,000 members in rural Maharashtra shows how savings and credit groups can be instrumental for women to come together to improve their livelihoods and incomes:

- Focusing on health promotion and disease prevention, rural grassroots women's collectives hold health providers accountable for delivering high quality health services to their rural communities. Over 1000 women are recognized as community leaders, trainers and experts who transfer strategies and create a platform of women practitioners to dialogue and collaborate with decision makers and providers for accountable services in the area of safe water, sanitation and health services. These measures have helped women and families to save money for their health, using promotive and preventive health care and reduced their dependence on loans from money lenders for medical emergencies. Also, Sakhi supported more than 10

> widows and single women to access land from local Panchayat and engage in collective organic farming that has helped poor women to gain control over small farm land and decision making in agriculture, thereby improving their food security. Presently, the women farmers' network includes 2000 members across water scarce and climate affected areas and builds on indigenous knowledge on farming. The grassroots women's network partner with the government to take information and programmes to rural communities and in turn, grassroots women leaders are advisers to the local authorities in matters of local level development. Sakhi has also broadened grassroots democracy through civil society participation in local governance. The key message is that we need to build capacities of women's groups to determine development priorities and use of resources and also remove legal barriers to promote community ownership of social services and infrastructures.

P.K. Joshi, Director, IFPRI in South Asia, New Delhi did not present any paper, but highlighted two very important points for empowerment of rural women. These are (i) women friendly technological innovations in agriculture, and (ii) education and skilled training for entrepreneurship as well as high paid jobs in the organized sector.

Finally **Bina Jain,** President, All India Women's Conference presented a note indicating the pathways to empower rural women by making them self-sufficient in their own villages, by giving them technical training in modern agricultural facilities, developing skills as artisans, using locally available raw materials and presenting their distress migration to urban areas. Rural women need to be educated and economically empowered as well as independent in their own places, as financial independence is one of the key reasons for their subordination and poor condition.

Part – I
An Overview

1

Empowering Rural Women in Developing Countries

Challenges and Pathways

T. Haque

Introduction

The role of women in socio-economic transformation of a country is now globally recognized. According to the World Development Report, 2012 'Gender equality is a core development objective in its own right. It is also smart economics. Greater gender equality can enhance productivity, improve development outcomes for the next generation and make institutions more representative' (World Bank, 2012). The Convention on the Elimination of All Forms of Discriminations Against Women (CEDAW) and other international treaties provide an umbrella framework delineating international norms for gender equality. Besides, some national governments have undertaken affirmative actions in the past few decades to improve the socio-economic status of women. However, women, especially those living in rural areas of developing countries continue to be marginalized and underprivileged for a variety of reasons. This chapter analyses the nature and extent of socio-economic deprivation of rural women in developing countries and examines the key challenges and pathways to their empowerment.

Defining Rural Women's Empowerment

Empowerment of rural women refers to a situation in which women living in rural areas have adequate independent and equal means of livelihood and other economic, social and political opportunities for growth and upward mobility. The work and living conditions of empowered rural women are as good as those of men and women anywhere in the society.

In other words, empowered rural women gain control over their lives and claim various rights as equals at all levels in the society. Unfortunately, the gender equality for rural women in developing countries remain a distant dream as they are not only in low level equilibrium trap like most rural men, but also the victims of unequal and exploitative social structure, institutions, values and belief that create and perpetuate women's subordination. An empowered woman will have the following qualities or characteristics:

(i) She should have independent and adequate sources of income and not dependent on husband or any other persons for sustenance and growth;
(ii) She should be educated and productively employed without facing any discrimination in schools and labour market based on sex, caste, religion or place of birth;
(iii) She should enjoy a healthy and happy life;
(iv) She should have necessary freedom to participate in various economic, social and political activities at par (if not more) with her male counterpart;
(v) She should be identified as an individual and not merely as part of a family;
(vi) She should be liberated from various superstitions, beliefs and traditional norms that force women to be subordinated to men.

Nature and Extent of Rural Women's Deprivation and Marginalization

Women in Agriculture

The average income levels of rural families in developing countries are low and when women do not either own or control the household incomes, they stay relatively poorer and deprived. The main source of rural income is agriculture and allied activities. Women's share of economically active in agriculture marginally increased from 41.9 per cent in 1995 to 42.7 per cent in the world as a whole and from 42.1 per cent to 42.9 per cent in the developing countries during the same period (FAO, 2011). However, in the agricultural sector, majority of women are employed as agricultural labourers and not as owner cultivators. In India, Nepal, Vietnam, Laos, Philippines and Burkina Faso, less than 11 per cent women own land. On the higher side, 27 per cent women in Thailand and 32 per cent in Malawi and about 19 to 20 per cent in Ethiopia, Tanzania and Zambia own land. In the absence of secure land right, women farmers fail to access institutional credit and apply modern inputs for productivity improvement. Even as agricultural labourers, they get comparatively lower wages than men for the same or similar nature of work. In the rural non-farm sector also, they are employed mainly in the low paid informal activities. Consequently, the socio-economic conditions of rural women in developing countries remain far from decent. According to Food and Agriculture Organization of the United Nations (FAO: 2011), globally gender inequalities in land right are pervasive. Not only do women have lower access to land than men, they are also restricted to so-called secondary land rights, which they hold through male family members.

To quote Diouf (FAO 2011-12), "Women control less land than men and the land they control is often of poor quality and their tenure is insecure. Women own fewer of the working animals needed in farming. They also frequently do not control the income from the typically small animals they manage. Women farmers are less likely than men to use modern inputs such as improved seeds, fertilizers, pest control measures and mechanical tools. They also use less credit and often do not control the credit they obtain. Finally women have less education and less access to extension services, which make it more difficult to gain access to and use some of the other resources, such as land, credit and fertilizer...the obstacles that confront women farmers mean that they achieve lower yields than their male counterparts. Yet women are as good at farming as men. Solid empirical evidence shows that if women farmers receive the same level of resources as men on the land they farm, they would achieve the same yield levels. The yield gap between men and women averages around 20-30 per cent, and most research finds that the gap is due to differences in resource use. Bringing yields on the land farmed by women upto the levels achieved by men would increase agricultural output in developing countries between 2.5 and 4 per cent. Increasing production by this amount could reduce the number of undernourished people in the world in the order of 12-17 per cent...achieving gender equality and empowering women is not only the right thing to do, it is also crucial for agricultural development and food security." The actual gains from closing the gender gap in access to resources would be greater in countries where the gender gap is wider.

Education and Employment

Aside from farming, rural women can take up well-paid non-farm jobs in the organized sector if they have access to adequate level of quality education and skills. Unfortunately, the availability of non-farm employment in rural areas is very limited in most of the developing regions. Besides, rural women's low access to adequate level of quality education and skill along with restrictive socio-cultural norms prevent them seeking jobs in the organized manufacturing or service sectors. It would be seen from Table 1.1 that female population with at least secondary education was as low as 5.8 per cent in Afghanistan, 0.9 per cent in Burkina Faso, 5.6 per cent in Tanzania, 1.5 per cent in Mozambique, 7.4 per cent in Rwanda, 7.6 per cent in Yemen, 10.3 per cent in Central African Republic, 17.9 per cent in Nepal, 18.3 per cent in Pakistan and 18.0 per cent in Myanmar. Even in countries having medium human development status like India, Vietnam, Thailand and Syria, the female population with secondary level of education was less than 30 per cent. Women's access to education is low in both absolute and relative terms. Table 1.1 also shows that women's participation in the labour market is relatively low in most of the less developed or developing countries. It is more so in countries where the women's access to at least secondary education is low.

Table 1.1: Secondary Education, Labour Force Participation Rate of Gender as well as Share of GDP spent on Education in Developing Countries

HDI Rank	*Countries*	*Population with at least secondary education (%ages 25 and older)*		*Labour force participation rate (%ages 15 and older)*		*Education (% of GDP) 2005-2010*
		2006-2010		*2011*		
		Female	*Male*	*Female*	*Male*	
101	China	54.8	70.4	67.7	80.1	—
103	Thailand	29.0	35.6	63.8	80.0	3.8
104	Maldives	20.7	30.1	55.7	76.8	8.7
114	Philippines	65.9	63.7	49.7	79.4	2.7
121	South Africa	68.9	72.2	44.0	60.8	6.0
127	Viet Nam	24.7	28.0	73.2	81.2	5.3
135	Ghana	45.7	61.8	66.9	71.8	5.5
136	India	26.6	50.4	29.0	80.7	3.1

(*Contd.*)

Table 1.1 (*Contd.*)

HDI Rank	Countries	Population with at least secondary education (%ages 25 and older) 2006-2010 Female	Male	Labour force participation rate (%ages 15 and older) 2011 Female	Male	Education (% of GDP) 2005-2010
138	Cambodia	11.6	20.6	79.2	86.7	2.6
138	Lao People's Democratic Republic	22.9	36.8	76.5	79.5	3.3
140	Bhutan	34.0	34.5	65.8	76.5	4.0
142	Congo	43.8	48.7	68.4	72.9	6.2
145	Kenya	25.3	52.3	61.5	71.8	6.7
146	Bangladesh	30.8	39.3	57.2	84.3	2.2
146	Pakistan	18.3	43.1	22.7	83.3	2.4
148	Angola	—	—	62.9	77.1	3.4
149	Myanmar	18.0	17.6	75.0	82.1	—
150	Cameroon	21.1	34.9	64.2	77.4	3.5
152	Tanzania (United Republic of)	5.6	9.2	88.2	90.3	6.2
153	Nigeria	—	—	47.9	63.3	—
154	Senegal	4.6	11.0	66.1	88.4	5.6
155	Mauritania	8.0	20.8	28.7	79.2	4.3
156	Papua New Guinea	6.8	14.1	70.6	74.1	—
157	Nepal	17.9	39.9	80.4	87.6	4.7
158	Lesotho	21.9	19.8	58.9	73.4	13.0
159	Togo	15.3	45.1	80.4	81.4	4.5
160	Yemen	7.6	24.4	25.2	72.0	5.2
161	Uganda	23.0	23.9	76.0	79.5	3.2
163	Zambia	25.7	44.2	73.2	85.6	1.3
165	Gambia	16.9	31.4	72.4	83.1	5.0
166	Benin	11.2	25.6	67.4	78.2	4.5
167	Rwanda	7.4	8.0	86.4	85.4	4.7
168	Côte d'Ivoire	13.7	29.9	51.8	81.2	4.6
169	Comoros	—	—	35.1	80.4	7.6
170	Malawi	10.4	20.4	84.8	81.3	5.7
171	Sudan	12.8	18.2	30.9	76.5	—
173	Ethiopia	—	—	78.4	89.8	4.7
174	Liberia	15.7	39.2	57.9	64.4	2.8
175	Afghanistan	5.8	34.0	15.7	80.3	—
177	Sierra Leone	9.5	20.4	66.3	69.1	4.3
178	Burundi	5.2	9.2	83.7	82.1	9.2
178	Guinea	—	—	65.4	78.3	2.4
180	Central African Republic	10.3	26.2	72.5	85.1	1.2
182	Mali	11.3	9.2	36.8	70.0	4.5
183	Burkina Faso	0.9	3.2	77.5	90.4	4.0
185	Mozambique	1.5	6.0	86.0	82.9	5.0
186	Congo (Democratic Republic of the)	10.7	36.2	70.2	72.5	2.5
186	Niger	2.5	7.6	39.9	89.9	3.8

Source: Human Development Report, 2013, UNDP.

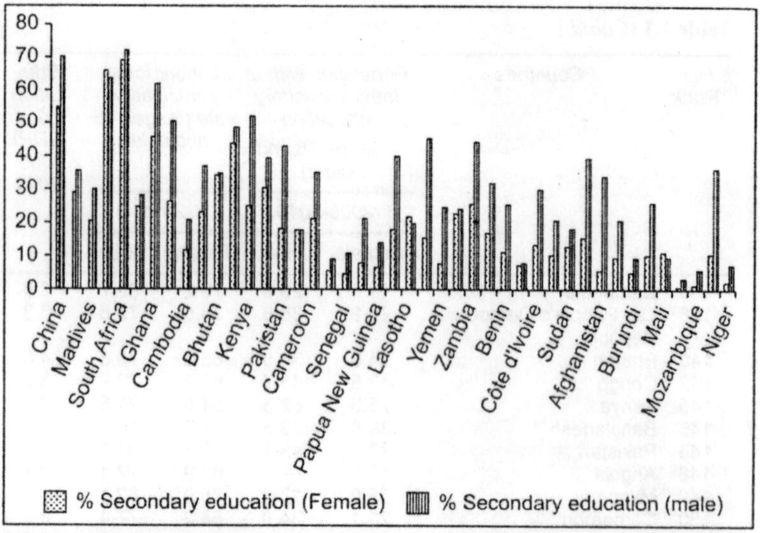

Fig. 1.1: Population with at least Secondary Education (%age 15 and above) in Developing Countries–2006-2010

Women's Health Status

According to latest available data (UNDP 2013), the maternal mortality rates are very high in most of the developing countries. About 3.9 million women under the age of 60 years are estimated to die every year. About two-fifths of them are never born, one sixth die in early childhood and the rest die in their productive years. This number is growing in sub-Saharan Africa and in countries hit by HIV/AIDS epidemic. Also the proportion of adult women affected by HIV/AIDS is relatively higher in developing countries (Table 1.2). Besides, the average adult mortality rate among women was above 400 per 1 lakh population in South Africa, Swaziland, Madagascar, Lesotho, Zambia, Cote d I'voire, Malawi, Zimbabwe, Burundi, Central African Republic and Mozambique (Table 1.2). It would be further seen that most of the developing countries spend relatively much lower proportion of gross domestic product on health care than the developed countries. As a result, both women and men suffer from ill health. But women suffer relatively more. Using inter-country data the correlation co-efficient between female labour participation rate and per cent of GDP spent on health was positive, while maternal mortality rate was negatively correlated with per cent of GDP spent on health.

Table 1.2: Adolescent Fertility Rate, HIV, Mortality Rates as well as Share of GDP spent on Health in Developing Countries

HDI Rank	Countries	Adolescent fertility rate (births per 1,000 women ages 15-19) 2012	HIV Prevalence, Youth (%ages 15-24) 2009		Mortality Rates (per 1,000 adults) 2009		Health (% of GDP) 2010
			Female	Male	Female	Male	
101	China	9.1	—	—	87	142	2.7
103	Thailand	37	—	—	139	270	2.9
104	Maldives	10.2	0.1	0.1	70	97	3.8
114	Philippines	46.5	0.1	0.1	130	240	1.3
121	South Africa	50.4	13.6	4.5	479	521	3.9
127	Viet Nam	22.7	0.1	0.1	107	173	2.6
136	Equatorial Guinea	114.6	5	1.9	355	373	3.4
136	India	74.7	0.1	0.1	169	250	1.2
138	Cambodia	32.9	0.1	0.1	190	350	2.1
138	Lao People's Democratic Republic	30.1	0.2	0.1	251	289	1.5
140	Bhutan	44.9	0.1	0.1	194	256	4.5
142	Congo	112.0	2.0	1.2	320	400	1.1
145	Kenya	98.1	4.1	1.8	282	358	2.1
146	Bangladesh	68.2	0.1	0.1	222	246	1.2
146	Pakistan	28.1	0.1	0.1	189	225	0.8
148	Angola	148.1	1.6	0.6	353	377	2.4
149	Myanmar	12	0.3	0.3	188	275	0.2
150	Cameroon	115.1	3.9	1.6	409	420	1.5
151	Madagascar	122.7	0.1	0.1	198	273	2.3
152	Tanzania (United Republic of)	128.7	3.9	1.7	311	456	4.0
153	Nigeria	111.3	2.9	1.2	365	377	1.9
154	Senegal	89.7	0.7	0.3	218	266	3.1
155	Mauritania	71.3	0.3	0.4	262	315	2.3
156	Papua New Guinea	62	0.8	0.3	221	274	2.6
157	Nepal	86.2	0.1	0.2	159	234	1.8
158	Lesotho	60.8	14.2	5.4	573	676	8.5
159	Togo	54.3	2.2	0.9	278	338	3.4
160	Yemen	66.1	—	—	180	237	1.3
161	Haiti	41.3	1.3	0.6	227	278	1.5
161	Uganda	126.4	4.8	2.3	348	539	2.0
163	Zambia	138.5	8.9	4.2	477	580	3.6
165	Gambia	66.9	2.4	0.9	246	296	2.9
166	Benin	97	0.7	0.3	246	385	2.0
167	Rwanda	35.5	1.9	1.3	258	304	5.2
168	Côte d'Ivoire	105.7	1.5	0.7	456	528	1.1
170	Malawi	105.6	6.8	3.1	496	691	4.0
171	Sudan	53	1.3	0.5	275	291	1.9
172	Zimbabwe	53.4	6.9	3.3	574	672	—
173	Ethiopia	48.3	—	—	379	445	2.6
174	Liberia	123	0.7	0.3	337	389	3.9
175	Afghanistan	99.6	—	—	352	440	0.9
177	Sierra Leone	104.2	1.5	0.6	363	414	1.5
178	Burundi	20.9	2.1	1.0	407	424	4.4
180	Central African Republic	98.6	2.2	1.0	470	461	1.4
183	Burkina Faso	117.4	0.8	0.5	262	443	3.4
185	Mozambique	124.4	8.6	3.1	434	557	3.7
186	Congo (Democratic Republic of the)	170.6	—	—	331	442	3.4
186	Niger	193.6	0.5	0.2	224	229	2.6

Source: Human Development Report, 2013, UNDP.

Adolescent Fertility Rate

Adolescent fertility rate is one of the indicators of poor health of women. It would be seen from Table 1.2 that adolescent fertility rate (births per 1000 women aged 15-19 years) was comparatively very high in developing countries. It was above 100 in Congo, Angola, Cameroon, Madagascar, Tanzania, Nigeria, Uganda, Zambia, Cote d I'voire, Malawi, Liberia, Sierra Leone, Central African Republic, Mali, Burkina Faso, Mozambique, and Niger.

Gender Inequality Index

Looking at the gender inequality index (UNDP 2013), reflecting inequality between women and men in three dimensions, i.e., reproductive health, empowerment and labour market, countries like Yemen, Afghanistan, Niger, Democratic Republic of Congo, Liberia, Central African Republic, Mali, Sierra Leone, Mauritania, Cote d I'voire, Cameroon, Zambia, Benin, Congo, India, Burkina Faso, Kenya, Sudan, Gambia, Haiti, Mozambique, Malawi, Pakistan, Ghana, Tanzania, Lesotho, Bangladesh, Uganda, Nepal, Botswana and Laos are at the bottom with very high levels of gender inequality (Table 1.3). Most of these countries are also on low human development index, excepting India, Iraq, Ghana, Guatemala, Swaziland and Laos which have medium human development index. Besides, most

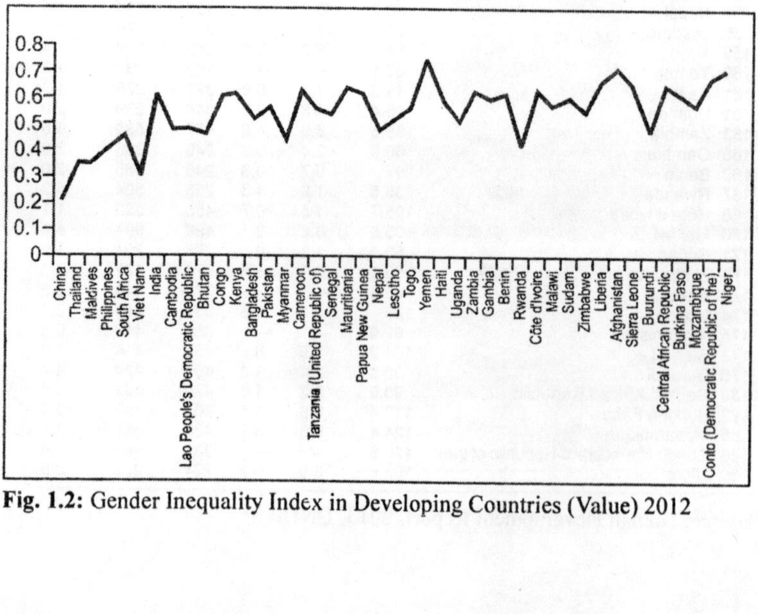

Fig. 1.2: Gender Inequality Index in Developing Countries (Value) 2012

of these countries have comparatively high incidence of poverty, measured both in terms of national and international poverty line.

Table 1.3: Gender Inequality Index in Developing Countries

HDI Rank	*Countries*	*Gender Inequality Index (Value) 2012*
101	China	0.213
103	Thailand	0.360
104	Maldives	0.357
114	Philippines	0.418
121	South Africa	0.462
127	Viet Nam	0.299
136	Equatorial Guinea	—
136	India	0.610
138	Cambodia	0.473
138	Lao People's Democratic Republic	0.483
140	Bhutan	0.464
142	Congo	0.610
145	Kenya	0.608
146	Bangladesh	0.518
146	Pakistan	0.567
148	Angola	—
149	Myanmar	0.437
150	Cameroon	0.628
151	Madagascar	—
152	Tanzania (United Republic of)	0.556
153	Nigeria	—
154	Senegal	0.540
155	Mauritania	0.643
156	Papua New Guinea	0.617
157	Nepal	0.485
158	Lesotho	0.534
159	Togo	0.566
160	Yemen	0.747
161	Haiti	0.592
161	Uganda	0.517
163	Zambia	0.623
165	Gambia	0.594
166	Benin	0.618
167	Rwanda	0.414
168	Côte d'Ivoire	0.632
170	Malawi	0.573
171	Sudan	0.604
172	Zimbabwe	0.544
173	Ethiopia	—
174	Liberia	0.658
175	Afghanistan	0.712
177	Sierra Leone	0.643
178	Burundi	0.476
180	Central African Republic	0.654
183	Burkina Faso	0.609
185	Mozambique	0.582
186	Congo (Democratic Republic of the)	0.681
186	Niger	0.707

Source: Human Development Report, 2013, UNDP.

Key Challenges and the Pathways

Improving Women's Access to Land and Water as well as Other Inputs

Rural women's access to ownership and control over land, forests and other natural resources, is the first prerequisite for their empowerment. Experience from India shows that mere legal provisions for equal distribution of land among men and women will not be enough. The Hindu Succession Amendment Act 2005 provides for equal distribution of land between sons and daughters. But in practice, this rarely gets executed due to a variety of reasons, namely poor systems of governance as well as lack of adequate awareness and sensitivity on the part of both men and women. Therefore, strong legal provisions should be supported by an effective system of implementation as well as creation of conducive conditions for it, through effective organization and voice of rural women. Even the redistributive land reform measures undertaken in the past were gender biased as women hardly benefited from them. Discriminatory land laws which lie at the root of agricultural productivity gaps in many countries should be reformed to provide for at least joint titling of agricultural land as well as homestead land. The post-2015 Millennium Dvelopment Goals should recognise the transformative nature of women's land and property rights build an equitable, secure and sustainable world. Besides, service delivery institutions such as land registry, bank and agricultural extension can help improve women's access to economic opportunity in many countries. In addition, mandatory joint titling on redistributed land would be important. Moreover, Government should help build women farmer's organizations to access technology and other inputs on equal basis.

Providing Education

Even though gender gaps in education have reduced in recent times in many countries, rural women, especially those disadvantaged by other adverse circumstances–remoteness, ethnicity, caste, race or disability, continue to lack adequate access to education, especially quality education. The situation and demand based solutions would be required, such as building more schools in remote areas recruiting local teachers and providing incentives conditioned on girls' school attendance.

Discrimination in Labour Market

Since majority of rural women are engaged as agricultural labourers and they are paid lower wages than their male counterparts, often for the same or similar nature of work, enforcement of equal pay for equal work and policy of non-discrimination in the labour market is a big challenge. In most of the developing countries, the labour laws and policies provide for equality of men and women in labour markets, but hardly these get implemented. Besides, technical change in agriculture in the recent past has not been gender neutral. In fact, the women workers in most cases do not possess the skills to operate tractors, threshers, harvesters, etc., and therefore, employers often think that women are not suitable workers. Any employability skills training programme can help in this regard. In addition, supporting the creation of women's networks can be effective where gendered networks hinder women workers, farmers and entrepreneurs (The World Bank, 2012). One good example is Self-Employed Women's Associations (SEWA) in India which organizes a large number of informal sector workers, providing information, support and training services to its members. Thus, removing discriminatory treatment in labour laws and regulations along with active labour market policies and creation of women's network can promote women's economic opportunities.

Increasing Women's Voice within Households and in Society

The muted voice of rural women within their households result from their limited access to economic opportunities, traditional social norms as well as lack of proper legal framework and poor enforcement of any provision of good law, if there is one. Increasing women's control over household resources, making the legal systems more responsive to women's needs, reducing domestic violence and increasing women's control over their fertility would help raise their voice within household. Besides, increasing women's voice in the society is constrained by social norms and beliefs which do not encourage women to participate in formal social and political institutions. Reservations and other types of affirmative action often help in promoting women's political representation. The 33 per cent to 50 per cent reservation for women in Panchayati Raj institutions in India can be quoted as an example in this regard.

Policies to Prevent the Inter-generational Reproduction of Gender Inequality

Acquisition of assets, education, health outcomes and economic opportunities by women largely determine their freedom from vicious circle of gender inequality trap. Appropriate policies to prevent the inter-generational reproduction of gender stereotype and inequality would include: (i) ensuring land rights to women, (ii) scholarships and other incentives to increase girl's school enrolment and attendance, (iii) vocational training, (iv) health education as well as health care facilities, and (v) affirmative actions for ending gender discrimination in labour market.

In India, the National Policy for Empowerment of Women 2001 was formulated as the blueprint for the future with the express goal of addressing women's felt needs and bringing about their advancement, development and empowerment. The government also made several affirmative laws and programmes for gender justice but women especially rural women could not benefit from them, due to their poor implementation.

Some of the important interventions in India could be listed as follows:

(i) The Dowry Prohibition Act 1961,
(ii) Hindu Succession Act (Amendment 2005),
(iii) The Protection of Women from Domestic Violence Act (DWDVA) 2005,
(iv) The Indecent Representation of Women Act 1986,
(v) Equal Wage for Equal Work,
(vi) Reservation of Job for Women under MGNREGA,
(vii) Reservation of seat for women in Panchayati Raj Institutions,
(viii) National Commission for Women
(ix) National Mission for Empowerment of Women
(x) Rajiv Gandhi Scheme for Empowerment of Adolescent Girls-Sasha 2010,
(xi) Indira Gandhi Matritva Sahyog Yojana,
(xii) Support to Training and Employment Programme for Women (STEP),
(xiii) Hostel for working women,
(xiv) Women Empowerment and Livelihood Programme in Mid-Gangetic Plains–Priydarshini, aiming at holistic empowerment of vulnerable groups of women,

(xv) Swadhar–to provide primary need of shelter, food, clothing and care to the margainalised women/girls living in difficult circumstances;

(xvi) 'Ujjawala'–a comprehensive scheme to combat trafficking.

Global Agenda

India signed the convention on the elimination of All Forms of Discrimination against Women in July 30, 1980 and ratified it on July 9, 1993. However, despite global concerns for employment of women, gender equality, especially for rural women is largely missing in development countries.

Global action for gender equality should focus on the following priority areas:

(a) Ensuring women's secure land, water and forest rights;
(b) Improving rural women's access to quality education and skills;
(c) Reducing maternal mortality rate as well as all female mortality;
(d) Improving rural women's access to economic opportunities;
(e) Increasing women's voice and agency in the household and in society;
(f) Ending the reproduction of gender inequality across generation;
(g) Providing financial support for improving the delivery of clean water, sanitation and health services;
(h) Sharing of good practices across various countries;
(i) Leveraging effective global partnerships for upstreaming and strategic mainstreaming;
(j) Improving the levels of economic development and poverty reduction in rural areas;
(k) Sustained advocacy and campaigns for change in socio-cultural norms; and
(l) Releasing women's time.

Some International Success Stories

Reducing Maternal Mortality Rates in Sri Lanka and Malaysia

The maternal mortality ratio in Sri Lanka declined from above 2000 per 100,000 births in the 1930s, to 500 in 1950 and 24 in 1996. In Malaysia, it dropped from 534 in 1950 to 19 in 1997. They did it with modest total public expenditures on health, i.e., 1.8 per cent of GDP on average, since the 1950s. Health programmes in both countries utilized synergic interactions of health care, with basic education, water and sanitation, malaria control and integrated rural development–including building rural roads which helped deal with emergencies. Better organizational management improved the supervision and accountability of service providers. Both countries were strongly committed to improving the status of women as female education received special attention. (The World Bank, 2012)

Catalyzing Women's Employment in Jordan

Despite growing education levels, labour force participation rates for women in the Middle East and North Africa remains very low. In Jordan, only 17 per cent of 20 to 45 years old women work, compared with 77 per cent of men. This labour force participation gap holds among the more educated. These low employment rates make it difficult for new graduates seeking to enter the labour market. With few women employed, young women lack role models to follow into employment as well as the network connections to help them find jobs.

The Jordan New Opportunities for Women Programme is a pilot to rigorously evaluate the effectiveness of two policies (i) short term wage subsidies; and (ii) employability skill training (The World Bank, 2012).

The short term wage subsidies give firms an incentive to take a chance on hiring young female graduates and an opportunity to overcome stereotypes by directly observing young women working for them. The subsidies can also give young women more confidence to search for work and to approach employers. In the pilot, each voucher has a value equal to the minimum wage for six months.

The employability skills training augments the technical skills that graduates learn in community colleges with the practical skills to find and succeed in employment. Early results from a mid line evaluation suggests that job vouchers have significant employment effects. Employment rates among graduates who received vouchers alone or vouchers plus training are between 55 to 57 per cent compared with 17 to 19 per cent among those who received training alone or received neither training nor vouchers. Follow up surveys will determine whether these employment effects of job vouchers are sustained in the long run.

Intervening Early to Overcome Future Labour Market Failures—The Adolescent Girls Initiative

This is a public-private partnership which promotes the transition of adolescent girls from school to productive employment through innovative interventions which range from business development skills training and services to technical and vocational training, targeting skills in high demand. In all projects girls receive life skill training to address the most important barriers to their economic independence. Underway in Afghanistan, Jordan, Laos PDR, Liberia, Nepal and South Sudan, the initiative targets about 20,000 adolescent girls and young women ages 16-24. Each country intervention is tailored to local context and specific needs of adolescent girls. The skills training programme aims to equip girls with technical skill that has proven demand in the labour market. While the focus is on matching skills to the market, the results in many cases challenge norms for gender appropriate occupations. (The World Bank, 2012)

Organizing Poor Rural Women as Neighbourhood Groups—Kudumbashree Experiences in Kerala (India)

There are several examples of organizing poor women in the form of self-help groups by Government and non-governmental organizations in India. Recently the Kudumbashree experience in Kerala can be cited as success stories.

Launched by the Government of Kerala in 1998 Kudumbashree is the largest women empowering project in India today. It has 4 million members, covering nearly 50 per cent households in Kerala. The main objective of the Kudumbashree Mission was to eradicate poverty through coordinated community actions initially by encouraging thrift and investment, vocational training, skill upgradation for self-employment and wage employment and later through other integrated development measures. In 2004 a new component, called collective farming by joint liability groups (JLGs) was added. Under this component, Kudumbashree Mission of the Government of Kerala has been assisting the poor women to lease in land in a group and thereby create an income source for them. This is promoted as an important livelihood activity of Kudumbashree neighbourhood groups, comprising small and marginal women farmers and landless agricultural labourers. The Gram Panchayats help the JLGs by providing inputs, basic infrastructure, irrigation facilities, one time land development for farming under Mahatma Gandhi National Rural Employment Guarantee Scheme and also assist in marketing of the produce. Besides, the primary agricultural credit societies provide interest free loans. In 2010-11 about 23,970 hectares of land was cultivated by 38,054 groups, benefitting about 0.23 million rural women. The experience shows that with handholding support by the government, the poor landless women engaged in lease farming and other activities in Kerala could overcome the poverty trap and move on the growth path. (Kudumbashree Mission Hope, 2011)

Allocation of Homestead Plot to Landless Women in West Bengal and Odisha (India)

The States of West Bengal and Odisha have initiated schemes in the past few years, involving allocation of homestead plot of 5 to 10 cents in size in the name of either the woman or jointly in the name of the woman and man which enable a beneficiary to construct a house if she does not have one and use the additional space for taking up some economic activities such as cultivation of vegetables, fruits, goat rearing, poultry, etc., thereby enhancing her food and nutritional security as well as social status. In West Bengal, over 0.12 million families received land through the Nijo-Griho-Nijo-Bhumi (NGNB) Scheme implemented by the State Governemnt with support from Landesa (Rural Development Institute) upto December 2013.

The Jalpaiguri district alone provided secure land rights through NGNB to 7000 rural landless families jointly in the name of both wife and husband till November 2013. Convergence support for the beneficiary families in the form of housing, water and sanitation, sapling of fruit and timber trees helped the families to initiate their journey out of poverty.

Beneficiaries of Land Distribution in Jalpaiguri (West Bengal)

Similarly, the Vasundhara Scheme introduced in Odisha in 2005-06 aimed at allocating homestead plot of 4 to 10 cents to about 0.25 million homesteadless households in the State. As per Government record, by 2008, about 92 per cent of the targeted households had received *Pattas* (land titles) in the name of either woman or jointly in the name of woman and man. The Government of Odisha with the help of Landesa, is also piloting a Rural Women's Resource Centre in the district of Gunjam and working out a model for empowerment of rural women by way of productive utilization of land and livelihood convergence.

Conclusions and the Ways Forward

Majority of rural women in developing countries are in poverty and low level equilibrium trap due to several factors including (i) low level of overall economic development, (ii) women's lower access to quality education and skills, (iii) poor health facilities, (iv) lack of secure land rights, (v) lack of proper access to institutional credit, technology and marketing, (vi) lack of proper policies for affirmative actions and to prevent the intergenerational reproduction of gender equality and (vii) unequal, albeit gender biased social structure, institutions, values and beliefs. The ways forward would include the following:

(i) Provide secure land, water and forest rights to all rural women, including homestead and agricultural land along with necessary provisions for modern inputs, technology, credit, marketing and insurance;
(ii) Provide at least 10 cents of homestead land to all landless and semi-landless rural women;
(iii) Develop and provide women friendly technology and institutions for removing the rural women's drudgery and improve their productivity and income;
(iv) Provide compulsory and free education to all rural girl children upto the higher secondary level, by establishing modern schools, colleges and skill training centres in all clusters of villages, along with proper infrastructure and incentives and trained teachers. More importantly, employability skills training programme for rural adult girls and women should be efficiently undertaken;
(v) Provide reservations and a proper system of effective affirmative actions to help improve rural women's active participation in politics as well as economic activities. This is particularly important for empowerment of *dalit*, tribal and other underprivileged women;
(vi) Make focused efforts for reducing maternal mortality rate as well as overall female mortality rate by way of improvement in rural health care facilities, including quality hospitals, sanitation, clean water, etc.;
(vii) Launch sustained advocacy and campaigns for change in

socio-cultural norms and beliefs which help perpetuate gender bias against women;

(viii) Improve overall income and employment opportunities for both women and men in rural areas which will help empower rural women;

(ix) Recruit more female extension workers for extending new agricultural technologies;

(x) Organize rural women on the line of self-help groups, neighbourhood groups, producers' cooperatives etc.; and

(xi) Provide leadership training to rural women in afforestation, environment protection, water conservation and climate change.

References

Food and Agriculture Organisation of the United Nations (2011), State of Food and Agriculture, Rome (Italy).

Kudumbashree Mission (2011), Government of Kerala.

United Nations Development Programme (UNDP, 2013), Human Development Report, New York.

The World Bank (2012), The World Development Report 2012, Washington, D.C.

2

Gender Inequality in Developing Countries

The Case of South Asia

Seema Gaikwad[1]

Gender equality and the right to empowerment is first and foremost a human right. Despite the fact that gender inequality has been publicly reverberating through society for decades and there is a worldwide consensus that gender equality is a prerequisite, a necessary condition, for sustainable development and poverty reduction, gender inequalities persist.

Gender inequality is not one homogeneous phenomenon, but a collection of disparate and interlinked problems[2]. The first Human Development Report in 1990 and subsequent reports over the years have highlighted the persistent gender gaps in several High, Medium and Low Human Development countries. Analytical frameworks such as the OECD's Social Institutions and Gender Index (SIGI) and the Gender Inequality Index (GII) discussed in the recent Human Development Report 2013, The Rise of the South: Human Progress in a Diverse World and the Women's Economic Opportunity Index (WEOI) 2010, capture the loss of achievement due to gender inequality. The GII captures gender inequality in three dimensions: reproductive health, empowerment and labour market participation. The higher the GII value, the greater the discrimination. Based on 2012 data for 148 countries, the GII shows large variations across countries, ranging from 0.045 (in Netherlands with a GII rank of 1) to 0.747 (in Yemen with a GII rank of 148). India, Pakistan, Bangladesh and Nepal rank 132, 123, 111, and 102 respectively. High gender disparities persist in Asia especially in South Asia, where the three driving factors are low female representation in parliament (18.5%), gender imbalances in educational achievement (28% of women have completed at least secondary education, compared with 50% of men) and low labour force participation (31% of women are in the labour force, compared with 81% of men) as compared to East Asia and the Pacific which has lower female representation in parliament (17.7%) but fare higher in educational achievement (49.0% of women have completed at least secondary education, compared with 63.0% of men) and a higher labour force participation (65.2% of women are in the labour force, compared with 80.6% of men)[3].

Countries with very high human development rank in 2012 show greater parity in educational attainment of women and men. In Norway (HDI rank 1) 95.6 per cent of women have completed at least secondary education, compared with 94.5 per cent of men, in Australia (HDI Rank 2) 92.2 per cent of men and women have completed at least secondary education and in Germany (HDI rank 5) 96.2 per cent of women have completed at least secondary education, compared with 96.9 per cent of men[4]. This high attainment in education parity has not translated to reducing high gender gaps in parliamentary representation. In 2012 Norway had 39.6 per cent of females in the national parliament, while Australia had 29.2 per cent, Netherlands 37.8 per cent and Germany 32.4 per cent. Other High Human Development countries like the United States of America, Japan and Ireland have very high gender gaps in parliamentary representation (17.0%, 13.4% and 19.0% respectively)[5].

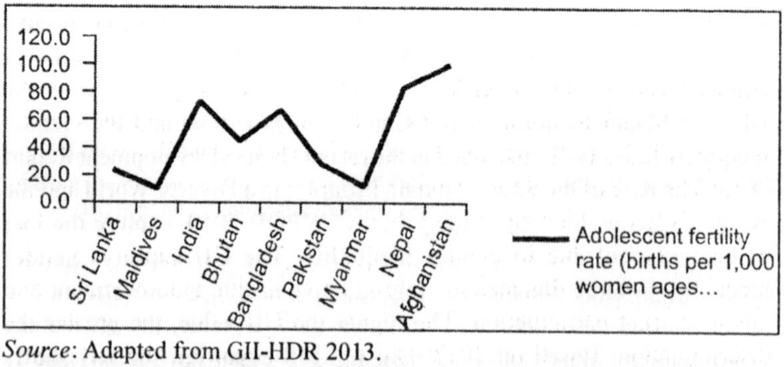

Source: Adapted from GII-HDR 2013.

Fig. 2.1: Adolescent fertility rate (births per 1,000 women aged 15-19) in 2012

While some countries in South Asia have shown an improvement in their GII ranking between 2008 and 2012 such as Bangladesh which moved from its position at 116 to 111 and Nepal moved from its position at 110 to 102, there are several countries which have moved lower in their ranks during the same period such as India (moved from its position at 122 in 2008 to 132 in 2012), Pakistan (moved from its position at 112 in 2008 to 123 in 2012)[6]. It is worth noting that these countries continue to have high maternal mortality ratios (deaths per 100,000 live births), high adolescent fertility rates (births per 1,000 women aged 15-19) and poor education attainment of population with at least secondary education (%ages 25 and older). In 2010 India had a maternal mortality ratio (MMR) of 200, during the same year Pakistan had an MMR of 260, in Bangladesh the MMR was 240 and in Nepal 170. The adolescent fertility rates (births per 1,000 women aged 15-19) in 2012 were 74.7 in India, 68.2 in Bangladesh and 86.2 in Nepal. During the period 2006-2010 these countries also fared very poorly in education attainment of population with at least secondary education (%ages 25 and older) India with 26.6 per cent, Bangladesh with 30.8 per cent, Pakistan with 18.3 per cent and Nepal with 17.9 per cent fared the poorest[7].

The concern I wish to flag here are twofold: (a) the increasing proportion of adolescent mothers in the country and (b) the increased likelihood of a correlation between the lack of education, inadequate access to health, high adolescents fertility rates and the combined associated of these of neonatal deaths and infant morbidity and mortality rates. The high under five mortality rates (the probability per 1,000 that a newborn baby will die before reaching age five) in India (61) Bangladesh (46), Pakistan (72) and Nepal (48)[8] may be a manifestation of high mortality rates, high adolescents' fertility and poor education attainments.

Types of Gender Inequalities

Natality Inequality: In some countries the preference for boys over girls has manifested itself in the form of families wanting the newborn to be a boy than a girl. Sex selective abortion has started to become a statistically significant phenomenon in countries like India, China and Korea. As a result the gender ratio is skewed in some Asian countries. In 1990, Amartya Sen suggested that worldwide, particularly in Asia, millions of women were "missing" from the population totals of many countries. "Nearly four million poor women go 'missing' each year in developing countries", said the 'World Development Report 2012: Gender Equality and Development', released by World Bank. The sex ratio in India is 940.27 females per 1000 males; China's sex ratio is dipping and stands at 884 females per 1000 males, with Bangladesh, Pakistan and Nepal having the same sex ratio of 961.53 females per 1000 males. These high sex ratios at birth are now attributed to sex-selective abortion and infanticide due to a strong preference for sons. This will affect future marriage patterns and fertility patterns. These imbalances can be addressed by ensuring greater participation of women in economic, political spheres, decision making at the household level and other levels of governance.

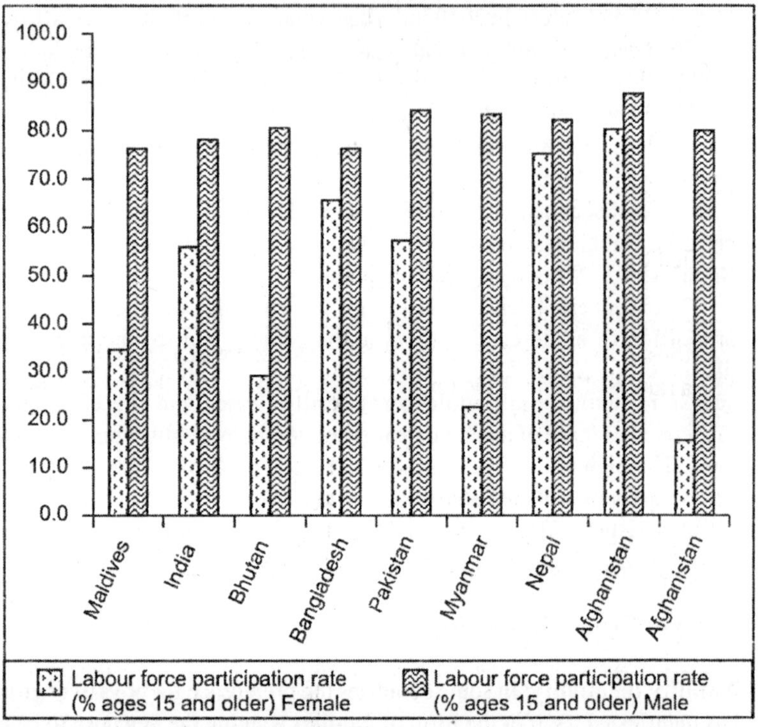

Source: Adopted from GII-HDR 2013.

Fig. 2.2: Labour Force Participation Rate, 2011

Household Inequality: It is quite common in societies that men work outside the home whereas women do the household chores. As stated by Amartya Sen, it is "quite common in many societies to take it for granted that while men will naturally work outside the home, women could do it if and only if they could combine it with various inescapable and unequally shared household duties"[9]. This inequality stems not from the fact that women are incapable for taking work outside the house but due to deep rooted patriarchy and uneven division of labour. There are several factors that have attributed to the low labour force participation rate (%ages 15 and older) for women and men in medium to low human development countries. In India, the labour force participation rate (%ages 15 and older) for women is 29.0 as compared to 80.7 for percentages 15 and older for men, in Bangladesh labour force participation rate (%ages 15 and older) for women is 57.2 as compared to 84.3 for %ages 15 and older for men, in Pakistan labour force participation rate (%ages 15 and older) for women is 22.7 as compared to 83.3 for %ages 15 and older for men. China and Nepal have a lower imbalance. In China, the labour force participation rate (%ages 15 and older) for women is 67.7 as compared to 80.1 for %ages 15 and older for men and in Nepal labour force participation rate (%ages 15 and older) for women is 80.4 as compared to 87.5 for %ages 15 and older for men.

Economic Inequality: According to the ILO, "[W]omen are too often trapped in insecure employment situations with low productivity and low earnings ... [and] face persistent earnings gaps which cannot always be justified by differences in skills, experience, or tenure"[10]. According to the new global index and ranking by the Overall Women's Economic Opportunity Rankings Table[11], India with a score of 42.7 ranks 22 of 33 countries in Asia, Bangladesh ranks 30 with a score of 32.6 and Pakistan with a rank of 32 scores the lowest (29.9). According to the International Trade Union Confederation (ITUC), the average gender pay gap was 22.4 per cent in 2008, based on a survey of 20 developing and developed countries[12]. A number of countries also have differentiated retirement age for men and women, while this on the one hand can be perceived as a social protection measure on the other, combined with the gender wage gap labour force participation and higher life expectancy adds up to lower pensions for women, which affects their financial security in later life[13].

Ownership Inequality: Inequality in ownership of property exists in most parts of the world. The dominant role played by cultural and customary practices in depriving women's rights and the non implementation of laws and rights have further exacerbated the ownership inequality. Gender biases are also inherent in land markets. Lacking access to credit facilities, women have poor purchasing power. In countries where only a few women have legal land rights in their names access to land markets, credit facilities and technical assistance services is difficult with the result that increasing number of women are landless or are dependent on men for their tenurial security. In rural South Asia, where arable land is the most important form of property, any significant improvement in women's economic and social situation is crucially tied to their having independent land rights. Despite progressive legislation few South Asian women own land; even fewer effectively control any. A complex range of factors—social, administrative, and ideological—are found to underlie the persistent gap between women's legal rights and their actual ownership of land, and between ownership and control. Eight countries in the Women's Economic Opportunity Index (2010) do not have such rights three Asian countries Indonesia, the Philippines, Sri Lanka also make it to the list[14]. In India, the **matrilineal social system** is found in small pockets in south and the north-east India. The Nairs and Mappillas in Kerala, the tribal groups of Minicoy Island and the Khasis and the Garos of Meghalaya still follow the matrilineal system. Many communities in coastal Karnataka and Kerala practice matrilineal system of property inheritance.

Women's Legal and Social Status: Some countries have taken positive steps to legislate women's rights by formally acknowledging the principle of gender equality. The Women's Economic Opportunity Index, 2010 includes an indicator that considers whether countries are signatories to the Convention on the Elimination of All Forms of Discrimination against Women (CEDAW), and whether they signed the accompanying Optional Protocol, which allows a key committee to hear complaints from individuals or groups of women about violations of their rights, and to conduct inquiries into grave violations of the Convention. 187 countries, out of 194 countries, have ratified the treaty. Seven countries that have

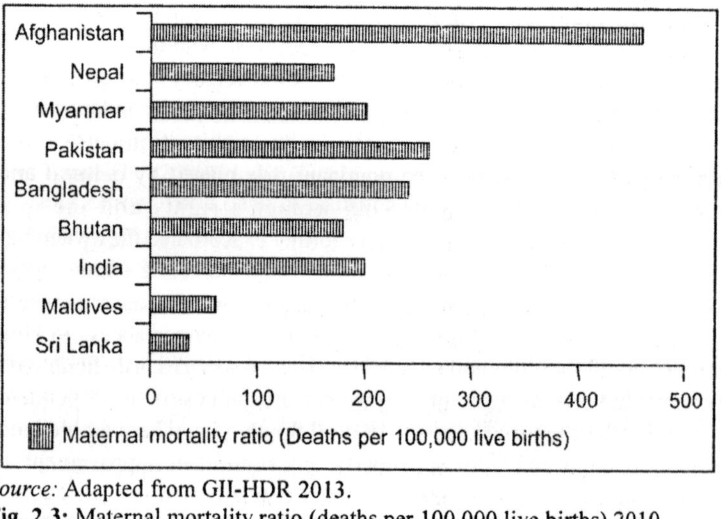

Source: Adapted from GII-HDR 2013.

Fig. 2.3: Maternal mortality ratio (deaths per 100,000 live births) 2010

NOT ratified CEDAW, including the United States, Iran, Somalia, Sudan, South Sudan, and two small Pacific island nations (Palau, and Tonga)[15].

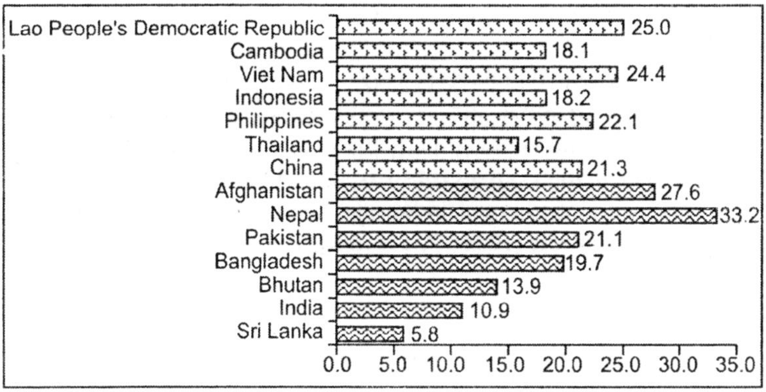

Source: Adapted from GII-HDR 2013.

Fig. 2.4: Seats in National Parliament (% female) 2012

Maternal Mortality: Medium and Low Human Development Countries continue to have low Maternal Mortality—the number of maternal deaths per 100,000 live births, is directly related to women's access to life-saving reproductive healthcare[16]. In terms of Maternal Mortality Afghanistan, Pakistan, Bangladesh and India are close to the bottom of the league. Early marriage is prevalent in the region. In Bangladesh 48 per cent of 15-19 years old girls and 32 per cent of 15-19 years old girls in Nepal are married[17]. Only Bhutan and Nepal have an equal minimum age of marriage for women and men; only Nepal, India and Bhutan grant women and men equal parental authority. There are several barriers in availing the health services especially for hard to reach and underserved regions of India, Nepal, Pakistan and Bangladesh. Some of these are the availability of health personnel, proper antenatal and postnatal check-ups, and availability of trained informal health personnel like midwives.

Public and Political Participation: National legislations and International declarations promoting the public and political participation of women from local to national and international levels have borne some dividends. India along with Bangladesh, Sri Lanka and Pakistan has had female heads of government and in the case of Bangladesh the leader of the opposition and the Prime Minister are both women.

There are several factors that constraint women's participation in public and political forum, some of these are economic dependency and lack of adequate financial resources, illiteracy and limited access to education and the same work opportunities as men, lack of access to information, discriminatory cultural and social attitudes and negative stereotypes perpetuated in the family and in public life. South Asia has however made impressive progress in the introduction of political quotas: India, Afghanistan, Bangladesh, Nepal and Pakistan have introduced quotas at both national and sub-national levels. Women's political representation in the national parliament is low in South East Asia; in China, women held 21.3 per cent seats, in Vietnam women held 24.2 per cent seats, in Cambodia and Indonesia women held 18.1 per cent and 18.2 per cent seats respectively[18]. This trend is similar across all countries in the region.

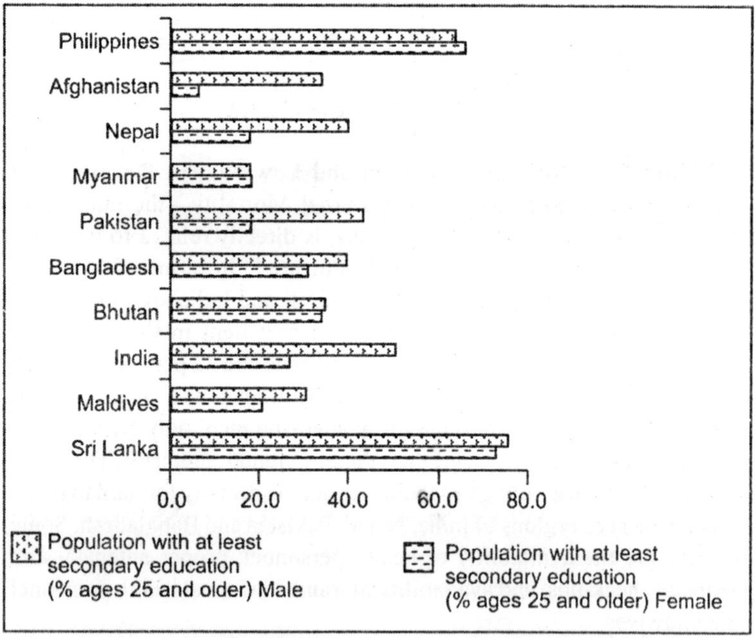

Source: Adopted from GII-HDR 2013.
Fig. 2.5: Secondary Education Attainment 2006-2010

Freedom of Movement: According to the UN Children's Fund (UNICEF), to "provide for their own needs, as well as those of their children, women require the ability to move freely within and outside the household"[19]. Only a few governments have laws that prohibit women from leaving their homes or the country in which they reside without the permission of a male relative or guardian (this includes restrictions on a woman's ability to obtain a passport). These include Oman, Saudi Arabia, Syria and Yemen. But cultural attitudes prevalent in Western Asia may prevent some women from easily leaving their homes on their own or without permission[20].

Education Attainment: In terms of elementary school most low HDI countries have achieved or are achieving full enrolment in elementary schools and more than 50 per cent enrolment in secondary school. Philippines and Sri Lanka are closer to achieving gender parity in percentages of 25 and older with at least secondary education[21]. In other South Asian countries female percentages of 25 and older with at least secondary education fall short of achievements made by male in the same age group. The issue that still need to be addressed is that of 'completion rates', 'learning outcomes' and the quality of education. The gap in education attainment, therefore, becomes a critical factor in addressing the inequalities and a key factor in eliminating poverty and aiding development.

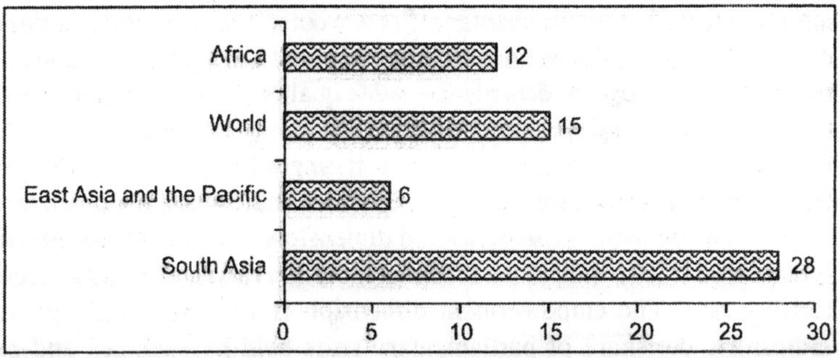

Source: Improving Child Nutrition: The Achievement imperative for global progress, 2013.

Fig. 2.6: Percentage of infants weighing less than 2500 grams

Under Nourishment of Girls and Women: Child malnutrition and undernutrition can manifest stunting, underweight, low birth and maternal malnutrition. Low birth weight data shows that 14 countries have the highest number of children under 5 years of age who are moderately or severely stunted. In South Asia 39 per cent of children under 5 years of age are stunted. Of these India ranks 1 with 48 per cent stunting prevalence in 2005-2006; followed by Pakistan with 41 per cent stunting prevalence in 2011; China with 10 per cent as per 2010 data; Indonesia with 36 per cent as of 2010 data and Bangladesh with 41 per cent as of 2011[22]. South Asia has also the highest underweight prevalence (59%) and also has by far the greatest regional incidence of low birthweight with one in four newborn weighing less than 2500 grams at birth. India alone accounts for 7.5 million, followed by Pakistan 1.5 million, Philippines 0.5 million and Bangladesh 0.7 million[23]. Nutritional status before and during pregnancy influence the maternal and child outcomes. As stated in the preceding pages women's low educational levels, unequal social status and limited decision-making power can negatively influence the nutritional status of their children and that of their own. Nutritional inequalities will also have intergenerational and long-lasting consequences impacts on a country's physical, social and economic well-being. It is, therefore, imperative for governments to commit to addressing the above issues and stress the need for equitable development.

Measuring Gender Inequality

There are several indices that measure gender gap using different indicators and parameters. The data from Gender Inequality Index (GII)[24] largely referred to in this chapter reflects women's disadvantage in three dimensions—reproductive health, empowerment and the labour market—for as many countries as data of reasonable quality allow. The index shows the loss in human development due to inequality between female and male achievements in these dimensions. It ranges from 0, which indicates that women and men fare equally, to 1, which indicates that women fare as poorly as possible in all measured dimensions. The health dimension is measured by two indicators: maternal mortality ratio and the adolescent fertility rate. The empowerment dimension is also measured by two indicators: the share of parliamentary seats held by each sex and by secondary and higher education attainment levels. The labour dimension is measured by women's participation in the work force. The Gender Inequality Index is designed to reveal the extent to which national achievements in these aspects of human development are eroded by gender inequality, and to provide empirical foundations for policy analysis and advocacy efforts[25].

The Gender Inequality Index faces major data limitations, which constrains the choice of indicators. For example, GII uses data of national parliamentary representation that excludes participation at the local government level and elsewhere in community and public life. The labour market dimension lacks information on incomes, employment and on unpaid work mostly done by women. The Index misses other important dimensions, such as time use—the fact that many women have the additional burden of care giving and housekeeping, which cut into leisure time and increase stress and physical exhaustion. Asset ownership, gender-based violence and participation in community decision-making are also not captured, mainly due to limited data availability. To get a comprehensive understanding of the Gender Inequality it would be worthwhile also to refer data from the Women's Economic Intelligence Unit's Economic Opportunity Index (WEOI) which focuses on laws and regulations about women's participation in the labour market and social institutions that affect women's economic participation. It has five dimensions–labour policies and practice, women's economic opportunity, access to finance, education and training, women's legal and social status, and general business environment[26]. The World Economic Forum developed its own indicator, the Global Gender Gap Index (GGGI) which measures social areas: economic participation and opportunity, educational attainment, general health and political empowerment.

Summing Up

The far reaching consequences that gender inequality has on both men and boys and women and girls and on a country's social, economic and political well-being has been enumerated in this chapter as well as several empirical studies. Greater gender equality is correlated not only with higher growth outcomes, but also with lower poverty rates[27]. The importance of understanding the complexity of women's agency is crucial for development practice, because women's capacity to exercise choice, as well as to act, is determined by their particular country, social and cultural systems and norms. Women's Empowerment interventions should be able to address the inhibitions by cultural dictates on seclusion, restrictions on mobility, or the unequal division of labour within the household. Similarly, it is important to assess how legislation and its administration work in terms of women's inheritance rights. It is also necessary to assess how changes in social practice might protect or endanger people's livelihoods. If change is to be effective, a systematic approach to implementation of plans, policies, programme's needs to be in place along with creation of a conducive environment for freedom of action and thought which promotes informed and critical women's agency for combating inequality of all kinds.

Notes

1. Seema Gaikwad is the Regional Advocacy Advisor, Asia and the Pacific, at VSO International, New Delhi. The views in this chapter are those of the author and do not necessarily represent those of VSO. This chapter was presented at the International Summit on Empowerment of Women, held at the India International Centre, New Delhi on September 2-3, 2013 and has been written to elicit comments and to further debate.
2. "Many Faces of Gender Inequality", Amartya Sen, *The New Republic*, September 17, 2001.
3. *Human Development Report 2013*, The Rise of the South: Human Progress in a Diverse World.
4. *Ibid.*
5. *Ibid.*
6. Gender Inequality Index 2012.
7. *Ibid.*
8. Improving Child Nutrition, The achievable imperative for global progress, UNICEF April 2013.
9. A. Sen, "The many faces of gender equality", *Frontline*, Vol. 18, Issue 22, October 27th-November 9th, 2001.
10. "Global employment trends for women", International Labour Organisation, Geneva, March 2009.
11. *Women's economic opportunity Index is a new global index and ranking*, presents the results of a global benchmarking model built and scored by the Economist Intelligence Unit.
12. Gender (in)equality in the labour market: An overview of global trends and developments", International Trade Union Confederation: Brussels, March 2009.
13. E. James, A. Cox Edwards and R. Wong, "The Gender Impact of Pension Reform", *Journal of Pensions Economy and Reforms*, Vol. 2, November 2003.
14. *Women's economic opportunity Index is a new global index and ranking*, presents the results of a global benchmarking model built and scored by the Economist Intelligence Unit.
15. www.cedaw2013.org
16. Bangla *et al.*, 2011:1043.
17. *Status of Adolescents in SAFOG Countries*, Saria Tasnim, 2009.
18. Gender Inequality Index 2012.
19. http://www.unicef.org/ sowc07/profi les/inequality_household.php
20. Women's Economic Opportunity Index, 2010.
21. Gender Inequality Index 2012.
22. Improving Child Nutrition: The achievements imperative for global purposes, UNICEF, 2013.
23. *Ibid.*

24. http://hdr.undp.org/en/statistics/gii/
25. *Ibid.*
26. *Ibid.*
27. A Morrison, D Raju and N Sinha, "Gender Equality, Poverty and Economic Growth", World Bank Policy Research Working Paper World Bank: Washington DC, 2007.

3

India's Twelfth Five Year Plan Approach to Reducing Gender Disparities in Development

Sudha P. Rao

The vision of the Twelfth Five Year Plan (2012-17) is 'Faster, Sustainable, and More Inclusive Growth'. The simultaneous achievement of each of these elements is critical for the success of the Plan. The Plan aims at an 8.2 per cent growth per annum. A full Chapter in the Plan is devoted to Women's agency and child rights. Besides, because gender is a cross cutting issue, specific concerns of women are addressed in the individual sectoral chapters also.

The orientation towards gender concerns has evolved over plans from a purely welfare approach to a development approach and subsequently to empowerment and now recognizes women's agency where women are acknowledged as agents of change. The Twelfth Five Year Plan recognizes the primacy of India's Women and Children who constitute over 70 per cent of India's people. The Twelfth Plan strategy of inclusion envisages the engendering of development and making it more child friendly. The ending of gender based inequities, discrimination and violence is an overriding priority in the Twelfth Plan.

The Prime Minister of India addressing the 57th National Development Council Meeting held to endorse the plan on 27th December, 2012, New Delhi emphasized that

> "Gender inequality is another important aspect which deserves special attention. Women and girls represent half the population and our society has not been fair to this half. Their socio-economic status is improving, but gaps persist. The emergence

> of women in public spaces, which is an absolutely essential part of social emancipation, is accompanied by growing threats to their safety and security.... There can be no meaningful development without the active participation of half the population and this participation simply cannot take place if their security is not assured."

Gender disparities are starkly brought out by the Census data and social indicators. According to 2011 Census, the population of women (including girls) is 586 million and they account for 48.5 per cent of the total population in India. The overall sex ratio is 943 and Child Sex Ratio (0 to 6 years) of 919 is even lower. The literacy rate for women is 64.6 per cent as against 82.1 per cent for males. The gap between female and male infant rate mortality is 49 for girls to 46 for boys as reported by Registrar General of India is a matter of concern. There is Gender differential in under 5 child mortality with 64 for girls against 55 for boys per 1,000 live births. There is a high prevalence of anaemia as brought out by National Family Health Survey among women with about 55 per cent (in 15-49 age group) suffering from it. According to Census 2011, as against the male worker participation rate of 53.1 per cent, the female participation rate is only 25.5 per cent. From 1993-94 to 2009-10 women's participation of the labour force has decreased substantially from 36.8 per cent to 26.1 per cent in rural areas and from 17 per cent to 13.8 per cent in urban areas as indicated by National Sample Survey Organization. Another major concern is the gender gap in the educational level of the labour force. Whereas in 2004-05, 60 per cent of employed females were illiterate and 3.7 per cent were graduates for men it was 28 per cent and 8 per cent, respectively. Female hourly wage rates in agriculture vary from 50 per cent to 75 per cent of male rates, and are insufficient to overcome absolute poverty.

Many women and children live in difficult circumstances. There are many faces of vulnerability and deprivation, which the Twelfth Plan strategy for Women and Children addresses. The intergenerational cycle of multiple deprivation and violence faced by girls and women is epitomized by the adverse child sex ratio in children under 6 years of age. The ending of gender based inequities, discrimination and violence is an overriding priority in the Twelfth Plan, and improvement in the adverse and steeply declining child sex ratio is, therefore, recognized as an overarching monitorable target of the Twelfth Plan for Women and Children. The key strategies for women's agency in the Twelfth Plan have been identified as: (i) Economic Empowerment; (ii) Social and Physical Infrastructure; (iii) Enabling Legislations; (iv) Women's Participation in Governance; (v) Inclusiveness of all categories of vulnerable women, (vi) Engendering National Policies/Programmes. Further, strategies for the inclusion of vulnerable women such as those belonging to the Scheduled Castes (SC), Scheduled Tribes (ST) and minorities; single women, differently abled women; migrant and trafficked women have also been identified.

Monitorable Targets

The Monitorable Targets of the Twelfth Plan for Women and Children are:

- Improve the Child Sex Ratio from 914 in 2011 to 950 by 2017.
- Prevent and Reduce Child Undernutrition (percentage of underweight prevalence in children 0-3 years) by half (50%).
- Reduce anaemia in girls and women by half (50%).
- Ensure that all children receive a protective environment at family and community level and through health and child care centres, schools and other facilities.
- Ensure that 80 per cent or more Panchayats, districts and cities progressively become child friendly.

Addressing violence against women, in both public and private sphere, is a major challenge recognized in the XII Plan. The XII Plan has accordingly recommended that implementation of Protection of Women from domestic violence (PWDPA) and Dowry Prohibition Act (DPA) will be improved with the help of appointment of Protection officers under a new scheme for the purpose as well as appointment of sufficient number of full time Dowry Prohibition officers. New initiatives such as One Stop Crisis Centres for providing shelter, police desk, legal, medical and counselling services and Women's Helpline will be implemented. A scheme for providing restorative justice to victims of rape through financial assistance as well as support services will be implemented in the Twelfth Plan in pursuance of the Supreme Court of India directives.

There is need for inclusion of vulnerable women especially widows, elderly women, women affected with HIV/AIDS, Migrant Workers, women in disturbed areas, trafficked women, women in prison and transgendered communities in the development process. The Plan envisages better implementation of the Scheduled Castes and Tribes (Prevention of Atrocities Act, 1989), Good quality house sites in the joint names of both the wife and husband, PDS outlets in SC *bastis* and support for education for girls belonging to minority community including collective transport facilities.

The Plan strategy focusing on health, education, sanitation and infrastructure development will create many productive jobs, a large proportion of which will be in the formal sector. This must be accompanied by measures to ensure that women have adequate access to these new job opportunities including transportation facilities and housing.

There has been an increase in literacy amongst women from 53.67 per cent (Census 2001) to 65.46 per cent (Census 2011). The challenge however remains in bridging the gender gap which stands at 16.68 per cent. The gender differential in education has been declining, particularly at the primary level. There is still a need to address the issues of retention of girls' in school, quality of education and the provision of separate toilets and sibling care facilities. In the wake of Right To Education, a child tracking system would be adopted. Providing hostel facilities and scholarships for girls as well as including nontraditional vocational training as part of the overall education curriculum are instruments for engendering the education strategy so on. The Plan will also ensure the provision of toilets with water in all schools and Anganwadi Centres and the active involvement of women in determining the location of sanitation facilities.

For economic empowerment, the plan expects to increase women's employability in the formal sector and focus on women's work participation. Employment generation with equity in work conditions will be ensured by strengthening the implementation of the Equal Remuneration Act and the Maternity Benefit Act. Skill development will enable women to move from traditional skills to emerging skills to help women to break the gender stereotypes. To improve livelihood opportunities, there is need for promotion of enterprises of home-based workers and small producers. In addition Self Help Groups (SHGs) need to be classified as priority sector and given loans at concessional rates, technology transfers to take place to women in all aspects of farming, farm management, animal husbandry, forestry, sustainable natural resource management. Other measures for empowerment proposed are granting Joint land titles in all government land transfers, assistance to purchase land in groups for group cultivation and incentives to women farmers/SHGs for group farming. Special emphasis has been laid on skill development of women belonging to marginalized sections. Women's workforce participation would be more active particularly in secondary and tertiary sectors by ensuring decent work for them.

Engendering Development

The Twelfth Plan takes cognizance of the fact that policies and programmes have different impact on men and women and it is necessary to strengthen gender mainstreaming efforts and pursue gender responsive budgeting at all levels of Governance. State governments have been requested to integrate gender budgeting and gender assessment outcome in Planning Process. This includes Gender Assessment Survey to ensure that women's needs are addressed right at the design and planning stage. and engendering flagship programmes. The strengthening of Gender Budgeting and its extension to all Ministries is proposed. It is proposed to bring in gender concerns in Results Framework Document (RFD) of Ministries. Gender being a cross cutting issue, the Results Framework Document of Ministries would explicitly reflect gender concerns in their vision, mission and objectives, especially those pertaining to equity, inclusiveness and empowerment and also gender disaggregated *inter se* priorities, targets/success indicators to make the gender outcome accountable and visible. There should be mandatory collection of sex disaggregated data wherever feasible.

Effective participation of women in institutions of governance is an effective way of empowering women. The elected women representatives need to be equipped to ensure delivery of public services. The Panchayats should be strengthened to enforce registration of births, marriages and migration to address the issues of trafficking and child marriage. Urban local bodies need Gender focal points and, citizen report cards with ratings on meeting women's needs in services such as provision of water and sanitation, widows pensions Effective participation of women in institutions of governance is an assured way of empowering women and integrating gender concerns in development.

The Twelfth Plan seeks to make the fulfilment of women's rights an inalienable condition to achievement of rapid and sustainable economic growth. The Plan endeavours to provide a nurturing, protective and safe environment for women to facilitate their entry into public spaces. According the highest priority to ending gender based inequities, discrimination and violence faced by girls and women is the prerequisite to the objective of the Plan. The Plan calls for structural transformation, not only in the direct policy and programme interventions for women and children but also in the policies and programmes of different sectors that impact upon women and children.

Part – II
Land and Property Rights of Women

4

Women's Land and Property Rights and the Post-2015 Development Agenda

Mayra Gomez and *D. Hien Tran*

Introduction

Secure rights to land and property for women are widely regarded as fundamental to ensuring effective and sustainable human development. Rights to land and property include the right to own, use, access, control, transfer, exclude, inherit and otherwise make decisions about land and related resources. *Secure* rights to land are rights that are clearly defined, long-term, enforceable, appropriately transferable, and legally and socially legitimate. For women, exercising these rights should not require consultation or approval beyond that required for men.

Globally, there is an evident correlation between gender inequality, societal poverty, and the failure to respect, protect and fulfil these rights for women. This failure entrenches gender inequality by reinforcing women's dependence on men, and prevents poor countries from finding a sustainable and equitable path to development. Strengthening women's secure rights to land can help empower them to reach their potential as citizens and as economic actors, and enable them to take control over their own lives. According to a World Bank report, "only independent or joint ownership can ensure that women have access to [and] control over land-based earnings.[1] Additionally, as the World Bank recognizes, "[r]ights to land and natural resources increase a woman's bargaining power within the household, which results in increased allocation of household resources to children and women as well as increased household welfare."[2]

The link between women's land and property rights and sustainable human development is evident for a wide range of issues. For example, from the perspective of women's empowerment, food security and poverty alleviation, the Swedish International Development Cooperation Agency (SIDA) has noted that "Women's access to land and property is central to women's economic empowerment, as land can serve as a base for food production and income generation. Agricultural production and food security also increase when women are granted tenure security:"[3] The United Nations Food and Agriculture Organization (FAO) estimates that if women had the same access to productive resources as men, they could increase yields on their farms by 20-30 per cent.[4] These gains in agricultural production could lift some 100-150 million people out of hunger.[5] The FAO, however, noted:

> [T]he potential production gains calculated by this method are *based on the existing distribution of land.* This implies that countries where women control proportionately more land could achieve the greatest potential gains. It may be the case, however, that the overall gender gap in access to agricultural resources is, in fact, wider where women control less land. The actual gains from closing the gender gap in access to resources would be greater in countries where the gender gap is wider. *Increasing women's access* to *land* as *well* as *complementary inputs in that case would generate broader socio-economic benefits than those captured in this analysis* (emphasis added).[6]

On HIV, the United Nations Development Programme (UNDP) has noted that women's rights to inheritance of property are "a crucial factor in reducing women's vulnerability to violence and HIV, as well as empowering women to cope with the social and economic impact of the epidemic at the household level."[7] And on environmental sustainability, women's farming practices are typically less likely to contribute to environmental degradation and natural resource loss."[8]

Without the basic recognition of women's capacity and right to make fundamental decisions about their lives, women will remain relegated to the sidelines of society, among the first to suffer hardship and homelessness, violence and exploitation. For women to become active and valued participants in the lives of their communities, every woman's right to land and property must be respected, protected, fulfilled and enforced—and this must be done on the basis of equality with men. It is also clear that the global gains to be made through improving women's land and property rights are significant. These rights contribute to women's equality and well-being, and go hand in hand with many sustainable human development goals, including women's social and economic empowerment, poverty eradication, food security, and sustainable agriculture. The gains to be made would lift up women, first and foremost, as well as entire families, communities and societies.

International Recognition of Women's Land and Property Rights

Despite the potential gains, the current Millennium Development Goals (MDG) framework does not directly address women's land and property rights. Goal 3, to Promote Gender Equality and Empower Women, does not contain any specific target in relation to these rights. Similarly, Goal 1, which seeks to eradicate extreme poverty and hunger, provides no specific target in relation to these rights. This silence has led organizations including the DECO Development Centre to note that women's control over resources, including land and property, is one of the "missing dimensions" of the current MDG framework, and that examining this issue can in part "shed light on the bottlenecks that hamper further progress across all the MDG targets."[9]

More recently, however, international policy documents have addressed women's land and property rights. In May 2012, the Committee on World Food Security officially endorsed the Voluntary Guidelines on the Responsible Governance of Tenure of Land, Fisheries and Forests in the Context of National Food Security. The Guidelines recognize the importance of gender equality in land tenure as critical to the strategies to reduce hunger and poverty and support sustainable development.[10] They exhort States to "ensure that women and girls have equal tenure rights and access to land, fisheries and forests independent of their civil and marital status", and to ensure that policy, legal, and organizational frameworks for tenure governance are "non-discriminatory and promote social equity and gender equality"[11].

The United Nations Conference on Sustainable Development held in June 2012 (Rio +20) also visibly raised the importance of women's land and property rights. In the Rio +20 outcome document, 'The World We Want', women's land and property rights are explicitly reflected at paragraphs 58(k), 109, and 236-244. Paragraph 240, for example, clearly notes:

> We are committed to equal rights and opportunities for women

> in political and economic decision-making and resource allocation and to removing any barriers that prevent women from being full participants in the economy. We resolve to undertake legislative and administrative reforms to give women equal rights with men to economic resources, including access to ownership and control over land and other forms of property, credit, inheritance, natural resources and appropriate new technology.

This recognition of the centrality of women's land and property rights builds upon the increasing attention that the issue has received in recent years despite their exclusion from the current MDG framework. In fact, women's land and property rights have been recognized in dozens of international human rights instruments and related standards. In 1997, the former United Nations Sub-Commission on the Promotion and Protection of Human Rights adopted the first resolution by an international body directly addressing women's housing and land rights specifically, urging governments to:

- Take all necessary measures in order to amend and/or repeal laws and policies pertaining to land, property and housing which deny women security of tenure and equal access and rights to land, property and housing;
- Encourage the transformation of customs and traditions which deny women security of tenure and equal access and rights to land, property and housing; and
- Adopt and enforce legislation which protects and promotes women's rights to own, inherit, lease or rent land, property and housing."[12]

In 1998, the Commission on the Status of Women adopted its first resolution on women's housing and land rights, resolution 42/1 on *'Human rights and land rights discrimination/*recognizing that "secure land rights are key rights for the economic empowerment of *women."* During the early to the mid-2000s, the former United Nations Commission on Human Rights (now the Human Rights Council) also adopted a series of resolutions on *'Women's equal ownership of, access to and control over land and the equal rights* to *own property and to adequate housing'* (resolutions 2000/13; 2001/34; 2002/49; 2003/22; 2005/25).[14]

Beyond these resolutions, international bodies and experts relevant to women's land rights have adopted a number of additional pronouncements. The General Comments and Recommendations of the UN Treaty Bodies are particularly instructive. The Committee on the Elimination of Discrimination against Women stated that "there are many countries where the law and practice concerning inheritance and property result in serious discrimination against women. Such provisions contravene the Convention on the Elimination of All Forms of Discrimination against Women and should be abolished."[15]

The UN Committee on Economic Social and Cultural Rights (which monitors States party compliance with the International Covenant on Economic, Social and Cultural Rights) has stated in its General Comment No.16 that "women have a right to own, use or otherwise control housing, land and property on an equal basis with men, and to access necessary resources to do so"[16] and has highlighted women's equal inheritance rights.[17] On food security, the Committee has said that national strategies to ensure food and nutrition security for all should "give particular attention to the need to prevent discrimination in access to food or resources for food. This should include: guarantees of full and equal access to economic resources, particularly for women, including the right to inheritance and the ownership of land and other property, credit, natural resources and appropriate technology."[18]

The United Nations Human Rights Committee (which monitors States party compliance with the International Covenant on Civil and Political Rights) has similarly said: "Women should also have equal inheritance rights to those of men when the dissolution of marriage is caused by the death of one of the spouses."[19] The Committee has also stated unequivocally that "The capacity of women to own property. may not be restricted on the basis of marital status or any other discriminatory ground."[20]

This commitment from the international community is an important foundation on which to build, and must be urgently translated into reality for the world's women. The post-2015 process represents a critical moment to ensure that women's land and property rights receive the attention that they deserve on the international development agenda.

The Status of Women's Land and Property Rights Worldwide

The FAO has recognized that, globally, "Gender inequalities in land rights are pervasive. Not only do women have lower access to land than men. They are often also restricted to so-called secondary land rights, meaning that they hold these rights through male family members. Women thus risk losing entitlements in case of divorce, widowhood or their husband's migration. Evidence also shows that women's land parcels are generally of smaller size and lower quality" than men's.[21] Single women or those whose marriages are not formally recognized also typically have more tenuous rights to land.

While women's land and property rights are vital to development, the reality remains that in many parts of the world these rights are often not shared equally between men and women, and are routinely violated, denied, and given insufficient protection and enforcement. The obstacles which prevent women from effectively enjoying these rights equally with men are complex, and at times context specific. They range from inadequate legal standards and implementation of laws, to discriminatory social norms, attitudes, and programmes at the national, regional and local levels which taken together result in wide discrepancies in practice between development outcomes for men and women.

In many countries, the result of gender biased statutory laws, customary law, traditions, and social norms and attitudes is that women cannot or do not use, access, control, own, rent, lease, or inherit land and property without consent from a man. This results in a form of social exclusion which constrains a woman's ability to participate fully and equally with men in their homes and their communities. Certainly, secure rights to critical resources are connected to broader social concerns of power, status, personal autonomy, and economic independence. These issues are in turn related to patterns of gender discrimination in education, work, income, family responsibilities, and participation in decision-making processes at all levels; a cyclical pattern of discrimination which exists in both developing and developed countries.

Women's exclusion from formal and customary systems of property inheritance has received increasing attention over the past few years. Because property inheritance is fundamental to how wealth is transferred within a society, it directly relates to the protection of a woman's economic livelihood and long-term security. This issue is especially vital because it addresses some of the systemic reasons for women's disproportionately high levels of poverty around the world and disproportionately insecure land and property rights. Some formal laws do not recognize equal inheritance for women and men and for daughters and sons. Moreover, in many systems of customary law, primary property rights are allocated to the males in the household, and widows are not permitted to inherit those rights from their deceased husbands. Protections for women which may have existed traditionally are eroding as land pressures increase.

For instance, widows may have traditionally retained the right to use matrimonial land and remain in the matrimonial home until her death, remarriage, or while her children are unmarried. Over the past several decades however, widows, particularly those who are younger, have found themselves especially vulnerable to their in-laws taking the land, leaving them landless and homeless.[22]

In many parts of Africa where customary systems predominate, men control household land (and the house which sits on that land). Community authorities, who are predominantly male, generally allocate land to male household heads for use with their households. These rights to land are then most commonly passed down to male heirs. And because most women move to their husband's home at the time of marriage, this means that for many women, access to land and property is entirely dependent on a relationship to male relatives (usually husbands and fathers). A husband may be obliged to provide arable land to his wife to farm, but he has ultimate authority to decide which piece of land the woman can use, for what purposes, under what conditions, for how long, and what she can do with the proceeds from that land. It also means that if their relationship breaks down, she must rely on his family's goodwill (which is often tenuous) or return to her father's/birth family's land (which is often not possible) to continue to provide for herself and her children.

In countries where women have the statutory right to own, rent, lease and inherit housing, land and property, tradition and dominant social attitudes may still prohibit these rights from being claimed or enforced in practice. For example, in India, women have considerable legal rights to own and inherit land, yet few women are able to claim these legal rights.[23] Although India has a fairly progressive legal framework with respect to gender, this legal protection rests precariously upon a foundation which is fractured by a lack of political will at some levels and widespread gender inequality. Even in the cases where a woman does legally own land, gender discrimination and social stigma often serves to thwart a woman's ability to effectively exercise genuine "control" over her land. Similarly, in Nigeria, although the "Land Use Act" does not explicitly exclude women from being landowners, only a husband's name is expected to appear on land and house titles, putting women's claims on land on unequal footing with men's.[24] Furthermore, where gender-sensitive laws exist, progress can be constrained by the lack of resources necessary to reach rural communities through practical, low-cost, and culturally acceptable means.

The Transformative Development Potential of Women's Land and Property Rights

Gender inequality in secure rights to land and property impedes progress in achieving inclusive economic and social development, environmental sustainability, and peace and security-four dimensions the UN System Task Team on the Post-2015 UN Development Agenda identified as requiring progress to build an equitable, secure, and sustainable world. This gender disparity leaves women and the households they manage economically and socially vulnerable. Data analyzed by the DECD Development Centre show that countries where women lack rights or opportunities to own land have on average 60 per cent more malnourished children than countries where women have some or equal access to land.[25]

It has become increasingly clear that when women have secure land and property rights, the improvements in household welfare are even more pronounced. Secure land and property rights are a foundational building block for agricultural productivity, household food and nutrition security, education, and poverty reduction and promote more inclusive and stable societies. However, it is not only important that *households* have secure rights to land and property, but also that *women,* as well as men, hold these rights. This is crucial, first and foremost, for ensuring women's equality and empowerment, but it has other beneficial effects in terms of lifting households out of poverty. When men alone enjoy secure land rights, women and their children may not be able to fully reap the benefits of those rights.

Inclusive Economic and Social Development

The UN Task Team Report, *Realizing the Future We Want for All,* recognized that ensuring access, use and control of land is critical to supporting the smallholder agricultural growth that is needed for poverty reduction, particularly where families—and women—depend on farming for their livelihoods. In addition, it identified land tenure security as a key element to help eradicate hunger and guarantee food and nutrition security.[26] That the Report identified the significant role of secure rights to land in achieving inclusive economic and social development is not surprising, given the clear linkage between those rights and improved agricultural productivity and food security.

Smallholder farmers with secure land and property rights have greater incentive to make productivity-enhancing investments because they have greater confidence that they can recoup their investments over the medium and long term. Secure rights also provide improved opportunities for families to access financial services, and sometimes are prerequisites to access government programmes and assistance.[27] As numerous studies have shown, secure rights to land and property thus can lead to increased agricultural productivity and production.[28]

The increased agricultural productivity and production can in turn enhance household food security and nutrition through two avenues: directly, through increased food production for consumption, and indirectly, through increased incomes permitting the purchase of more and better quality food and supporting livelihood diversification. In both ways, secure rights to land help moderate the impact of food price volatility on poor households.

A growing body of research points reveals the link between secure land and property rights and improved household food and nutrition security. When women have secure property rights—including rights over the land they cultivate—they gain improved social status which leads to their empowerment and greater influence over household decisions. For instance, a study in Central America found that women with land rights are more likely to exercise control over household income and have access to credit.[29] In Nicaragua, women with either individual or joint title control over 50 per cent of the crop income while women who have no land rights control only 14 per cent of that income.[30] In Nepal, researchers found that women who own land are significantly "more likely to have the final say" in household decisions.[31] Similarly, a study in Brazil showed that women's secure land rights are associated with a woman's increased ability to participate in household-decision-making.[32]

The enhanced status of women is an important step to empowering women and achieving gender equality and economic and social development, as it leads to women's increased decision-making power, greater autonomy, and greater participation in the community. Secure rights to land improve women's ability to diversify livelihoods, better plan for the future, and escape the cycle of poverty and social exclusion.

Beyond that, it also translates into improved nutrition for women and for their children. Data from South Asia, Sub-Saharan Africa, and Latin America and the Caribbean "leave no doubt that women's status plays a positive role in determining child nutritional status."[33] Women with higher status have better nutrition and enjoy better prenatal and birthing care than those with low status, especially in South Asia.[34] Their children, in turn, are more likely to be born at higher birth weights and receive better care critical to their nutritional well-being[35] This study identified several public policies to improve women's status-including reforming legislation to give women equal rights to own and inherit land.[36]

Furthermore, when women own land, their purchasing decisions are likely to benefit the household's food security and their children's nutritional status. Indeed, a World Bank report points out that "*lithe* income and resources that women control wield disproportionately strong effects on health and nutrition outcomes generally."[37]

- A study in Nicaragua and Honduras found that families spend more on food when the woman of the house owns land.[38] The study also found that when women have land rights, children have higher levels of educational attainment.[39]
- A study in Ghana showed that when women own a larger share of the household's farmland, families allocate a larger proportion of their household budget to food.[40]
- In Nepal, research demonstrated that the likelihood that a child is severely underweight is reduced by half if the child's mother owns land. The Nepal study suggested that the route to better child nutrition was through the greater income and resources provided by the women's right to land.[41]

Women's improved status benefits not only their children and families, but also the well-being of women themselves. This is paramount both to combat gender inequality and promote women's empowerment. One study in Botswana and Swaziland found that women who faced food insufficiency were more likely to engage in sexual risk-taking behaviours, such as selling sex for money or engaging in unprotected sex, putting them at greater risk of HIV infection.[42] Some research suggests that land and property rights for women may help prevent the further spread of HIV by promoting women's economic empowerment, thereby reducing their vulnerability to some forms of gender-based violence and exploitation, unsafe sex, and other HIV-related risk factors.[43] For example, women's increased economic empowerment through secure land and property rights can enhance their sexual autonomy. And because secure land rights can lead to increased household food security, women are less vulnerable to engaging in transactional sex as a means of survival. In fact, some have suggested that the way to make sex safer for women is by ensuring that they have access not only to condoms, but to title deeds[44] Furthermore, land and other property can also serve as an income source to cover costs associated with HIV, improving women's ability to cope with the economic and social impact of the disease.

Environmental Sustainability

Population growth and poverty both place enormous pressure on the growing problem of land and natural resources degradation. When land rights are insecure and land users fear eviction or expropriation[45] or when natural resources are publicly owned and managed,[46] incentives exist to overuse the land and to convert non-arable land into farmland. As the UN Task Team Report noted, an immediate priority in preserving environmental sustainability is the sustainable management of natural resources, particularly with the full cooperation of local populations.[47] Traditional knowledge is a major asset for promoting this sustainability.

With secure rights to land, users have incentives to make the land more productive and sustainable. By providing those who use land with long-term interests in the land's fertility and sustainability, secure land rights can create incentives to invest in measures such as erosion control.[48] Furthermore, secure land rights have been shown to reduce demographic pressures on natural resource areas such as forests, wetlands, and rangelands, thus minimizing the uncontrolled conversion of such areas to farm land where that is inappropriate.[49] This is especially important for the protection of common resources, which constitute a critical factor in providing women pastoralists, gatherers, and fishers, with secure access to food.

Lack of secure rights to land for women can cause land—and women's productivity—to suffer. As the people most often involved in day-to-day farming, it is critical that women have a vested interest in protecting natural resources.[50] When a woman's rights to use land are derived from and dependent on a relationship with a male, she may fear that not using the land for one season will impact her longer-term access to the land. For example, a study in Uganda found that when women farmers did not have secure rights to the land they farmed, many chose not to let it lie fallow during the most beneficial periods, contributing to soil degradation.[51] In Rwanda, a study found that women are the primary farmers but are granted only temporary and insecure use rights to the land they farm. These weak land rights contribute to a lack of investment in land that has led to severe problems with soil erosion.[52]

However, where women have secure rights to use and access land, there is evidence that they use resources sustainably. Research shows that many women practice "traditional conservation methods such as 'managed' fallow, crop rotation, intercropping, and mulching," and "[b]ecause of their particular household responsibilities for obtaining food, fuel, and water, women who get these products directly from natural resources have a vested interest in protecting them."[53] The benefits to the environment are thus two-fold when women have secure land rights: as farmers, women will be able to make good long-term land use decisions, and as women, they are often more likely to use ecosystem based approaches to land management.

Peace and Security

Around the world, land rights disputes within countries and between countries have led to political instability, violence, and displacement, which all have profound human costs and also undermine economic growth and poverty reduction. Disputes over property and land also have grave, and sometimes fatal, results at the community level. Intuitively, it is clear that secure rights to land and property provide families with greater security: secure rights decrease fears of eviction and displacement and provide families a solid stake in society.

The UN Task Team Report also pointed out that a development agenda that recognizes the centrality of human security must include efforts to prevent and reduce all forms of violence and abuse, particularly that of marginalized populations such as women and girls, calling gender-based violence "one of the worst and most pervasive manifestations of inequality and discrimination."[54] Efforts to address women's lack of secure rights to land and property is one key way to help reduce gender-based violence. By providing women enhanced status in the household and community, secure rights can in a very real sense protect women against domestic violence, and ensure that women who do face abuse are able to leave violent relationships. Land and property rights can strengthen a woman's status and bargaining power within marriage, which serves to deter violence. Additionally, because these rights can enhance a women's self-worth and increase her sense of autonomy and options, they can thereby increase her ability to stand up to violence.

For example, a study from India indicated that women who own land or a house face a significantly lower risk of marital violence. In Kerala, 49 per cent of women without property reported experiencing long-term physical violence and 84 per cent reported long-term psychological violence. However, significantly smaller percentages of women with land and a house reported physical and psychological violence—7 per cent and 16 per cent respectively. In addition, 71 per cent of propertied women who suffered violence left home compared to 19 per cent of women without property, and a much smaller proportion of propertied women subsequently returned home.[55] In West Bengal, the story is similar. Women with property were much less in number than women without property who experienced physical violence—15 per cent *versus* 40 per cent—and psychological violence—28 per cent versus 50 per cent.[56] Surveys conducted in Nicaragua indicated that women's land ownership increase their power and control within a marriage, which in turn reduces domestic violence.[57] While more studies are needed, these findings point to an important outcome linked to secure land and property rights for women.

Recommendations for the Post-2015 Development Agenda

The "persistent inequalities and struggles over scarce resources are among key determinants of situations of conflict, hunger, insecurity and violence."[58] Gender inequality in secure rights to land and property is intimately tied to all of these development-related problems, which are key factors impeding efforts to achieve equitable and sustainable human development.

Indeed, women's enjoyment of secure rights to land and property is essential to several of the current MDGs, including improvements in poverty and hunger, gender inequality, environmental sustainability, universal primary education, and combating HIV.

But without secure rights, women are relegated to a lower social status and more vulnerable to poverty, hunger, and violence as compared to men. Moreover, women cannot fully participate in the economy and cannot realize their full potential as individuals. Unfortunately, the lack of attention given to land rights issues has translated into less meaningful gains in achieving several of the current MDGs.

The very cross-cutting nature of women's secure land and property rights represents a substantial opportunity: Efforts to strengthen and enforce such rights can help achieve multiple goals in a post-2015 development framework. But, without focused and explicit attention to women's secure land and property rights that opportunity could be squandered. Accordingly, the post-2015 framework must:

- Recognize the transformative nature of women's land and property rights with respect to a range of development goals related to advancing women's empowerment, gender equality, food security and environmental sustainability;

- Include specific targets related to advance and secure land and property rights for women, as well as targets related to women's access to productive resources more generally (such as credit, agricultural extension services, and agricultural inputs). Such targets should be crafted to address *de jure* protection of women's land and property rights, as well as their *de facto* enjoyment of these rights;
- Ensure that these targets are themselves informed by, and aligned with, relevant international human rights standards protecting women's land and property rights, (including as they relate to women's access to, use of and control of housing, land and property; gender equality; equal inheritance rights; and equal rights in marriage); Ensure that affected women and women's organizations are able to meaningfully and effectively participate in the articulation and monitoring of these targets.

These recommendations address both substance and process for the post-2015 framework. The good news is that there are many things that States can do to improve the status of women's land rights and property, both *de jure* and *de facto.* While it is beyond the scope of these recommendations (and this article) to discuss fully all of the effective strategies which have been shown to advance the enjoyment of women's land and property rights in practice, it should be noted that such practices certainly do exist. Several important approaches will be discussed in greater detail in a Handbook on Effective Strategies to Realize Women's Rights to Land and Other Productive Resources that UN Women and the United Nations Office of the High Commissioner for Human Rights (OHCHR) is currently developing following an expert group meeting convened in June 2012.[59]

For their part, States can address the problem of gender inequality in land and property rights in at least three ways. First, States should design and revise laws to ensure that women are accorded full and equal land and property rights with men, and should undertake administrative reforms and other necessary measures to give women and men the same access to credit, capital, appropriate technologies, markets, and information. Adequate enforcement mechanisms must also be put in place.

In this respect, part of the solution lies in removing discriminatory barriers in law and policies which exclude women from access to these resources, be they overtly or covertly discriminatory. It is important that all relevant laws—for example, personal laws, marriage and family laws, and land laws, etc.—are clear and consistent in their support of women's land rights. Laws which seem on their face to be 'gender neutral' must also be examined for their discriminatory impact. For example, the CEDAW Committee in its recent Concluding Observations on Sri Lanka underscored this point when they noted "that discriminatory practices prevent women from acquiring ownership of land since only the 'head of household' is authorized to sign official documentation such as land ownership certificates and receive pieces of land from Government,"[60] because in Sri Lankan society the 'head of the household' was most often deemed to be male. The Committee urged the Government of Sri Lanka to abolish the concept of 'head of household' in administrative practice and recognize joint or co-ownership of land and to amend its national legislation to ensure joint or co-ownership.

Second, States should also support the transformation of customs, traditions and patriarchal practices and norms that deny women secure land tenure. Awareness-raising campaigns and community dialogues can be effective ways to build understanding and support for women's land rights. Customs and traditions which support women's equal rights to land and property should be championed and shared.

Third, States should take proactive measures to ensure women's equality and to ensure that policies related to and affecting land and property rights actively promote gender equality and prioritize women's needs. In this regard, States should adopt temporary special measures as needed.

In all of the above, it is vital to ensure genuine and effective participation by women (especially the poor and marginalized) in the design, implementation, monitoring and evaluation of all laws, policies and programmes that relate to land and property. Furthermore, States should specifically monitor the gender-differentiated impacts of their laws, policies and programmes, in particular those concerning rural development and food security, with a special emphasis on women's land rights.

These strategies are fully consistent with international human rights laws and standards noted above, and would go a long way towards advancing these rights for women in both law and practice. Gains in increasing the number of women with secure land and property rights across the world will help achieve progress in a post-2015 development agenda that seeks to eradicate poverty, address gender inequality, and build an equitable, secure and sustainable world. The world must not allow this opportunity to pass by again.

References

1. World Bank. (2005). Gender Issues and Best Practices in Land Administration Projects: A Synthesis Report, 3.
2. World Bank, United Nations Food and Agriculture Organization (FAO), and International Fund for Agricultural Development (IFAD) (2008). The Gender in Agriculture Sourcebook, Module 4,125-171. See also: Fong, M. and Bhushan, A. (1996). *Toolkit on Gender in Agriculture. Gender Toolkit Series No. 1.*
3. Swedish International Development Cooperation Agency (SIDA). Quick Guide to What and How: Increasing Women's Access to Land. *Women's Economic Empowerment Series.*
4. United Nations Food and Agriculture Organization (FAO) (2011). *The State of Food and Agriculture: 2010-2011.*
5. United Nations Food and Agriculture Organization (FAO) (2011). *The State of Food and Agriculture: 2010-2011.*
6. United Nations Food and Agriculture Organization (FAO) (2011). *The State of Food and Agriculture: 2010-2011.*
7. UNDP (2008). Voices and Visions: The Asia Pacific Court of Women on HIV, *Inheritance and Property Rights.*
8. Mehra, R. (1995). *Women, Land and Sustainable Development.* ICRW Working Paper No. 1.
9. OECD Development Centre (2010). *Gender Inequality and the MDGs: What are the Missing Dimensions*?
10. United Nations Food and Agriculture Organization (FAO) (2012). *Voluntary Guidelines on the Responsible Governance of Tenure of Land, Fisheries and Forests in the Context of National Food Security.*
11. *Ibid.*
12. UN Sub-Commission on the Promotion and Protection of Human Rights, 'Women and the right to adequate housing and to housing and land,' UN Doc. E/CN.4/SUB.2/RES/1997/19 (27 August 1997). A subsequent resolution (1998/15) was adopted the following year under a similar title 'Women and the right to land, property and adequate housing,' (UN. Doc. E/CN.4/SUB.2/RES/1998/15).
13. UN Commission on the Status of Women, Report on the Forty-second Session (2-13 March 1998), Economic and Social Council Official Records, 1998, Supplement No.7, UN. Doc. E/CN.6/1998/12 (1998).
14. UN Commission on Human Rights, 'Women's Equal Ownership, Access to and Control over Land and the Equal Rights to Own Property and to Adequate Housing,' UN Doc. E/CN.4/2005/RES/25 (15 Apr. 2005).

15. Para. 35, Gen. Rec. 21, adopted by the CEDAW Committee at its thirteenth session (1994).
16. UN Committee on Economic, Social and Cultural Rights, General Comment 16, Article 3: the equal right of men and women to the enjoyment of all economic, social and cultural rights (Thirty-fourth session, 2005), U.N. Doc. E/C12/2005/3 (2005).
17. UN Committee on Economic, Social and Cultural Rights, General Comment 16, Article 3: The equal right of men and women to the enjoyment of all economic, social and cultural rights (Thirty-fourth Session, 2005), U.N. Doc. E/C12/2005/3 (2005).
18. UN Committee on Economic, Social and Cultural Rights, General Comment 12, Right to adequate food (Twentieth Session, 1999), U.N. Doc. E/C12/1999/5 (1999), reprinted in Compilation of General Comments and General Recommendations Adopted by Human Rights Treaty Bodies, U.N. Doc. HRI/GEN/l/Rev.6 at 62 (2003).
19. United Nations Human Rights Committee (2000). General Comment 28: Equality of Rights between Men and Women (Article 3).
20. United Nations Human Rights Committee (2000). General Comment 28: Equality of Rights between Men and Women (Article 3).
21. United Nations Food and Agriculture Organization (FAO) (2010). Gender and I and Rights: Understanding Complexities, Adjusting Policies. Economic and Social Perspectives Policy Brief 8.
22. Raradza, G., International Land Coalition (2011). Securing Women's Access to Land: Linking Research and Action—An Overview of Action-Research Projects in Eastern Africa; Adoko, J., Land and Equity Movement in Uganda. *How Does Land Grabbing Happen: Experiences from Northern Uganda.*
23. Rao, N. (2012). Good practices in realizing women's rights to productive resources, with a focus on land: The case of India. Paper presented at the UN-Women/OHCHR Expert Group Meeting on good practices in realizing women's rights to productive resources, with a focus on land. Geneva, Switzerland. 25-27 June 2012. 15
24. USAID (2010). Nigeria: USAID Country Profile: Property rights and resource governance.
25. OECD Development Centre (2012). At Issue: Do Discriminatory Social Institutions Matter for Food Security?, 4; *see also* OECD Development Centre. Coding of the Social Institutions Variables. Retrieved from http:/ /genderi ndex.org/sites/default/files/G ID _variables.pdf.
26. UN System Task Team (2012). Realizing the Future We Want for All, 27, 29.
27. Prosterman, R., Mitchell, R., and Hanstad, T., (eds.) (2009). *One Billion Rising*, at 17-18.
28. *See, e.q.,* Deininger, K. (2003). Land Policies for Growth and Poverty Reduction 42-48. World Bank.

29. Katz, E. and Chamorro, J. (2002). Gender, Land Rights and the Household Economy in Rural Nicaragua and Honduras 11. Paper prepared for the Regional Workshop on Land Issues in Latin America and the Caribbean.
30. Katz, E. and Chamorro, J. (2002). Gender, Land Rights and the Household Economy in Rural Nicaragua and Honduras 11. Paper prepared for the Regional Workshop on Land Issues in Latin America and the Caribbean.
31. Allendorf, K. (1980). Do Women's Land Rights Promote Empowerment and Child Health in Nepal? *World Development,* 35, 11.
32. Mardon, M. (2005). Land Rights, Collective Action and Household Gender Relations in the Brazilian Agrarian Reform. University of Massachusetts, Amherst.
33. Smith, L.; Ramakrishnan, U.; Ndiaye, A.; Haddad, and L., Martorell, R. (2003). The Importance of Women's Status for Child Nutrition in Developing Countries. International Food Policy Research Institute Research Report 131, p. 58.
34. *Ibid.*, p. 79.
35. *Ibid.*, pp. 8-9, 60, 79.
36. *Ibid.*, p 131.
37. World Bank (2007). *From Agriculture to Nutrition: Pathways, Synergies and Outcomes*, xiii.
38. Katz, E., and Chamorro, J. (2002). Gender, Land Rights and the Household Economy in Rural Nicaragua and Honduras 15. Paper prepared for the Regional Workshop on Land Issues in Latin America and the Caribbean.
39. Katz, E., and Chamorro, J. (2002). Gender, Land Rights and the Household Economy in Rural Nicaragua and Honduras 15. Paper prepared for the Regional Workshop on Land Issues in Latin America and the Caribbean, 11.
40. Doss, C. (2006). The Effects of Intra-household Property Ownership on Expenditure Patterns in Ghana, *Journal of African Economics,* 15(1), 149.
41. Allendorf, K. (1980). Do Women's Land Rights Promote Empowerment and Child Health in Nepal? *World Development,* 35, 1985.
42. Weiser, S.D.; Leiter, K.; Bangsberg, D.; Butler, l.; Percy-de Korte, F.; Hlanze, Z.; Heisler, M. (2007). Food Insufficiency is Associated with High-Risk Sexual Behaviour among Women in Botswana and Swaziland. *PLos Medicine* 4:10: 260.
43. Strickland, R. (2004). To Have and To Hold: Women's Property and Inheritance Rights in the Context of HIV/AIDS in Sub-Saharan Africa. International Centre for Research on Women (ICRW) Working Paper. See also: Panda, P., (2002). Rights Based Strategies in the Prevention of Domestic Violence. ICRW Working Paper No. 344.
44. Sweetman, C. How Title Deeds Make Sex Safer: Women's Property Rights in an Era of HIV: *From Poverty to Power*: Background Paper, Oxfam, 2008.
45. Mendolsen, R. (1994). Property Rights and Tropical Deforestation. *Special Issues on Environmental Economics,* Vol. 46 Oxford Economic Papers

750-755; Deacon, R. (1999). Deforestation and Ownership: Evidence from Historical Accounts and Contemporary Data. *Land Economics* 75(3), 341.

46. Gibson, C.; Lehoucq, F.; and Williams, J. (2002). Does Privatization Protect Natural Resources? Property Rights and Forests in Guatemala. *Social Science Quarterly* 83(1). 207; Bassey, E. (2003). The Effects of Land Tenure on Natural Resource Conservation in the Nigerian Rainforest Ecosystem, FAO.
47. UN System Task Team (2012). Realizing the Future We Want for All, 27-28.
48. Mitchell, R. (2006). Property Rights and Environmentally Sound Management of Farmland and Forests, in Bruce, J. *Land Law Reform,* 183; Deininger, *Land Policies for Growth and Poverty Reduction: Key Issues and Challenges Ahead,* UN, FIG, PC IDEA Inter-regional Special Forum on the Building of Land Information Policies in the Americas (Oct. 2004).
49. Deacon, R. (1999). Deforestation and Ownership: Evidence from Historical Accounts and Contemporary Data. *Land Economics* (75)(3), 341; Jaramillo, C. and Kelly, T. (1997). Deforestation and Property Rights in Latin America, *IADB.). Retrieved from* http://www.iadb.org/sds/publication/publicationl030e.htm;
Deininger, K. and Byerlee, D. (2011). Rising Global Interest in Farmland. *World Bank.*
50. *See, e.g.* Jacobson, J. (1992). Gender Bias: *Roadblock to Sustainable Development.* Worldwatch Paper 110.
51. Giovarelli, R. and Wamalwa, B. (2011). Issue Brief-Land Tenure, Property Rights, and Gender: Challenges and Approaches for Strengthening Women's Land Tenure and Property Rights. 2 (citing Mason, K. and Carlsson, H. (2005). The Development Impact of Gender Equality in Land Rights. *Human Rights and Development: Towards Mutual Reinforcement).*
52. Randolph, S. and Sanders, R. Constraints to agricultural production in Africa: A survey of female farmers in the Ruhehgeri prefecture of Rwanda. Studies in Comparative International Development 13(3): 78-98 (1988).
53. Mehra, R. (1995). Women, Land and Sustainable Development. ICRW Working Paper No.1, 24.
54. UN System Task Team (2012). *Realizing the Future We Want for All,* 31-32.
55. Panda, P. and Agarwal, B. (2005). Marital Violence, Human Development and Women's Property Status in India, *World Development* (33)(5), 823-850, at 836, 842.
56. Gupta, J. (2006). Property Ownership of Women as Protection for Domestic Violence: The West Bengal Experience, in ICRW (2006) *Property Ownership and Inheritance Rights of Women for Social Protection—The South Asia Experience,* at 45.

57. Grabe, S. (2010). Promoting Gender Equality: The Role of Ideology, Power, and Control in the Link Between Land Ownership and Violence in Nicaragua. *Analyses of Social Issues and Public Policy,* 10, 146-170.
58. UN System Task Team (2012). Realizing the Future We Want for All, p. i.
59. For more information, please see: http://www.unwomen.org/events/54/expert-group-meeting-good-practices-in-realizing-womens-rights-to-productive-resources-with-a-focus-on-land/
60. UN Committee on the Elimination of All Forms of Discrimination against Women, 'Concluding Observations on Sri Lanka,' Forty-eighth session, 17 January-4 February 2011, UN Doc. CEDAW/C/LKA/CO/7, at paras. 38-39 (4 February 2011).

5

Gender Differentials in Access to Land

Constraints, Enabling Factors and Impacts on Women's Status

Nitya Rao

Introduction

The importance of land and other productive resources to women's livelihood security as well as recognition of social identity is now well established (Rao, 2011). In India, women own about 11 per cent of cultivable land, though they constitute over 60 per cent of the total agricultural work force (FAO, 2011) and 84 per cent of all rural female workers (NSSO, 2010: H-ii)[1]. Stagnation of agriculture has led to growing male migration in search of alternate employment, and despite increased urbanisation, 66 per cent of the population remains rural and dependent primarily on farming for their livelihood. Reports of malnutrition and persistent rural poverty and disadvantage (World Bank, 2009, GHI, 2011), alongside the reality of a feminised agricultural sector, have called for refocusing policy attention to ameliorate the constraints faced by women farmers, a key one being the lack of control over productive assets, including land. This would improve productivity, food security, incomes and wellbeing, but more importantly, provide recognition to gender equality as a policy priority (Kelkar, 2011).

In India, starting with the Constitutional Fundamental Rights and Directive Principles of State Policy, that assured equality before law irrespective of sex, race, caste and religion, there has been a slow but systematic effort to make the legal framework both gender-equitable and gender-just. The Hindu Succession Act (1956) was amended in

September 2005 to remove gender discriminatory provisions and provide daughters and sons equal entitlements to agricultural land, the Domestic Violence Act was passed in 2005, and efforts to reform the marriage and divorce laws are currently underway. Additionally, the Scheduled Tribes and Other Traditional Forest Dwellers (Recognition of Forest Rights) Act 2006 seeks to recognize the rights of forest-dwelling communities to forest land and other forest resources, and the 73rd and 74th Constitutional Amendments 1992, granted women one-third reservation in all local government institutions. Further, a host of policies have been formulated from the Sixth Plan onwards (1980-85) to strengthen the entitlements of and support to women farmers (including joint titles to land) (Rao, 2013)[2].

Implementation of these laws and policies has, however, been slow, if not near absent. This is not surprising, given that land represents more than a physical asset and a source of material wealth; rather it refigures the meanings of power and authority in society. Pressures on land add to the complexities mediating women's access such as its location (natal/marital), mode of acquisition (inheritance, markets, state), the type and extent of rights (legal, use), and the larger religious and political economy context that shapes state policies and priorities within which claims are negotiated (Rao, 2011).

Actualising claims have involved struggles at different institutional levels, from the family and community to the markets and state, confronting a host of social, religious, political and economic resistances, rather than technical fixes. The spaces for struggle have been both formal (e.g., panchayats, law courts) and informal (e.g., SHGs, grass roots collectives, networks) (Rao, 2013), and involved diverse and context-specific strategies, recognising that women (and men) are not autonomous individuals, but embedded within wider social structures (Rao, 2008). Equitable laws are then an essential starting point for ensuring women's rights to land and gender equality. However, laws alone are not sufficient. The rule of law requires mechanisms for implementation, which are resourced and monitored, but also creative and dynamic, to be put in place, to ensure accountability, legitimacy and voice.

This article seeks to examine the relationship between women's ownership of and access to assets and an expansion in the opportunities (especially livelihoods) available to them, as well as wellbeing and status outcomes. In order to do so, the first section maps out the gendered differences in access to land and other resources, specifically technology, information and credit. The second section then moves on to examining the two-way links between women's employment and their asset ownership status. In Section 3, I examine some of the more unintended consequences of women's access to assets, in particular the links to violence and empowerment. Section 4 concludes.

Methodology

Given the complexity of gender relations in India, it is impossible to generalize for women across the country. Women are not a homogeneous category and their access to assets is mediated by a host of factors: their class, caste, ethnicity, age and stage in the life cycle, marital status, regional location (culture), to name a few. Data is not available across all these variables. Nevertheless, existing data, both quantitative and qualitative, do allow for certain hypotheses in relation to the gendered access to productive assets, in particular land, to be made. This chapter uses data from the Agricultural Census, National Family Health Surveys (NFHS 2 and 3) and the National Sample Survey Organisation's Employment and Unemployment Surveys to map women's access to land and work. All calculations have been done by the author, unless otherwise stated. Apart from national-level analysis, data is provided for a few States, where possible, to illustrate regional differences and similarities in landholding patterns. Southern India for instance is seen to support more gender equitable social relations in contrast to the northern States. Similarly, there is also an attempt to disaggregate data by caste/ethnicity to illustrate the effects of social identity on women's access. This is supplemented by an analysis of micro-studies.

One important point needs to be noted in relation to the data. Asset data is usually collected at the household rather than individual level, making it difficult to gain a precise understanding of women's access to and control over productive assets. At best, it is classified by the sex of the head of the household. While providing some insight into the possible differences between male and female-headed households, this data however tells us little about the access of a majority of rural women, who live in male-headed households, to assets. Unlike in the case of employment, it is, therefore, difficult to establish precise relationships between asset ownership and a range of empowerment and decision-making variables.

SECTION 1
GENDERED DIFFERENCES IN ACCESS TO LAND AND PRODUCTIVE ASSETS

(a) Mapping Access to Land

I use the agricultural census data over three time periods, i.e., 1995-6, 2001-2 and 2005-6-to set out the trends in terms of operational holdings, disaggregated by head of household and social group, to locate the nature of landholding patterns in the country.

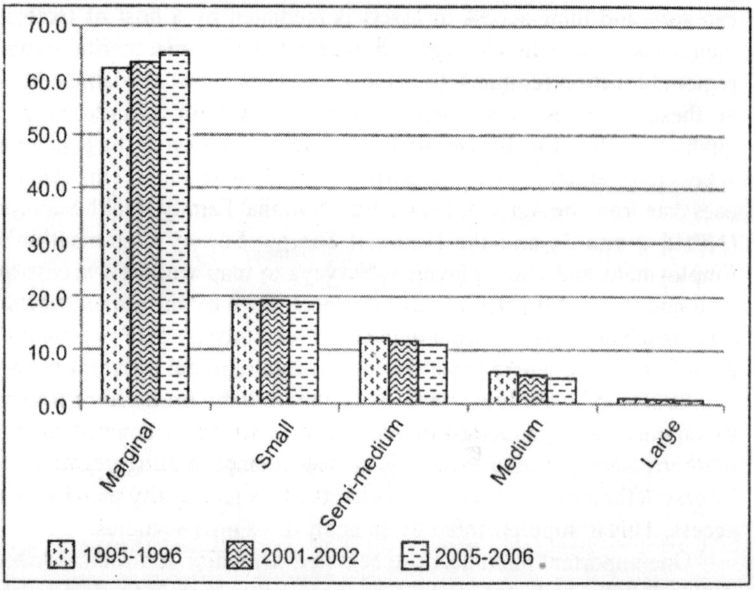

Fig. 5.1: Number of Operational Hoidings by Size and class (All India)

Figure 5.1 (and Table 5.1a) demonstrates the changing patterns of agricultural holdings since the mid-1990s, with an increase in marginal holdings of less than an acre from 62 to 65 per cent of total holdings and a decrease in both medium and large holdings. Yet, when compared with the area of holdings in Figure 5.2, the inequality is apparent, with 65 per cent of marginal farmers owning 21 per cent of the total operational holdings, while less than 1 per cent of large farmers own over 9 per cent of the holdings. This inequality in the ownership of land also emerges from micro-studies such as Ramachandran *et al.* (2010: 38), who find that landlords and big capitalist farmers in their three study villages in Andhra Pradesh owned 25, 22 and 19 per cent of the land, though constituting only 2, 3 and 1 per cent of households in the respective villages.

Table 5.1a: Number of Operational Holdings (in %) by Size Class and Head of Household

Size class (in %)	*1995-1996*			*2001-2002*			*2005-2006*		
	MHH	*FHH*	*Total*	*MHH*	*FHH*	*Total*	*MHH*	*FHH*	*Total*
Marginal	61.3	69.6	62.1	62.0	69.5	63.2	64.3	70.4	65.0
Small	19.0	17.2	18.8	19.2	17.4	19.1	18.9	17.6	18.7
Semi-medium	9.2	6.1	12.1	9.1	5.5	11.6	8.7	5.0	10.8
Medium	3.5	1.1	5.9	3.2	0.9	5.2	3.0	0.8	4.7
Large	1.1	0.5	1.0	0.9	0.4	0.9	0.8	0.4	0.7

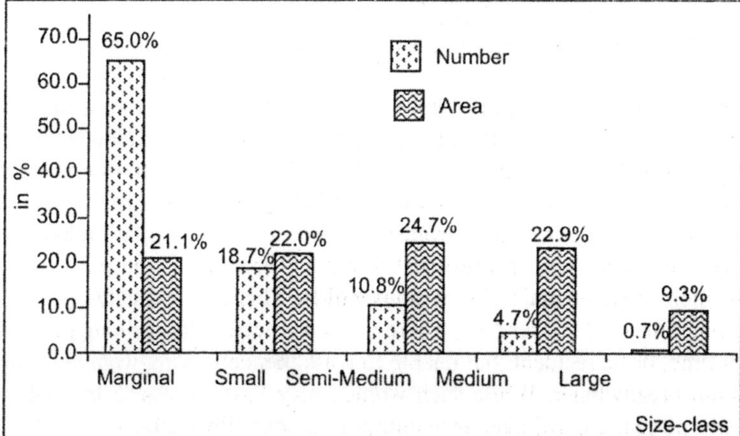

Social Group	*Number of holdings (in million)*	*Area of holdings (in million ha)*
Marginal	72.6	27.6
Small	20.9	28.9
Semi-Medium	12.1	32.3
Medium	5.3	30.0
Large	0.8	12.2

Fig. 5.2: Number and Area of Operational Holdings by Size Class (2005-2006)

Disaggregating this by gender, two interesting findings emerge. First, there has been a total increase in the number of operational holdings held in the names of women (classified by household headship), pointing

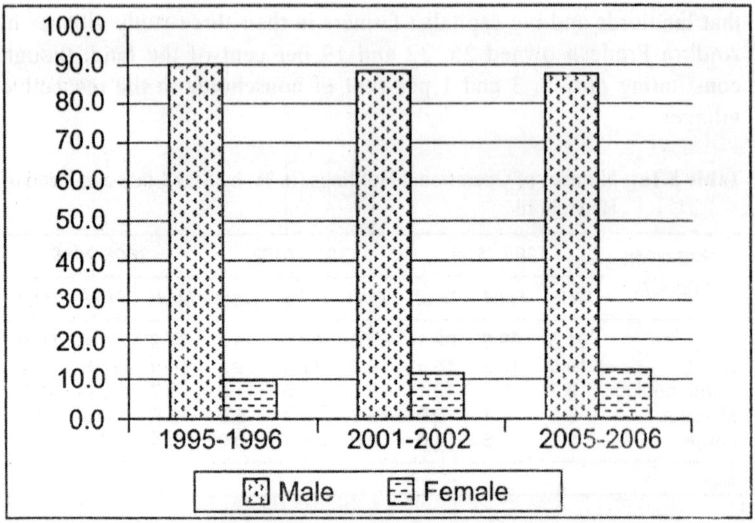

Fig. 5.3: Gender-wise Change in Number of Operational Holdings

towards the increase in the number of female headed households in rural India[3] (Figure 5.3). A detailed analysis of three villages in Tamil Nadu by Harriss-White and Janakarajan (2004:153) points to the definitional problems associated with female headship. While landlessness varied between 47-82 per cent in women-headed households (that included a man, may be a son or a brother), it ranged between 71-90 per cent in women only, or male-absent households. This still excludes *de jure* women-headed households, where men may be migrant for long periods of time, or be resident, but unable to work, hence leaving women as the main breadwinner. While such women may have access to land, they have no real control over agricultural decisions (Rao, 2012).

Secondly, the average size of holdings for women has always been less than men (Figure 5.4). Over the past decade, the decline in the number of operation holdings has been much faster for women at 26 per cent relative to men at 8 per cent (Table 5.1b). While the actual amount of land held by men has marginally increased, women's share of land also shows a substantial decline by 24 per cent. While 12.4 per cent of women were operational holders, they only controlled 9.8 per cent of the total land area. This too varies by social group, with women of the Other (OBC and General) category controlling 8 per cent of the land held by their social group (though constituting 12.8 per cent of owners), STs 8.4 per cent (9.6% of owners) and SCs 9.6 per cent (11.5% of owners). Caste

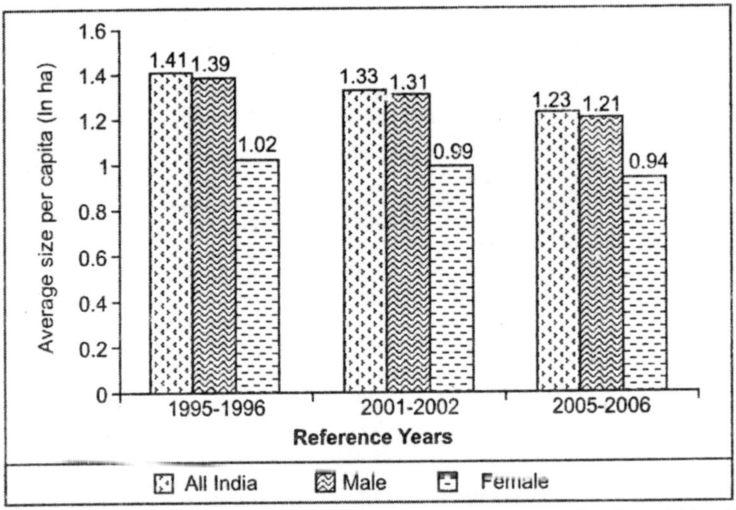

Fig. 5.4: Average Size of Operational Holdings (in ha) by Gender within all Social Groups and Size Class

seems to play a role, as the widest gap between ownership *per se* and area operated is found amongst non-SC/ST women.

One also finds a huge variation by State, with Haryana and Maharashtra demonstrating holdings of both men and women above the national average, while West Bengal and UP are much below. Interestingly, the gender gap in average landholding size is the lowest in UP, despite being the patriarchal heartland of India (Figure 5.5). This gender equal distribution of land could reflect attempts to overcome land ceiling laws through the division of property amongst the old Zamindari Estates. West Bengal and Kerala present an interesting contrast. Both States underwent land reforms; in Kerala this appears to have gone in favour of women, while West Bengal reveals the highest adverse gender gap in landholding size at the level of marginal and small-holders (Table 5.2). While not necessarily demonstrating an expected pattern, these regional differences highlight the importance of paying serious attention to both cultural and kinship variations and the political economy imperatives across contexts.

Livestock ownership data is not gender disaggregated, yet it is interesting to note that the possession of both milch and draught animals increases with size of landholding, the critical point determining the ownership decision appears to be in the size class of 0.41-1 hectare. In

Table 5.1b: Change in Individual Holdings by Size Class and Head of Household (All India)

Size of Holding (in ha.)	*Gender*	*Individual Holdings (in numbers, hectares and percentage of the total)*			*% change (in ha)*	*% change (in nos)*
		1995-1996	*2001-2002*	*2005-2006*		
Marginal (below 1.0)	M	55370150 (0.4) [61.3]	57296251 (0.4) [62.4]	62900007 (0.38) [64.3]	–1.7	–8.3
	F	7100692 (0.4) [69.6]	8384351 (0.4) [69.3]	9728450 (0.35) [70.4]	–8.9	–19.0
Small (1.0-1.99)	M	17196705 (1.4) [19.0]	17681857 (1.42) [19.2]	18481719 (1.38) [18.9]	–0.9	–1.4
	F	1753507 (1.4) [17.2]	2166462 (1.41) [17.9]	2432134 (1.36) [17.6]	–7.9	–4.9
Semi-medium (2.0-3.99)	M	11273027 (2.7) [12.5]	10953379 (2.72) [11.9]	10913108 (2.67) [11.1]	1.3	0.4
	F	942421 (2.7) [9.2]	1100479 (2.67) [9.1]	1196694 (2.61) [8.7]	–5.7	–1.8
Medium (4.0-9.99)	M	5530297 (5.8) [6.1]	5065104 (5.79) [5.5]	4855328 (5.71) [5.0]	3.6	0.7
	F	359529 (5.8) [3.5]	387063 (5.71) [3.2]	411516 (5.6) [3.0]	–2.3	–0.4
Large (10 and above)	M	1002298 (15.9) [1.1]	859673 (15.63) [0.9]	741596 (15.46) [0.8]	3.6	0.3
	F	52068 (16.6) [0.5]	51973 (15.44) [0.4]	51068 (15.21) [0.4]	0.9	0.0
All Groups	M	90372477 (1.39) [100]	91856264 (1.31) [100]	97891758 (1.21) [100]	5.9	–8.3
	F	10208217 (1) [100]	12090328 (0.99) [100]	13819862 (0.94) [100]	–24.0	–26.1

OH—Operational Holdings.

Note: (i) Census was not carried out for Bihar, Jharkhand, Maharashtra for the year 2005-2006

(ii) Figures outside of brackets are the number of individual holdings, in round brackets are average size of holding and in square brackets are percentage of the total in a given year.

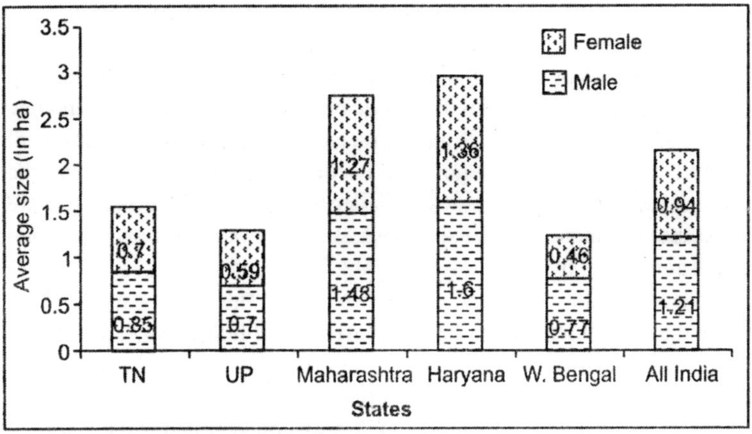

Fig. 5.5: Average Size (in ha) of Operational Holdings by Gender for Select States (Agricensus 2005-2006)

Table 5.2: State-wise Distribution of Average Size per Holding in Hectares (2005-2006)

State	*Gender*	*Marginal*	*Small*	*Small-Medium*	*Medium*	*Large*	*All sizes*
Kerala	M	0.06	1.31	2.44	0.6	—	0.07
	F	0.06	1.37	2.58	—	—	0.06
Tamil Nadu	M	0.35	1.36	2.62	5.42	14.83	0.58
	F	0.35	1.36	2.61	5.42	14.33	0.53
Uttar Pradesh	M	0.34	1.35	2.64	5.40	15.25	0.51
	F	0.34	1.36	2.61	5.33	16.85	0.45
Maharashtra	M	0.45	1.30	2.63	5.65	12.15	1.17
	F	0.48	1.31	2.59	5.54	12.73	1.09
Haryana	M	0.40	1.44	2.75	5.84	13.48	1.63
	F	0.42	1.44	2.78	5.75	15.87	1.35
West Bengal	M	0.46	1.53	2.68	4.85	—	0.65
	F	0.29	1.36	2.55	5.02	—	0.38
All India	M	0.37	1.38	2.66	5.73	15.93	0.84
	F	0.34	1.36	2.61	5.68	15.48	0.69

Source: Agricensus 2005-6.

Note: Within every size class, the average size per holding of land for female farmers is slightly less than for male for the States under consideration except Kerala. However, large farmers in the case of certain States like Uttar Pradesh, Maharashtra and Haryana, the average land size of land holding is more for the female than for the male.

India 70 per cent of female headed and 64 per cent of male-headed households have less than one hectare of land and hence are unlikely to own either milch or draught animals. This is partly related to the need to provide fodder to such animals, a large part of it being the stalks and hay from foodgrain cultivation. What then seems clear is that there is a minimal level of land ownership required to encourage both cultivation and the maintenance of larger livestock. Smaller livestock on the other hand are much more manageable for the landless or near-landless and are often assets controlled by women (Rao, 2002; White, 1992).

Disaggregating by social group, two observations can be made. First, while the Scheduled Tribes have a share in land-holdings proportionate to their share in the population (8%), this is not the case for the Scheduled Castes, over 50 per cent of whom are landless (16% population share) (Figure 5.6). Secondly, 91 per cent of SCs are concentrated in the marginal and small-holder categories; this is 76 per cent for STs and 73 per cent for others (Figure 5.7).

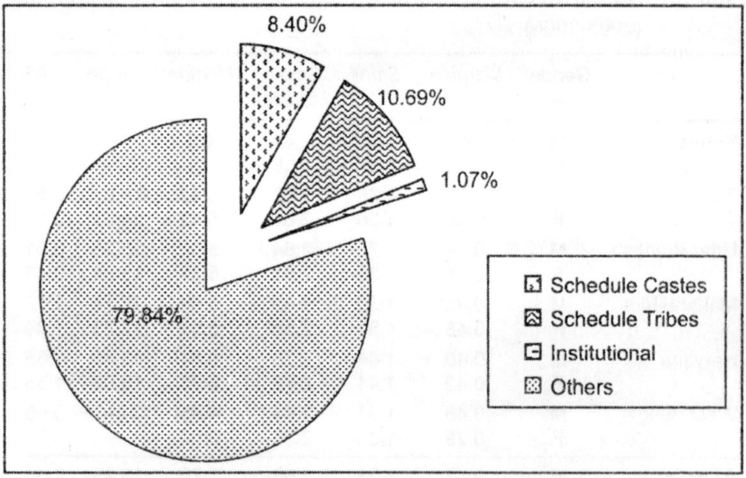

Source: Author's calculations, Agricensus 2005-6

Fig. 5.6: Percentage Share of Different Social Groups in Area of Operational Holdings

Land constitutes the most important asset for rural households, accounting for between 60-75 per cent of household wealth. Village studies reveal that SCs and STs (in non-Scheduled Areas) are often landless, with their average level of asset/landholdings varying between 1-5 per cent of Other Caste households (Ramachandran *et al.* 2010: 43-44)[4].

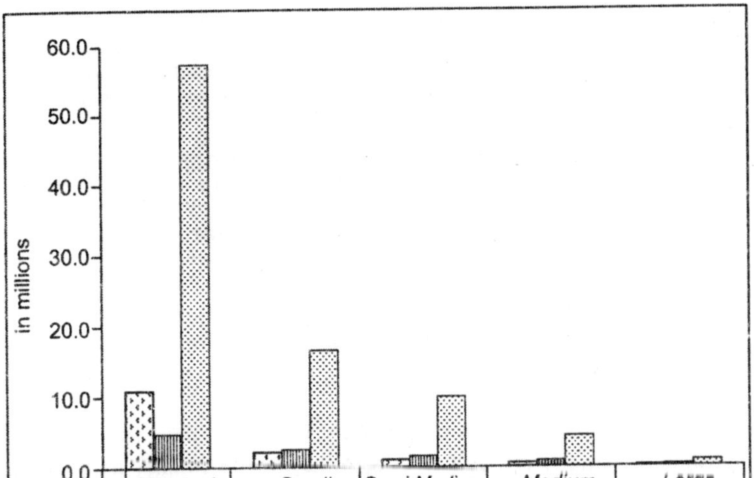

	Marginal	Small	Semi-Medium	Medium	Large
SC	10.7	2.2	0.9	0.3	0.0
ST	4.8	2.5	1.5	0.7	0.1
Others	57.1	16.3	9.7	4.3	0.7

Size class and social group

Source: Author's calculations, Agricensus 2005-6.

Fig. 5.7: Number of Operational Holdings by Size Class and Social Group in Millions (2005-2006)

In Scheduled Areas, STs do own land. What is, however, not often mentioned is the quality of land—the Scheduled Tribes largely inhabit forested, hilly and rainfed land—the productive capacity of which is much lower than the land in the plains, often irrigated. Even STs with over 5 acres of land can fall much below the poverty line, due essentially to low productivity. As Rao (2008: 147-9) found in her Jharkhand study, 25 per cent of the cultivable land area in Dumka district was classified as lowland (paddy producing), 33 per cent midland and the remaining 42 per cent upland. Less than 15 per cent of this land was irrigated. The villages demonstrated an average output of 500 kg per acre (1.2 tonnes per ha), less than half the all-India average of 2.85 tonnes per hectare in 1998-9 (Table 5.3). Landholding on its own, without reference to the quality, is then not a good indicator of the value of assets or indeed of well-being.

What then is clear is that while 84 per cent of rural female workers are engaged in agriculture, as also a majority of SCs and STs, their share of operational holdings remains small and even the land they have is

Table 5.3: Area, Production and Productivity of Rice in India

	Irrigated	*Rainfed Lowland*	*Rainfed Upland*	*Flood Prone/ Deep Water*
Area (m.ha)	17.8	15.0	7.0	2.4
	(42.0)	(35.5)	(16.8)	(5.7)
Production (m.t)*	52.0	22.0	4.7	3.3
	(63.5)	(26.8)	(5.7)	(4.0)
Productivity (t/h)*	2.97	1.47	0.67	1.37

Source: Siddiq, E.A., 2000, Bridging the rice yield gap in India, National Professor, Directorate of Rice Research (ICAR), Hyderabad-500030 (AP), India. http://www.fao.org/docrep/003/x6905e/x6905e09.htm, accessed on 13/8/12.

largely characterized by low productivity. Of course, there are variations by State, making it difficult to generalize for the country as a whole. Women headed households typically own less than male headed households; the data does not however provide any insight into women's access to land and assets in a majority of 'male-headed' households, or indeed the reasons for possibly lower productivity. Before examining the constraints to enhancing investments and productivity faced by women farmers, I briefly examine the data from a few micro-studies for insights into women's access to and control over land even within male-headed households.

(b) Insights from Micro-studies

In a survey of 4,110 households in four agro-climatic regions of Karnataka, conducted in 2009-10, that sought specifically to identify the patterns of asset ownership by men and women and the extent of their rights over these assets, Swaminathan *et al.* (2011) found that in rural areas, 71 per cent of all agricultural land was owned by men, 14 per cent by women and the rest was in joint titles between different household members. 72 per cent of women owners were widows. Much greater gender equity existed in the ownership of other assets, especially livestock, agricultural tools and consumer durables. Jewellery was overwhelmingly owned by women (69%). Secondly, women's share tended to decrease as the size of landholding increased: amongst marginal farmer households, women owned 18 per cent of the land, this was only 11 per cent amongst medium and large farmer households[5] (see also Tables 5.1a and 5.1b). While this does point to a class effect, with women owning a much smaller share of land amongst the upper classes, the reason for greater equity amongst the poorest is also because of the low level of assets owned by the household in the first place (this is not true in the case of UP, Haryana and Maharashtra as discussed in the last section (Table 5.2).

The Working Group on Women's Land Ownership (WGWLO), a network of 23 NGOs and CBOs, working for women's rights in 12 districts of Gujarat, conducted a study in 23 villages, to understand the status of women in agriculture in Gujarat (2004). They found women accounting for roughly 12 per cent of total land-holders (561 women *versus* 4,188 men). Of these 561 women, they conducted in depth interviews with 403 women to identify the reasons for their ownership and the process by which they acquired land. 48 per cent were widows who had claimed a share in their husband's property, 41 per cent were wives who had received titles with a view to claiming particular State announced tax benefits or for their husbands to escape land ceiling laws (many did not even know they held land titles) and less than 5 per cent had inherited a share of their natal property and this too because their parents had no male heirs. Several women reported having poor quality of land—degraded, unirrigated, or at a distance from the village. Yet, close to 20 per cent of them did cultivate their own land, take decisions on cropping and sale, despite confronting a host of difficulties in terms of access to irrigation, credit and technical information (less than 10 per cent had access to credit or agricultural cooperatives), negative attitude from their family members, and lack of support from the State revenue bureaucracy.

A similar story emerges from a study of 504 households across 19 villages in Andhra Pradesh and Bihar (UN Women and RDI, 2011). A key problem in women's ownership is one of recognition and legitimacy. Surprisingly, husband's had a more supportive view, with 85 per cent indicating that women had the legal right to own land, compared to women themselves, 40 per cent of whom denied this right. Despite supportive husbands, 60 per cent of the women felt that they would be unable to operationalise the ownership of inherited land, due to lack of community recognition. In practical terms, the study found that 70 per cent of land in male-headed households was acquired through inheritance; this was the case for only 57 per cent of female headed households. 29 per cent of them reported buying their homestead plot. A study of 254 deserted women in Pune district of Maharashtra found even more dismal results. Half the women were married into landless households, but from those married into landed households, only 2 per cent women were able to secure a small plot of land following separation. Natal families were better, giving 4 per cent of women their land. A slightly larger 17 per cent of women were able to secure house property in their own name (Kulkarni *et al.*, 2008). Women in general then own and control a much lower share of agricultural land across States, despite their extensive participation in agriculture.

(c) Access to Inputs, Technology and Services

Even where women do own land, they face substantial barriers—socio-cultural and institutional—in their access to knowledge, information or financial assistance that considerably constrains the potential benefits from this land. The WGWLO (2004) study found that 45 per cent of women owners had changed their cropping pattern in response to the difficulties they faced as women. Rao (2008) points to the comparatively lower productivity of female headed households due to a range of problems: inability to get labour to plough their land on time, lack of cash to pay for inputs and labour, apart from harassment from male marital kin and community leaders. Opposition was particularly intense *vis-à-vis* inheriting daughters and young widows. I briefly examine the evidence available on gendered input use, access to information/extension, and access to agricultural credit to provide an insight into the nature of constraints faced by women.

(i) Input Use

In one of the few studies of gender difference in agricultural decision-making in India, especially investments in land through the use of manure and fertilizers, improvement in drainage and irrigation, and agricultural inputs, Chen *et al.* (2011) find a positive relationship between the proportion of male children in a family and investments, based perhaps on the expectation that male children will inherit the land and take care of their elderly parents, in the absence of alternate social security mechanisms[6]. Households with only boys had double the amount of irrigated land (2.61 ha) compared to those with no boys (1.28 ha); their fertilizer use too was 214 *versus* 128 kgs, and these relationships were significant. They, however, do not disaggregate input usage by the sex of the head of household or indeed the gender of the farmer. Nevertheless, the meaning of land as a male asset is clearly signalled.

Studies on access to technical inputs (seed varieties, fertilisers) and natural resources, (such as water and soil fertility), have largely focused on Sub-Saharan Africa, but most of these find that there is no significant difference in resource use and technology adoption between male and female farmers, once land, education and labour are controlled for (Peterman *et al.*, 2010). A study in Ethiopia (Tiruneh *et al.*, 2001, quoted in Peterman *et al.*, 2010) on gender differentials in agricultural production and decision-making, highlights this point further: while farm size and extension service contact positively affect adoption in male-headed households, farm size and asset ownership are critical in female-headed households.

Despite the absence of quantitative analysis, this insight seems to hold largely true for India. State subsidised inputs, such as seeds for horticultural crops, are often dependent on the size of landholding, disadvantaging many small and marginal farmers and women, who are over-represented in this group. A medium farmer in Varanasi pointed out, 'the Horticulture Department distributes seeds, which give good yields, but only to medium and large farmers with more than two hectares of land. The marginal and small farmers lose out' (Rao, 2012). The agricultural census (2006-07) confirms that 28 per cent of marginal farmers had access to certified seeds in comparison to 37-40 per cent medium and large farmers. Input use and technology adoption then depend on both access to land and security of tenure (Doss, 2001).

(ii) Information and Extension

A second element in improving production is the access to information and extension services. A World Bank and IFPRI (2010) study of 676 households in Karnataka on access to extension services, found that 20 per cent of female headed households and a slightly higher 27 per cent of male headed households reported extension visits in the previous year. Here too, asset/wealth variables seem to be more important than gender variables, a result confirmed by Rao (2005)'s micro-study of agricultural extension in one district of Jharkhand, where the better off groups benefited much more than the poorest Scheduled Tribes, who owned land (though remote and marginal), but lacked access to other resources, financial and social, critical for accessing information around new technologies[7]. Lack of land titles however does exclude women from membership of and decision-making within farmers' organisations, irrigation societies and other development projects. It is possible that in some parts of India, such as Uttar Pradesh, the gender of the extension agents, primarily male, could influence the degree of interaction with female farmers and consequently their access to information[8].

ICTs are increasingly becoming an important tool for information dissemination: women in South Asia are 37 per cent less likely to own a mobile phone compared to their male counterparts (GSMA Development Fund, quoted in Peterman *et al.* 2010). The recent Government of India announcement to provide mobile phones to all BPL households can potentially have a transformatory effect on access to information for the poorest households, including women[9], provided adequate attention is given to gender relations in the distribution of these phones (http://telecomtalk.info/india-govt-to-give-mobile-phone-free-bpl-family-200-minutes-talk-time/98114/ 8th August 2012, accessed on 17th August 2012).

(iii) Credit

Credit is often a prerequisite for input use, and the ability to obtain credit is linked to having land as collateral. Table 5.4 presents some interesting insights. Credit access has improved considerably over the last decade, for farmers across size classes, both in terms of the amount of loan and the numbers availing of loans. Loans are predominantly short term, taken from institutional arrangements such as the PACS (Primary Agricultural Credit Society), PLDB (Primary Land Development Society), CBB (Commercial Bank Branch) and RRBB (Regional Rural Bank Branch). This improved access to a large extent reflects government emphasis on financial inclusion, achieved through the expansion of the institutional structure of formal-sector lending institutions, engaging with directed lending schemes (through the Integrated Rural Development Programme or IRDP in the 1990s followed by the Swarnajayanti Gram Swarojgar Yojana or SGSY post-2000)[10] as well as the provision of *kisan* (farmer) credit cards (that provides farmers a credit limit based on the size of their landholding).

Despite improved access, the amount of loans taken by small and marginal farmers remains comparatively low. Women are over-represented in these categories, as are the SCs and STs. While gender disaggregated data is not available, it is likely that only a small proportion of this went to women due to most women not having land titles as collateral for agricultural credit.[11] Long term fieldwork in Jharkhand's Dumka district revealed that women and men engaged equally with cultivation, but only 4 per cent of *kisan* credit cards were issued to women (Rao, 2008); in Gujarat this was only 2 per cent (from amongst 349 women farmers

Table 5.4: Institutional Credit for Agricultural Purposes by Class Size

Size class	*OH that had access to credit in 2001-2 (in%) Group*	*Amt*	*OH that had access to credit in 2006-7 (in%) Group*	*Amt*	*Average amount of loan taken in 2001-02 (in INR)*	*Average amount of loan taken in 2006-7 (in INR)*	*% change in credit amount between 2001-02 and 2006-07*
Marginal (below 1.0)	14	24	19.6	38	4892	7843	60.3
Small (1.0-1.99)	27.7	25	32.8	20	7843	8639	10.2
Semi-medium (2.0-3.99)	31.6	26	34.5	20	11285	13932	23.5
Medium (4.0-9.99)	33.1	20	39.4	17	17502	21138	20.8
Large (10 and above)	29.4	5	40.1	5	26042	30321	16.4
All Groups	20		25	—	8499	10445	22.9

Note: OH—Operational Holdings.
Survey was not conducted in Bihar, Jharkhand and Maharashtra

interviewed across 9 districts of the State only 7 women had *kisan* credit cards, pers. comm., Sejal Dave, Convenor, WGWLO, 20/6/2010).

One of the explanations for women's exclusion from formal credit has been the rapid expansion of targeted microfinance (through Self-Help Groups), which is aimed precisely at overcoming problems of accessibility, high transaction costs and poor repayments. There is, however, little evidence that micro-credit contributes substantially to poverty reduction or indeed to women's empowerment, given the small amounts of loan provided, insufficient for most productive investments, especially in the absence of supportive infrastructure (Duvendack *et al.* 2011). They are mainly used to support the household's family farm (controlled by men) or for consumption.

Input use, access to extension services and credit are all directly related to the size of holding, with larger landholders having better access to larger amounts of credit, but also information, compared to smallholders. As women's landholding size is generally smaller than that of men, and also in the absence of titles (as wives of farmers), they are disadvantaged in terms of the investments they can make.

SECTION 2
ASSET OWNERSHIP AND WOMEN'S WORK FORCE PARTICIPATION: EXPLORING THE LINKS

Gendered labour force participation and the changes it has undergone over time has perhaps been the one area that has been analysed indepth in the case of India, given the availability of individual level data. The NSSO employment-unemployment surveys are the best source of information on labour use across sectors and activities. What has been less explored is the relationship of workforce participation with asset ownership. In this section, I briefly set out the gendered division of labour in farming (based both on the NSSO data and long-term studies of rural change), and then examine the possible linkages with asset ownership.

(a) Women's Employment in Agriculture

Analysis of NSSO data from 1977-78 to 2007-8, shows that male participation, either as cultivators or labourers, has sharply declined from 80.6 to 66.5 per cent over this period, as compared to female participation, that has declined only marginally from 88.1 to 83.5 per cent (NSSO, 2010, Statement 15: 43). Male workers have steadily diversified out of agriculture (accounting for 75% of increase in self-employed in non-agriculture), while women have remained in this sector (60% of total increase in self-employed in agriculture) (Himanshu, 2011). A longitudinal survey of two villages in Mahbubnagar district of Andhra Pradesh reveals that while agriculture contributed 87-97 per cent of household income in 1975-76, this had fallen to 27-32 per cent in 2000-01. Interestingly, the share of non-agricultural income, which was 3-12 per cent in the earlier period, was now 67-72 per cent (Rao and Bantilan, 2003). This shift in the livelihood portfolio needs to be understood not just in terms of the size of holding, but also the type of employment available in agriculture and the returns to labour, especially in the context where the agriculture sector has more or less been stagnant over the last decade.

If we look at different types of employment in agriculture, roughly 65 per cent of both men and women are classified as self-employed and the remaining as casual workers. The share of regular workers is negligible (Srivastava and Srivastava, 2010). While there has been optimism in some quarters about the increase in self-employment reflecting the opening up of new productive opportunities, a deeper analysis reveals that it has involved a downward spiral for women in terms of investing more labour and time for lower returns, a form of distress employment (Unni and Raveendran, 2007). The category of self-employment includes both own-account workers and unpaid household helpers. In a disaggregated, sectoral analysis of self-employment, using NSSO data, Neetha (2010) makes several interesting points: across sectors, there has been a decline in women own-account workers and expansion in women's unpaid work as helpers in household enterprises, both farm and non-farm. Within the agricultural sector, unpaid female family labour constituting close to 70 per cent of women categorized as self-employed, have replaced hired wage workers (see also Djurfeldt *et al.,* 2008), as evident also in the declining number of casual agricultural labourers. In manufacturing too, the increase in self-employment is largely due to the expansion of the putting out system leading to an increase in the number of home-based women workers, their conditions of work being much worse than those of casual wage workers, reflecting a decline overall in the quality of work available (*c.f.* Himanshu, 2011)[12]. In the absence of assets such as land and other productive resources, SCs in particular are less able to engage with self-employment compared to other caste groups, and remain confined to casual wage work.

When it comes to casual wage labour, one finds agricultural work receiving much lower wages than non-agricultural work; yet amongst female casual workers, 90 per cent were concentrated in agricultural work as against 71 per cent of male casual workers (Srivastava and Srivastava, 2010, Harriss *et al.*, 2010). In their socio-economic survey of three villages, Ramachandran *et al.* (2010) show that women in labouring households are almost entirely confined to agricultural wage-work, but also earn roughly half that of men, even for activities such as harvesting and threshing that use both male and female labour. Half of the female casual labourers belong to SCs and STs, nearly twice their share in the population. Even within this, there is a gender wage gap, with women on average earning 71 per cent of male wages in 2007-8 as compared to 65 per cent in 1993-94 (NSSO, 2010).[13]

A final comment needs to be made about the extent of joint work in farming by men and women within households. The contribution of rural men to joint work in the domestic domain (production and reproduction) has been steadily declining across the country from 81 per cent in 1983 to 49 per cent in 1993-94 and 42 per cent in 2004-5 (Rao *et al.,* 2008). In Andhra Pradesh, just 6 per cent of male labourers engaged in joint tasks, compared to 54.5 per cent of all female workdays spent on joint work (Garikipati, 2008: 635). Government of India's time use study (GoI, 2000), conducted across six States, further shows that male contributions to farm work as well as domestic work are declining in both rural and urban areas, with women now performing 53 per cent of total work done. Women remain the mainstay of agriculture, both as 'household helpers' and agricultural labour. I now turn to examine the relationship between female work participation and asset ownership, drawing mainly on small-scale surveys and long-term studies of rural change.

(b) Does Asset Ownership by Women Improve the Terms of Work Participation?

One reason that a majority of women appear confined to casual work in agriculture or indeed low paid, informal sector work, while men (especially those with some assets) are able to diversify, appears to be their lack of productive assets, be it land or capital (Kapadia, 2000). Even when they do own land, the size of holding is much smaller than that of men. Fewer women have bank accounts or control over the money they earn (Table 5.5)[14].

Table 5.5: Women's Access to Money and Credit

	Percentage who have a bank account	*Percentage who know of a micro-credit scheme*	*Percentage who have taken a loan from a micro-credit scheme*
SC	11.6	38.1	4.7
ST	9.0	30.1	3.1
OBC	13.3	38.5	4.8
Other	20.5	41.0	3.0
West Bengal	14.1	41.4	2.7
Uttar Pradesh	13.2	14.1	0.4
India	15.0	38.6	4.0

Source: NFHS-3 Report (from Rao *et al.*, 2008, Table 7.3).

Srivastava and Srivastava (2010), based on NSSO's informal sector enterprises survey, 2001, show that in rural areas, female proprietary enterprises are very small in size, a majority home-based (81%) with an average fixed investment of less than ₹ 8,000 or one-third that of male enterprises. Returns too are low, with 89 per cent of such enterprises (42% for men) giving daily returns less than the minimum wage. In conclusion they note that higher work force participation for women *per se* (self-employment and casual work) does not lead to improved welfare, unless this is accompanied by higher educational capabilities and/or other assets. Jayaraj (2004) points to the importance of gender, caste and access to land for engagement with higher return, rural non-agricultural employment. Such engagement also becomes crucial for making further investments in land and agriculture (such as wells, irrigation and farm equipment) and contributes to a positive spiral of upward mobility (Djurfeldt *et al.,* 2010). Women, the lower castes and the landless are then clearly at a disadvantage in their levels of investment in or engagement with non-farm employment. Garikipati (2009:537) through her micro-study in Andhra Pradesh confirms that if a woman owns productive assets, the probability of her participation in household processes and of receiving a better wage and working conditions increase. This relationship is strongest for women from the labouring classes (both landless and small-holders)[15].

(c) Does Women's Work Participation Result in Increased Purchase of Assets by Them?

Except for the upper decile, women's work participation then needs to be understood in the context of male migration, and pressures for survival. In such circumstances, women's resources are almost entirely directed to household survival and subsistence (Mencher, 1988), rather than asset accumulation, more so, in a context of low wages and low returns for women's work, price rise and increasing cost of living. Withdrawal of women from the workforce is then potentially a sign of household status and wellbeing.

Evidence presented so far seems to suggest that land ownership is crucial for gaining access to all other assets, especially in rural contexts. In the absence of land, what do poor rural women invest in? Heyer (1989, 1992) in her Coimbatore study found that landless womens' asset strategies included investing in the education of their children, in gifts and dowry exchanges (as a way of building social capital) and in jewellery or other mobile assets. Labour was their biggest asset, hence they sought to both increase the productivity of labour and also its flexibility. Land or livestock they felt would tie them down to the village. Swaminathan *et al.* (2011) in their study of gendered assets in Karnataka also note that jewellery was the only asset where individual ownership by women dominated; they owned 69 per cent of all jewellery in rural areas. This was primarily secured as gifts at the time of marriage (*c.f.* Garikipati, 2009); they, however, also purchased it from their own earnings. While pointing to the natal family as the source of women's wealth, especially jewellery, they do not, however, discuss the larger political economic context of globalization and dowry inflation, and its implications for women's status and very survival.

Interestingly, inheritance was the major channel for acquisition of assets, especially landed property, men from their natal family, and women from their marital households, especially after the death of their husbands. Self-acquisition was less common, except in urban areas, and was dominated by men, who had greater resources available to purchase land or property than women. In rural areas, women could also acquire housing through government schemes targeting women such as the Indira Awas Yojana. With their limited earnings, what women seem to look for in assets is something moveable and liquid that can provide them security, especially in times of crisis.

SECTION 3
UNEXPECTED IMPACTS—WOMEN'S RIGHTS TO LAND, VIOLENCE AND EMPOWERMENT

While clearly women's asset ownership has some positive outcomes as discussed above, studies exploring the links between women's property status and violence report contradictory, and often conflicting, results. While Rao's (1997) study in Karnataka showed that a wife's income is associated with reduced lifetime violence, Jejeebhoy (1998) found in Uttar Pradesh and Tamil Nadu that women's employment had no significant impact on their experience of violence. Kishor and Johnson (2004), in fact, report that as compared to non-working women, women earning cash were more likely to have experienced physical violence. In fact, change in husband's employment status and male (in) security, alongside alcoholism and a growing consumer culture, remains a major driving factor behind violence.

Similarly contradictory examples can also be found in the case of land ownership. Research in two States of India, i.e., West Bengal and Kerala, conducted by the International Centre for Research of Women reveals that irrespective of productivity effects, asset ownership enhances a degree of social protection apart from substantially lowering the risk of violence. Non-propertied women are much more likely to experience violence than propertied women (who account for roughly 30% of the study sample), both physical (38.5% against 15%) and psychological (50% against 28%) (ICRW, 2006). Panda and Agarwal (2005) in their Kerala study found 49 per cent property less women subjected to violence as against 18 per cent among landowning women and only 7 per cent amongst those owning both a house and land, pointing to the much more significant effects that ownership of a house has in this context. In the ICRW study too, as against 61 per cent of women with land, only 13 per cent of women with a house faced any form of violence (2006: 79).

Bhattacharya *et al.* (2011:1680) in their Uttar Pradesh study find greater ambiguity in outcomes. While an increase in male assets leads to a reduction in violence, an increase in assets owned by the wife, while reducing household economic stress, and providing women an exit option from an abusive relationship, may induce additional control-fuelled marital violence. They too, however, find that ownership of a house has a violence reducing effect. Several qualitative studies provide a more nuanced understanding of the relationship between women's ownership of property and violence. Chowdhry (2011) notes in the case of Haryana, that it is precisely because property is seen to give women leverage, that it is opposed. Kelkar and Nathan (1991) as well as Rao (2008) in their Jharkhand studies find that it is women who have claimed rights to land who are harassed, subjected to violence and even branded as witches, rather than women who accept patriarchal norms of male control.

There is a second crucial issue and this relates to the nature of property, whether marital or natal, and the legitimacy of women's subject-position in relation to her land claims (Rao, 2008). While a widow's claims to her marital property are largely seen as legitimate, unless widowhood is triggered by unusual circumstances such as HIV/AIDS (see, for instance, Swaminathan *et al.* 2009), a daughter's claim to a share in her natal property, even though a legal right, is seen as illegitimate, as claiming a 'double share' (Chowdhry, 1997), almost as breaking social relations with her brother and natal family. An exception here is the practice of *ghar jamai* (resident son-in-law), when a daughter inherits land, but this is usually in the absence of brothers. Gender relations do change, but this is because property inheritance is also accompanied by the fact that women continue to live in their natal village with their husbands, with social support from their own friends and kin. *Ghar jamai* rights are, however, increasingly under attack and subject to violent confrontations, especially in a context of land scarcity and rising land prices, contributing to growing competition amongst men (Rao, 2005, Chowdhry, 2011). Amongst wealthier households, women may be given land in their names in order to escape State taxes or the land ceiling structure (Chowdhry, 2011; WGWLO, 2004; Rao, 2012), but with little control in practice.

Given the key role of housing in providing women protection against violence, however, a few studies have explored the unintended effects of housing rights on intra-household gender relations. In the case of Chandigarh, the major impact of joint titling in an upgraded urban slum was security-from abandonment, in old age, for children and against an alcoholic husband (Datta, 2006: 282). Further, joint titling here made women more assertive in their domestic relationships, gained them respect from their spouse and also the courage to protest if her preferences were overlooked (*ibid.*, 292). In Ahmedabad, women were more interested in secure tenures and attached to their homes, not just for the security, stability and prestige it gave them (compared to living in rented accommodation in slums), but also the opportunity to raise their children in clean and hygienic environments (Baruah, 2007: 2101).

In India, neither inheritance nor markets have been effective in enabling women to gain access to property. State redistribution, especially through housing rights, could help change this situation. Nielsen *et al.* (2006) in evaluating Karnataka's rural housing programme, which required house titles to be provided only in the names of women since 2000, indicate physical security to be the main gain articulated by women, alongside the potential for income diversification, increased status, comfort, confidence and the cessation of domestic violence. While legislation or policies alone may not change rural practices, they do create a legal space for social change.

In terms of women's autonomy and decision-making status, while there is in general a move towards joint decision-making, especially in the context of male migration, this is mediated by a host of social and cultural factors, and it is hence difficult to make generalizations, or isolate particular causal factors. In Tamil Nadu, for instance, irrespective of their work or asset status, women still exercise considerable agency in decision-making, compared to Uttar Pradesh, where despite being active farm-workers, they lack power *vis-à-vis* their men (Jejeebhoy, 2000; Luke and Munshi, 2011; Rao, 2012; Bhattacharya *et al.*, 2011). Swaminathan *et al.* (2011) too found that while women who owned a place of residence or some agricultural land had more individual decision-making rights as well as access to outside spaces, with respect to employment, health and use of money, decision-making was usually a consultative process, irrespective of women's asset ownership status.

Decision-making is one area where socio-cultural norms matter; economic participation is clearly not the only contributory factor. It is a complex process involving a series of negotiations, and these vary across different domains and dimensions of life (productive, reproductive, social, economic). Property inheritance and ownership nevertheless can and does strengthen women's power, status and mobility, and hence needs priority attention if gender equality goals are to be met.

SECTION 4
CONCLUSIONS—WOMEN'S RIGHTS TO LAND AND GENDER EQUALITY

This concluding section will briefly summarise the key findings from the data presented in this chapter, and present a few possible ways forward.

Despite the lack of gender-disaggregated data on land and other assets, the inequalities in their distribution is obvious. Women own and control only a small share of total household assets, if at all, even though they contribute a disproportionate share of labour to the maintenance of the household. This starting inequality disadvantages them across different spheres of life and work, whether in accessing other productive resources and services, seeking decent employment, setting up an enterprise, or even just bargaining for better outcomes within the household. Without access to adequate land or security of tenure (even those who own land have marginal holdings), they are unable to access inputs, extension services or markets, that can help enhance productivity. To ensure subsistence, they then engage with a range of low paid, often hazardous, home-based, informal employment. Steps for financial inclusion are underway, yet women remain largely under-represented in the credit accruing from formal institutions.

Women's channels for asset acquisition, especially land, are limited. Despite having legal inheritance rights, this is not seen as a legitimate claim by the family or community, making it difficult to operationalise. Marriage is seen as the ultimate goal for all women, so while there is support for a share in marital property, claims to natal property are seen as a sign of greed, of claiming a 'double share', signalling a breakdown of social relationships with her natal family. Markets too do not work for women, given their initial lack of resources for investment; rather they often serve to dispossess women owners. State policies and transfers then become crucial for transforming this situation, giving women a 'new' resource, one that is not contested, at least at the time of transfer. Policy anomalies however need to be addressed to avoid leaving women in a vulnerable situation.

Assets, especially land, do contribute to strengthening women's voice and say in household decisions. Yet this relationship can at times be contradictory and women with resources, while often assertive, also become targets of male violence. Of course, this is linked to social norms and cultural ideologies of what is considered appropriate or legitimate for women in different subject-positions, with South India being considered much more women-friendly than the North. The process of decision-making too is more complex than has been assumed, with consultation and negotiation taking place, often backstage, while maintaining the façade of male dominance and female subservience. These processes also vary across the productive and reproductive domains, with women often having control and final say over the latter irrespective of their asset status, with production and investment remaining contested.

An enabling environment in terms of equitable laws and affirmative action policies are an essential starting point for women to make and secure their claims. Laws alone, however, are inadequate. Mechanisms for implementation, which are resourced and monitored, are needed to ensure accountability, legitimacy and voice, indeed the rule of law. In a large country like India, where the problems of implementation are huge, this can only be realized by a combination of bottom-up action and top-down responsiveness. An active civil society which contributes both to public awareness and mobilization, as well as sensitization of the bureaucracy and ruling elite, has demonstrated that this task is difficult, but not impossible.

References

Agarwal, B. (1998), Widows *versus* Daughters or Widows as Daughters? Property, Land, and Economic Security in Rural India Modern Asian Studies (1998), 32: 1-48.

Agarwal, B. (2003), Gender and land rights revisited: exploring new prospects *via* the state, family and market. *Journal of Agrarian Change* 3 (1 and 2): 184-224.

Baruah, B. (2007), Gendered Realities: Exploring Property Ownership and tenancy relationships in urban India. *World Development*, 35(12): 1096-2109.

Bhattacharya, M, A. Bedi and A. Chhachhi (2011), Marital violence and women's employment and property status: Evidence from North Indian villages. *World Development*. 39(9): 1676-89.

Chavan, P. and R. Bedamatta (2006), Trends in agricultural wages in India: 1964-65 to 1999-2000. *Economic and Political Weekly*, 41(38): 4041-51.

Chen, S.E., P. Bhagowalia, *et al.* (2011), Input choices in agriculture: Is there a gender bias? *World Development*, 39(4): 561-568.

Chowdhry, P. (1997), Ideology, culture, and hierarchy: Expenditure-consumption patterns in rural households. In: Chakravarti, U. and K. Sangari (eds.) *From Myths to Markets: Essays on Gender*. New Delhi, Manohar, pp. 274-311.

Chowdhry, P. (2011), Reduction in violence against women: property ownership and economic independence in rural Haryana. New Delhi, *UN Women*.

Datta, N. (2006), Joint titling-a win-win policy? Gender and property rights in urban informal settlements in Chandigarh, India. *Feminist Economics*, 12(1-2): 271-298.

Dave, S. (2010), Women's land ownership in Gujarat—What has worked and what needs to be looked at! Paper presented at the Expert Group meeting on gender and productive resources: Women's Entitlements to Land, Livestock and Energy. 17-18 August. New Delhi. UN Women.

Djurfeldt, G., V. Athreya, *et al.* (2008), Agrarian change and social mobility in Tamil Nadu. *Economic and Political Weekly*, 43(45): 50-61.

Doss, C.R. (2001), Designing agricultural technology for African women farmers: Lessons from 25 years of experience. *World Development*, 29(12). 2075-92.

Duvendack, M., Palmer-Jones, R. *et al.* (2011), What is the evidence of the impact of microfinance on the well-being of poor people? Systematic Review, DFID http://www.dfid.gov.uk/R4D/PDF/Outputs/SystematicReviews/Microfinance2011Duvendackreport.pdf

FAO (2011), The state of food and agriculture 2010-11: Women in agriculture. Rome. *Food and Agriculture Organisation*.

Garikipati, S. (2008), 'Agricultural wage work, seasonal migration and the widening gender gap: evidence from a semi-arid region of Andhra Pradesh'. *The European Journal of Development Research*. 20(4): 629-48.

Garikipati, S. (2009), Landless but not assetless: Female agricultural labour on the road to better status, evidence from India. *Journal of Peasant Studies*. 36(3): 517-45.

Government of India (2000), Report of the Time Use Survey—1998-99, New Delhi. Central Statistical Organisation, Ministry of Statistics and Programme Implementation, Government of India.

Gupta, J. (2002), Women Second in the Land Agenda. *Economic and Political Weekly*, 37(18): 1746-1754.

Harriss-White, B. and S. Janakarajan. (2004), Rural India facing the 21st Century: Essays on Long Term Village Change and Recent Development Policy. Anthem Press, London.

Heyer, J. (1989), Landless Agricultural Labourers' Asset Strategies. *IDS Bulletin* 20(2): 33-40.

Heyer, J. (1992), The role of dowries and daughters' marriages in the accumulation and distribution of capital in a south Indian community. *Journal of International Development*, Vol. 4, No. 4, pp. 419-36.

Heyer, J. (2010), The marginalisation of *dalits* in a modernising economy. In: Hariss-White, B. and J. Heyer (eds.) *The Comparative Political Economy of Development*. London, Routledge: 225-47.

Himanshu (2011), Employment Trends in India: A Re-examination. *Economic and Political Weekly*, 46(37): 43-59.

ICRW. (2005), Property ownership and inheritance rights of women for social protection: the South Asian Experience-Cross-site analysis. *International Centre for Research on Women*. New Delhi.

ICRW (2006), Report on violence against women. International Centre for Research on Women. Available online www.icrw.org/html/issues/violence.htm.

IFPRI (2011), Global Hunger Index 2011: The challenge of hunger. *International Food Policy Research Institute*, Washington D.C.

Jayaraj, D. (2004), Social institutions and the structural transformation of the non-farm economy. In: B. Harriss-White and S. Janakarajan (eds.) Rural India facing the 21st Century: Essays on long term village change and recent development policy. London, Anthem: 175-94.

Jeffery, P. and R. Jeffery (1994), 'Killing my heart's desire: Education and female autonomy in rural North India'. In: Kumar, N. (ed.) Women as subjects: *South Asian Histories*. pp. 125-70. Kolkata, Stree.

Jejeebhoy, S. (1998), Wife-beating in Rural India: A husband's Right? *Economic and Political Weekly*, 33(15): 855-862.

Jejeebhoy, S.J. (2000), 'Women's autonomy in rural India: Its dimensions, determinants and the influence of context'. In H. Presser and G. Sen, (eds). *Female Empowerment and Demographic Processes*, Oxford, Clarendon Press.

Jensen, R. and E. Oster (2009), 'The Power of TV: Cable Television and Women's Status in Rural India', *Quarterly Journal of Economics*, 124(3): 1057-94.

Kapadia, K. (2000), Responsibility without rights: Women workers in bonded labour in rural industry in South India. In: D.F. Bryceson, C. Kay and J. Mooij (eds.) Disappearing peasantries? Rural Labour in Africa, Asia and Latin America. London, IT Publications: 247-61.

Kelkar, G. (2011), Gender and productive assets: Implications for Women's Economic Security and Productivity. *Economic and Political Weekly*. 46(23): 59-68.

Kelkar, G. and D. Nathan (1991), *Gender and Tribe: Women, Land and Forest in Jharkhand*. New Delhi, Kali for Women.

Kishor, S. and K. Johnson (2004), Profiling Domestic Violence: A Multi-Country Study. Calverton, MD, MACRO International.

Kishor, S. and K. Gupta (2009), *Gender Equality and Women's Empowerment in India*. Indian Institute of Population Studies, Mumbai.

Kulkarni, S., S. Tiwari, *et al.* (2008), Women and land rights in Maharashtra: Exploring the facilitating and constraining factors in achieving resource rights. Pune, Society for Promoting Participative Ecosystem Management (SOPPECOM).

Lee, D. (2009), The impact of mobile phones on the status of women in India. Stanford, California, Department of Economics, Stanford University.

Luke, N. and K. Munshi (2011), Women as agents of change: Female income and mobility in India. *Journal of Development Economics*, 94: 1-17.

Mencher, J., P. (1988), Women's work and poverty: women's contribution to household maintenance in South India. *A Home Divided: Women and Income in the Third World*. D. Dwyer and J. Bruce. Stanford, California, Stanford University Press: 99-119.

Mitra, A. (2008), Convergence of agricultural interventions in Maharashtra's distressed districts. Working Paper 1 on Social and Gender Aspects, Rome, IFAD.

National Farmers Commission (2006), *Serving Farmers and Saving Farming*, New Delhi. Ministry of Agriculture, Government of India.

Nakkeeran, N. (2003), 'Women's Work, Status and Fertility: Land, Caste and Gender in a South Indian Village' *Economic and Political Weekly*, 38(37), September 13, 3931-39.

National Sample Survey Organisation (2010), Employment and Unemployment Situation in India 2007-08-NSS 64th Round (July 2007-June 2008), New Delhi. National Sample Survey Office, Ministry of Statistics and Programme Implementation, Government of India.

Neetha, P. (2010), 'Self-employment of women: Preference or compulsion?', *Social Change*, 40(2): 139-156.

Nielsen, R., N. Bhatla, *et al.* (2006), Increasing women's property ownership through rural housing programmes in India. New Delhi, ICRW and RDI.

Padmaja, R., M.C.S. Bantilan, *et al.* (2006), Gender and Social Capital Mediated Technology Adoption. Hyderabad, ICRISAT.

Panda, P.K. and B. Agarwal (2005), Marital Violence, Human Development and Women's Property Status in India, *World Development*, 33(5): 823-50.

Peterman, A., B.J., *et al.* (2010), A review of empirical evidence on gender differences in nonland agricultural inputs, technology, and services in developing countries. Washington D.C, IFPRI.

Ramachandran, V.K., V. Rawal, *et al.*, Eds. (2010), *Socio-economic Surveys of Three Villages in Andhra Pradesh: A Study of Agrarian Relations*. New Delhi, Tulika Books.

Rao, K.P.C. and M.C.S. Bantilan. (2003), *Rural Development in India: Response in ICRISAT Villages*. Hyderabad, ICRISAT.

Rao, N. (2002), Standing One's Ground: Gender, land and livelihoods in the Santal Parganas, Jharkhand, India. School of Development Studies. Norwich, University of East Anglia. PhD.

Rao, N. (2005), Agricultural Research and Extension in India: Changing Ideologies and Practice. *Economic and Political Weekly*, 40(3): 1371-75, March 26.

Rao, N. (2008), "Good women do not inherit Land": *Politics of Land and Gender in India*, Social Science Press and Orient Blackswan, New Delhi.

Rao, N. (2011), Women's access to land: An Asian perspective. Paper presented at the Expert Group Meeting on 'Enabling rural women's economic empowerment: Institutions, opportunities and participation', Accra, Ghana, 20-23 September.[1]

Rao, N. (2012), Male 'providers' and female 'housewives': A gendered co-performance in rural North India. *Development and Change*. 43(5)

Rao, N. (2012b), Caste, Kinship and Life-course: Rethinking Women's Work and Agency in Rural South India. Paper accepted by *Feminist Economics*.

Rao, N. (2013), Gender and productive resources: Claiming women's entitlements to land. In: Kelkar, G and Krishnaraj, M. (eds.) *Women, Land and Power in Asia*. New Delhi. Routledge.

Rao, N.; Verschoor, A.; Deshpande, A.; and A. Dubey (2008), Gender, Caste and Growth Assessment-India, April. Report to DFID. http://www.uea.ac.uk/dev/publications/RPP8

Rao, V. (1997), Wife-beating in rural South India: A qualitative and econometric analysis. *Social Science and Medicine*, 44(8): 1169-1180.

Srivastava, N. and R. Srivastava (2010), Women, work and employment outcomes in rural India. *Economic and Political Weekly*. 45(28): 49-63.

Swaminathan, H.; N. Bhatla, *et al.* (2009), Women's property rights and HIV/AIDS in India. *Economic and Political Weekly*, 44(17): 101-108.

Swaminathan, H.; Suchitra, J.Y. and R. Lahoti (2011), Karnataka Household Asset Survey: Measuring the gender asset gap. Bangalore. Indian Institute of Management. Bangalore.

UN Women and RDI (2011), Gender and land tenure security: Challenges and barriers to women's entitlement to land in India. *UN Women*. New Delhi.

Unni, J. and G Raveendran (2007), Growth of Employment (1993-94 to 2004-05): Illusion of Inclusiveness? *Economic and Political Weekly*, 42(3): 196-99.

WGWLO (2004), *Study on Status of Women and Agricultural land Ownership in Gujarat*. Ahmedabad. Working Group for Women and Land Ownership.

World Bank, The (2009), *India Undernourished Children: A Call for Reform and Action*. World Bank. Washington D.C.

Notes

1. The total cultivable land in India was 182.57 million hectares in 2005-06 (60% of total land area), declining from 185.09 million hectares in 1980-81, mainly due to its diversion to non-agricultural purposes. The total workforce in the same year was 509.3 million, of whom 60 per cent were engaged in agriculture. http://www.financialexpress.com/news/indias-cultivable-land-falls-marginally/282603/ accessed on 10/6/12.
2. The most recent of such policies is the Mahila Kisan Sashaktikaran Pariyojana (MKSP) or Women Farmers' Empowerment Programme,

launched in 2010-11 with a budget of ₹ 100 crore to enhance women's productive capacities in agriculture.

3. NFHS data reveal an increase from 9 to 14 per cent between 1995-56 and 2005-6. While 25 per cent female headed households belonged to the lowest wealth quintile, this was only 20 per cent for male headed households (Kishor and Gupta, 2009: 55).
4. The National Sample Survey's Indebtedness Report that calculates the value of total assets per social group (land, livestock, buildings, equipment, household durables and financial assets) confirms this in revealing that the SCs and STs own about half the value of assets of the OBCs and about a third that of Others (Rao, *et al.* 2008:91). See also Harriss, *et al.* 2010, Heyer, 2010, Harriss-White and Janakarajan, 2004, Ramachandran, *et al.* 2011, Deininger, *et al.* 2010 for data on asset inequality across castes.
5. Mitra (2008), finds a similar result for the Vidarbha region of Maharashtra based on the Agricultural Census.
6. The study was undertaken before the Amendment was made to the Hindu Succession Act.
7. Padmaja, *et al.* (2006), in a case study from Maharashtra, point out that women have stronger bonds with kin and family, while men have cross-cutting ties with farmers, friends and acquaintances, expanding their sources of information considerably.
8. In Karnataka, none of the 41 extension agents were female, 1 or 41 junior engineers and 4 of 40 veterinary assistants (World Bank and IFPRI, 2010).
9. Lee (2009), cites evidence that not only points to the improvement in agricultural and fish markets through better market information, but also the beneficial effects of mobile phones on reducing domestic violence and improving women's mobility and economic independence. It does not however improve women's autonomy or decision-making within the household. The results are similar to Jensen and Oster's (2009) study of cable TV use in India, which attributes shifts in social norms to exposure to such media.
10. IRDP loans were mainly targeted at men, and it was only with the introduction of a special scheme, namely, Development of Women and Children in Rural Areas or DWCRA within the IRDP ambit, that some of the resources were directed to women.
11. Gender-disaggregated data on crop loans for Dumka district, Jharkhand, revealed that 3.9 per cent of all crop loans were disbursed to women in 2000-01, doubling from 2 per cent the previous year (Rao, 2002:282).
12. Rao (2012), found in her Uttar Pradesh study that female agricultural work largely constituted work as unpaid household helpers on family farms, so to earn some cash, especially in the absence of migrant husbands, women supplemented this with low paid, home-based, bead-making work.
13. NSSO (2010: 50), Statement 21 reveals female wages of ₹ 48 *versus* ₹ 66 for men in 2007-8, increasing from ₹ 15 and ₹ 23 respectively in 1993-4.

Nakkeeran (2003) argues that wage gaps reflect the hierarchies between the ideological valuations of male and female work.

14. NFHS 3 data also provides some insights into women's control over income and its use. Only 15 per cent of women in the 15-49 age-group had bank accounts which they could manage, though this increased with wealth, education and employment status (Kishor and Gupta, 2009: 65-66).
15. Luke and Munshi (2011), Specify that female income effects on household decisions and marital violence are only obtained for certain sub-castes, even amongst the SCs, pointing to the importance of caste and social background in mediating women's autonomy, decision-making and empowerment.

6

Land Rights for Women

Planning Gender Inclusion to Address Gender Resource Gap

Shivani Bhardwaj

Introduction

The 2013 draft land policy of India which gives women preferential treatment in further land distribution is an official recognition that the gender resource gap remains in most important means of production. The mention of group land rights for women is a way to get resources for women outside family and community resource control. The issue of gender resource gap and its link with patriarchal control of the powerful on resource base (Katrak, 2009) is a complex contestation rendering most inclusion efforts to lessen impact. Yet historically rights are realized when a system of demand is consistent with legal and moral arguments. This paper analysis the issue of land rights for women from the perspective of planning gender inclusion to address gender resource gap.

From Land Rights to Gender Resource Gaps

The Consult for Women and Land Rights (CWLR) gathered voices of women across different cultures to advocate and lobby for change in law, policy and programmes in 2003. Within no time, many networks emerged that created the human resource for organizations to support ground level work, research and policy reform work on women and land (UNIFEM and SAFP, 2008). The discourse has certainly evolved for the issue to be recognized at all levels and many groups have earnest successful pilot programmes on women and agriculture, homestead and right to the commons. Few studies have indicate the gains in reducing the control ownership and access of land women and men have at district and national level. It is time to gather data on how much land and assets have been transferred to women from 2002 to 2012 and this should be computed against a gender resource gap in spaces, sector and household to form base line for future development plans.

A land title in woman's name requires credit, access to services and asset base to sustain ownership and control while trying to make land productive and regenerating. The discourse on women and land right focused on agriculture, as if all women were farmers alone. A farmer belongs to a village, caste and class who has abilities and roles within their spatial and community setting. A farmer works cross sector as farming families shift to urban areas as unorganized sector workers. Women migrating due to marriage or with their work have to negotiate their right to land differently than men thus remain vulnerable as their ownership to housing and services is even less secure than their land right. The discourse of women and land thus incorporates housing and livelihood resources. For this reason most people working on women and land began to focus on related assets that help sustaining land once it is got on women's name. All along the role of women as caretakers of the young and elders of the household was upheld to compute the cost and gain of this gender role. The leadership of single women on housing and land rights asked for further disaggregation of data on land and assets which called for clarity on planning to be done for women and men as individual citizens rather than as people within a household as a unit of planning. However, when single women were defined as never married, married and divorced, deserted, widowed and in partnership with other women/men the planning unit remained household with addition of the category of women headed households. The conceptual clarity on what land rights constituted thus has had a long process which further got qualified on the basis of gender roles on management of land, assets and related resources. Households have reproductive role, productive role and community roles that need to be negotiated between its members on the basis of capabilities and opportunities different members of the household get to experience multiplicity in performing gender roles.

Skills to manage land and productive assets was a gap. Dr. Nitya Rao was one the first to expound in 2003 with CWLR members that related resources such as skills, access to forest and water as well as housing, livelihoods and credit are a prerequisite to get to realization of woman's land right (Rao, 2006). While working on the issues since the

1990 one realized the importance of working at both individual, local and district level. This realization becomes more acute after the passing of gender equal laws on private property. Most cases referred to members of CWLR had a very difficult time getting lawyers and judgments in a gender equal manner. Even after Hindu Succession Act amended in 2005 superseded the ZA act in Uttar Pradesh the local land recording officials i.e. *patwaris* still refuse to shift their operational work pattern related to land registration in women's name.

The work on gender resource planning was evolving under the policy concerns for gender equality (Beal, 1999). In 2011 consultations were held on urban development flagship programme—The JNNURM but this policy discourse did not lead to tangible gain for planning for increased access for women to urban infrastructure. Token allocations for land planning for a vending zone for women were attempted by town planners in 2011 and this was a welcome sign. However the rural and urban development ministries did not adopt a holistic method to compute gender resource gap as the basis of planning projects and area development plan. The demand for this planning was raised by Sathi all for partnership (SAFP) but sans an academic and written proposal of how gender resource gaps can be understood at micro and macro level the justification for this advocacy was weak. Pioneering research was to be conducted to establish the link of women resource rights gap and local planning as it was clear that private property will not be easily transferred to women by families. If they were to acquire skills in property management they had to first learn it from outside the family structure in their own neighbourhood.

How can women gain and increase skills to manage property and how can women get more access to property to manage is a question that the author explored for the past decade. Through an organizational and individual efforts of many people an attempt was made to look at inclusion of women land and related resource rights within planning at different levels. The organization that the author belongs to, is called Sathi All For Partnerships (SAFP) which also is the coordinator of CWLR. The individual efforts that are mentioned in this article are of those people who partnered with SAFP on the journey to increase understandings to change perceptions on realization of women's land and resource rights. The initiatives are enumerated in 3 different sections ahead that build the understanding of gender resource gaps at different levels of planning that needs to plan for resource equity between and within each community based in urban and rural locations to foster gender equal sectoral and spatial planning in practical terms.

This article thus shares a journey which women and land rights that meandered into understanding gender resource gap differentials in urban and rural locales with its implication on a *dalit* and tribal women whose lack of resource base should form the slices of local, district and national planning process and end with a possible plugging in of the concepts in the urban and local planning process that should result in an increased realization of women's right to land and resource equality.

Locating Gender Resource Gap at Different Levels in Multiple Forms

In 2009, the author computed Gender Resource Gap (GRG) in a rural area and a district through a doctoral thesis called "Differential resource access—An exploratory study of gender gaps in Delhi.

This section provides learning from the thesis. The unequal distribution begins from the smallest unit of our society that is the family. GRG epitomizes disparity in the society and economy. If the gap is known planning can ensure to reduce the same. The objective of the thesis was to map the multi forms in which gender resource gaps exist; to locate the gender resource gaps at different levels; to measure the quantum of GRG through Harvard Analytical Framework (Evertzen, 2009) to propose ways in which gender resource gaps framework could be accommodated at macro and micro levels. gaps in the thesis were explored in space, services and spousal income as forms of gender gaps to find out that women use and access 31 per cent less space and avail 3 per cent less services on an average.

Multiple forms of gender resource gaps provided evidence to identify the socio-economic worth of women and men at different levels, i.e. the familial level, the socio-economic level and at the level of governance. These levels decide gender roles of a household that works within a community to govern and impact lives of individuals living in an area. The quantification showed that married men have 130 per cent more income than women. A 14 per cent asset gap showed that women can buy fewer assets, sustain them less when they buy it and inherit less than men. GRG at the familial level can be understood at a 7 per cent in literacy in favour of men. However among those who get education gender gap favoured women in professional education. The men had 10 per cent and 7 per cent more access to resources within the house and institutions of governance, while women had 7 per cent more access to schemes. At the level of economy the gender gap favoured men by 10 per cent more in access to resources outside the house, 30 per cent access to livelihood opportunity and equipment and 7 per cent control of resources. Qualitative data was collected as on perceptions about space needs, services and participation at socio-economic and governance levels that were explored across high, middle and lower income categories. These were documented and shared with stakeholders who suggested different kinds of interventions that may minimize gender resource differentials.

The gender resource gap form was most in spousal income, livelihood opportunities and space. Therefore, a spatial plan was proposed to make gender resource centres with livelihood interventions connected through safe roads with many public infrastructure for care and production spaces. Outcome of this exploration is a methodology to compute gender resource gaps at a spatial unit level that clarify the forms of gender resource gaps and the output of the research are micro and macro plans with a set of next steps in form of recommendations for stakeholders at different levels (Exhibit 6.1).

This research explored ways on how inclusive planning can be manifested at a local area level. Towards this end discussion with respondents was evolved to develop gender resource increase options within a local area level plan that is linked to district planning. The exploration of the research thus demonstrated that cities and villages within a district could be planned to make areas and its inhabitants regenerative.

Exhibit 6.1: Gender Resource Centre

State & National level	FORMS and levels OF RESOURCE GAPS		
District level	Governance and political control for inclusion	Socio-economic transaction worth of electors	Quality of services from Local Body and network for security
Neighborhood level	Socio-economic transaction worth in community	Emotional and economic worth decides status of women and men in households	Access and control of public space
Household level	Familial bonds and culture.	Individual space can impact personal aspiration more	Knowledge and skill base for livelihood and care

Note: The Exhibit 1 depicts that GRG exist at different levels and these gap correlate with each other.

This regenerative plan was termed as a sustainable development zone within which a women resource zone exists. This research proved that balancing inclusion and development is possible. Specific projects could be developed to promote gender equality as a result of this work in rural and urban settings.

Relation between Gender Resource Gaps and Spaces

Women have less worth in terms of assets and income so they get to build and design fewer spaces. Spaces if co-created with men and women's participation in neighbourhoods could provide a different visual image of inclusive design. Participation in a project from its inception builds web of relationships that can influence utility, usage and design. Attitude based on gender equality first needs to be imbibed in both women and men. A simple solution to closing the gender gap in space is to provide spaces that women can access more or even access exclusively. Changes can be brought at the level of public visibility. This visibility will help in transforming patriarchal attitudes.

> *"If many women are visible moving around and interacting openly with men with purposeful confidence, men will also get opportunity to interact enough, leading to less of eve teasing and VAW"*
>
> —Dr. Baraan Farooqui, Faculty Jamia Millia Islamia

An example of government action is the Delhi Metro rail women compartment and example of exclusive space for women is the Balak Mata centre of Jamia University where children and mothers get educated under one facility (SAFP and NCW 2011). Such a convergence can be done for old age care as well as production needs.

Relation between Gender Resource Gaps and Services

One of the outcomes of the research was articulation of people in the locales who co created options after knowing about gender gaps in services through FGDs on cluster planning and green transport.

> *"If mobility, habitation and economic activity is planned with services and market areas in a sustainable way through projects*

it will benefit all at different levels within the district".

—Ms. Mamdooha Majid,
Member, Muslim Personal Law Board

Architecture students guided by Equal Saree a young women architect team from Barcelona, designed a solution of a safe road network for the neighbourhood spaces and road networks and this plan was called the Okhla gender plan. Thus the 130 per cent GRG in income could be reduced by providing 3 per cent services improvement linked through a network of roads and social relationship web in 31 per cent spaces that women could manage to lessen their occupation and care role supports through a planning that promotes wellness and provides nurturing environment to build skills and mobility.

"The women view environment in relationship of family health and as a public health issue. Men exercise caution as they experience the effect of environmental laws on their business and jobs."

—Dr. M. Khalid,
Climate Change Expert, Resident of Okhla.

Balancing growth and development against protecting the environment and preserving open space needs to be done in the solutions we seek that may close the gender gaps. Training for men to increase their livelihood and rejuvenation options near home will also help interchange of gender roles. Young women said "If boys get engaged in learning skills they have less time to follow us around and if men are educated on development needs they can take decisions that favour all equally".

The Solution: Inclusive Development Zone: Towards this inclusive spatial planning was developed (Bhardwaj and Ghosh, 2012) that included a Women Resource Zone (WRZ) proposal among other transformative projects proposed. Towards this focus group discussion was held at micro level and experts were consulted at macro levels with as respondents of this study to suggest solutions. These stakeholders were policy planners, academics and leaders responsible for the local and national development process who would rather respond to concepts like sustainability and inclusion than GRG and its reduction by a WRZ and other integrated development projects. A critical conclusion of the research process was to understand inclusion as a process inclusive for women and sustainability as an inclusive agenda. Thus sustainable inclusive development zone was a reformulation that was recommended to stakeholders at different levels within the locales and institutional systems responsible for decreasing GRG.

Gender Resource Gaps at Micro and Macro Levels can be Addressed by Planning in Rural and Urban Local Administrative Units that should also be Planned within Watershed Boundaries

To reduce gender gaps at household levels a macro plan was required that provided care services and training and employment to women near their housing. An example of this kind of a plan was developed the Shivpuri Rural WRZ and Okhla Gender Plan as shown in Exhibit 6.2 which depict that a woman resource centre provides training and production space to women, while the vending space/social forestry and land based SMEs can provide market avenues for women locally. Different groups of women and men could manage the production units, labour centres and rickshaw pullers parking and wet kitchen to have access to labour and financial resource. The space could also work itself as a green project by developing horticulture, fish farming, livestock, poultry, forest regeneration and agriculture production options. Many such projects need to be planned in different parts of the district that plan the linkage between rural and urban areas for the macro plan together with participation of local people in the planning.

Exhibit 6.2: Green Pilot in Okhla gender plan in Haji Colony: Gender resource centre, Jamia haat, rickshaw stand and night shelter

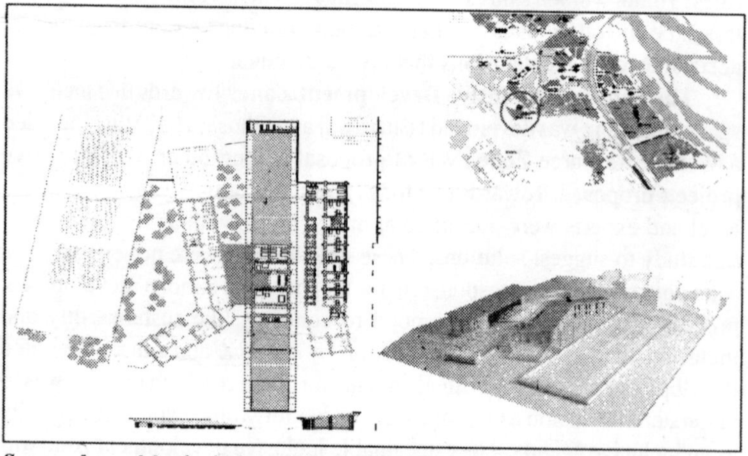

Source: Laura Manford Master Thesis Equal Saree http://equalsaree.tumblr.com/

Many local level discussions led to recording aspirations of different people in the locales to make a Macro Plan with myriad projects that links local development with a district plan. Urban local bodies, city level leaders, academia and national planners were informed about the research results. Discourse thus has been generated from local to higher levels. Rural WRZ was later explored in two rain fed villages in Shivpuri Madhya Pradesh as rural area in Delhi was different than these remote tribal and *dalit* villages.

The macro plans need to be linked to planning process of the city and village development. Exhibit 6.3 is a part of rural marco plan to show how GRG lessening agenda can become a part of an ongoing development project that is truly aimed at inclusion (SET 2013). The draft Land policy 2013 has special implication for land-use planning in context of rural area and while JNNURM and RAY can be applied in urban areas. Planning for gender and inclusion, space for children, elders and for workers can solve many gender role related tensions as well as build peace between distribution of space between marginalized and vulnerable. The more resourced will be able to willingly invest in enterprise should they understand that they could get workforce who are well fed and well trained in a neighbourhood workers centre, care centres, space for relaxing and rejuvenating. A person who needs to spend time earning needs to have services near home that could be within distances to be covered in a day. With services and livelihood planned well in each local area gender relations can be ne renegotiated without fearing house work or work outside the house. With all less fearful the security of being one with the environment may set in to reduce feelings that generate violence in households and within communities.

The urban daily route is provided on the right hand side with the proposed infrastructure in the middle in Exhibit 6.4.

In Okhla the urban area, the 'Metro' is being introduced and transport systems will be reviewed for it. This opportunity could be used by the socio-economic actors to carry forward proposals that have emerged as a result of the research process. In Okhla an elderly women and children centre, a vending area, Yamuna river bank revival, women resource zone, multipurpose halls, health and education centres are proposed as macro plan. The Shivpuri rural plan gave a combination of social forestry livestock and watershed plan for soil and water conservation that made women in charge of regenerating watertable with increasing vegetation cover while gender resource gap reduce through women getting resources in groups to work on MSE with infrastructure credit and training provided within local planning (SET, 2013).

The thesis as well as SET report did not cover all areas and suggested further research. SAFP undertook three other parallel studies to understand the *dalit*, the Muslim and the tribal women's resource gaps. The section ahead will explain the context and preliminary learning from the *dalit* woman's resource gap study as an example of this work.

Research on GRG for Women in Different Communities and Work Sectors

SAFP partnered with CWLR members, Women Struggle Committee and NACDOR to compute the *dalit* woman's resource gap (SAFP, 2013). The research supported by Ministry of Women and Child was spread over 5 States and the sample of 1000 *dalit* and non-*dalit* women drawn from rural and urban settings in Uttar Pradesh, Rajasthan, Bihar, Tamil Nadu and Punjab. Each location and each State had a different rate of landlessness and resource equation.

In India *dalit* women constitute 16.3 per cent of which 18 per cent women live in rural areas and they rarely own any land but work as agricultural labourers as unemployment among them is high. In 1991, about 71 per cent of *dalit* women workers in rural areas were agricultural labourers. Only 19 per cent of them owned land (Tirmare, 2004). *Dalit* women have been at the forefront of *dalit* land rights movements and whenever they have participated in these campaigns they have been much more successful (Nicholas, 2005). About 90 per cent of women working in unorganized sector are mainly from lower castes (Jogdand, 2005). MNREGA workers are largely *dalit* women as workers from another caste are not willing to work on the low wage offered by the flagship programme (interview with Geetha R. of women struggle committee in 2012 for the SAFP *dalit* women resources study).

The preliminary results of the SAFP *dalit* women and resource study show that non-*dalit* women have more access to resources such as 19.66 per cent more land, 66.67 per cent more shop/workshops and 60.63 per cent more livestock besides having more access to health care and transport The research found that *dalit* women lag behind in education and skills, credit, access to natural resources in particular land, housing and services when compared to non-*dalit* women. Even where schemes exist such as the SCP only 25 per cent of *dalit* women knew about it. Women's schemes, which did not seem to reach *dalit* women, with the exception of those with political patronage had an awareness of around 58 per cent among *dalit* women where as only 33 per cent non-*dalit* women

Exhibit 6.3: Hypothetical Route for Gender Equal Net

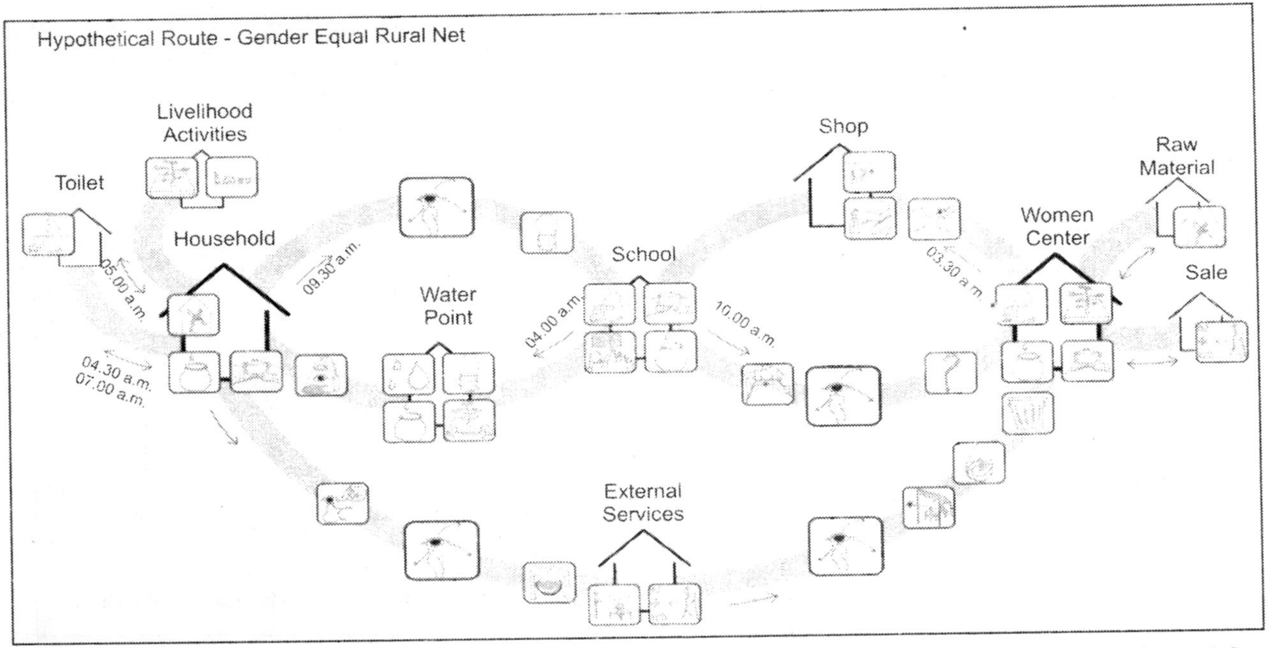

Source: Master thesis of Helena Cardona Tamayo from Barcelona School of Planning and Architecture and Equal Saree equalsaree@gmail.comhttp://genderequalurbanplanning.tumblr.com and SET report 2013

Exhibit 6.4: Global Proposal Net of Equipment and Services

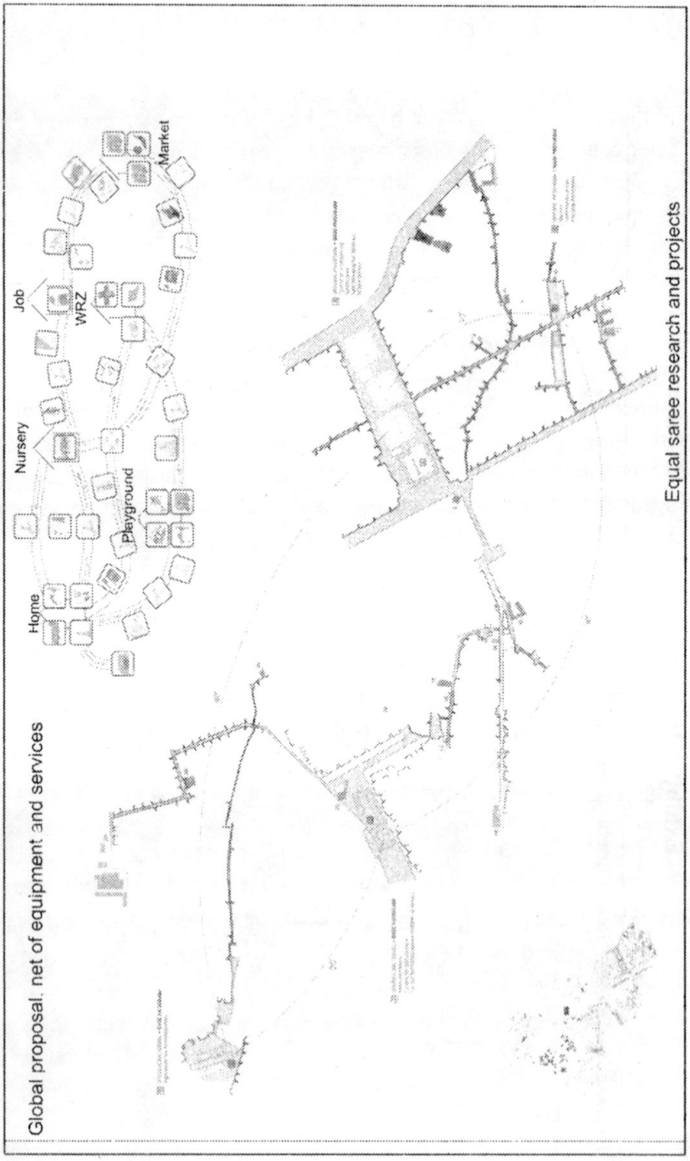

were not aware. The *dalit* women resource gap in access to schemes was 25 per cent with 46 per cent non-*dalit* women reporting that say that they have not been benefited from the government or NGO schemes, where as more than 71 per cent *dalit* women say the same. This is also a huge gap when in addition 33 per cent more *dalit* women feel deprived services like health, transport and social get together and 20 per cent *dalit* women feel that they have not been benefited by education as compared to only 11 per cent non-*dalit* women responding on the same.

Discrimination across different institutional sites, from the household and community to the State and markets, and the pervasive violation of their human rights, implies that even when *dalit* women gain access to resources, they are unable to translate it into improved welfare and wellbeing over a period of time. *Dalit* women are more agricultural labour, and less home makers as compared to non-*dalit* women. The missing social networks seem to be a clear gap for *dalit* women to get better employment who continue to work in their caste based occupations. About 33 per cent *dalit* women say that being *dalit* is an obstacle to reform as compared to only 11 per cent non-*dalit* women saying so. The need to organise special awareness programmes on government schemes for *dalit* women and promote their collectives and organizations to empower them and facilitate reduction in resource gap was felt by both *dalit* and non-*dalit* women.

Considering the resource gaps found out by the study it is recommended that the success and failure of every government programme should be measured by their reach and impact on *dalit* women. All government interventions should provide disaggregated data by sex, caste, income and minority households living in each electoral constituency. The computation of gender resource gap and caste and minority based resource gap then can be present for proper utilization of SCP. The allocation and monitoring of the SC Sub-Plan with mechanisms need to be improved to ensure that 50 per cent of the SCP should be earmarked for *dalit* women. Since *dalit* people are 16 per cent of the population of India the Gender Budget Guidelines of the Government of India needs to make proportionate provision for SC/ST/Minorities women. In this case, 16 per cent allocation for the Scheduled Caste women should be mandatory under the Gender Budgeting by the Government of India or the States. District development plans should be audited for gender and *dalit* equity gaps. Towards this end the monthly action taken report of the District Collector should be utilised to monitor the reduction of resource gaps for *dalit* women by tracking implementation of all schemes including SCP and Women component of budgets. Other recommendations included setting up an empowered government body to deal with *dalit* women's development and protection of livelihood opportunities with special protection mechanism for the *dalit* women who have filed police complaints. The right to livelihoods of *dalit* women needs to be protected for specific sectors where *dalit* women work as unorganized sector workers in urban and rural areas. Social audit of MNREGA, developmental projects as well as other schemes that can enhance land or infrastructure base related to adequate housing and right to livelihood needs to be led by *dalit* women's organisations.

To increase skill base of *dalit* women and girls an award of 100 per cent pre-Matric and college scholarship with hostels should be granted as the current scholarship amounts are too small to cover quality education in addition to self-employment schemes for manual scavengers. Public distribution system and services be made people and *dalit* women-centric by facilitating their access to safe spaces for active participation in decision-making at all levels. Special schemes should be created to increase the resource base of *dalit* women, including land. All existing schemes should be redesigned towards this focus. The study recommends that land grants for *dalit* women in groups needs to be accompanied by infrastructure and training support to begin group enterprises as land and agriculture alone cannot give *dalit* women the reason to shift out of traditional degrading occupations.

Creating Space for Gender Equal Spatial Planning

While inclusion in planning appears in official documents (NPC, 2012), concrete examples are needed to be developed and presented to stakeholders for action. SAFP in collaboration with Equal saree and partners who work with State government has made sustainable planning models that were addressing gender resource gaps. This planning includes a detailed gender resource plan within the urban or rural plan of any development project.

Each local area will have different levels of exclusion that need to be lessened for fostering inclusion as is clear from the SAFP *dalit* women and resource gaps research. If these gaps are worked through the gender lens two levels of vulnerability are dealt with simultaneously exclusion at the socio-economic level gaps that could be addressed through area development projects that can impact status of women within their own households. The resource gaps at the familial or the household level will be addressed through local climate change adaptation and care services projects that benefit both the community and the household in each neighbuorhood. This plans should make visible contribution of women through local governance structures. Greater gender equality can enhance productivity, improve development outcomes for the next generation, and make institutions more representative.

The next short terms steps that are:

- Getting a constituency and stakeholders active to take on the process to understand gender resource gaps of different communities and neighbourhoods they live and work in.
- Planning inclusion with owners, users and participant people by livelihood, care and development visioning exercise to map a way forward benefiting all but keeping the women incharge in 50 per cent of development activity.
- Making the Detail Project Report for projects with ULBs and Gram Punchayats to own the process.
- Secure financial, building and natural resource for neighbourhood wellness projects that connect with each other as a district inclusion and gender equality plan.

The long term steps are:
Formulate the area and neighbourhood plans:

- Setting up information and training service to improve access to resources for community under women's ownership.
- Data generation for community livelihood based on regeneration of local resources through women's cooperatives (for placement and productive and care services).
- Establishing neighbourhood care services through gender resource centres that are linked with district-wise social infrastructure development that increases productivity and safety.

SAFP partner organization Drishti offers its land in Sitamarhi in Bihar to develop a gender resource centre with a adolescent girls centre as the core to make a building that will link to the inclusive zone. This work was possible as SAFP partners in Delhi, i.e., Muslim Women's Organization and Taal in Shivuri Madhya Pradesh had worked out sustainable development area development plan for a urban district and two village locations to look at rural connotations of gender equal planning. The basis of any planning needs rationale and clarity on the quantum of resources required with the need to have implementation mechanisms for the same. The first step here is to understand what inclusive planning entails before the need for computing gender resource gap is clarified. The unit for each such planning could be the local constituency of each elected leader. Leaders and members of households need to be sensitized to invest in gender equal planning. SAFP has trained Urban Local Bodies (ULBs) in 5 cities in Bihar to plan an inclusive development zone where women's participation in decision-making levels could evolve sustainable development in a local area of a counsellor. Of the five the Mayor of Hajipur was most willing to carry forward the plan (IPE 2012). This planning now needs to be developed as a pilot to demonstrate the building and natural resource management projects as a reality. The projects could be differently designed housing, transport, production spaces and wellness spaces in a neighbourhood to include everyone's concerns in the habitat. The next steps need to be taken at different levels of governance to propose different women resource increase projects with a DPR or a Detailed Projects Report of each women resource increase enterprise with its infrastructure, care services or a natural resource revitalization process to suggest the planning of such a zone. Thus each WRZ needs a basic programme that will link care roles support to help households to manage work at their level effectively and a specific programme for all human beings to manage their productive and community roles efficiently. The next short term and long term work in any area where local leadership gets trained is listed as a way forward and recommendations for institutions, civil society and academia circulated to shared research finding, outcome and output. This practical application is a way forward to work upon lessening gender inequality in the resource base that makes daily work easier for everyone.

Conclusion

Resources have been maintained differentially within communities through a State supported patriarchal structure which needs to now demonstrate that it wears a constitutional hat of equality. This research offers possibility of a transformation seen desirable by myriad protestors who thronged the streets after the Delhi Gang Rape in December 2012. The recommendations of Justice Verma's report (Verma, 2013) calls for individual virtuosity and virtuosity of institutions of governance. This virtuosity should make each person work on their own individual transformation. The practical application that emerged from the research can produce new solidarity among women and men and draw them together to work in public spaces near homes. Addressing sexual division of labour requires daily hard work while transforming a social order additionally requires infrastructure. In tandem these can make it easier for both women and men to perform their roles equally and bring growth, prosperity and peace to our land. The research for the thesis clarified that many form of resources at different levels are divided unequally between women and men and this can change peacefully through virtuous planning. The existence of a Gender Resource Gap is a violation of constitutional obligation of the State. The gender resource gap will vary at different levels such as at the household level, at work level and community level for women and men differently. The resource requirement for each person and each geographical area varies. Therefore, forms of gender gaps can be multiple. For example, when women have less mobility at family level they are exposed to less information and situations to make informed decision as compared to men. Thus resource gap at the basic unit of society impacts the resource gaps at all the other levels. Gender resource gaps exist in services, access to income, asset base and credit. These gaps indicate that the work required to reduce gender resource gaps is yet to become a priority for stakeholders as they are not aware of the nature and quantum of gender resource gaps. Stakeholders have made themselves aware that they are constitutionally bound to reduce the gender gaps. However, policy and planning level solutions proposed at macro level, i.e., at National Planning Commission level or local or district, city or of village level require training to document gender resource gap in smallest area to monitor the reduction of the gap. Towards this social, economic and political will, to impact local area plans with inclusive planning is essential. The SAFP research process offered ways in which a local area plan can impact gender resource gaps at local level. This local level can easily inform the district and the national level planning.

References

Beall, Jo, (1996), "Urban Governance: Why gender matters". *UNDP Gender and Governance Programme*.

Bhardwaj, S. and Ghosh. (2012), "Women Resource Zone: A Sustainable Approach to Governance" Annual Land Conference of the World Bank, Washington USA. April.

Bhardwaj, S.; Ghosh R.; Kumar, S.; and Dhavid, D. (2008) "Overview of civil societies engagement with women's control and ownership of productive assets and resource". SAFP and UNIFEM Discussion Paper, New Delhi.

Evertzen A. "Gender tools" Netherlands Development Organization http://gade-gender.nl/Bibliographies/Gender%20 tools.htm 2009 (accessed on 9.9.2010).

FWSCI (2013), *Food and Water Security: A Micro Study on Food and Water Security at Household Level in Tribal Areas of Madhya Pradesh and Rajasthan*, by Sewa Mandir, TAAL and SAFP.

Jogdand (2005), *Dalit Women: Issues and Perspectives*, Gyan Publication, New Delhi.

Katrak Ketu H., (2006), *Politics of the Female Body: Post Colonial Writers of the Third World.* Rutgers University Press, New Brunswick, New Jersey and London.

NCW *Gender data gaps in application of equality of resources*, SAFP, Delhi, 2011.

National Planning Commission, Government of India, "Faster, sustainable and more inclusive growth: An approach paper to the 12th Five Year Plan". http://planningcommission.nic.in/plans/planrel/12appdrft/appraoch_12plan.pdf. 2011 August, 2011. (Accessed on 12.09. 2011).

Nicholas (2005), "National Federation for Dalit Land Rights Movement", Seminar Speech at the India Social Forum, New Delhi.

Rao, N. (2006), "Women's Rights to Land, Assets and Other Productive Resources: Its Impact on Gender Relations and Increased Productivity". IFAD-UNIFEM Working Paper 4, South Asia Regional Office, New Delhi.

Swaminathan, H.; Suchitra, J.Y.; Lahoti, R. (2011), *Karnataka Household Asset Survey: Measuring Gender Asset Gap*, Indian Institute of Management, Bangalore.

SET (2013), (Sathi All For partnerships, Equal Saree and TAAL) "The next steps towards rural women resource zone in Shivpuri, Madhya Pradesh. Delhi September.

Tirmare, P. (2004), "Violation of Human Rights of Dalit Women: Issues and Facts", paper presented in the seminar on "Gender and Human Rights by College of Social Work, Nanded Maharashtra,UNDP "Human Development Report" http://hdr.undp.org/reports/global/1999.

Verma, J.S.; Seth, L.; and Subramanium, G. (2013), "Report of the Committee on Amendment to Criminal Law" GOI, New Delhi, 23 January.

Zahidi, S. Tyson; D.L., Hausmann R. (2011), "The Global Gender Gap Report 2011" World Economic Forum. Geneva Switzerland.

7

Negotiating Gender and Land Rights in Pluralistic Terrains with Tribal Women in Southern Rajasthan

Soma Kishore Parthasarathy

Locating Pluralism Gender and Land Rights in Southern Rajasthan

A discussion on local level institutions invariably begins and ends with the constitutional provisions of the Articles of the Constitution of India which give us a three tier Panchayati Raj system of governance. Local governance structures and institutions, however, comprise not only the Constitutionally constituted PRI system but also consist of traditional institutions which have existed and prevailed on the lives of communities for centuries; these provide the normative structure of governance and rules to live by and conduct one's social relations in the given social structure such as the '*jaati panchayat*' in Hindu caste based society, or the traditional forum of the tribal communities known by different names such as "*Palli Sabha*" *or* "*Patti Sabhas*" etc., in the regions of the country where tribal populations are dominant. These traditional governance structures on the one hand, have evolved over the centuries as societies have also transformed and adapted their customary practices to the challenges the environment presents from time to time. These traditional structures are embedded in the socially stratified structure of their communities, and serve even to maintain the hierarchies of these societies. They wield considerable power over their societies through their prescriptive pronouncements from time to time, as well as the interpretation and implementation of the customary law of the community which they pronounce and adjudicate on the basis of. They are significant in that they represent the evolving ethos of communities that have governed themselves and their interface with the elements as well as with others through a system of rules, practices and norms. Invariably we find that these systems have evolved in a context of pluralism, where other cultures and social groups have also evolved with their own set of rules and institutions in close or distant proximity depending upon the local context This is the justice delivery system most accessible to the communities, and function as a first point of reference in the settlement of trivial disputes, family quarrels and incidents of conflicts.

On the other hand are the constitutional structures, emerging out of the pre- and post-colonial configurations of politics and conceptions of modernity in a newly independent nation. The colonial regime established its rule of law over the region, establishing its authority over most areas of governance, but left the terrain of family and personal laws largely untouched, given the complexities of the diversities of personal and family laws and practices across the country, varied by religion, ethnicity, region, etc., with independence the Constitution of India provided for individual freedoms to citizens and introduced a civil law structure, to run parallel with the specific personal laws of each community. The codification of Hindu personal law, the belief in Muslim personal law by followers of that faith and the pursuance of their reigning customary law by people of other faiths and denominations and by tribal people in their own regional forms and context continue to be the prevailing dominant paradigm even as the constitutional provisions offer an alternative, giving citizens the legal right to an alternative, even while the faith and pursuance of the particular belief system continue to dominate in most cases of personal custom, law and belief. In the present context, India is, therefore, a nation that hosts a varied multiplicity of co-exisiting customary or traditional legal systems and authorities and institutions alongside a statutory constitutional structure of formalized and codified family law.

This chapter presents the insights gained from a study on "Tribal Women and Land Rights". The study was conducted with researchers from five CBOs in collaboration with Asthaa an NGO located in Southern Rajasthan. The study was undertaken in 10 villages from 5 Blocks of 5 districts in the tribal dominant Fifth Schedule areas of Southern Rajasthan. The primary objective of the study was to capture the status of women with respect to land rights and rights to land based resources; to enable the participating Community Based Organizations (CBOs) to gain insights to the significance of land and resource rights in the lives of Adivasi women and to enable them to address the impediments that emerge to their gaining such rights through their efforts to engender their agendas for collective action[1]. Beyond seeking women's participation in agitations and campaigns to stake claims to forest resources and to strengthen governance, the attempt was to understand the issues and constraints to women's entitlement to land. This chapter is part of the larger study done in this connection. Based in the feminist framework, Structured Questionnaire and FGD methods were used in the conduct of the study, apart from interviews with political actors and functionaries of the State machineries to elicit their responses to the important question of women's rights to land and resources. Participant observation methods enabled the research team to gain insights into the perceptions and realities of women's status in relation to land and resource issues, and to examine means of negotiating the same. Each research team spent about a month in each village to garner insights and elicit responses.

A broad overview of the household data and status of the population across the 10 villages studied through stratified purposive selection, reveal that:

- Average household size is 5-6 members.
- Households consist of parents and unwedded children. Girls are married and sent to marital homes. Distance of marital homes varies, but is usually within the *adivasis* regions of the southern Rajasthan region. The sex ratio is higher here than elsewhere in the State, but has recorded a decreasing trend as compared to previous decades, which is a matter of concern, The Education status is significantly worse for girls than for boys–about half the boys are educated upto an elementary level.
- Apart from their incomes from the land a large majority of tribal households depended on migration as a means of income earning in the lean and dry season.
- Landholding size of the households is small and the family is patrilocal and patrilineal. Households are patriarchal, with sons provided a house on their marriage, but continuing to work with the father on the household landholding and receiving a portion of the produce for his family.

This chapter is an attempt to unravel, for actors in the region, the nuance of tribal people's land relations and land rights from a gender perspective; and while it may unearth facts already known and evidences of changes in perceptions regarding women's status in regard to land and social marginalization, the effort is to understand and identify the means and possible areas for these CBOs and their support organizations to traverse between the customary and legal institutional frameworks towards entitling women. The major attempt is to recast findings within the entitlements framework, and to reinterpret and analyse the findings from recent studies in order to understand the implications of these shifts for the poor and the marginalized groups.

Legal Rights to Land and Property for Tribal Women—Perspectives and Perceptions

Tribal communities have sustained their lives in a shared economy, where the concept of private property is traced only to a few decades ago, and its footprint has become more explicitly imposed upon their way of life in the post-independence decades since the 60s, with the establishment of the modern Indian State. This was also the period when the forest department established its control over vast majority of forest lands in their vicinity as its domain, and leaving only small pockets of land as settlement or cultivated lands of individual households, and demarcating the boundaries of villages in somewhat arbitrary fashion to appropriate much of the forest land as its own.

Tribal peoples' ownership of property on individual names is a relatively new practice; traditionally the common lands, forests and other resources therein has been the domain of these societies, their norms and practices of sharing of which have evolved over the centuries through a reciprocal relationship ecologically embedded within nature in all its variations and seasonal and spatial vagaries; and their social relationships evolved in relationship to the sharing of its abundance. With the incursion of agrarian settlers and rise of kingdoms in the neighbouring regions the tribal lands were delimited but continued to be held by them. Prabhu records how traditional tribal lands were left out of the records in the settlements made by the Bristish colonial government simply because the British could not fathom the method of governance of the land among the tribal's, hence "in the process of declaration of the forest into areas of reserved forest it was the State who was the encroacher" It encroached on the community lands just because the community lands did not fall into their concept of ownership"[2]. In the wake of such settlement followed the independence movement and the declaration of independence, followed by the withdrawal of privy purses and the end of the Maharajas rule, by which due to lack of documented evidence of the *adivasis* rights in the region, large tracts of forests that were occupied by the tribal's were taken over in the process of "rebellions"[3] as part of the forests under the forest department including those regions that were considered the domain of the tribal's by the Maharajas. Once more the tribal rights remained unrecorded as the State department established its control over large tracts.

In this process, however, especially in the newly independent India, some tribal leaders and dominant elements had gained knowledge and an understanding of the means by which the new land regime could be used to gain rights over tracts of land in individual names, and the outsiders or non-*adivasis* for trade commerce and as government functionaries in the region worked in collusion with such persons to usurp large tracts of land in their individual names and left the more infertile land to the *adivasi.* Even as this process of forest land was being registered in the names of *adivasis* and non-*adivasis*, the dominant custom of mainstream tribal society came to prevail as the norm for ownership of land and women's rights followed the pattern of the dominant Hindu caste society, and the laws related to the Hindu community came to be applied to the *adivasis* in the new interpretations of the Constitution of India and the legal systems adopted from the British.

Since women were not in positions of power and decision making in the transforming structures of governance or in the traditional systems of adivasi justice systems in these parts of the country, there was little scope for them to either raise the issues of depleting access to common property resources from which they were the primary members of their communities to draw sustenance or could they file their own claims or challenge the predominance of men in claiming land rights in the process of individual claim making during the land settlement process. Their lack of exposure to the mainstream societies and vulnerabilities in instances of interface rendered them at risk to partake in parleys with the mainstream and it was the men, especially the more powerful, and those with contact with the new government and the traders and money lenders who settled in the region who benefited most. The trend to declare criminal the tribes of Rajasthan and the restrictions on the *adivasi* from entry into the tribal region all worked against their interests and women were the most marginalized in this process of land grab by private parties—non-*adivasi* and *adivasi*—and the inroads made by the Forest Department and the Contractors into their traditional territories. Women found the commons quickly receding and the rule of the government often in conflict with their own practices of collection and grazing and cultivation, etc., such that they became encroachers in their own land.

Several legislations provided the means for the forest department to strengthen its stronghold[4] on the forest lands in the region despite pronouncements about protection of the traditional rights of the *adivasis*. This trend coupled with the encroachment by other parties and the acquisition of land for government infrastructure created pressure on the *adivasi*, who continued to then privatize for their own use the lands in their vicinity—the open lands, the forests, etc., in the absence of access to the forests and grazing lands, and women found it increasingly difficult to fend for the family and find adequate grasses and food and MFP to ensure a level of economic wellbeing. These processes have led to the situation now of the impoverishment of the *adivasi* and their having to migrate out in distress as the abundant natural resource around them is either destroyed and does not provide a means for sustenance or the forest that exist and its resources are controlled by the State and *mafias* in the timber and MFP trades.

Despite the relatively recent advent of the concept of private property, deep-rooted beliefs exist that women do not have property rights. This may be attributed to the appropriation of mainstream ideas that accompanied the adoption of the mainstream concept of private property; since the interface was invariably controlled by men and the interpretation of laws and rules was dominated by men, protection of their own interests and reinforcing the idea of male privilege in this sphere too as an extension of the dominance of men in decision making realms is assumed as an automatic progression. Women rights were accepted in the realm of the forests, since women did much of the foraging and gathering and could negotiate those rights on the basis of their dominance of that sphere of work, whereas rights to the private land were considered as entirely a male domain and was justified as such an act of lineage—the forest could be owned commonly, whereas the private land was the households, and the household the man's domain, so how could land ownership be claimed by the women?

Inherent in this argument by men in several villages, was also the acknowledgement of women's work in foraging and collection of MFP, etc., for household sustenance, but a refusal to acknowledge women's contribution to the work in agriculture. Dominant stereotypes had made deep inroads into the mindsets of these communities with the increasing dependency on agriculture and the depletion of forest land and resources. In fact women reported that whereas earlier men would respect their rights to any income that would accrue from the sale of MFP, recent shifts has occurred in trying to usurp even that income from women and children, in an attempt to control all assets as a means of enhanced control over women's labour. In Kanpur, Banswara men acknowledged that women had rights earlier and these rights had in fact eroded over the decades. Their reference was to the fact that prior to the privatization of land and its transference from forest land to agricultural use, such land was actually controlled and accessed in much greater measure by women. This also relates to an observation made by women that to demonstrate their authority and status in the community, men had gradually usurped control over larger tracts of forest land, and bigamy and polygamy practices enabled them to manage such lands through the unpaid labour of multiple wives. Only in one village, (Bhilai—a prosperous village with larger average landholding size) did women report an improvement in their status regarding rights to land and ownership of property even in the private domain with the claims being recorded as joint titles under the FRA. Since forest cover still exists in this village unlike other sample villages, greater dependency and visibility of women in forest related activities and greater control over their resources and incomes may be attributed to account for such a positive response.

Despite the reportedly recent shift to private property regimes, women and men in almost all villages referred to only to the parcels of agrarian land as that upon which private ownership rights could be claimed. Tribal communities in this region have perceived of the forests as a shared and common heritage and culturally do not perceive it as an alienable, divisible object of property. Hence, they do not include the forest and common lands in their conception of private lands—only those which have been brought under agriculture are owned and considered as property. Women and men espoused the view that men were given rights to ownership of property primarily because they were the carriers of the patrilineal lineage, and that men's acceptance of women's rights to land and property were inconceivable in the current circumstances, as it would cause too much change in the social equation and men would not tolerate it. The majority of men claimed ignorance of the recent amendments of the Hindu Succession Act Amendment (HSA 2005) and were of the opinion that land rights for women would imply that girls/daughters would then demand their share of property which could prove to be a serious threat to society. Both espoused in most villages (60%) that women were given entitlement in the event of their husband's demise, and this was adequate provision for women. Women in some villages were of the opinion, however, that this was not enough and nor was such land actually given to women, although they are aware of the provision by which the local *patwari* is required to record the land in the woman's name immediately following the death of the husband. In effect, however, the family pressure comes to bear on the women and seldom is land recorded accurately, nor does she gain any power over it except in rare cases.

Land rights for women are a contentious issue and several men restricted the women from their households from participating in our discussion for this reason. Most men expressed the opinion that girls must go to the marital home and this was the order of things since the ownership of land as a fixed asset should remain with those who are in the family and girls are *paraya*. Although the reasons cited in the responses for denial of land and property rights to women were similar among men and women, women expressed this fact with subdued anger about the situation while men took on rigid postures and refused to engage in any discussion. Even on the issue of the widow's rights to land for instance men felt that "giving women a little land to survive was enough, she should be happy with that", claiming once more the right to determine what was "enough".

While disputes are usually resolved by customary law provisions, they are sometimes taken to court of law when resolution was not satisfactory through the customary provisions of their community; and it was the Hindu Succession Act and provisions of the Hindu Personal Law which would then be applied for arriving at a judgment on these matters and all parties would accept these decisions as final. Only in **cases where women's rights were concerned, however, several instances were brought to our notice wherein the defending council invariably take recourse to tribal customary law to reject any proposal that may go in women's favour, citing the fact that tribal customary law does not give land rights to women.** Thus while on all other matters of dispute on land are allowed to be adjudicated on the basis of the Hindu law, discretion is applied to deny women their rights whenever the question of land rights for women are claimed, and they are then compelled to accept these judgments as the courts are quick to succumb to such references to customary law.

Participants in the study were unable to give specific information but did site instances of women who had sought to claim land rights after the demise of their husbands, and they were also aware of instances where daughters with difficult or estranged marital relationships or who had been widowed were bestowed with a small piece of land by the father or brother from his property to enable her to survive. This was seen as a largesse rather than entitlement. Men also reported that other men would protest and would even dissuade anyone proposing to entitle their daughters even to this meagre extent, lest it set a wrong precedence and encouraged women to demand such consideration as a right.

The predominant opinion which was asserted emphatically by the men in our study was that "men are the ones from whom the family continues and it is, therefore, their right to inherit. Girls will go away they will live in another home that is the way it is" men drew upon this patrilineal reference more frequently to establish their precedence in the matter of property rights.

On our query whether women should be given equal rights to land and property (ancestral), while the majority of men and women were in favour of women having land rights at least at a conceptual level, with about 80 per cent of women and 60 per cent of men reporting a positive attitude towards women's land ownership rights, subsequent queries revealed that none had actually transferred land to their wives' name; several (50% of participant men) cited the fact that since land remained in their fathers' name during his lifetime they were constrained from doing so. However, the average age of the men in the study being about 10 years older than the women participants, a larger number (50%) have received their shares in inheritance already, and the fact that none had transferred land title to his wife was hard evidence to the resistance to entitling women despite the current rhetoric. The unanimity in this trend also spoke of a structural resistance to any shift from the traditional position lest one such event lead to a trend. In six villages, however, 60 per cent of sample, women were unanimously emphatic about claiming land rights in matrimonial property and any initiative that provided them with information or enabled them to grapple with the issue collectively was likely to reap results (Dharni, Devgarh, Nichlagarh, Ramgarh Dhamod and Jagabhor).

Among the women the reasons for land rights being necessary for them related to security: of livelihoods and of assured residence in the marital home; women from 3 villages felt that "this is women's right, they contribute significantly to the wellbeing and work in the household" (Ramgarh, Neechalagarh and Dharini). Among the men in favour of women's land rights, recognition of the contribution that women made to the household, and men in Jagabhor were unanimous in their opinion. Could this be converted into a positive outcome in favour of women by encouraging such men to act upon their conviction is a matter that the efforts of the *sangathans* involved in the study can only tell.

The opinions of men resistant to women rights to joint title in matrimonial property–the majority in 4 villages and totally opposed in one (Ghirwar in Sirohi district) bear interesting insight on how land rights act as a means of asserting control over women.

The reasons quoted for men's opposition to women's land rights by men were All these imply a need to control women's mobility, control her in the interest of the household as if her denial is the means to ensure her obedience, the major reason for resistance was, however, the unwillingness to disturb a social structure that was based on a hierarchy of relationships based on the subordination of women; denial of land rights keeps women dependent and subservient and, therefore, kept the possibilities of dissent and conflict minimal as women would remain subservient and dependent on the authority of men. Thus individually while men may speak in favour of land rights for women the larger societal pressure prevents them from actually giving those rights for women and of disturbing a social order of inequality, which is viewed as being in the interest not only of the men but also in the interest of society and its sustained wellbeing.

While we found a wider dissent among men to women's ownership or women's land rights, only in one village was there a vociferous opinion among women against women's land rights. In Ghirwar, in Bhalai and Ghartara a small minority of women did not favour this right for women but did not give reasons for their opposition. It is pertinent to note that all those not in favour of womens rights to land in matrimonial home were older and had either married sons or sons of a marriageable age! Patriarchal values transcend gender boundaries when women themselves take on the mantle of ensuring that values are reinforced to maintain the current hiatus of power relations in order to claim greater power within the prevalent household and societal dynamics; concerns about their own security and power may be assigned as the reasons for this resistance.

Men in most villages expressed fear at the idea of women's gaining entitlement to land and articulated implications far beyond the realm of the economic or the security that women speak of land and its ownership is the one factor that is obviously invested with the entire gamut of potential to impact power relations in every sphere. The entitlement of land to women implies the possibility of women challenging the entire power structure and its impositions on women's lives, and hence men collectively and individually resist the claims of women through assertions of lineage and denial of knowledge and resources to claim these rights; methods are also evolved to declare women without a male as incapable of dealing with land, or to ostracize women through practices such as witch-hunting if women assert their claims, lest other women also assume such assertions.

Queries about whether women should be entitled to land from their paternal home (from the father), or the marital home, from both or neither, revealed contrasting responses once again with women unanimous in and willing to claim rights to land entitlement in the marital home rather than in the parental home. A third of women participants felt that such rights should be given in both places. Among those who were in favour of making such claims, however, about 22 per cent expressed the opinion that it would not be possible to claim these rights since their husbands too did not have such ownership rifts at present, the title being in their father's name. The layers of hierarchy that needed to be surmounted to actualize the rights itself presented a daunting hurdle for some while others were willing to struggle and make claims at both ends.

Among the male respondents, 20 per cent remained entirely opposed to women's land claims, while others were more in favour of women claiming land title from the fathers' land than from matrimonial property. Men were willing to give women land rights so long as it did not in any way impose a sharing of their own rights, or disturb the power relations within their own households. Husbands were willing to support women for a claim to land in the parental home while resisting a claim to entitlement in the marital home, despite their previous declarations that women were the ones who ran the house and managed the home even in their absence—when it came to actual claim they would prefer the claim being made elsewhere. Women in contrast felt more justified in making the claim in their marital homes and felt that this could be a means of their security as well as strengthen their position in the household where they now lived and contributed to its wellbeing.

Have women received land rights? Women in Jagabohr and Ghirwar had not heard of any such case. ***"Even if she claims society will not allow it to happen", was the refrain from men in Ghirwar,*** marking once more their resistance to the idea. Men from 4 villages were unaware (or feigned any such knowledge?) of any cases, but women were able to cite and narrate instances and circumstances wherein women had received land title on the death of the husband, on the death of her brother when she took the responsibility of care for her parents; fathers had bequeathed the daughters with some land in the marital home in the event of her husband's constant harassment and violence to enable her to leave him; or in instances where she was left destitute as the husband took another wife. In one village land was transferred to the wife's name to prevent the land from being grabbed by others in the village. ***Men from Devagarh showed more positive attitudes and were of the opinion that while such instances were few and in dire circumstances, land rights need to be accorded to women as a means of establishing equality***! Perhaps people in this village are ready to take on the issue and to bring about some transformatory changes that can serve as a positive example to others, and strategies may be considered to help them work in this direction to demonstrate how this can be done, using the customary and legal frameworks as required!

Men and women were aware of women gaining land rights only on the demise of the husband as it has now become mandatory for the transfer of title to be recorded by the local revenue functionary as soon as the husband passes away in the name of the wife. However seldom have other claims been made, and even if made these are not granted. Women cited problems of lack of awareness and education and lack of knowledge of the law to challenge obstacles and resistance to their claims; men on the other hand felt that it was only right that women be given the land right to secure the wellbeing of her family on the demise of her husband, but that if she made a demand there would be a backlash and she would be targeted for ridicule and social boycott. Widows have tried to make their claims on the demise of the husband but despite government orders have a difficult time pitted against the family members and society in her matrimonial home. Men in most villages felt it was lack of awareness and education and the inability to negotiate with confidence that denied women their rightful share.

Only few women even view rights over property/assets brought from their parental home as their right, whereas in the majority they view this property as joint title rights, with jewellery being one asset that women wear and hold as the single security for themselves, but even as a tradable resource for family crisis. Girwar was the one village where men were of the opinion that whatever the woman brought with her was his entitlement and that she had no right over it! Whereas elsewhere the understanding was of this being joint property. It is interesting to note that resources and assets from the paternal home were quite spontaneously assumed to be joint in the context of marital sharing, whereas the woman could claim no right to such a spontaneous inclusion in her husbands property by virtue of marriage-indication once more of the gendered duality of power relations embedded in the ownership and control of assets and resources.

Women report that men often invoke the fear of marital and family discord to dissuade any women from claiming rights to land. Such warnings of discord are issued with a veiled threat, as men view these transgressions as a challenge to their dominance and authority. Women do not claim a rightful entitlement and caution from the wisdom of their experiences that the mere provision of rights to land is important but insufficient condition for women to face the onslaught of the families, leading to greater insecurity. "We will have to demand it cautiously and slowly, it will take some time; otherwise there will be more trouble for us. Women will be given the right on paper but will be unable really benefit". Women are more than aware of the resistance but are also optimistic of change however gradual.

There were a few women who had also inherited land from their maternal family. A difference was found in perceptions among men and women regarding ownership of property acquired by men and that acquired by women. On the ownership of property or assets acquired by the men, whereas women view such properties as joint along with their spouse, only 40 per cent of the men reported that they considered such property or assets as jointly owned. Some even went to the extent of stating emphatically that land ownership was a male purview, even if the woman inherits, it is the men who will determine the use.

Have women asserted rights over family property, and related decisions? Is there a consultative process before the decision to sell a property is taken and how does this transpire? The unanimous response was that this is viewed as men's domain, and women **are** only consulted as a measure of appeasement or conflict avoidance. While most men and women were in agreement that women need to be consulted and consented to sell the property or land, before men can dispose of any property, men and women in 3 villages acknowledged that men went ahead with the sale even if the women disagreed. Women spoke about men threatening to leave them or throw them out if they disagreed to their decision; they would anyhow go ahead for the sale irrespective of their opinion. Only in Devgarh did men report that women's agreement was a necessary condition to sell an asset. In Bhalai women said "some men would be there in every community who would sell the property/asset without even consulting irrespective of the woman's wishes due to habits of indulgence to alcohol, etc. They assume that they alone had the right to take such decisions". Overall women's opinion may be sought but is not a reason why men would change a decision to dispose an asset, reflecting and assuming a dominant position in the matter. Even now when women's names are being included in the claim forms, the customary view remains that women do not own property and that any discussion on the matter is only likely to create family and societal discord.

Acquisition, disposal of land continue to be considered the domain of men traditionally and women's rights have not been a matter of debate hitherto among the *adivasis*. Their own culture does not allow it and the practices of private land ownership adopted over the years have been so modelled on the mainstream model to disallow the inclusion of women since *adivasi* family patterns are also primarily patrilocal and patrilineal.

Thus gender relations related to land-rights to own, sell, dispose, or use have gradually moved to the private domain in the wake of transitions from a forest and resource gathering based ecological footprint to an agrarian character, and in the process the patriarchal character of land relations has only been reinforced.

Social Justice Mechanisms and *Adivasi* Women's Rights

In this section we explore the traditional/customary mechanisms of justice delivery and decision making among the Bhil and Girasia *adivasis* of Southern Rajasthan and the implications and efficacy of these mechanisms from a gender viewpoint as well as their accessibility for *adivasi* women. The queries addressed are:

- What are the customary and constitutional justice delivery mechanisms?
- Which system do men and women approach for what kind of problems? What considerations inform their decisions?
- Are women able to assess them? What are the constraints they experience?

What are the customary and constitutional justice delivery mechanisms in the village? Do these consider women's perspectives and are women included? This section describes how the systems of traditional justice delivery work and what are their processes and constraints based on the responses of men and women included in this study. Traditional leadership lies in hand of the *Mukhiya*—always a man—and he selects his *Panch. Mukhiya* is an inherited role transferred from one generation to the other in a family that has been assigned with such authority over the generations. Roles of the *Gamethi,* as the *Mukhiya* is also known in some parts, include settlement of marriage/death related conflicts; land related decisions and problems, punishment of crime and settlement of Mohtana.

He appoints members of the community as his *Panch* for support in the work of village governance, taking care to represent the hamlets and interest groups in the village. The village *Patel* is the *Mukhiya* and is usually a person who has traditionally enjoyed the trust and faith of the community and the aggrieved parties approach the *Mukhiya* to settle matters of conflict.

They may not, however, call on them for justice delivery if their credibility is in doubt. Hence, according to the men, the Patel tries to maintain his credibility for unbiased justice delivery. In Ramgarh women report the committees in the village sits in the leadership of *'tadavi'*, based on need when a conflict arises. Such persons are selected who have higher respect in the community.[5]

Only men are nominated on the customary '*Panch*' forum and even in matters related to women they seldom consult women or and may only hear their views. Parties in the conflict may also nominate their own representatives to the *Panch* on the hearing of their case in order to keep the balance. Customary practice, therefore, eliminates women from such forum of justice delivery and decision making and cases are settled without women's voices or opinion being heard. Implicit in the role of the *Mukhiya*/ Gamethi is the continuance of the system of justice delivery based on the traditional principles and values of the tribal community. He is expected to be the holder of this tradition, and the person who then lays the normative structure of how the community lives together. He works with men from his community to strengthen their culture and practices and reinforce structures of governance (with the *Panch*); he would, therefore, be cautious and even resistant to practices that may threaten his authority or reduce his credibility in the community. Thus on issues of gender justice for instance, the accepted practices are likely to inform his path of action and adjudication in order to maintain his credibility. Through such a process, therefore, the structural constraints of justice delivery are maintained by keeping women out of the forum, and the practices maintained with minimal challenge to established gender and power relations. Inquiries into the reasons for this from those in positions of power and serving as *Panch* revealed a belief that women's presence will disrupt the delivery of justice as women are not capable of being unbiased. This serves as an excuse to exclude women from these structures and perpetuate gender bias and discrimination in the hearing and delivery of justice. While some women also report that informal practices are sometimes adopted to consult them outside the formal structures to integrate some measure of justice related to gender rights, but the structures and systems remain largely gender discriminatory.

The system wherein the *Panch* sits on a case is called a *'Bhanjhara'*. This meeting is held in a common central place and relates to a village or community matter. On intra-family or inter-family disputes the *Panch* will sit at the home of the aggrieved complainant and the other party separately for a personal hearing. *Patels* have been the first point of contact for government. functionaries traditionally and have, therefore, strengthened their position through their interaction with *Patwaris,* etc. They have also used this privilege of access to claim lands into their control so that now they are relatively better off than others, and the new systems of governance and hierarchy in post-Independence era have helped them to negotiate the structures of power, representation and asset distribution in their favour. Many *Patels* are also known to have more than one wife as symbols of their power and economic status.

The formal constitutional structures include the Gram Sabha and the Panchayat, with Ward members and Sarpanch at village level; at the Block level are the Panchayat Samitis which are also representative structures. Women now have 50 per cent representation in the Gram Sabha, which has given women the space to enter the decision making and justice delivery process and make her presence and allow for her to assert agency. However, men often dominate this domain too by proxy, by preventing women from actual participation or by marginalizing her voice. The State has witnessed several initiatives to build capacities of women members of Panchayats by NGOs through the Hunger Project and by the State Panchayati Raj department; the consequences of these are evident in the increased awareness and participation of women in Panchayats and Gram Sabhas and their capacities to take initiative, but these are as yet limited. People's campaigns such as the NCPRI have undertaken intense activism in the region to formulate and monitor/social audit programmes such as the NREGA and RTI and RTF. These have enabled peoples representatives to have greater access to information and to have greater accountability to their electorate in the performance of their responsibilities. The region is the node of several such movements and this has also provided an impetus to awareness and activism and engagement with systems of governance in the region. The permeation of these processes into the tribal region is ongoing but will take a while before adequate empowerment occurs to enable men and women to claim these spaces and demand their rights.

Currently the PR system runs parallel to the customary practice and tradition. In the absence of the implementation of the PESA Act, despite the notification of the rules by the State government the processes of implementation of Tribal Self Governance, which calls for strengthening the traditional mechanisms of decision making and justice delivery is yet to be wholly understood by the State government and to be put in place. The shortcomings of the PESA enactment in its lack of gender inclusion and redressal of gender concerns will also need to be addressed lest it reinforce traditional patriarchal modes of decision making and representation to the detriment of women and of justice.

Apart from these customary decision making and social justice systems, and the legal formal system of the State are the institutions and forums set up by people's organization at the initiative of local NGOs; these village structures include the Adivasi Samaj Sudhar Samiti in Sirohi and Udaipur which works towards strengthening governance and justice within the traditional forum and serve as a space where women have been able to raise their issues. This study, however, does not focus on these villages, but on those that have no such forum since the effort is to view the current situation and design for means to address gaps and needs that arise especially to take action on the gender concerns.

What are the current practices?

In Pratapgarh and Devgarh women report that formal constitutional structures have begun to make inroads into the traditional mechanisms of governance and the Panch and Sarpanch also sit in the decision making and conflict resolution, although the leadership remains that of the Mukhiya Patel. Even so the Mukhiya and Panch continue to prevail upon the justice and governance systems. Women expressed resignation that any justice sought from the customary forum was bound to be conferred in the traditional belief pattern that did not consider women's needs or point of view; the decision of the customary leaders would prevail and women would not get a hearing but have no choice in the matter. Women from Dharini, however, were of the view that with greater interface with the constitutional system women will be less vulnerable and are likely to be less prone to corruption as decision makers.

In Kanpur and Nichalagarh women say, "We go to the Mukhiya mostly. This **tradition has been in existence for a long time**. A police process causes **excess expenditure. Mukhiya listens to both sides, he is fair.** These days **some people go to the formal system but finally they too have to bear high costs and wait for a long time for justice** and **there too women remain vulnerable to manipulation by the police and the court functionaries** so who is to decide that which is better".

> The traditional system for all its limitations is quicker and approachable for immediate relief. Women from Kanpur say "we prefer the village tradition only, **expenditure is minimal** and the **problems is resolved locally** itself, keeping the **village honour** intact". **Women rely on the local traditional system of justice delivery but observe at the same time that they have no choice or voice. Violation of the honour of the village is a serious offence and may in fact bring other consequences.**

Issues of land are addressed only at local level but serious crimes are likely to be taken to the formal level. The customary practice of ***Mohtana***, where the customary Panch was referred to for settlement of murder and such disputes, continues to function but there is greater chance of recourse to formal structures for such crimes. **For crimes against women however, women are likely to seek local resolution due to lower cost and less outreach to police. Among men we found a higher willingness and acceptance of police intervention. Women believe that even when they appeal to police they are finally compelled to accept local decisions.**

While we may conclude that the traditional justice system is preferable due to its access and understanding of local issues, women are constrained from their customary leaders and dread the retribution of being considered as betrayers of the tribal honour by appealing to other sources. Women fear that they may be ostracized and declared as evil (*dakan*) with no recourse to any support. Women do, however, use constitutional means when resolution is not in their interest but only in situations where men from the family support their appeal to external justice agencies and the Panch grants them permission. Without this it is difficult for women to appeal to Police or Court authorities. They are compelled to accept the decision of the local Gamethi and Panch.

Access and Agency of Tribal Women in Local Justice Delivery Mechanisms and their Role in Women's Lives and Land and Resource Rights

In this section we examine the extent to which women are able to access the justice delivery systems, whether their views are taken into account in the delivery of justice in cases involving them and whether they exercise any agency in the delivery of justice on issues of women's lives and women's rights in their communities. We also examine the availability of alternative recourse in the legal institutional framework for justice delivery and when and how women are able to access those in the quest for justice.

Domestic Violence and Harassment in the Marital Home

Our queries on how issues of domestic and other forms of conflict are resolved elicited varied responses from men and women across the villages. The only point of agreement was that women did not go to external parties or legal institutions for such resolution, and depended on the community based social justice systems to resolve the issues of domestic violence and violence. The reasons for this dependency on traditional justice delivery systems was understood differently by men and women and were located in the power relations within their own communities as much as in the impediments in accessing the information about legal and other procedures of law enforcement agencies. While women felt that they may have a better solution from the courts and the institutional justice system, their knowledge and exposure to the same was too limited as to any other formal institutions due to other limited spheres of mobility and exposure to these. While men viewed the traditional justice delivery system as adequate to deal with these cases, women felt constrained by the lack of alternatives but also felt that there was more of a chance of being heard in these systems today than there was in the past.

Most villages (90%) reported that the decision making process of all forms of conflict including matters of domestic violence were referred to the Patel and the Panchayat in the village. Only in one village (Bhalai) did women participate in the decision making processes and as active Panchayat members and as the Sarpanch. Men from the same village reported "we don't have any such cases of this sort so there is no problem so the question of going to any other authority does not arise" but do not recognize the impact of women's being in the decision making and social justice structures as impacting the incidence of violence against women or placing constraint on harassment against women. Women from the same village, however, saw a direct relationship between the participation of women in the justice delivery system and the low number of cases in the village of this nature and felt that cases were being dealt with fairly as their views and problems were addressed properly.

Customarily, however, women were not accepted in positions of decision making and nor were they consulted even in cases relating to violence or charges against them. Men and women in five villages reported that women were neither consulted nor were they allowed to be present or speak during the discussions, being represented by the male members of their families when their cases were discussed. Women in जगाबोर, धामोद,

देवगढ़, निचलागढ़ ने बताया कि उन्हें बोलने की अनुमति नहीं है और निर्णय ले लिए जाते हैं। Other villages—Ghartara, Ramgarh, Jagabhor, Dharani, Devgarh, however, men reported that although women were not allowed to be present there was an attempt to take their opinion or to talk to them by the Patels prior to passing a judgment on the case. Ramgarh, Ghartara, Jagabhor Dharini and Devgarh women report that they get an opportunity to interact with the decision makers prior to decisions being made for them.

Women and men were also entitled to seek the presence of the Panchayat to hear their case, and both sides were entitled to nominate a person on their behalf to represent their interest on the Panchayat. In such instances the Patel and Panchayat would sit at the house of the person who called the case, and would need to be catered for by that party until the satisfactory resolution of the case. This itself would act as a deterrent for women from calling for such a hearing except in extreme circumstances, given that they were usually in vulnerable situations already and would not be in a position to make these provisions. Since all the Panchayat members are men, women seldom had a chance of being heard adequately and would have to accept any judgment meted out for them. In the instance of judgment not being acceptable attempts are invariably made to counsel both parties to resolve disputes and this is often to the disadvantage of women, since they are compelled to accept a compromise and have little means to assert their rights due to the deeply embedded patriarchal structures of decision making and marital relationships as well as property relations which divest women of independent rights in the event of a dispute. Men from one study village in Sirohi district reported that there was also an incident where the man was found to be errant and when he did not accept the verdict of the Panchayat, then he was turned out of the village.

The situation above reveals that changes are permeating into the tribal justice delivery systems in the region, but the final authority for the settlement of marital conflicts and disputes remains the traditional structure of the Patel and the Panchayat. These structures are now being influenced by the new Panchayati Raj Institutions which provide a space for women to participate in decision making processes. There is also an increasing incidence of women being conferred with or being consulted in the resolution of cases of marital conflict. This is, however, in the midst of a patriarchal family and decision making structure, wherein some measures of access are being addressed, but delimit the space for women to negotiate their rights by the limited nature of rights and entitlements women are accorded in the marital family.

The above processes reveal that traditional systems are hugely biased against women. They view such crimes against women as an assault upon the family and its honour rather than an assault upon the woman, hence, the measures for settlement are also embedded in patriarchal solutions of compromise where '*daappa*' allows the woman's family to retain its dignity and the marriage of the girl to the rapist becomes a means of compromise without addressing the injustice to the victim of the crime or the criminal nature of the act itself. The woman in question is seldom the subject of discussion, nor is she or other women allowed to speak or participate in deliberations, indicating the deep rooted patriarchal values of the system of justice delivery in tribal society in these regions. Women expressed deep anguish and resentment at being kept away and silenced from the justice delivery, whereas men believe the system was responsive and addressed the needs of the community adequately without causing disruptions in the cultural beliefs and practices. The gendered structure of the justice delivery system and its control by men serves to maintain the hierarchies. Given these limitations of the justice delivery systems at both levels, cases of rape and sexual assault are invariably settled informally, or are hidden to avoid shame to the family, thereby suppressing women and the crime they are subjected to.

Harassment on Suspicion of Witchcraft (Dakan)

Cases of women being accused of being witches also occur often, and women viewed this as a cultural practice to keep off evil omen across the villages studied. Only few women across the villages viewed this as a means of dispossessing women of their status and rights, most were convinced that there was in fact some truth in the practice. Men viewed this as an instance of women's rivalry and a means of ostracizing women whom others feared in many cases. There is a gender bias in the difference in perception between women declared as witches and men. Women accused have a negative connotation since this is seen as an evil eye on the victim, whereas men suspected of being possessed of such powers is viewed as positive as it gives them the insight to view people from a position of superior perceptional ability and this gives them the right to pronounce judgments whereas women's heightened ability is viewed as a curse.

Women from 4 villages–Jagabhor Dharini and Devgarh—reported that they participate in discussions involving cases of women being suspected of witchcraft and that women's presence is necessary since it involves a social sanction to the judgment. Whereas women from Bhalai and Nichalagarh and Girwar were allowed to be present but could not participate in the discussions. Only in Bhalai did women have the freedom to participate actively and express opinions and represent their interest in such cases.

Women's presence is a means to sanction the harassment of a woman, based on a suspicion and is in fact a perpetuation of the superstitions and blind faith of communities in such rituals. What is important is to provide an opportunity for such women to be able to understand and unravel for themselves how these acts are discriminatory against women in order to be able to challenge such rituals and practices. As it is their acceptance in the hearings on such cases is a means of validating and reinforcing the practices to subordinate women who may for any reason be considered a threat to a community or a family, by claiming rights or by questioning structures of domination and patriarchy.

Men spoke in greater detail about the practices in hearings on such cases; families of the accuser and the accused are required to be present in these meetings, and accusations are made by men and women. The Panch hears the views of both parties including the accused, but decisions are taken in the absence of women accused. If the verdict is acceptable to both parties the matter is resolved amicably; if it is not acceptable cases may be taken to the formal legal system.

Although these practices of witch-hunting are reducing yet they are a means of ostracizing women through socially sanctioned legal processes from various rights, especially in relation to entitlements. Often women may not be in a position to protest or contest a verdict of the traditional justice systems and may be compelled to accept the conditions. Women who are declared witches are invariably women whom members of the community fear (older women) for their outspokenness or who pose a threat to their families (widows) and are already in situations of vulnerability. These allegations of witchcraft, etc., often work to further ostracize them and marginalize them so that they may not be in a position to claim a status in the family and community or its resources.

Ownership and Access to Land and Property

Our discussions with men and women revealed that as in the non-tribal communities, property rights and issues related to property and land are generally considered the domain of men in this region, but transitions are evident with the changing policy and socio-cultural environment. According to women decisions related to land are taken by the family without their being consulted. Women in Deogarh and Jagabhor are themselves engaging in discussions related to land and property resources but are not consulted in decisions related to these resources even when women are engaged with land based activities. The majority of women from 8 villages stated that they have an opportunity to represent their views in disputes related to land, but in two villages, since women's stakes to land were not considered an issue that needed to be engaged with at all "what is there to discuss about it? Women have no rights, it has been like that for ever". Here, women responded with a sense of resignation and despondency to our queries and even with sharp retorts, indicating a sense of futility in a discussion on such a contentious issue. Men from a significant numbers from several villages (about 60%) opined that women can even appeal to the formal legal system for their rights if they wished. They saw no reason or requirement however for women to intervene in matters of land and property as these were matters of the male domain. This contradictory view seems to indicate a distance between an awareness of the legal provision and the attitudinal resistance of men to admit this as an issue for discussion.

Women's Land Rights and Depleting Forests

An interesting relationship emerges between women's engagement with common land and their assertion for rights in matters of private property among the tribal community. **We found an inverse relationship between access to forest and common property resources and women's assertion of claims.** In areas where the livelihoods depend to a large extent on the forests, and land and agricultural activities are limited we found that women's involvement in discussions and resolution of matters related to land is much higher and disputes are less. Women were more agitated and willing to grapple with justice delivery systems for their rights in those villages where the forest resources that they depended on have depleted over the past couple of decades and they see the need to address their reducing control over resources as a necessity towards augmenting resources for the family. This would also enable them to assert their position in their communities. **However the dilemma is that even as women are willing to struggle and assert their rights in the situation of crisis, where forests have been destroyed or are no longer the primary source of livelihoods sustainability, there the resistance from men to their participation in public forums as actors in the citizenship space is higher; in such regions men opine in larger number that the**

engagement of women in land discussions is irrelevant, since their roles in management of land and natural resources is either invisible or at best marginal as household labour.

Land Rights and Women's Work in the Forest Economy

Our analysis reveals a changing scenario with regard to women and men's relationship with land and natural resources. Women in forested areas for instance are more concerned about their access to forests, where they depend on it to a large extent for fuel and fodder needs, and are struggling to retain their access where such access is being denied especially in areas where agricultural lands are less productive or of smaller scale and dependency on agriculture is not paramount.

Men on the other hand are less vexed with issues of the receding control over forests except in the context of timber, but their attitudes towards women's work also varies with the level of engagement and dependency of the family economy on forest resources for daily subsistence and, therefore, on women's visible work. Men recognize their contributions to the household more in regions of greater forest dependency and women in such communities report a better status in the community by virtue of this role. Women also report a better ability to cope with struggles for survival and sustenance in the areas of survival of forest cover; their work and opinion is also respected in such communities where forest is accessible and the dependency on forest based economic activity is higher. Women and girls are valued more in these forest based economies, where the questions of distribution of private property do not implicate the girl as a burden in a patriarchal structure of society. There is also a greater space for them to engage in the discussions of land and resource allocations and ownership. In regions where the forest wealth has depleted and the economy has become more dependent on private land and agricultural resources, women's status in terms of respect for their labour contribution has decreased and their role is minimized in the issues of land ownership management and allocation. Even in regions where forests exist but the dependency is greater on agriculture, women are not consulted in matters of land and nor are their rights and status respected (as we found in one village named Ghartara).

The discourse around the Forest Rights Act has created opportunities for tribal women to file claims to land jointly as part of their families (although women reported that only the names of wives and mothers have been included, and not those of unmarried daughters) or individually as single women and female headed households, while such claims to joint title may be more significant notionally than in any substantive way, this has had a significant impact on how women view their land rights and status; this was especially so in areas where the *sangathans* have actively promoted the inclusion of women's names in claim documents. The discussion and momentum around inclusion of their names as joint title holders and claimants has created space for women to reflect on their worth as workers and contributers to the household economy and inform themselves about their rights to land in other contexts as well. Single women have also been encouraged to file their claims independently or as part of a household depending upon their residential status whether residing independently or with the son.

Community claims are also being filed to the forest areas that have commonly been used by communities around the settlements for foraging and MFP collection, etc. and in some areas women are claiming a higher stake in these by virtue of their greater engagement in the collection and gathering activities from forests for livelihoods purposes. In some areas it has also enabled single women to make claims despite resistance from some men who have sought to discourage them in several ways lest they begin to interject into negotiations on land and its transfer and ownership at the family and community level, which would upset the balance of power in gender social relations. Women have also been at the forefront of struggles to claim common property resources and prevent the incursion by others and in the process have gained knowledge of the processes and means of protecting their rights. An exposure to these issues has given them a heightened awareness of their rights over these as well as other resources and they have now begun to understand and grapple with the means by which to negotiate these rights gradually. Structural and cultural impediments to their rights are, however, mounting and changing the environment in ways that women themselves are unable to fathom as new developments related to infrastructures and the economy in their vicinity and beyond impact their lives.

Impediments to Justice for Women

Adivasi women in the region are subjected to similar structures of governance and justice as their male counterparts, but are greatly impeded by the gendered nature of these institutions and structures of justice delivery. Women are impeded from access to the system and their views and rights are negated at various levels through systemic and structural constraints that operate at family, community and society levels.

At the family level, women are ever-conscious of the threat and fear of repercussions in terms of oppression which constrain them from claiming land rights in the maternal as well as the marital family. Women's claiming a share to parental property is more conceivable to the men than their claiming a share in the marital property. "Here they get the right to cultivate and live in the home and care for everyone. What more do they want?" said an elderly man from the Udaipur region. Women reported how "threat and derision about women's limited capabilities are used to instil a sense of helplessness in the marital home. Fear is used to control women from making demands and claims in the family, and the fear of being thrown out or abandoned keeps women silent". Disallowing the women from interacting with us was one such means of impeding women's access to any information on the subject, even as they themselves considered it necessary to participate and state their claims and views emphatically!

Women reported about how women are denied access to information and denied mobility as a means to keep them ignorant and dependent, "if a woman makes a complaint against any family member or tries to gain her rights, the entire family will try to silence her with threats and abuse or even throw her out".

"Widows are forcibly thrown out and abandoned so that their land rights can be usurped. Since she is not aware of the legal position or requirements and cannot approach anyone, she has no choice. Standing crop is destroyed and pension is denied in order to restrain her from operating freely or complaining." (village name withheld on request from the women). Men reported a double duress that operates against women claiming their land rights. On the one hand men within the family restrict her from any free social interaction, on the other they prevent others from supporting her by use of their authority and treats to other women.

Other men especially those vested with governance and decision making power, reinforce this position by ignoring or undermining women's views in their decision on disputes in the family. "The Gamethi does not listen to women's views, they ignore women deliberately in order to ensure they do not overstep their position and start asserting themselves." Men from Pratapgarh district reported that Gamethi would try to control women " women will assert themselves (if we do not control them) so it is best to silence her before she can make any allegations. They fear that women will start asserting authority, show her ego, deride men, it is better to disallow them from doing so". Patriarchal structures are used to subordinate women by restricting their spaces and roles within the family so that justice is rendered inaccessible.

At societal levels too men and women report different means by which the ostracization occurs, by demeaning or making accusations on women's character, by introducing customary practices that deny women access and rights, and delimit their boundaries of work and claims. Customs and rituals are used to silence women in public spaces and reduce their roles to ceremonial roles rather than substantive ones, for instance by disallowing them to speak before elders, or speaking in public forums. Women's advancement and claims to rights is seen as dangerous and disintegrative by leaders on the community who use coercive and threatening methods to silence them. A representation about injustice by women is interpreted as a slur on the honour of the community, and a reason to rally around the call for protecting the community by punishing or removing the woman from their midst.

At institutional levels the practice of disallowing women a position in the customary decision-making and governance forums works to assert absolute power in favour of men. Women are disallowed to speak, in the Bhanjhara and even if consulted separately this is more a cursory process than one that takes her interest seriously unless her family (the male members either her brother or her father or in-laws or husband) supports her to challenge the authority of the Panch. Since invariably she is in her in-laws house, any hearing will be dominated by men including men from her household and the opinion of the men will far outweigh any protest she may express, and the ruling will be in the favour of the family, while some measure of compromise will be suggested to the woman as a petty recourse to show that justice is done. The restriction on women's voices in the Bhanjara enables men to rule in the absence of women and override any demands in the interest of the family or patriarchal presence.

Men in 4 villages noted that changes are occurring and that women's opinions are now beginning to be taken seriously, as women are gaining awareness and mobility and learning about their rights. Despite formal justice systems however the situation for women to be able to appeal to the constitutional systems is far from easy. The efforts to restrain women from accessing the formal institutional structures is likely to be even more restrictive on matters of land claims as men consider land and property as their exclusive domain.

Another space that has been explored for women to gain visibility and access to development opportunity is through their participation in the SHG and micro credit programmes. This has not yet gained significant currency in much of this region, yet we did find that a number of commercial and NGO organizations have initiated such programmes but these are mostly at a preliminary level of savings[6]. There are several organizations which have been working in the region for more than 3 decades and have integrated savings programmes into ongoing programmes so that the institutional impact of such initiatives is minimized even as these programmes create some resources in the names of women. Such initiatives have seldom led to women being able to acquired land, etc. except through programmatic interventions and collective formation, given the micro scale of savings and lending for individual women even though this has enabled them to gradually slip out of debt crisis through cycles of mutual borrowing at reasonable rates of interest from their own groups. On the other hand are the new generation Micro finance institutions which had begun to make inroads into the region. Private NBFC and other micro finance promoters are also visible in the villages and are attempting to extend their outreach and influence with the tribal people to adopt the credit and micro finance development model. The lack of success of the government programmes for micro credit and group formation, the cautious approach of tribal's to a system centred on money, and their earlier experiences of exploitation at the hands of money lenders, has fortunately impeded the pace of the adoption of Credit based models in the region hitherto. Nevertheless the intrusion of such processes is likely to bring new actors and new paradigms into the region, supported by government programmes as well as neo liberal actors. The fear is that their presence in the area to spread credit may in fact result less in redressal of poverty and basic needs and more in the creation of greater debt in the absence of an empowerment and sustainable livelihoods approach to the distribution of credit.

Way Forward

The challenge before *sangathans* will be to nurture a genuine tribal leadership of men and women, who are able to arbitrate their interests with the external world to enhance opportunities for strengthening local sustainability, even while they grapple with the contradictions and complementarities of the present institutional structures and institutions to claim justice as marginalized communities and women strive for equality. Equality is a modernistic liberal term that women do not articulate in their context, instead they speak of dignity and self esteem of their rights as independent and rightful members of communities that have nurtured and been nurtured by them. The adoption of inclusive and gender just approaches that give women opportunities to enter governance spaces within the structures of pluralism along with their men, and efforts to strengthen the spaces for tribal self governance are likely to serve to ensure the sustainability of their region, and enable tribal societies to develop in an environment of equality, justice and rights.

Notes

1. This study comes at a time when each of these CBOs has been in existence for a significant period of time and have realized the need to recognize and incorporate gender issues into their strategic initiative.
2. Prabhu Pradip : Forests and Adivasis : This is our homeland—A collection of essays on the betrayal of *adivasi* rights in India, Equations Bangalore 2007, pp. 144-150.
3. Referred to by Pradip Prabhu as the process by which that does not belong to any individual.
4. Legislations such as the The Indian Forest Act 1927; the Conservation Act 1980; The Indian Forest Policy 1988 have given the Forest Department increasing control over the forest areas of the country.
5. Patel (Dungarpur), Tadavi (Banswara) or Pal are other names by which the Mukhiya is also known in different parts of the tribal region of South Rajasthan.

8

Huairou Commission's Land and Housing Campaign's Global Strategy as a Platform for Women's Security of Tenure

Becca Asaki

Introduction

For the past seven years, the Huairou Commission, through its Land and Housing Campaign, has provided a unique platform to establish grassroots women as key constituents in the land and property rights debate. The results of evidence-based monitoring of land processes and cases have demonstrated that interventions exist that can stop asset stripping, halt land grabbing, reverse evictions and influence policies and programmes that work for poor women.

The HC has supported groups to link together, share strategies and mechanisms and build strategic partnership with key stakeholders in the land and development community. Fifty-two grassroots women's groups across Asia, Africa and Latin America have joined together to advance their common concerns through collective actions. These achievements have been further enabled by Huairou Commission programmes and actions that have strengthened women's leadership, built organizational capacity, and scaled up successful practices. The aim has been to combat exclusion by positioning the missing voice of grassroots women in land policy debates from the community to the global level.

The premise of "land for development" embraces the Huairou Commission's position that women's access to land is a necessary, but not sufficient, condition for improving the social, political and economic well-being of grassroots women, their families and their communities. Ban Ki-moon, the United Nations Secretary General, confirmed the link between women's land rights and development when he stated:

> *"Rural women produce most of the world's food, yet they are often excluded from land tenure and the credit and business services they need to prosper. They are the primary users and custodians of local natural resources, but are seldom given a voice on national and local bodies that decide how these resources are managed. They are the care-givers and managers of households, but rarely share these responsibilities equally with men or have a say in major household decisions.*[1]"

The link to land tenure is an all too often overlooked aspect of life for rural women. Forced off the land by land grabbing and male-biased inheritance rights, women and their children are at risk of homelessness, food insecurity and poverty. Women within the Huairou Commission networks, regularly report that lack of access to land has made them: (i) food insecure; (ii) without safe housing; (iii) unable to develop resilience to shocks; and (iv) unable to procure loans to start or grow their business because they lack land or property to use as collateral.

The Huairou Commission's Land and Housing Campaign aims to build multi-stakeholder platforms for action in order to transform the legal and social barriers faced by women in accessing land into systems that provide and protect fairness and equality with men with regard to property and opportunities for development. The Huairou Commission aspires to strengthen grassroots women's access to their right to development[2] and all related physical livelihood assets.

Values and Development Principles

Women as Change Agents

The recognized role of women as agents changing the course of their own development is embedded in all Huairou Commission activities. Evidence confirms that secure land tenure and property rights provide grassroots women with a foundation to empower themselves and improve their own well-being and that of their families and communities.

Grassroots Women Centred

Established in 1995 at the Fourth World Conference on Women in Beijing, the HC has been committed since its founding to strengthening the capacity of grassroots women as community development leaders. Captured in the byline, "*for grassroots women, by grassroots women*", the Huairou Commission believes that grassroots women are legitimate advocates and interlocutors with policy makers and decision-makers from the local to the global level. HC members and partners across Asia, Africa and Latin America believe that partnerships with government and multilateral bodies should, among other purposes, open spaces in support of grassroots centred development. Through inclusive processes community women are empowered (Box 8.1) as advocates, policy partners and joint implementers of programmes that aim to reduce poverty and foster transformative change. The Huairou Commission interprets participation by grassroots women to mean "nothing for us, without us".

BOX 8.1: Empowerment

Empowerment has been defined by Huairou Commission member groups to signify women are empowered when they are full actors in the development process. This means they are able to articulate their work, situation and goals from a position of strength instead of as recipients of government services. In the regular course of internal monitoring and review throughout the Huairou Commission, the following quotes capture the empowerment concept:

- "It is the process of awareness and capacity building which leads to greater participation in transformative action."
- "Empowerment is based on factors such as capacity, the ability for strength and leadership but it is also rocused on factors such as self-esteem."
- "A woman who is empowered has self-respect. Self–respect and self esteem are often under-represented to build women's strengths as role models."
- "Everything we do now (voice, engage, dialogue, hold authorities to account) connects to the changes we are seeing in women and the men of our community. It is not just the result of a house, understanding what is ours, but attitudes are changing from men and how they work with women."

The Huaioru Commission believes the foundation for sustainable community development has three pillars: (i) gendered rights; (ii) opportunities; and (iii) participation. Gendered rights are the most challenging of the three pillars. While legislation may help to support rights, the HC recognizes that culture cannot be legislated. HC members whose communities have overcome cultural constraints confirm that the process, though gradual, can be successful. Progress has been most rapid where women have joined with forward-looking men who are willing to denounce practices, rules and customs that discriminate against women. The Huairou Commission sees gendered rights to be achieved where the social, political and economic relations between women and men are equal in relation to land and development. The exercise of this equality will be measurable not only in terms of legislation and judicial systems, but also in women's "on-the-ground" reporting on their rights of ownership, inheritance and other socio-economic forms of equality.

The Land and Housing Campaign aims to contribute to sustainable human development by strengthening the contribution that grassroots women can make to development within poor and marginalized communities by direct collaboration with State and non-State actors at local through global levels. In all too many reported cases, the voice of grassroots women has been suppressed or displaced by others who presume to represent them, including civil society organizations. The Huairou Commission promotes ABCD based on grassroots inclusion, equitable access, and gender justice.

Critical Issues, Challenges and Opportunities

The Huairou Commission Land and Housing Campaign was established in response to needs expressed by community women to gain effective influence over policies and programmes affecting their access to and control over land for development. The shift from "land and housing" to "land for development" captures the view within the HC membership that land is a necessary, but not sufficient, condition for women's human development that is inclusive of their social, political and economic empowerment. Land is seen as being *for* development in that it is the foundation for identity and dignity, for housing, for farming and as a base for seeking employment or operating a business. Furthermore, land is equally important to women living in rural, peri-urban and urban areas.

Despite policies, including international protocols, aimed at eliminating discrimination against women with respect to their rights to land and property, a common global need for grassroots women to gain visibility, voice and opportunity to participate in development decision-making as legitimate rights holders remains. The voice of grassroots women is far too often co-opted by those who presume to speak for them, denying grassroots women the right to represent themselves. The HC plays a critical role in countering this flawed process by ensuring that representation is by grassroots women for grassroots women.

Today, the Huairou Commission's Land and Housing Campaign is even more important than when it was founded in 2004. In a global world where women's rights continue to be denied, platforms such as the Land and Housing Campaign are increasingly critical. Food security at the country, community and household level is intimately tied to smallholder agriculture where women are the primary producers. Without security of land tenure not only are grassroots women vulnerable, but so is their contribution to aggregate food supplies for their community and the country at large. Without security of tenure it is not feasible for women to either restore degraded soils and to invest in land practices that will moderate climate change. The well-known risks of forced eviction without compensation and the selling and granting of land concessions to foreign investors further confirm the need to secure the land rights of grassroots women. Equally strong linkages between women's access to urban land and development are also well researched and documented.

Fortunately, understandings and opportunities are emerging that can inform the formation of pro-poor, women-led policies on land for development. These understandings are embedded in a wide and diverse range of ratified international agreements ranging from, *inter alia*, conventions on climate change and desertification, the elimination of all forms of discrimination against women and the right to food. While international agreements are imperative, government compliance with such agreements is frequently lacking. Without high levels of transparency and accountability within governments and intergovernmental bodies, the value of the international community as standard bearers for women's quality of life and human development will be compromised.

Goals

The goals of the Land and Housing Campaign are to: (i) raise awareness of the values, concerns and needs of grassroots women on land for development; (ii) heighten the influence of the Huairou Commission membership in global organizations, networks and venues of strategic importance to grassroots women; and (iii) offer opportunities for global actors to associate with Huairou Commission land and development initiatives and innovations.

Objectives

To fulfil its mission and realize its vision, the Land and Housing Campaign's strategies, actions and resources will be directed toward achieving the following four objectives. These objectives will be used to plan, prioritize, manage, evaluate results and identify strategic changes necessary to improve future performance and results.

Objective 1

The Land and Housing Campaign will be recognized as a global organizer of grassroots women with leaders of relevant multilateral organizations, globally and within regional structures in Asia, Africa and Latin America, for fostering constructive dialogue and forms of collaboration.

Objective 2

The Huairou Commission will become a "go to" network for grassroots women to work together to gain the land rights they have been systemically denied along with the respect, dignity and identity that land rights provide. Governments and multilateral bodies will go to WLD to ensure their policies and programmes respond to the demands of grassroots women and their communities.

Objective 3

The intergenerational knowledge and experience of grassroots women (Box 8.2) will be a valued asset in planning and decision-making, based on the evidence that when grassroots women are included in the allocation of human, social and physical resources, there are measurable and significant improvements in well-being and human development.

Box 8.2: Tools and Methodologies

Within the Huairou Commission network, we believe in the principle that grassroots women recognize and value their own knowledge, exchange skills and practices, and use it as the basis for advocacy. The following tools and methodologies are applied to achieve these strategic objectives.

Peer Exchange *is a strong tool for transfers of and consolidation of skills and tools between communities.*

Grassroots Academies *uses the principles of peer learning in a larger space with 30-100 women from multiple communities, organizations and often countries. Participants use participatory processes to reflect on larger political and development issues, starting from the positive place of their own successful development practices.*

Community Mapping *places grassroots women in the centre of information collection by empowering them to undertake critical evaluations of the state of their communities*

Local to Local Dialogues *are locally designed strategies whereby grassroots women's groups initiate and engage in dialogues with local authorities to negotiate a range of development issues to influence policies, plans and programmes in ways that address women's priorities.*

Objective 4

WLD will become a sustainable mechanism, providing a continuing foundation for grassroots women who undertake daring and challenging land and development work knowing they can rely on the solidarity, security and support embodied in WLD.

Huairou Commission Core Strategies

Women's Land Link Africa

Women's Land Link Africa (WLLA) is a pan-African platform on women's land and property rights coordinated by the Huairou Commission's Land and Housing Campaign and its regional partners. Since its founding in 2004 by African grassroots women and their partners, WLLA has grown into a coalition of 23 organizations in 13 African countries.

WLLA aims to influence the formation and implementation of land and housing policies for the benefit of grassroots women. It gives like minded, similarly placed organizations a space to gather, exchange information, and learn from each other. The Women's Land Link Africa initiative uses a development-based approach and grounded rights-based strategies to help grassroots women improve their access, control, and ownership of land, housing, and property in sub-Saharan Africa.

The Women's Land Link Africa platform utilizes three main strategies to promote its members' agendas:

1. To strengthen and expand the capacity of grassroots women to successfully campaign for their resource rights to land and housing.
2. To become a centre of excellence in support of women-led, asset based community development.

3. To open spaces for dialogue, negotiation and partnerships of grassroots women with public authorities.

WLLA gives grassroots women a platform then uses their knowledge to inform policy, frame practices, and strengthen the capacity empower women to be agents of change within their communities.

The ultimate goal of WLLA is to strengthen the capacity of grassroots women to reduce poverty and inequality. The Huairou Commission's role is to develop women-led grassroots organizations and grassroots nongovernmental organizations into a regional network and peer-learning community focused on housing, land, and property issues. Regional partnerships support and strengthen linkages among grassroots women's organizations and other stakeholders.

WLLA helps grassroots women learn about how their government works and grow their own leadership ability through self-directed mapping and dialogue. These processes increase women's groups' awareness of government obligations and understanding of how to monitor, measure, and evaluate government performance. This *monitoring and evaluation* is a powerful process for holding government decision makers accountable and for helping women see how to meet their own needs.

WLLA is a bridge between advocacy and development organizations and grassroots women's organizations and, therefore, between policy and practice. WLLA members respond to women's legal challenges daily and have demonstrated that informal community tools can resolve many injustices without reliance on the formal legal system. Women have become knowledgeable about using the systems that help them achieve the justice outcomes they seek. Large advocacy organizations can use local women's experience with customary law just as local women can use advocacy organization's experience with statutory law. Women's rights for land and property are advanced when global advocacy and local initiatives are complementary and interconnected.

As a direct result of WLLA member's advocacy and organizing efforts:

- Hundreds of women have secured land and housing through reversed evictions, registered marriage certificates, and individual, joint, and communal land titles.
- Over fifty community watchdog groups have formed to oppose the eviction of widows and orphans from their land.
- Over eight hundred plots of land have been acquired by women.

- Grassroots women leaders have exchanged practices in over twenty peer learning exchanges and regional Land Academies.

Through the WLLA, grassroots women have mapped out the process of community justice related to land and the work of organized groups of women to ensure that justice is accessible for women (See Roadmap below from *The Grassroots Women's Community Justice Guide*. New York, USA. Huairou Commission, 2013). This work has been documented in a forthcoming action research project on Access to Justice completed earlier in 2013 and will be published by the Huairou Commission and UNDP Democratic Governance Group.

Case Study on HC and WLLA Member in Tanzania-Maasai Women Development Organization

The Tanzanian Village Land Act of 1999 seeks to give customary rights of land occupancy equal legal standing to the statutory rights of occupancy. It sets out procedures for the management and administration of "village land" under customary tenure. As well as seeking to protect the occupancy rights of land users within customary regimes, it also contains provisions to promote and protect the rights of women within these regimes. It provides for both men and women to be registered as land owner, either together or separately, and promotes gender-balanced representation on local land related decision-making bodies.

GLTN supported the work of the Maasai Women Development Organization, a member of the Huairou Commission, to capitalize upon the opportunities both for Maasai communities as a whole to enhance their communal security of tenure in the face of competing demands for land in the Arusha and Manyara areas of Tanzania. It also enables women to enhance their security of tenure over land, and thus their economic and political status within these communities.

Despite the law, however, Maasai women are marginalized in terms of decision-making and denied their rights to land and property. Effective implementation of the Act is limited, particularly among the Maasai who, as pastoralists, do not have a long tradition of land rights at the village or household level. Provisions supporting the rights of women, in particular, lack effective implementation, and women are effectively excluded from village, Ward and district development plans. This situation is attributed to many factors: cultural attitudes, a lack of the required knowledge and skills, disempowerment, low literacy levels, as well as poor knowledge of their legal rights as prescribed procedures.

As part of its work to improve the women's livelihoods, the Maasai Women Development Organization facilitates the certification of village lands in a way that expressly defines the rights of women and not solely those of men. It fosters women leaders and promotes women's participation in village governance. The idea behind its approach is that if women know their rights, they will be empowered to change their living situation. That will benefit them as well as their households and community as a whole.

The approach has eight steps:

- Supporting the organization of women's groups within the umbrella of the Pastoralist Women's Forum.
- Training on the Village Land Act and land administration processes for women's groups.
- Training on leadership skills for women's groups.
- Awareness raising activities within the community on women's rights to land, e.g., on women's rights to representation within village decision-making bodies.
- Local-to-local dialogues between women's groups and local officials and government authorities on a range of development issues (UN Habitat and Huairou Commission 2004).
- Support in preparing applications for land under the Village Land Act.
- Facilitating plot demarcation with group members and district land officer.
- Ensuring that land documents are safely stored.

The organization of women's groups forms the starting point to give the women confidence by acting together. Men are more ready to accept their actions when women act in a group, rather than as individuals. The approach is also much more than helping women to apply for land: the group's awareness-raising and dialogue activities aim to inform the change the attitudes of communities as a whole, of community leaders, and of land officials up to the district level. In this pilot, the Maasai Women Development Organization worked with 500 women and 250 men in ten villages, and helped some 850 women to gain individual and collective land allocations. This demonstrates the village land committees' effective negotiation and monitoring process. It has also been a learning opportunity: a way for the organization to investigate obstacles to implementing the Village Land Act, and to ensure it is gender-responsive. That will guide its strategies in the future.

One difficulty is resistance by husbands and male community leaders to women's applications for land. Progress on this front has been made by explicitly including men in the process at an early stage to build their support, and by raising awareness on gender issues. But instances of discrimination continue. That underlines the need to ensure that both men and women see the benefits for households and communities.

Another difficulty is that community leaders do not understand the Village Land Act, even though they are supposed to implement it. Educating them about the Act also needs to be part of the approach.

A lack of the right paperwork is another problem. In many places, village officials do not have the correct forms and certificates. In other cases, letters and meeting minutes have been used as (legally acceptable) documentation of occupancy rights–but many officials do not know that this is possible. Plus, some villages and districts do not keep land registries. The Maasai Women Development Organization has supplied some village officials with forms from the district office, and works with them.

Many villages in the area do not have a certificate of village land issued by the Land Commissioner. Without this, land allocations within the village have no legal standing. Some village councils are also reluctant to allocate land before the village land-use plan is completed, as envisioned by the Land Use Planning Act of 2007. That implies a strategic need to ensure that village lands as a whole are secured, and that village land-use planning takes place and adequately reflects the needs of women.

While Tanzania has a legal framework and land administration which could facilitate access to land for Maasai women, a number of obstacles need to be overcome. Communities need to be empowered with knowledge on the law and how the land administration system works. They need to be in a position to put pressure on the government systems which create plans and undertake land certification.

Security of Tenure Initiative

In April 2013, Huairou Commission launched the *Global Initiative on Women's Security of Tenure*, a multi-stakeholder platform to advance an alternative approach on women's security of tenure that is informed and centred in grassroots women's lived experiences. HC leads this initiative with member networks and women's organizations working on engendering

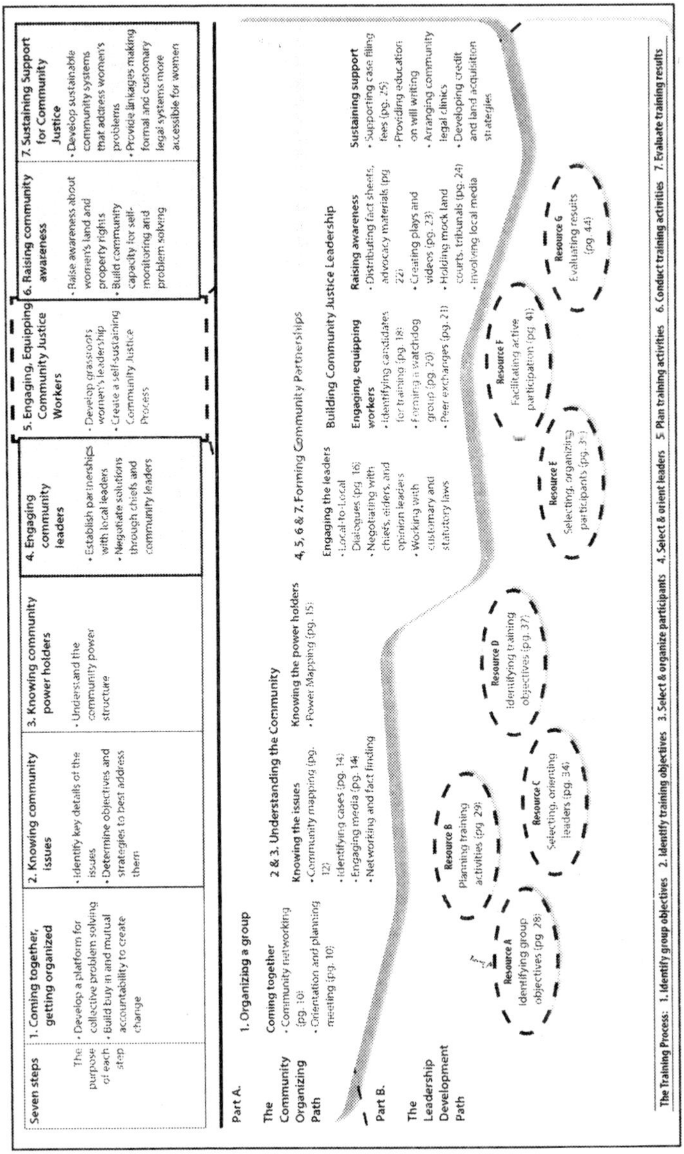

Fig. 8.1: A Roadmap of the Community Justice Process

land governance, land administration, policies and programmes. This effort aims to strengthen a multi-stakeholder platform that believes in the mission of securing women's tenure including young women of all marginalized groups.

Globally women are making progress in securing tenure to land and housing through different tenure systems and a variety of processes. Yet they still represent the largest group marginalized by development policies, land policy and land administration. Indicators of their marginalized status include their over representation in subsistence agriculture and the informal economy. Women typically also bear primary responsibility for community development, and are tasked with compensating for the withdrawal of or lack of provision of basic services. This gendered experience is a critical factor to be taken into consideration in efforts to win secure tenure to land and housing.

Overall, despite acknowledgment about gender inequalities in land, there is insufficient understanding of how women's lived experiences and realities affect the delivery of established forms of tenure, as well as of the strategies employed by underprivileged women to navigate their way across tricky cultural, economic and institutional terrains to secure tenure. Reviews of tenure for women remain focused on the legality or level of formality of the system or structure as the primary factor in providing security,[3] rather than on its political, social and economic characteristics. Most or all typologies of tenure do not explicitly identify gender as an axis of difference. For example, key aspect of UN Habitat's Global Land Tools Network's framework *Continuum of Land Rights*[4] goes from informal land rights to formal land rights (the continuum is perceived tenure approaches, customary, occupancy, anti-evictions, adverse possession, group tenure, leases, and registered freehold) with little understanding of how these different tenurial arrangements might be gender differentiated. This approach has led to a lopsided understanding of the various forms of tenure,[5] as well as of their capacity to trigger empowerment for women in different social, political and economic arenas, and of their ability to create the conditions for sustainable development.

After a series of consultations, it has been identified that there is an urgent need to broaden the discussion around women's security of tenure from product-centred (focused on titles), to process-centred. A process-centred approach draws attention to the socio-political conditions that enable women to win and maintain security of tenure. This recognizes the multi-dimensional character of security of tenure for women, which includes not only the legal dimension, but the social, political, economic, cultural and technical dimensions.

Conclusion

It is through platforms like the Land and Housing Campaign, Women's Land Link Africa and hopefully the new Global Initiative on Security of Tenure that grassroots women can strengthen their practice on the ground and add substantively to sectoral debates around security of tenure. The Huairou Commission's Land and Housing Campaign's Global Strategy lays out a vision for grassroots women's knowledge, organizing and expertise to be harnessed and strengthened to secure land for women as a productive economic asset. The Huairou Commission supports grassroots women to make concrete change in their communities and in turn serves as a platform for peer learning and institutional advocacy.

Notes

1. Ban-ki-Moon, Secretary-General's message on the International Day of Rural Women, New York, 15 October, 2010.
2. UN Declaration on the Right to Development, adopted by the General Assembly on 4 December, 1986.
3. For example, USAID Study on Best Practices on Women's Secure Tenure, 2006
4. Handling Land: Innovative Tools for Land Governance and Secure Tenure. Nairobi, Kenya. UN Habitat, 2012.
5. For example, from formal to informal, derived or direct, individual or communal, permanent or temporary.

9

Land Rights and Women's Empowerment

A Case Study of West Bengal (India)

Pinaki Halder

Secure right to land for women is now universally considered as fundamental to achieving effective and sustainable human development. Right to land includes rights to own, use, access, control and among other things make decisions about this productive asset. According to a World Bank Report "only independent and joint ownership can ensure that women have access to and control over land based earnings".

In India rural landlessness has long been identified as a key determinant of poverty and social exclusion. West Bengal is among a few States in India who believed and implemented land reforms as a means to address poverty, positive impact of which has been felt on income, consumption and asset accumulation.

Improving women's education, their knowledge on land matters can contribute to raising women's access to land. In turn, increasing women's access to land can be a powerful tool to fight poverty and hunger (FAO).

Gender dimension in women's access to land was given primary consideration in policy framing in West Bengal during the mid-years of land reforms era in 1992 when administrative instructions were issued for ensuring wife's name in the land titles when land distribution happened as per the provision of West Bengal Land Reforms Act 1955 to landless poor families.

Landesa, founded as the Rural Development Institute (RDI) in 1967, envisions a world free of poverty. It sees a future in which all who depend on land for their well-being have secure land rights—one of the most basic, powerful resources for lifting oneself and one's family out of poverty. It is driven by its mission of recognising that legal right to land is the foundation for prosperity and opportunity.

Research—Design—Advocate—Implement, constitute the four basic steps of Landesa's engagement in India, China and Sub-Saharan Africa. Landesa's land rights programmes are carefully crafted to fit the specific contexts of geography, political institutions, history and culture of that particular country. Special emphasis is placed on establishing and protecting land rights for women and inheritance rights for girls. Studies show that when women have secure rights to land, they are less likely to be victims of domestic violence and family nutrition and health improve. Also, they have better access to micro-credit and their participation in household decision-making increases. Moreover, their children are more likely to stay in school longer. Thus, connecting girls to land would help shape their future positively by delaying their marriage, continuing education and improving nutritional status.

In West Bengal, Landesa has been closely working with the government starting from policy advocacy, designing and providing technical support for implementation of the homestead plot allocation schemes, Cultivation and Dwelling Plot Allotment (CDPA) and later Nijo Griha Nijo Bhumi (NGNB) meaning My Home My Land. With the participation of beneficiaries, the government purchases land suitable for homestead development at the market price to be distributed to landless labourers, artisans, and fishermen for settling them in a cluster of minimum 10 families. The government has recently expanded the programme to also include allocation of ceiling surplus vested land. Women-headed households from Scheduled Tribes (ST) are given first priority, followed by women-headed households from Scheduled Castes, then minority communities, and finally those belonging to any other caste. Next priority is given to male-headed households in the same order with titles in joint names of wife and husband. There is a programme implementation committee at Block level to ensure certain quality aspects of the land distribution and title in the name of women. Along with government, revenue officials, elected representatives of the local self-government are members of the committee. Landesa also works towards improved knowledge enhancement on secure land tenure among the women beneficiaries to enable them exercise greater access and control over the land they are receiving.

The programme is based on research that shows that a small allotment of land, if of sufficient quality and with appropriate support, can contribute substantial benefits to sustain a household by providing them with both shelter and a means to meet their basic food needs. These plots, distributed by the State, are expected to enhance families' ability to access government services, agricultural inputs, and financial resources, thereby enhancing families' income, reducing their vulnerability, and improving their food security.

Landesa has provided technical support to the Department of Land and Land Reform since 2009 to pilot the CDPA/NGNB, identify best practices, and facilitate scaling it up to reach 150,000 households. In addition, and as part of an umbrella initiative to study the gender gap in asset ownership, Landesa has partnered with the International Food Policy Research Institute (IFPRI) to evaluate the impact on women and their families from this land allocation programme.

The key findings of the Gender, Agriculture, and Asset Project (GAAP) indicate that including women's names on the land titles matters– it significantly contributes to women's perceptions of increased tenure security and to women's involvement in food and agriculture decision-making. Women's report on tenure security outcomes improves up to 10 per cent when their names are included on the land documents. When their names are on the land titles, women are 14 per cent, 15 per cent, and 13 per cent more likely to participate in decisions about taking loans, purchasing productive assets, and food purchasing and consumption, respectively. Finally, women with land documents in their names have say over a larger share of their households' land when it comes to decisions on how to use the land, what to grow on it, and whether or not to sell the produce from that.

Moreover, the results indicate that if their households are CDPA beneficiaries, women are more likely to be involved in important food and agriculture decisions. Compared to their non-CDPA peers, women in CDPA households are: (i) 12 per cent more likely to be involved in decisions to take loans from an SHG or microfinance institution; (ii) 12 per cent more likely to be involved in decisions on whether to purchase productive assets; (iii) 9 per cent more likely to be involved in decisions related to food purchase and consumption; and, (iv) the share of the family land over which they are involved in decisions on how to use the land, what to grow on it, and whether to sell produce from it increased by 15 per cent, 14 per cent, and 11 per cent, respectively.

All these GAAP findings from the research corroborate the World Bank statements that the "right to land. increases a woman's bargaining power within the household, which results in increased allocation of resources to children and women as well as increased household welfare".

Landesa is also working with the women's groups targeting improved land literacy.This training focuses on legal literacy, and specifically focuses on the three factors necessary for secure land rights (having a title deed, having this recorded in the Record of Rights, and actual occupation of the land) and on the benefits of having wife's name on the title. Landesa has developed a module to hand out along with orientation to SHG leaders and a one-page handout to give to every female beneficiary for sustaining the learning. Most of the trainings are attended and partially conducted by local government revenue officials. This has provided substantial positive results, as it exposes the women to government officials and shows them that their rights to land are important to the government. Although the main target is women beneficiaries, where men showed interest they are included in the training.

Programme on Adolescent Girls Security through Land: Coping with Change

The Rajiv Gandhi Scheme for the Empowerment of Adolescent Girls, popularly known as SABLA, is being implemented in 200 pilot districts of the country, including six districts in West Bengal. The programme aims to empower adolescent girls through multiple interventions of nutrition support, life skill education, and vocational education with a goal of reducing their social and economic vulnerabilities. The programme is implemented through the ICDS system of the Women and Child Development and Social Welfare Department (WCD&SW).

Given Landesa's interest in working with adolescent girls, the government invited Landesa to implement SABLA in one Block. As a result Landes aaccepted and then secured permission from the department for an innovative joint pilot that includes four additional sub-components to the programme interventions, namely (1) property rights training within the life skills education, (2) land-based vocational skills within vocational skill education, (3) engagement with boys on property rights, and (4) engagement with communities on the value of girls in the family, the latter two targets aimed at creating an enabling environment for adolescent girls.

In 2012, RDI jointly implemented the pilot in 299 Anganwadi centres (AWCs) in close collaboration with 231 Anganwadi workers (AWWs) and 897 Sakhi-Sahelis (peer leaders) in Tufanganj-II Block of Coochbehar District. More than 7,000 girls benefited from the joint pilot, and the results were measured with qualitative and quantitative tools. The results clearly showed that adding the land-related sub-components significantly enhanced the programme impact, in terms of clear articulation of knowledge, immediate use of vocational skills, resultant increase and improvement of the girls' food basket, earning income, increased self-confidence, returning to school by dropped out girls, and determination to defer early marriage, along with slow but discernible change of mindset among the parents.

This pilot project of Landesa in partnership with the government is based on the rationale–increasing adolescent girls' access asset (land) and narrowing the gender-asset gap would directly improve well-being by reducing their vulnerabilities and enhancing their health, self-esteem and sense of control. Adolescence marks the significant transition from childhood to adulthood. World Health Organisation (WHO) categorises individuals in the age group of 10-19 years as adolescents. Globally, adolescents account for more than one-fifth of the world's population. In India, this age group constitute 21.4 per cent of the total population (National Youth Policy, 2000).

Rural adolescent girls in India lead particularly disadvantaged lives. They have to bear the burden of patriarchal and gender norms and certain other socio-cultural practices with detrimental consequences. Poor nutritional status, restricted access to educational and work opportunities, early marriages and early pregnancies become common features in their lives. Norms such as the need for paying substantial dowries during marriage and the preference for son make them even more vulnerable. These vulnerabilities are also exploited by traffickers who lure girls with prospects of a better life (through marriage or job opportunities).

The programme entails campaigns for increasing school attendance both at the primary and secondary level, delaying early marriages and pregnancies. Enhancing awareness among community stakeholders about the potential and agency of girls is also needed. Connecting adolescent girls to assets through equal inheritance of the family resources and land in particular would further help reduce their vulnerabilities and increase their status in the family. Moreover, it would help change the way the family perceives them. Further, sensitising girls on land rights, asset creation and equal inheritance and training them on land based livelihood skills creates opportunities for funding their own education. Livelihood skills such as growing vegetables in their home gardens also help to improve nutritional status of the girls. Encouraging girls to complete their schooling (at the least) would significantly reduce early marriages and pregnancies and promote smaller families. This would certainly aid them in breaking the cycle of poverty. Informed and empowered girls would be better prepared to resist temptations offered by traffickers and they would be able to secure a better future.

Impacts of the Joint Pilot

While implementing the pilot with the government, Landesa also concurrently studied the changes and impacts happening among the AGs and their parents. To study these changes, Landesa employed qualitative and quantitative techniques such as self-administered questionnaires, personal diaries, quantitative surveying, personal interviews and transcripts of community meeting. Several of the documented changes are reported below.

The following was found in the Landesa SABLA joint pilot areas, which included the additional land-related curriculum components:

1. 76 per cent of the girls are growing Bottle Gourd, 46 per cent are growing pumpkin, 47 per cent are growing green chilli, and 30 per cent are growing spinach.
2. 74 to 87 per cent of families reported lesser purchase of the above items compared to previous year.
3. 81-96 per cent of girls were able to cite the importance of assets in their lives, whereas most of the girls in a control area were unable to answer the question at all.
4. 40 per cent of girls could articulate what assets have been created by their parents compared to only 19 per cent in control areas.
5. 73 per cent of girls reported that they have or would in the next year create assets in their names.
6. 25 per cent of girls asserted that they would decide for themselves when to marry compared to 19 per cent in control areas.
7. 99 per cent of girls surveyed in one pilot area in November 2012 correctly reported that brothers and sisters have equal inheritance rights; 96 per cent correctly described what a *khatian* (land record) and *patta* (land title) are; and 94 per cent correctly named the Land Office as the institution that can change information on a *patta*.

Qualitative data from the joint pilot reinforce these findings and reveal slow but discernible changes in the girls' and parents' mindsets about the value of the girls in the family. These data also reveal that these changes are attributable to interventions with the AGs, boys, and parents.

> "One girl from my centre protested against her marriage. She is sixteen years old. One day, she informed me that her parents were looking to get her married and that she did not want to get married now. I encouraged her to talk to her parents on her own, and said that if they still didn't listen to her, I would talk to them. But finally, she was able to convince her parents on her own."
>
> *"Now, girls are expressing their views and opinions on their marriage and continuation of their studies. They are aware of the issues and also try to make their communities aware."* Anganwadi workers, Tufanganj II

An unexpected outcome of this innovative joint pilot surfaced when a group of landless AGs approached an AG with family land and requested to access it for developing a vegetable garden. With permission from the latter AG's parents, the others jointly cultivated a good quantity of carrots for household consumption and sale. While unplanned, this development presents a replicable mode for accessing assets and generating group cohesion and empowerment.

Activities like boys' group interactions, parents' meetings, community meetings and orientation of Gram Panchayats successfully helped to unravel significant misunderstandings linked with negative social norms. For example, numerous communities exposed to interactive sessions that examined the causes and effects of girls' vulnerabilities developed "action plans" and pledged not to practice or support adolescent marriage, to continue their girls' education until 18 years of age, and to create assets and follow equal property inheritance practices for girls.

The pilot experience found that adolescent girls can themselves play a powerful role in changing mindsets within their communities and families. The case study illustrates how a girl's ability to generate income and improve her family's food supply can help empower her to raise her voice within her family regarding early marriage.

Conclusion

The work of Landesa in West Bengal demonstrates that secure land rights for women create an extraordinary ripple effect that spreads to her family, village and beyond, such as:

(a) Family nutrition and health improvement;

(b) Children are more likely to get an education and stay in school longer;
(c) Women are less likely to become victims of domestic violence; and
(d) Women have more collateral to access micro credits.

Based on the above report, there are important lessons for improving land rights for women. To increase women's access and control of land we propose these follow up actions:

1. Develop monitoring mechanisms to ensure that women's name are always collected during field verification as a prelude to land allocation to include that the names are written in the title document and record of rights. Sensitise the elected representatives of local self-government about its importance and benefits;
2. Implement land literacy training for women, communities and political officials targeting the women beneficiaries of land allocation programmes. This effort needs to become part of the government services and included in every land scheme; and
3. Adopt the land rights and land-use modules developed in West Bengal as part of the national SABLA scheme. The SABLA partnership has provided enough of field evidences that access to land as an asset and its utilisation for improved livelihood in this era of feminization of agriculture could bring about a social change in respect of empowerment of adolescent girls. The module developed by Landesa on 'secure land tenure and land-based livelihood' has been well accepted at all the levels of pilot implementation which now covers five ICDS project areas of Coochbehar. This could be a viable means for bringing about positive change in the mindset of community in general about the perception of adolescent girls as a whole.

10
Potentials of Land Rights to Contribute to Gender Equality in Developing Countries

Nidhi Tandon

Introduction

Background and Objectives of the Study

The purpose of this research was to quantify and qualify the intended and unintended consequences arising from rural women's secure access to land and how that links to their empowerment and food security. The research drew on interviews from a small sample of women, evenly drawn from three countries namely Guntamala, India and Sierra Leone. The research participants comprised indigenous women in Guatemala, *dalit* women in India, and women living with HIV in Sierra Leone. All of these women face restrictions on land access or control due to their cultural or social status, and are restricted in their social interactions and in the scope of personal, social, economic or political choices they can make. The women were invited to self-assess using a number of variables such as social isolation, self-confidence, household decision-making, agency, leadership and collective voice, political ambition, influence and action.

Measuring Women's Empowerment through Security of Land Access

Empowerment refers to women's real or perceived ability to control or change different aspects of their personal, social, political and economic environment. 'Empowerment' is a relative measure, not an absolute one. It is a non-linear process of change rather than a targeted or defined outcome. Its interpretation is subject to complex contexts of culture, values, knowledge, relationships and behaviours; it is constantly negotiated and contested on an individual basis and at household and community levels. In sum, it is a measure of relative social status that is difficult to catalogue and compare. The study from Guatemala suggests that, "...rural women's empowerment has different features, depending on whether they are organised or not, whether they develop productive projects or not, and whether they have collective spaces to critically reframe the patriarchal reality."[1] What is perhaps most profound is the way women articulate their own interpretation of issues like 'autonomy', 'empowerment', 'food sovereignty' and what kind of future they foresee for themselves and their families.

Drawing on their interpretations of what empowerment, inclusion and agency means to them, this research gathered evidence from three distinct communities of women who share one common thread despite enormous cultural differences: they are communities of women who are extremely marginalised, even ostracised, in their social contexts. Adapting from the IFPRI's[2] Women's Empowerment in Agriculture Index[3] methodology, women's empowerment in this study is measured through economic/material, household food security/nutrition and social capital/political indicators. A questionnaire was developed to compile qualitative and quantitative data on 15 distinct indicators (see Annexure II for research methodology).

Profiles of Women's Relationship to Land

The field research findings are from three very different contexts—previously displaced indigenous rural communities who have returned to occupy farms and reclaim land in Guatemala; untouchable *dalit* women in India facing deeply embedded cultural barriers to their land claims; and women living with HIV in Sierra Leone where stigma associated with the condition compounds their social marginalisation.

There is a broad diversity in land tenure regimes globally; the issue of tenure is a complex, locally and historically embedded, and deeply political issue.[4] This makes it more difficult to secure the key determinants that shape women's access and rights to land. With regard to defining 'security of tenure', the Committee on the Economic, Social and Cultural Rights, in its General Comment No. 4, notes that, "notwithstanding the *type* of tenure, all persons should possess a degree of security of tenure which guarantees legal protection against forced eviction, harassment and other threats."[5] Ensuring security of tenure for women enables them to make decisions on how best to use the land for its resources and long-term sustainable investment, use land more efficiently, and gain greater access to economic opportunities.[6]

Guatemala

In Guatemala, most rural women are small-farm producers. Guatemalan peasant women (indigenous and non-indigenous) have the potential to be sustainable producers, but public policies are oriented toward macro-economic growth policies and small peasant economies receive almost no government support.

Women's rights to land and property have been recognised constitutionally since the 1996 Peace Accords that established the elimination of any form of discrimination against women in relation to access to land, housing, loans and participation in development projects.[7] In the past decade, rural peasant women have increasingly been demanding property rights. According to the research study, although changes are occurring, the women's land rights movement lacks a clear vision.

Portrait of Women Interviewed

The women in this study are from 13 communities in three municipalities (Ixcán, Río Grande, San Carlos Alzatate), in Quiché, Suchitepéquez, and Jalapa provinces. In total, 25 rural landowners were interviewed and three group discussions took place with women of varying ages and marital status who have access to land through either communal ownership or private property. Of the 25 women, 24 had an average five children, only one had no children. The women's ages ranged from 22 to 62 years old; ten women self-identified as mestizas[8] and 15 as indigenous.[9] Six are illiterate; 12 have incomplete elementary education; five had completed elementary education, one completed secondary education and one tertiary education. It may be seen from Table 10.1 that majority of the women in the Guatemala sample either own land on the basis of communal land share, or share ownership. Inheriting land is the least means of gaining ownership.

Table 10.1: Pattern of land ownership in Guatemala

Co-owner with Frontierras	28% (7)
Owner through Frontierras	32% (5)
Communal land share	20% (8)
Purchased on own	16% (4)
Inherited	4% (1)

Table 10.2: Percent share of women married or cohabiting

Married	40% (10)
Divorced/separated	12% (3)
Single	16% (4)
Widow	16% (4)
Cohabiting	16% (4)

Eight of the 25 women are community landowners, 15 have private property titles (eight individual ownership and seven co-ownership), and two are self-described as 'ownership in fact' (because of the lack of documents to support their land claim). Twenty-four women have had access to land in the past eight years; only one received her inheritance 12 years ago. The system of communal land share varies throughout Guatemala; in the town of San Carlos Alzatate, for instance, all of the town's land is considered common property. According to the General Property Registry, it is stated that the entire territory of San Carlos Alzatate is for the 'natural population.'[10] Despite this, the women of San Carlos Alzatate had to fight to change a community tradition that denied land owning to women.[11]

India

The sale or transfer of ownership of large tracts of land from Indian farmers to industrialists and estate agents is at the core of current land allocations. On the grounds that agriculture is no longer viable in large parts of the country, the government is 'reforming' the sector on the premise of 'the second green revolution' that encourages 'corporate farming.'[12] This, combined with 'mechanisation of labour' is dispossessing small and marginal peasants, who constitute 80.5 per cent of total farming households.[13] Today, the peasantry is engulfed in a deep and intractable crisis. Compared to the 7 per cent growth in the economy (2009-10), growth in agriculture and allied sectors was just 1 per cent.[14] As agriculture distress intensifies, more and more peasants are forced out of their generational livelihood practices and towards uncertain future at the cost of national food security.

As communities are dispossessed and more men migrate to find paid work, the feminisation of the agrarian crisis has affected every corner of the country. With farming livelihoods made increasingly vulnerable, the percentage of women joining the labour force has also increased.[15] Various social movements in India are critical of the systemic and trans-historically patriarchal role of the State.[16] The decades of struggles of these groups have revealed that, "the State is more gender-retrogressive than gender-progressive", as it derives its laws from the unwritten norms of patriarchal society. Women's perspectives remain underrepresented in various State policies, including land reforms and agrarian policies. Typical constraints to women's access to land include legal conditions and economic factors such as transaction costs, credit and land prices.

Portrait of Women Interviewed

Within this context and set of constraints, the confines that restrict *dalit* women's access to land become even more acute. Their economic and social status reflects the fact that they are members of the 'lowest' caste:

- Around 80 per cent of *dalits* and about 92 per cent of total tribal populations live in rural areas and account for 24.4 per cent of India's total population[17].
- *Dalit*'s control over resources is less than 5 per cent of total resources[18].
- 91 per cent of *dalit* households in rural areas are either landless or operate what are termed 'sub-marginal' or 'marginal' holdings[19].
- Less than 10 per cent of *dalit* households have access to sanitation[20].

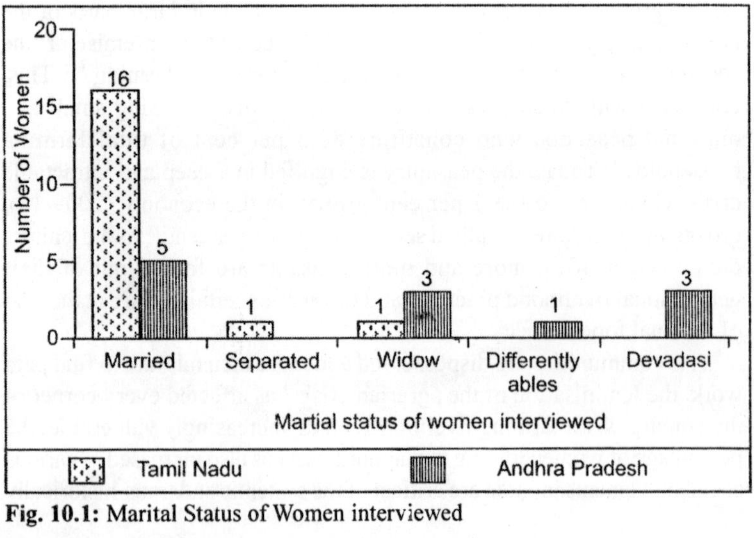

Fig. 10.1: Marital Status of Women interviewed

Thirty *dalit* women from Tamil Nadu and Andhra Pradesh participated in the research study;[21] they had access to land as follows:

- access to and control over land with ownership of land—18
- access to land without control and ownership—five
- access and control without ownership—three
- access and ownership without any control—three
- only ownership without any access and control—one

Table 10.3: Distribution of landholdings in India

State	*India research sample: Size of land holdings*					
	Up to 0.25 cents	*0.26 cents to 0.50 cents*	*0.51 cents to 1 acre*	*1 acre to 2 acres*	*> 2 acres*	*Total*
Tamil Nadu	2	3	1	9	3	18
Andhra Pradesh		4	1	4	3	12
Total	**2**	**7**	**2**	**13**	**6**	**30**

Table 10.4: Women's access, control and ownership over land in India

Category of land security	*Tamil Nadu*	*Andhra Pradesh*	*Total*
Full access, control and ownership	11	7	18
Access only	3	2	5
Access and control, but no ownership	2	1	3
Access and ownership, but no control	2	1	3
Women with only ownership-tokenistic	—	1	1
Total	18	12	30

The women from Tamil Nadu are members of Dalit Mannurimai Kootamaippu (DMK-Land Rights Forum promoted by the Institute for Research and Documentation in Social Sciences IRDS).[22] More than half of the women interviewed (57%) belong to the Paraiyar community (Tamil Nadu) or the Mala community (Andhra Pradesh); 40 per cent belong to the Arunthathiyar community in Tamil Nadu or the Madhika community in Andhra Pradesh. One woman, a *devadasi*, came from an inland fishing community.[23]

All *dalit* women who are members of the Land Rights Forum have made various protests in attempts to influence government policies with respect to land. The women from Andhra Pradesh are members of *dalit* Mahila Samakya, promoted by AARDIP,[24] and two are Jogini[25] women.

Assigned land and ceiling land allocated to the *dalit* community by the government is usually 'wasteland', which is also often the only land that *dalit* women can afford to purchase. In Tamil Nadu, out of the 18 women interviewed, nine *dalit* women purchased land, five had inherited land and three received government allocations. In Andhra Pradesh, out of 12 women interviewed, five had inherited land and five were assigned land by the government.

Of all the 30 women interviewed, 60 per cent grew only one crop in a year, dependent upon the monsoon rains, 30 per cent grew a second crop, and only 3 per cent of the women, i.e. only one woman, grew three crops in a year. In Thiruvallur district, the women who own land have not cultivated the land for three years, because of monsoon failure. Some women only grow cash crops, such as cotton, eucalyptus and tubers, due to pressure from the government.

Sierra Leone

Sierra Leone is a predominantly rural country caught between civil and customary laws. Traditional customary laws, for instance, treat women as 'chattels'[26] to be inherited. In other areas women are regarded as minors in need of guardianship from a male family member. Women face discrimination in the exercise of political, social, civil, economic and cultural rights. Under customary law, it is difficult for a wife to seek redress before the courts against her husband.

Women living with HIV face extreme vulnerability and stigma. They are ostracised from society and blamed for their illness. They live with extreme discrimination and little opportunity to earn income or contribute to society. Their main concern is not land ownership, but finding daily food and fighting against social stigma.

Although it is a signatory to several international treaties that promote gender equality, the Sierra Leone government has yet to institutionalise and effect any real change. Gender inequality and discrimination still exist at all levels of society.

The communal land system comprises both family-owned and community-owned land. Land is predominantly family-owned (83%) in all the districts. An older male member of the family holds the land in trust for the family. Access to family-owned land is granted by the head of the family, in consultation with other male family members. Similarly, the chief, who is the traditional leader, is the custodian of the community land.[27] The chief, in consultation with other community elders grants access to land. This ultimately means that less powerful members of rural communities, including women, do not have equal opportunities to access productive land. Customs relating to inheritance and property rights, such as the loss of a woman's right to keep her husband's land in the case of his death or absence, contribute further to the gendered challenges of land access and control in Sierra Leone.

Portrait of Women Interviewed

- 37 respondents (63.8%) had no form of education.
- In Kambia and Bombali, only 10 per cent of respondents had some form of education; in Tonkolili, none of respondents had any form of education.
- 30.4 per cent of respondents live in households with 16 or more people, compared to 21 per cent and 22 per cent of respondents living in households with 1-5 people and 11-15 people respectively.
- The lowest household size (1-5 people) was recorded in Freetown (75%) and the highest household size (16+) was recorded in Tonkolili (70%).
- 42 of the respondents have not had the opportunity to share their experiences of farming practices, health or food with others in a forum-type setting. Those who were able to participate felt it gave them a sense of empowerment and increased self-esteem.
- The focus group discussions indicated that women who are educated and married to wealthy men are more likely to have some form of control of land and property.
- 55 per cent of people aged 15-24 are either not in school, unemployed or economically inactive. Out of the 58 women interviewed, 26 are living with HIV. Six women living with HIV were interviewed in Moyamba, two in Freetown, six in Bombali, three in Tonkolili, six in Kambia and two in Bo.

There is a sense of limited opportunities for women to utilise and control land for any economic purpose of their choice. Circumstances for the single women are even worse. They are regarded as irresponsible

Table 10.5: Percent of women having private individual title deeds

District	Inheritance	Purchased/ bought	Unspecified	Total
Bo	50	50	0	100
Freetown	50	50	0	100
Kambia	90	10	0	100
Moyamba	60	20	20	100
Tonkolili	50	50	0	100
Bombali	80	10	10	100
Total	63.3	31.6	5	100

Source of land owned: Percentage distribution

women and may be allocated a very small portion of land, if any. This can lead to women entering into risky relationships just to secure a living, which adds to their low level of confidence and self-esteem, and they cannot safely engage in any community development discourse.

According to an FAO report, "Field interviews with members of women's farming groups reveal that there is a strong desire by women to be able to inherit land, but in many cases a continued inability to do so. This can be an important desire in a post-war context where many male head of households were killed in the war, or are unable or unwilling to return to home areas. In some locations, namely the east and south of the country, women enjoy greater rights, can inherit land and property and become paramount chiefs. In the north of the country this is not the case and women continue to enjoy substantially less rights than men."[28]

Some Country Data Comparisons

In the three countries studied, women's ownership of landed property is, to varying degrees, dictated by patriarchal forms of ownership. Of the three countries, Sierra Leone has the highest annual rural population growth rate, and the highest percentage of the economically active population in agriculture. Compared to India and Guatemala, Sierra Leone (see Table 10.6) also has much higher rates of illiteracy, higher levels of maternal and infant mortality, a larger proportion of the population living below the poverty line, a higher prevalence of HIV among adults, and very low mobile phone use. In all three countries, more than half of the total population lives in rural areas, and Sierra Leone and Guatemala both have a high GINI coefficient.

Table 10.6: GDP and human development indicators in Sierra Leone, India and Guatemala

Country comparators[29]	*Sierra Leone*	*India*	*Guatemala*
GDP (per capita, US$)	$966.49	$3,751.99	$4,757.23
HDI	0.298	0.602	0.663
GINI Index[30]	62.9	36.8	59.6
Population below poverty line (%)	70.2%	29.8%	54%
Population[31]	5,485,998	1,205,073,612	14,099,032
Proportion of the total population in rural areas (%)[32]	62%	70%	51%
Average annual growth rate of rural population (%)[33]	2.2	1.1	1.6
Economically active population in agriculture %[34]	60%	54%	38%
Literacy[35]	35.1	61	69.1
Average years of schooling adults	2.4	5.1	3.5
Arable and permanent cropland	550,000 hectares	169,700 hectares	1,905 hectares
HIV/AIDS–adult prevalence rate[36]	1.6%	0.3%	0.8%
HIV/AIDS–people living with infection[37]	49,000	2,400,000	62,000
Maternal mortality[38]	890 per 100,000	540 per 100,000	120 per 100,000
Infant mortality[39]	76.64 deaths/ 1,000 live births	46.07 deaths/ 1,000 live births	25.16 deaths/ 1,000 live births
Telephones–fixed lines per 100 people[40]	0.22	2.99	11.29
Mobile telephones in use per 100 people[41]	31.06	64.1	136.09

Case Studies: Synthesis of Key Findings

Despite differences in context and culture, and the study's limited sample size, shared elements of the case studies begin to create a comprehensive portrait of potential links between secure land access and women's empowerment and ability to fight hunger. Has secured access to a natural resource—in this case land increased or improved the probability of women achieving their aspirations, ambitions and sense of empowerment? To understand and assess empowerment, the study evaluated outcomes for women; and although outcomes in themselves are not measures of empowerment they validate the changes that land ownership make to women's lives. The study also assessed whether, in fact, women leveraged their land-based assets to secure other economic resources, including food security, to increase empowerment.[42]

(a) Land Ownership is Not Empowering if it is Insecure, if the Land is Insufficient or Infertile

The one underlying feature common to the three samples is that securing small parcels of land for cultivation continues to be an enormous, uphill and fraught struggle.[43] Despite national regulatory, legislative and programmatic efforts (e.g., consecutive Five-Year Plans in India),[44] deliberate programme initiatives (e.g., the Land Fund in Guatemala) or targeted awareness programmes (e.g., with women living with HIV in Sierra Leone), women face a tenuous hold over prime land. This means that the number of women who actually secure land is not only extremely small[45] (as evidenced by the proportionally small sample of women available for this study) but also that as other, more powerful, demands for landholdings increase, these women will find it more difficult to protect their interests without direct political support[46] and new land allocations to women will be more difficult to attain.

Despite the fact that women in the study[47] have who, in their own estimation, already secured some land, they continue to face challenges:

- They could lose the land at any time, sometimes because formal processes and documentation are incomplete,[48] or because they are pressured into selling. In Tamil Nadu, for instance, *dalit* lands have been mortgaged or sold for very meagre amounts to people of the 'dominant' caste.[49]
- Those women who have been involved in a longer struggle over time in Guatemala[50] are more likely to maintain control over the lands that they have fought for, and yet, with one exception, all participants in Guatemala reported that they faced opposition from male leaders in their communities as well as from their brothers, and had difficulty finding land to buy and accessing credit.
- The parcels of land these women are allocated or can afford are often of minimal productive value and size.[51] Out of the 30 women interviewed in India, only six owned over two acres[52] and 11 owned less than one acre; 13 women owned between one and two acres. This has direct implications for both the productive capacity of land and its economic value for leveraging loans or credit.

- Decisions on how to use the land might rest with more powerful interests—from male family members to national government policies. While the land might be in a woman's possession, she may choose not to cultivate it at all, "due to the threat of dominant caste men".[53] Systemic government support for farming production favours[54] cash crops (like cotton) for the market and use of industrial seeds and pesticides—as opposed to investing in local seed management practices.

Despite these challenges, the interviews and focus groups findings indicate that women very much value securing land for themselves and for future generations. Most, if not all, feel that secure access to land does empower them on an individual and communal basis.

(b) Expressions of Individual Empowerment

(i) Impact of Land Access on Decision-making

In expressing their assessments of individual choice and agency, almost all the *dalit* women felt that their decision-making had improved as a direct result of their secure access to land.

A more profound relationship with land developed when the women were able to work the land optimally and contribute to the overall wellbeing of their family and community. Women who produced more felt a much greater sense of self-worth than those whose relationship to land was limited to just asset ownership. In Guatemala, this was echoed by women who felt empowered particularly by what they could produce from the land and their contribution to the family's daily sustenance. The natural process of stewarding land and its productive capacity fosters a sense of pride and care. In Sierra Leone, this aspect is less apparent as more of the land is accessed through existing relationships with male family members.

Working, harvesting and caring for land is a matter of pride and dignity for many women. As a direct result of having a stake in land, they are spoken to, involved in meetings, treated with some degree of respect and feel a sense of status and acknowledged responsibility. In Guatemala, it is apparent that women's empowerment is represented in the ways they can produce—their pride lies in their contribution to the welfare of the family and community. In the majority of cases, the women were less likely to regard the land as a capital asset that might be leveraged—they did not consider themselves to be any wealthier as a landowner, but their sense of wealth is linked to what they can produce from the land.

It was apparent, too, that women struggled to keep their land optimally productive, primarily because they received minimal support to improve their farming practices. Almost all the women interviewed were quite confident of their farming knowledge but decried the absence of systematic government support for their activities. In Guatemala, close to half the women interviewed are uninformed about public policies and agrarian issues. Nonetheless, about a quarter of the women have forwarded demands related to land, participated in land protests and supported the adoption of an agricultural policy. Seven women have participated in Municipal Development Councils and eight in Community Development Councils.[55] This suggests that women can be conscious of their land claims without necessarily being informed of public policies related to agricultural issues.

(ii) Impact of Land Access on Food Security

Comparing land allocations, it appears that the women in Guatemala had fertile parcels that were large enough to supplement household food requirements, while the *dalit* women in India were dependent on rain and had poor quality land overall. Participant women in Sierra Leone had access to fruit trees and seasonal fish to supplement their land produce, but relied on the market almost entirely for their daily staples.

All three groups of women had a relatively low protein intake reflecting their low incomes. Of particular note, is that these groups of women did not consider borrowing against the value of their land. This is because their interpretation of the economic empowerment of land is limited primarily to what the land can produce, and reflects their difficulty in accessing loans or credit. Such difficulty is due to the perceived role and status of women in society, and to the use of such small land parcels (usually less than two acres) as collateral. How does this translate into measures of food security and the ability to stave off hunger? Experiences are mixed. Compared to those with no land security, women who have access to and control over land and its productivity are in a relatively stronger position to supplement family food requirements. The research indicates that *dalit* women want to grow more grains and use traditional farming practices to get nutritious food. However, in India, the data analysis and interviews with women indicate that there is increasing dependence on the market for food. This is ultimately because of insufficient resources to support agricultural self-sufficiency. Nonetheless, one participant in India says, "If I work in the field, you people (research team) can eat, but if you work I cannot eat, that is the status of farming community. If more land is brought under cash crops then there is no food security for all of us. Hence, government should take measures to improve the fertility of land and bring more land under the cultivation of food crops."

Of the women landowners who participated in the research, 93 per cent are active members of land rights forums and also engage in food sovereignty[56] issues in their community. They also feel that the possession of land has given them courage and social status in their community and between communities. The women who are part of the land rights movements are more aware of food sovereignty issues than the women who are not part of any forums. Similarly, knowledge of sustainable agriculture and collective farming is greater among those women who participate in forums.

In Guatemala, 80 per cent of the respondents practised traditional farming (corn, beans, chayote and herbs), and the management of native seeds. Sixteen women have incorporated new practices in order to produce food without the use of chemicals. Here, too, the survey results[57] indicated a strong correlation between implementing sustainable agricultural practices and an understanding of food sovereignty. Those who had not changed their practices in food production had also not participated in any training related to sustainable agriculture.

(c) Expressions of Cumulative Empowerment

Cumulative, or collective empowerment—in contrast to individual empowerment—goes beyond the private domain where the individual can now make meaningful choices that also benefit others in the community. Women who have access to, control over or ownership of land are more politically aware of their status and their peers compared to women who lack any of the above. *Dalit* women in control of productive land resources are more active in public forums, not only because they have a vested interest in community decisions, but also because their opinions are seen to count.

As evidenced from the case studies, all those women who were engaged in one way or another with organised movements or associations assessed their empowerment by their capacity to contribute to collective action and voice. In the same vein, women who engage in public forums become more involved and aware of other community struggles; for example, in Guatemala, women agitate together in solidarity for health rights or to regulate mining activities in their localities.

The absence of a land rights movement in Sierra Leone is noticeable; the instances where women have laid claim to land is where they have inherited land or purchased their own as individuals. The sense of empowerment and solidarity that then comes from working collectively to improve the land status of all women in the community appears to be missing. In the sample from Sierra Leone, only 16 out of 58 women felt they had something to contribute in public forums, although all 16 felt that this gave them a feeling of empowerment and self-esteem. In both India and Guatemala, a very small minority of women (one or two) stood for local elections, whereas this did not happen at all in Sierra Leone. This suggests that land rights movements are an important impetus for women's political empowerment.

(d) How Land Security Empowers Women

The study has established that the more precarious a woman's land rights are, the less capacity she will have to produce from, and reinvest, in the land and to advocate for representation. The converse is also true: the stronger a woman's claim over land, the greater her participation in the household and the community and the fulfilment of other rights. This aspect of empowerment is especially important, given the prevailing male preference in inheritance, male privilege in marriage and male bias in State programmes of land and resource distribution. The deeper a woman's vested interest in the land that she stewards, the deeper her ecological (and perhaps even spiritual) empowerment. Given her specific gendered roles, she is also more likely to be concerned with the welfare of the next generation.

The Significance of Land as seen through Women's Eyes

The stories from the women interviewed are rich expressions of various forms of repression and resistance, and how their claim over land gave them a platform for action, a sense of status and opened up possibilities for change. For women, secure access to land has great significance: land as a social and political mobilising force, land as security and legacy, and land as a status symbol and productive resource.

Land as a Mobilising Force

Mobilising around a newly created or a common identity may serve to secure other rights, including political ones. This points to the process of empowerment through collective voice. In sum, the experiences of the women interviewed indicate that:

- Formal organisation around land movements provides women with a recognised channel through which to voice their demands—land becomes a rallying focus for demanding legal and political rights.
- Land rights movements become more proactive in addressing the priorities of their women members as the critical mass of women's membership and women's collective voice rises.
- While title to land or security of access is a priority, it is not the sole objective for most women; they place a high value on being part of a representative organization or movement. In other words, the social capital aspect of land is invaluable to women landowners.

Where women are not organised (as part of movements or collective voice) they must defend their land rights individually and this can be extremely challenging (as evidenced by some *dalit* women and women living with HIV in Sierra Leone).

Land as Security and Legacy

Evidence from Guatemala suggests that women who use communal land and those who have documented access to private property (owned or co-owned) are similarly empowered. This is noteworthy because, arguably, communal property cannot be mortgaged or sold, unlike titled properties registered with the General Registry of Property. Land is the backbone of agricultural and pastoral livelihoods and, by extension, a communal safety net. Land provides a place of cultural and social belonging with symbolic and spiritual values as well as a place of residence, a registered address to allow people to vote in elections, and an inheritance for future generations.[57]

The experiences of the women reinforce this:

- Women are reluctant to borrow against the value of the land, aware that in doing so they could risk losing a precious asset to debt. At the same time, ownership of small parcels of land does not automatically make them credit worthy for loans.

- Women save to further invest in their land. This might include building homesteads, planting trees, and other long-term measures to steward the land and its natural assets.
- Women are able to break with tradition and consider leaving land to their daughters, and not just their sons (more so in Guatemala than in India, where a woman's inheritance might go to her husband's family). They are concerned to maintain the security of the next generation.

Interpreting Empowerment: Domains and Spheres

Figure 10.2 represents the levels of empowerment apparent in the research findings; these complement the evidence collected in the case studies.

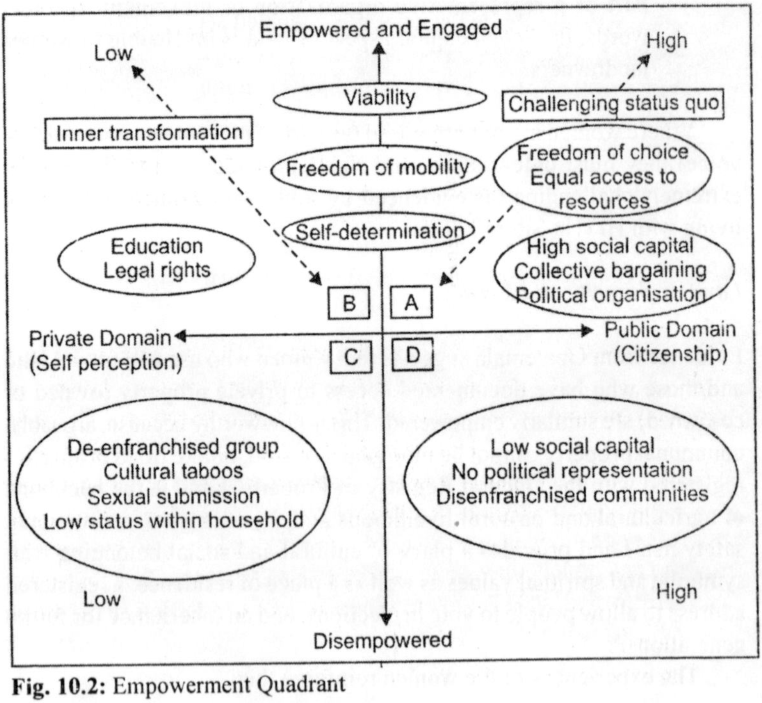

Fig. 10.2: Empowerment Quadrant

Figure 10.2 depicts four quadrants representing different domains and spheres of empowerment as experienced by the women in this study. The horizontal axis spans individual status to the concept of citizenry (private domain to public domain), the vertical axis represents degree of empowerment.

Quadrant A: Represents empowerment beyond the personal domain and into the collective and public realm-leading to structural changes in power relations as distinct from partial empowerment of certain individuals. Innovative forms of associations and mobilisation around issues are integral to the deepening of social capital and representation in political institutions so that women can engage in making decisions that affect the lives of others like them. Unlike Quadrant C, here women will reframe their relations to institutionalised power. At its highest point, political empowerment seeks to challenge and transform the *status quo.*

Quadrant B: Reflects a stage of inner-transformation, still in the private domain, but higher up the vertical axis of empowerment—a partial empowerment of individuals within an unequal system where women are collectively still at a disadvantage. Here women seek ways of *adapting themselves to the status quo.* On account of legal changes, and with awareness of these rights, women can claim, among other things, their land rights and they also gain a legal identity. They are best able to do this with government support and as a collective voice. Legal and policy frameworks are important elements in changing how are done as well as how women envisage themselves and are regarded by others, enhancing their capacity to act to bring about changes in their lives and those around them and stepping outside the labels they are given by society. The further along the horizontal axis they move, the more likely they are to gain visibility, freedom of mobility and self-determination. On gaining access to land, most of the women interviewed expressed more confidence about making decisions around food consumption at household level and how their children would be educated. What represents empowerment is the way they value what they produce.

Another important feature is that those women who had opportunities to gain practical training and literacy—and who were able to share lessons learned and update their knowledge—also felt a sense of empowerment. In San Basilio, Guatemala, seven out of ten respondents said they had not received such training and had no ability to participate in decision-making about community food or health issues.

Quadrant C: Represents women's disempowerment in the private domain, which women express as either an inability to make decisions on their own or a lack of autonomy—for instance, in relation to decisions on land-use or contraception use. Quadrant C represents women's sense of self in the private domain but still within the restrictions of their community, they face a combination of cultural taboos, a secondary status within the household; this can range from a state of fear, to low self-esteem, limited choices and a disproportionately heavy burden of work. *The social institutions around them shape their identities.* Placing land rights in the hands of women in this quadrant does not necessarily empower all of them since they still face suppression in the institutional contexts.

Quadrant D: Represents the contextual backdrop of social groups that for historical, cultural and other reasons have been displaced, disenfranchised, or systematically discriminated against. Women within these communities are, because of their gender, at the bottom of the social totem pole.

In sum, the women interview for this study had successfully claimed land in contexts where their identities are shaped, and even restricted, by social institutions and norms around them. With land now in their hands, some women seek ways to adapt to the *status quo*, to 'fit in' better while stepping out of labels given them by society. Within this small group, an even smaller percentage begins to reframe their relations to institutionalised power, and seek further rights on behalf of themselves and others. What is apparent is that controlling land is, on its own, an important—yet sometimes tenuous—step to women's empowerment.

Changes in one sphere of relations may not necessarily trigger changes in another sphere; at the same time, advances made over time can also be reversed or lost.

Although some women fought for their land rights in the public domain (as in Guatemala), only a few have chosen to take their actions into the political sphere or to mobilise around their individual and collective rights (into Quadrant A). While it might seem unlikely that individual rights can be lost or empowerment reversed once individual awareness is raised, it does not take much to undo progress. It is already evident that the few land rights that women have been able to claim are under siege by other powerful interests. Setbacks can occur in the private domain (illness, widowhood, droughts or floods) and in the public domain (if government policy changes direction, or social support is cut, or the freedoms of land movements are curtailed).

Conclusion and Recommendations

Maintain Support for and Strengthen Peasant Land Movements

Despite the limited sample size, this study provides some evidence suggesting that when women share in assets and land ownership there are positive correlations with higher food expenditure and rural productivity.[58] But in spite of this evidence, governments seem to be unable or unwilling to invest or commit to systemic changes that would boost women's control over land and its production. Given women's perceptions of the value of land, it is especially critical to maintain a high momentum in building rural women's collective agency particularly since governments rarely have the inclination to support disempowered groups. Communities have learned that in order to bring about change, there needs to be a collective force, a 'critical mass' of people working together to achieve it. Disenfranchised and historically subordinated groups need to be engaged in political processes through a combination of representative and deliberative institutions.

Within the broader framework of peasant land rights, the voices of women need to be amplified, not only in determining what their priorities are, but in supporting their active management of, and decision-making about, production, storage and local marketing systems. At the same time, land rights movements need to encourage and support more women members to represent women's priorities and needs at local elections. Civil society organisations need to equip membership groups with skills and knowledge to enter public and political arenas at various levels.

Invest in Women's Social Capital and Knowledge

Women's knowledge and self-confidence is multiplied when they learn to apply ideas and methods, including practical scientific farming and nutritional awareness, and can share such knowledge and awareness—this adds value to their community standing. It is also important that this is developed with the engagement and support of men in the community. Civil society and human rights organisations need to work with rural women and their representative organisations to build their social capital and collective voice to hold governments and investors to account. Investment in 'social capital' supports women's abilities to come together around a common goal and to build institutions that respond to their interests, as they define them.

Secure access to land needs to be supported with dependable channels of information, training and awareness, including, for instance:

- Information on farming methods: Farmer's development programmes and land rights movements should focus on providing information for farmers on food sovereignty, promotion of food crops, sustainable agriculture, diversified cropping and mixed-farming systems;
- Governments should promote access to information for all marginalised communities with respect to agricultural policies and government schemes on agriculture. Local government units, such as Grama Sabha in India, should be effectively used as forums for dissemination of information to the *dalit* community.

Most of the women who participated in this study showed a willingness to share their experiences and continue updating their knowledge. Their perspectives and narratives should be translated and shared with other rural women's associations and land movements in order to strengthen solidarity among women and land advocacy groups.

Governments Need to Recommit to Food Security Policies and Women's Rights to Land

In countries where women play a central role in rural livelihoods, there is an important role for governments in facilitating coordination with civil society to protect the poor and to regulate and counter market-based exploitation.

Of immediate concern to *those women who currently do have secure claims to land,* the following recommendations are submitted:

(a) *In the face of growing pressure for arable land,* existing land claims need to be protected, with proper surveys and documentation made accessible to the public. As part of gender-sensitive land reforms, national land audits and publicly accessible land registries should be established, and reinforced by community mapping programmes that engage women. Secure access to productive land and related natural resources is absolutely critical to people living in rural areas who depend on agriculture, livestock or forests for their livelihoods. It reduces their vulnerability to hunger and poverty, increases the likelihood of their investing in the land and in the sustainable management of their resources, and helps them to develop more equitable relations with the rest of society.

(b) *In the face of industrialisation of agricultural production,* governments need to stipulate and commit the necessary budgetary support for rural investment models that increase local food production, improve land stewardship, and contribute to ending poverty. The UN Committee on World Food Security (CFS), the central body of the global governance system for food and nutrition security, recommended in 2011 that governments and international organisations "ensure that agricultural policies and public investment give priority to food production and nutrition and increase the resilience of local and traditional food systems and biodiversity, with a focus on strengthening sustainable smallholder food production" (see box on IAASTD). Governments need to commit to policy changes that will promote water-harvesting farming methods and other small-scale water management practices to ensure that small-scale farming can be optimised (and not be entirely dependent on rains). Women's cooperatives, community registries, seed banks and participatory plant-breeding systems are a few of the institutions that need substantial investment. This implies that policies should promote cultivation of foodgrains rather than directing farmers to grow more cash crops like cotton (with the required seeds, fertilisers and pesticide use that comes with commercial farming).

(c) *In the face of growing privatisation of landholdings,* governments and land rights organisations need to consider alternative models of ownership that provide communities with land and natural resources held in trust for future generations (see box 'Alternative models of ownership'). Customary laws may need to be strengthened to protect the interests of all women and especially of widows and other vulnerable groups.

(d) *Of concern to women who have not yet claimed their land rights,* while recommendations are on a case-by-case basis and are highly contextualized for the countries involved in this study, the following recommendations stand:

- India needs to recommit to implementing the Land Ceiling Act, redistribute fertile land to Dalit women and put in place simplified processes that enable them to claim their land rights. (The land reform process initiated in the post-independence period allocated land to only a few *dalit* men who have since lost those allocations to other dominant communities through coercion, distortion, encroachment, etc. Now *dalit* women are much more aware of their rights, but the State is not prepared or ready to meet their demands.)

- The government of Sierra Leone recently formulated and adopted a number of legislative instruments[59] and plans, including the National Gender Strategic Plan. Implementation, however, is progressing slowly due to the lack of technical and human resources. Rural women need to be made aware of the rights that they can claim, so that they can begin to make demands of the government. They also need to form stronger associations and begin to work with the men in their communities and the traditional chiefs to consider models of land tenure (drawing on examples from countries such as Mozambique). There is clearly a strong need for 'legal literacy' to inform women about new land legislation and their negotiated security within it. Landowning families need to be represented on the Land Commission, not only at national and provincial levels, but especially at district and town council levels.

Opportunities for Further Research

While the evidence gathered in the three studies indicates clear trends, as well as imparting a better understanding of the relationship between women's access to land and increased empowerment, the small sample size is a clear limitation of the research. There is certainly scope for a widening of this study through a greater number of participants and an examination of other countries.

This report has indicated that empowerment comes from having *used* the land accessed for production, rather than from simply having *access* to land. This important finding opens up various avenues for further research. In a similar respect, while it has been touched upon within this report, a more thorough analysis of the links between women's access to land and their ability to fight hunger and withstand food crisis shocks would contribute greatly to current knowledge on women's land rights and empowerment.

As a final note, Amartya Sen makes the case for societies to regard women less as passive recipients of help, or as property or secondary citizens requiring custodians, and more as dynamic promoters of social transformation, a view strongly supported by a body of evidence suggesting that the education, employment and ownership rights of women have a powerful influence on their ability to control their environment and contribute to economic development.[60] That influence is their empowerment.

Notes

1. Action Aid International (2013), *'Guatemala: Linkage between Land Rights and Rural Women's Empowerment'*, Internal Study, unpublished.
2. International Food Polity Research Institute.
3. WEAI. See http://www.ifpri.org/publication/womens-empowerment-agriculture-index.
4. Hirsch, C.; Aguilar-Støen, M.; and McNeill, D. (2012), '*REDD+ and Tenure Rights,*' University of Norway: Oslo. Accessed 12/02/13 at: www.sum.uio.no/forskning/publikasjoner/2012/tenure_redd.pdf.
5. UN Committee on Economic, Social and Cultural Rights (CESCR), *General Comment No. 4: The Right to Adequate Housing* [*Art. 11 (1) of the Covenant*], 13 December 1991, E/1992/23, accessed 12/03/13 at: http://www.unhcr.org/refworld/docid/47a7079a1.html.
6. UN Women (2012), 'Promoting security of tenure for women,' Virtual knowledge centre to end violence against women and girls, accessed 12/03/13 at: http://www.endvawnow.org/en/articles/770-promoting-security-of-tenure-for-women.html.
7. Lopez, MLM (2006), 'Indigenous Women and Governance in Guatemala,' FOCAL. Accessed 11/03/13 at: http://www.focal.ca/pdf/mujer_indigena_e.pdf.
8. A person of mixed racial ancestry, especially of mixed European and Native American ancestry.
9. From Mam, Q'eqchi', Popti', K'iche', and Kaqchikel clans.
10. Action Aid International (2013), *'Guatemala: Linkage between Land Rights and Rural Women's Empowerment'*, Internal Study unpublished, p. 7.
11. *Ibid.*, p. 23.
12. Ramachandraiah C. and Srinivasan R. (2011), 'Special economic zones as new forms of corporate land grab: experiences from India,' in *Development* 54, 59-63. Accessed 12/03/13 at: http://www.palgrave-journals.com/development/journal/v54/n1/pdf/dev201099a.pdf.
13. Chandra, P. (undated). *Labour File,* Vol. 6, No. 2 and 3, Labour and the Union Budget (Article-Debt Waiver and Rural Labour-pp 19-23).
14. World Bank (2010), '*India Economic Update.*' Accessed 12/03/13 at:

http://siteresources.worldbank.org/INDIAEXTN/Resources/295583-1268190137195/India_Economic_Update_June_23_2010.pdf

15. Bhalla, Surjit and Kaur, Ravinder (2011), *'Labour Force Participation of Women in India: Some Facts, Some Queries'*, Working Paper, 40. Asia Research Centre, London School of Economics and Political Science, London, UK, p. 18.
16. Ekta Parishad is a non-violent social movement in India working on land and forest rights at a national level. It has been built up over 20 years, growing from the local, to the State, to the national and increasingly, to the international level. The purpose of 'amassing' a larger and larger grouping of poor people into a movement has been to put pressure directly on the central government, which is resisting reform and structural change. The structural change that Ekta Parishad is calling for is a complete land redistribution to enable the marginalised and downtrodden to get out of poverty. National Federation of Dalit Land Rights Movements (NFDLRM) is a nationwide mass movement initiated by more than 250 *dalit* land rights movements/struggles/networks/organisations from 16 States, primarily to focus on issues of land and livelihood of *dalit* communities in India from 2006. It is part of the four national movements: All India Dalit Mahila Adhikar Manch (AIDMAM), Dalit Aarthik Adhikar Abhijan (DAAA), National Dalit Movement for Justice (NDMJ) and National Federation of Dalit Land Rights Movements (NFDLRM) promoted by National Campaign on Dalit Human Rights (NCDHR). Dalit Mannurimai Kootamaippu in Tamil Nadu and Dalita Mahila Samakya in Andhra Pradesh are regional land rights movements in India.
17. Census of India (2001), available at: http://censusindia.gov.in/
18. Andharia J. (2009), *'The Dalit Women's Movement in India: Dalit Mahila Samiti'*.
19. National Campaign on Dalit Human Rights, (2012), 'Caste Based Discrimination in India,' accessed 13/03/13 at: http://www.indianet.nl/upr-caste-2012.html
20. Sadangi, H.C. (2008), '*Dalit: The Downtrodden of India*' Isha Books, p. 211.
21. This is not a representative sample; however, it is a well-known fact that *dalit* women have hardly any access to land in Tamil Nadu and Andhra Pradesh. An average of three to four women have land ownership in each village. The first criteria in selecting the women for this research was legal ownership, followed by access and control. Women were selected from a geographically diverse selection of villages where women have land and from a diversity of social standing within the *dalit* caste system. It was also important to identify women who could articulate empowerment through land rights—the selection was managed by the Action Aid India partner in both States.
22. One participant, Muniammal, from a non-Action Aid intervention area, has full access, control and ownership of land but is not a member of any

land rights forum, and Rani, from Vellore, also has not been part of DMK so far.

23. The *dalit* community has different sub-caste systems. This research included two predominant sub-caste systems of *dalit* community: Paraiyar or Adhidravidars community in Tamil Nadu and Mala community in Andhra Pradesh. Arunthathiyar community in Tamil Nadu and Madiga Community in Andhra Pradesh are at the bottom level of the social ladder. They are discriminated by the Paraiyars/Adhidravidar/Mala communities in social activities in addition to the pressures they face from the dominant caste.
24. www.aardip.org AARDIP was started in 1988 and is working with multi-pronged developmental activities and starting to bring social, economic and cultural justice to marginalised people in Kurnool District, covering 360 villages and expanded to other districts, e.g., Prakasham and Kadapa.
25. Jogini women are bonded to serve prostitution As part of the village religious customs. Both women are members of JVVP, a women's movement promoted by AASHRAY working for the eradication of the Jogini system. These Jogini women are also members of a right to food committee in their village.
26. In common law systems, personal property may also be called chattels women are treated as property in this case.
27. USAID (2010), Country Profile: Sierra Leone, *Property Rights and Resource Governance*, p. 3. Accessed 13/03/13 at: http://usaidlandtenure.net/sierra-leone
28. FAO (2006), *'Land Tenure, Food Security and Investment in Postwar Sierra Leone,'* Livelihood Support Programme Working Paper 22. Accessed 13/03/13 at: http://www.fao.org/sd/dim_pe4/pe4_061201_en.htm
29. *Source*: Nation master statistics (http://www.nationmaster.com/statistics).
30. The GINI index measures the extent to which the distribution of income (or, in some cases, consumption expenditure) among individuals or households within an economy deviates from a perfectly equal distribution. A Lorenz curve plots the cumulative percentages of total income received against the cumulative number of recipients, starting with the poorest individual or household. The GINI index measures the area between the Lorenz curve and a hypothetical line of absolute equality, expressed as a percentage of the maximum area under the line. Thus a GINI index of 0 represents perfect equality, while an index of 100 implies perfect inequality.
31. *Ibid.*
32. *Ibid.*
33. *Ibid.*, between 2005-2010.
34. *Ibid.*
35. *Ibid.*
36. *Ibid.*
37. *Ibid.*
38. *Ibid.*
39. *Ibid.*

40. *Ibid.*
41. *Ibid.*
42. Drawing on Uphoff (2003).
43. In the target areas under study in Guatemala, the land was actively reclaimed by displaced peasantry. In 2000, women and men from nearby farms organised to recover lands in San Basilio Hacienda. At first, 62 families started the recovery movement and there was a lot of pressure to remove them. The CUC organisation called on its members to join this struggle and increase the number of beneficiaries, and in a few days the number of applicants doubled. A three-year occupation movement faced off the Guatemalan army. Those farmers without land faced eviction attempts and violence by security forces. "The 'antimotines' (special police force) came to throw us out but we won; now we are landowners." The applicant families were able to recover most of the extension of San Basilio Hacienda through an official institution, FONTIERRAS. In Ixcán, Quiché highly organised cooperative groups rejected the presence of oil companies on their land in the 1970s because it represented a threat to peasant production. Following the counterinsurgency policy between 1980 and 1982, thousands of residents were displaced; some fled to Mexico, and some to the mountains—living as refugees in the Mexican states of Chiapas, Campeche and Quin-tana Roo. In 1990 a rural women's organisation, Mamá Maquín, was formed and 1992 saw the return of organised families—among the first were Cuarto Pueblo, Pueblo Nuevo, Mayaland communities. Some 23,000 people returned to the country as a collective movement, "20 per cent came back to their own land, other people received land in compensation or credits for purchase a parcel," 43,000 returned as dispersed mobilisation. FONTIERRAS (the official Land Fund) participated in the provision of some land.
44. In the late 1970s—UN women's decade (1975-1985)—women's organisations demanded joint title. This was reflected in India's Sixth Five-Year Plan (1980-85). In 1985-1990, the Seventh Plan, the 'national perspective plan for women,' committed to upgrading rural women's skills and women's access to land. The next Five-Year Plan called for joint title to spouses in productive assets, houses, and homestead sites. It also directed States to allocate 40 per cent of surplus land to women, particularly women-headed households, under the Land Ceiling Act. The Tenth Five-Year Plan talked about increasing women's productivity while increasing work opportunities, regularising leasing and share-cropping of uncultivated agricultural land by women's groups.
45. In Tamil Nadu, out of 144,703 women in 300 villages, just 1,314 (0.91%) women own land and of this number only 0.4 per cent own agricultural land (*Source*: India Base Line Study).
46. In Gadivemulu Mandal, 1,500 acres of wetland has been allocated to Jindal Cement Factory. But in the same village, there are 170 landless *dalit* families who depend on agriculture but are denied land rights. The *dalit*

families are constantly struggling against the factory and have organised several protests. However, there has as yet been no response from the State (findings from field research).

47. In India, interviews were conducted with the few women who have ownership of, control and access to land from the operational area. Focus group discussions were held with landless women and landed women separately.
48. In Tamil Nadu, some of the women were in possession of land but had not received the title deed (*patta*), while others had title deeds but the land measurement, survey and transfer had not taken place. Those without title deeds are not legible for any government credit support.
49. In Tamil Nadu, agricultural land (some of it fertile with the potential of an irrigation well) had been assigned to *dalit* communities as Panchami Land during the British period. This access is now threatened by encroachment from other communities and business interests.
50. The women of St. Basilio occupied a farm for three years, pressuring the government until they gained possession. The women of Ixcan began their fight from Mexico as refugees and later in Guatemala until they were recognised as landowners or co-owners. Women in San Carlos Alzatate fought to change a community tradition that denied land owning to women.
51. Most of the land assigned by the government is 'wasteland' and dry land (rain fed). In Andhra Pradesh the assigned land and ceiling land allocated by the government is wasteland, including the recent assignments given to women in poor households. *Dalit* women purchasing land can only afford wasteland with the very meagre savings they have.
52. One hectare is equivalent to 2.4 acres.
53. ActionAid India, Baseline Study, November 2012.
54. Women interviewed in Andhra Pradesh in Adoni Region noted particularly that they are urged to use pesticides and cash crops by the government and seed companies. This result in very poor access to foodgrains and entire families in the villages are dependent on the market for their food. "There needs to be a ban on the company seeds and more encouragement and investment should be for traditional seeds," say the women.
55. Article 1. The Development Council System is the primary means of participation for Mayan, Garifuna and Xinca and non-indigenous people in governance to carry out the process of democratic development planning, taking into account principles of national unity, and the multi-ethnic and multilingual Guatemalan nation. Article 14. Functions of Community Development Councils (COCODE). Promote policies, programmes and projects to protect and promote comprehensive childhood, adolescents, youth and women. *Councils Act Urban and Rural Development*. Decree 11-2002 of the Congress of the Republic of Guatemala. Guatemala, 2002.
55. Loosely defined here as the rights of people to determine what they grow and for what purposes.

56. Action Aid International (2013), *Guatemala: Linkage between Land Rights and Rural Women's Empowerment,* Internal Study (unpublished), p 20.
57 *Action Aid* International (2013), *Guatemala: Linkage between Land Rights and Rural Women's Empowerment,* internal study, unpublished.
58. World Bank (2012), *World Development Report 2012.*
59. The Local Government Act of 2004 provided an opportunity for the empowerment of rural women specifically. The local councils are mandated, through the ward committees, to promote all empowerment initiatives/programmes for rural women.
60. Sen, A. (1999), *Development as Freedom,* Oxford University Press.

References

Action Aid India (2012), *Establishing linkages between land rights of Dalit women and their empowerment,* internal study, unpublished.

Action Aid International (2013), *Guatemala: linkage between land rights and rural women's empowerment*, internal study, unpublished.

Action Aid International Sierra Leone (2013), *Establishing linkage between land rights and women's empowerment*, internal study, unpublished.

Action Aid International (2012), *What works for women? Proven approaches for empowering women small-holders and achieving food security,* more publication details.

Andharia J. (2009), *The Dalit women's movement in India: Dalit Mahila Samiti,* more publication details.

Bhalla S. and Kaur R. (2011), *Labour Force Participation of Women in India: Some Facts, Some Queries,* Working Paper, 40, Asia Research Centre, London School of Economics and Political Science, London, p. 18.

Chandra P. (undated) 'Debt waiver and rural labour', *Labour File*, Vol. 6, No. 2 and 3, 19-23, Labour and the Union Budget.

Eyben R., Kabeer N. and Cornwall A. (2008), *Conceptualizing Empowerment and the Implications for Pro-Poor Growth—Report to DAC POVNET on Empowerment,* Institute of Development Studies, Sussex, UK.

Food and Agriculture Organization (2006), *Land Tenure, Food Security and Investment in Postwar Sierra Leone.* Accessed 13/03/13 at: ftp://ftp.fao.org/docrep/fao/009/ah243e/ah243e00.pdf

Government of India (2001), *Census of India 2001*. Accessed 13/03/13 at: http://censusindia.gov.in/

Hirsch C., Aguilar-Støen M. and McNeill D. (2012), REDD+ and Tenure Rights, University of Norway, Oslo. Accessed 12/02/13 at: http://www.sum.uio.no/forskning/publikasjoner/2012/tenure_redd.pdf

IFPRI (2012), *Women's Empowerment in Agriculture Index.* Accessed 13/03/13 at: www.ifpri.org/publication/womens-empowerment-agriculture-index.

Kabeer, N. (2012), 'Empowerment, citizenship and gender justice: A contribution to locally grounded theories of change in women's lives,' *Ethics and Social Welfare*, 6:3, 216-232.

Lopez, MLM (2006), 'Indigenous women and governance in Guatemala', FOCAL. Accessed 11/03/13 at: http://www.focal.ca/pdf/mujer_indigena_e.pdf.

National Campaign on Dalit Human Rights (2012), *Caste-based Discrimination in India*, accessed 13/03/13 at: http://www.indianet.nl/upr-caste-2012.html.

Ramachandraiah C. and Srinivasan R. (2011), 'Special economic zones as new forms of corporate land grab: Experiences from India,' in *Development* 54, 59-63. Accessed 12/03/13 at: http://www.palgrave-journals. com/ development/journal/v54/n1/pdf/dev201099a.pdf.

Sadangi, H.C. (2008), *Dalit: The Downtrodden of India*, Isha Books, p. 211.

Sen, A. (1999), *Development as Freedom*, Oxford University Press.

UN Committee on Economic, Social and Cultural Rights (CESCR) *General Comment No. 4: The right to adequate housing* (*Art. 11 (1) of the Covenant*), 13 December 1991, E/1992/23. Accessed 12/03/13 at: http://www.unhcr.org/refworld/docid/47a7079a1.html.

UN Women (2012), *Promoting Security of Tenure for Women*, Virtual knowledge centre to end violence against women and girls, accessed 12/03/13 at: http:/ /www.endvawnow.org/en/articles/770-promoting-security-of-tenure-for-women.html.

Uphoff, N. (2003), *Some Analytical Issues in Measuring Empowerment for the Poor, with Concern for Community and Local Governance*, Cornell International Institute for Food, Agriculture and Development.

USAID (2010), Country Profile: Sierra Leone, *'Property Rights and Resource Governance'*, p. 3. Accessed 13/03/13 at: http://usaidlandtenure.net/sierra-leone.

World Bank (2010), *India Economic Update*. Accessed 12/03/13 at: http://siteresources.worldbank.org/INDIAEXTN/Resources/2955831268190137195/India_Economic_Update_June_23_2010.pdf

World Bank (2010), *Support to Land Administration and Land Redistribution in Central America*, Report No: 55341, An IEG Performance Assessment of Three Projects: EL SALVADOR, Land Administration Project (LOAN NO. 3982) GUATEMALA, Land Administration Project (LOAN NO. 4415), GUATEMALA, Land Fund Project (LOAN NO. 4432).

World Bank (2012), *World Development Report 2012*, Washington, D.C.

World Economic Forum (2005), *Women's Empowerment: Measuring the Global Gender Gap*.

11

Lease Farming as a Livelihood Option for Rural Landless Women

A Case Study of Kerala

T. Haque and *Jaya Lakshmi Nair*

Introduction

Rural women in India are generally resource poor and marginalized because the majority of them do not possess either any landed property or education and skill for gainful employment which can result in their economic independence and upward mobility (Haque, 2012). Despite so much talk about growing feminization of Indian agriculture, women employed as wage labour receive lower wage than men do and even when women are categorized as cultivators, their limited ownership or control over land and access to water, credit, technology, market, education and skill put them in a disadvantageous position. According to Eleventh Five Year Plan (Government of India: 2007), the incidence of income poverty among women tended to be higher in rural areas. It increased from 28 per cent in 1993-94 to 29 per cent in 2004-05. In addition, about 42 per cent scheduled caste women, 46 per cent of scheduled tribe women and 30 per cent of other women were malnourished. Besides, measured in terms of person days of usually employed persons, according to current daily status about 4.6 per cent of women in rural areas were unemployed and 31.1 per cent were not in labour force for lack of gainful employment opportunities (Government of India, 2010). The average wage rate of casual women labourers in the country (as of 2007-08) was only ₹ 51.17 against the male wage rate of ₹ 75.30. The low wage income and high incidence of poverty among women demand that additional income opportunities be created for them. Besides, lack of education and skills prevents them to take up higher paid jobs in the organized non-agricultural sector. In view of these facts, it would be useful to explore whether lease farming could provide gainful employment to unemployed and underemployed, albeit landless rural women. The recent initiatives taken by the Governments of Kerala to help promote lease farming by joint liability (JLG) groups of women as well as some NGOs and independent enterprises throw some light in this direction. This chapter aims primarily at examining the potential and viability of lease farming as a livelihood option for the rural poor, especially women.

This study is based on both secondary and primary data. While the secondary data were collected mainly from National Sample Survey Organization (NSSO) and Government of Kerala, a field survey was undertaken in three districts of Kerala. The purposively selected districts were Alappuzha, Ernakulam and Thiruvananthapuram in Kerala. About 200 individual farmers and 50 Joint Liability groups (JLG) groups of women in Kerala were interviewed with the help of duly structured questionnaire schedule.

Landholding Status of Women

According to Agricultural Census 2005-06, women constituted about 9.6 per cent of the total operational holdings, covering 7.2 per cent of the total land. Although this does not clearly say whether land operated by women was also owned by them, it broadly indicated the same. Of course, it varied from region to region. In Andhra Pradesh, women shared about 22.0 per cent of total number of individual operational holdings, covering 18.1 per cent of area, while the corresponding figures for Kerala women were 19.4 per cent and 15.2 per cent respectively. Also women's access to land market remains highly restricted. A study by Rural Development Institute (RDI) in West Bengal indicates that women rarely purchased land on their own because of culturally constrained gender roles and lack of financial resources, while some women held independent rights to a portion of their household's purchased land (Haque, 2012). Moreover, women did not directly benefit from redistributive land reforms undertaken by various State governments since Independence. In fact, in a State like Kerala, more than one-fourth of those who lost land were widows (Sardamoni, 1983; Haque, 2012). Tenancy law even curtailed women's leasing right.

Another striking feature of the post-land reform era is that incidence of landlessness among rural households continues to be high in several

States. According to official estimates based on 59th Round of NSSO, the landless households constituted about 10.0 per cent of the total rural households in India. But disaggregated analysis of the NSS household level data (Rawal, 2008) shows that proportion of household that did not own any land other than homestead was as high as 41.6 per cent in the country. It was 68.4 per cent in Kerala and 53.2 per cent in Andhra Pradesh. Such high incidence of landlessness probably justifies the need for improving the land access of rural poor, especially women by way of activating the land lease market, if not through transfer of land ownership by way of redistribution of ceiling surplus land. Access to land is critical for poverty alleviation in many areas. In this context, leasing could provide lower income people, including women with an economic opportunity for improving their livelihood. Unfortunately, however, tenancy laws in various States in India are highly restrictive in nature (Haque, 2012b). In Kerala, the Kerala Land Reforms Act 1963 as amended in 1969 prohibits future leasing without any exemption being granted even to defence personnel or the disabled or the widows as is the case in some other States (Haque, 2001).

However, despite restrictions, informal tenancy exists in almost all parts of the country. According to 59th Round of NSSO (Government of India: 2006), about 11.5 per cent rural households in India leased in land and nearly 6.5 per cent of the total operated area was under lease farming.

Lease Farming in Kerala

According to 59th round of National Sample Survey, about 6.6 per cent operational holdings leased in land during the kharif season and 5.35 per cent during the rabi season. The total leased in area as percentage of total operated area was about 4 per cent. However, these estimates are considered to be underestimated (Nair and Menon, 2006). Tenancy being illegal, neither landowners nor tenants report their lease arrangements properly. Besides, the NSS data was collected mainly for seasonal crops, while there is widespread leasing of annual and perennial crops in Kerala, especially banana, pineapple, betel vine, etc. It is not certain that leasing in all of such crops was captured in NSS survey. Moreover, NSSO concentrated mainly on households, while leasing in of land by Self-Help Groups are quite widespread in the State (Nair and Menon, 2006).

In fact several micro level studies conducted in the past show the incidence of land leasing in Kerala to be much higher. John's study (2004) in seven Panchayats in Kottayam district, covering rice, rubber, coconut, tapioca, vegetables and banana revealed that tenant holdings accounted for 61 per cent of the total holdings, about 46 per cent of the tenants being landless agricultural labourers. Cherian's study (2004) of three Panchayats in Pathanamthhitta district, covering coconut, rice, betel vine, rubber and tuber crops points out that tenant holdings constituted about 52 per cent of total holdings, 70 per cent of the tenants being reporting agricultural labour as the main occupation. The duration of lease was for one year in all the cases and the rent varied from crop to crop. It was ₹ 11,000 per acre for betel vine and ₹ 9,000 per acre for banana.

Thus, these studies do point out that the incidence of tenancy in Kerala was higher than what was reported in NSS of 2003 (NSSO: 59th Round: Government of India, 2006). It was also observed in all these studies that income from lease farming of banana and vegetables was quite attractive and had helped in some cases, the small tenants to purchase small plots of land and move up in the socio-economic ladder as owner cultivators (Nair and Menon, 2006). One of the reasons for expansion of land leasing in Kerala is that lot of migrants who bought land through remittances do not cultivate land by themselves and prefer to give land on lease than to keep them fallow. Also the large scale entry of self-help groups in land lease market, encouraged by government, is helping the expansion of lease farming.

Lease Farming by Women

In 1998, the Government of Kerala had launched a Poverty Eradication Mission, called Kudumbashree which broadly means welfare or prosperity of the family. The main objective of the Kudumbashree Mission was to eradicate poverty through coordinated community actions initially by encouraging thrift and investment, vocational training, skill upgradation for self employment and wage employment and later through other integrated development measures. In 2004, a new component, called collective farming by joint liability groups of Kudumbashree was added. Under this component, Kudumbashree Mission of the Government of Kerala has been assisting the poor women to lease in land in a group and thereby create an income source for them. This is promoted as an important livelihood activity of Kudumbashree neighbourhood groups, comprising small and marginal women farmers and landless agricultural labourers. Joint Liability Groups (JLGs) of women farmers are formed under the collective farming initiative to help women cultivators' access agricultural credit from the banking system. The guidelines issued in this regard are as follows: "Groups should consist of Kudumbashree members ranging from 4-10 who are interested in farming. Groups can be formed from the same neighbourhood groups (NHG) or different NHGs within a Ward who are interested in farming. The farming area for a JLG should be a minimum of 50 cents and a maximum of 5 hectares and can be a maximum of three plots. For vegetables and medicinal plants, the minimum area is 25 cents. The Gram Panchayat helps the JLGs by providing inputs (seed, fertilizer, manure, and pesticide), basic infrastructure, machineries, irrigation facilities, one time land development for farming, using National Rural Employment Guarantee Scheme (MGNREGS) labour and also assists in marketing of the produce. The Primary Agricultural Co-operative Societies (PACs) provide interest free loans for selected crops, while nationalized banks and other private banks provide crop loan for the JLGs at 7 per cent rate of interest, out of which 5 per cent is provided as interest subsidy from Kudumbashree.

The lease farming by JLGs under Kudumbashree Mission is intended to help eradicate poverty, and improve food security and incomes of the poor and marginalized women through their participation in agriculture. The mission works in all the 14 districts of Kerala. The JLGs are engaged in lease farming, using land of members from within the groups, government land and also land leased in from private land owners. Originally the term 'lease land farming' was used for such group cultivation. Now it is called collective farming.

In 2010-11, about 23,970 hectares of land was cultivated by 38,054 groups, which produced 2,07,694 tonnes of agricultural produce, worth ₹ 297 crores. The women who were once just agricultural labourers are farmers today. About 2.3 lakh women have reportedly benefited from the scheme so far.

Results of Field Survey in Kerala

A field survey was conducted in three districts of Kerala, namely, Thiruvananthapuram, Alappuzha and Ernakulam to assess the impact of lease farming by women. About 201 individual farmers, who were tenant-cum-owner cultivators and 50 Joint Liability Groups, were interviewed. The district-wise details are given in **Table 11.1**.

The average area leased in by JLGs (per group) was 1.86 acres in Thiruvananthapuram, 3.58 acres in Alappuzha and 4.38 acres in Ernakulam. On per member basis, it worked out to 0.32 acre in Thiruvananthapuram, 0.42 acre in Alappuzha and 0.96 acre in Ernakulam

Table 11.1: Selected Districts/Sample Farmers/JLGs in Kerala

District	*No. of JLGs Interviewed*	*No. of Landless pure Tenants*	*No. of Marginal Farmers (owner-cum-tenants) interviewed*
Thiruvananthapuram	19	36	29
Alappuzha	12	21	53
Ernakulam	19	20	42
Total	50	77	124

(Table 11.2). In the case of individual lessees, the average leased in area was 1.06 acres in Thiruvananthapuram, 1.74 acres in Alappuzha and 3.13 acres in Ernakulam.

Table 11.2: Average Area Leased in and Income from Lease Farming by Lessee Category in Kerala

District	*Average area leased in (acre)*		
	Per JL Group	*Per Member in JLG*	*Per Individual (individually leased land)*
Thiruvananthapuram	1.86	0.32	1.06
Alappuzha	3.58	0.42	1.74
Ernakulam	4.38	0.96	3.13
Total	3.27	0.57	1.98

Source: Field Survey.

The main crops grown in both women's group leased land and individually leased in and self-operated land were banana, paddy, tapioca and vegetables. In fact, the yields and returns of crops varied from district to district. The average area of banana cultivated by JLGs was 1.83 acres in Thiruvananthapuram, 0.91 acre in Alappuzha and 2.13 acres in Ernakulam and for individually leased land, the average area of banana was 0.87 acre in Thiruvananthapuram, 1.13 acres in Alappuzha and 1.81 acres in Ernakulam and in the case of ownership cultivation, the average area under banana was 0.62 acre in Thiruvananthapuram, 0.60 acre in Alappuzha and 1.10 acres in Ernakulam. In Thiruvananthapuram, the average yield of banana was 90.0 quintals in group leased land by women, ₹ 87.3 quintals in individually leased land and 82.6 quintals in self-cultivated land. The average return per acre was ₹ 85,000 in group leased land, ₹ 40,000 in individually leased land and ₹ 55,000 in individually owned and self-cultivated land. Thus Joint Liability Group (JLG) of women cultivators did generate higher yields and higher returns per acre of banana cultivation compared to individual lessees as well as owner cultivators. A similar situation could be observed in Alappuzha where the average yield and returns from banana cultivation were higher in women's group operated leased land than individually operated leased land as well as self-cultivated land (Table 11.3). The average returns per acre of banana cultivation were ₹ 45,000 in women's group leased land, ₹ 35,825 in individual leased land and ₹ 37,756 in self-cultivated land. In Ernakulam also, both average yields and returns were higher in women's group leased land than individually leased and self-operated land. For tapioca, the results were mixed. In Thiruvananthapuram, the average yields and returns were slightly better in self-cultivated land than women's group operated leased land and individually operated leased land. In Alappuzha, the yields and returns of tapioca were higher in women's group operated leased land than individually operated leased land but in Ernakulam, both yields and returns were relatively higher in self-operated land than either individually leased land or women's group leased land. In the case of paddy, the women's group operated leased land showed better performance than both individually operated leased land and self-operated land. For vegetables, the women's group performance was better than individually leased or self-operated land in Alappuzha, while in Thiruvananthapuram, women groups' performance in terms of yields and returns were comparatively lower (Table 11.3).

In the surveyed villages, about 76 per cent of the group leased land was owned by private land owners, 18 per cent was owned by JLG members and 6 per cent by others (Table 11.4). In Ernakulam about 95 per cent group leased land was owned by private land owners, while in Alappuzha 33 per cent of group leased land was owned by group members.

Nearly 60 per cent leases were written but not registered and 28 per cent lease agreements were just oral/informal. The informal leases were as high as 75.0 per cent in Alappuzha district and as low as 5.3 per cent in Thiruvananthapuram district (Table 11.7).

On average, in about 76 per cent cases, the terms of lease was fixed cash and only about 10 per cent was under share cropping. In Ernakulam, about 89.5 per cent leases were on fixed cash basis and 10.5 per cent was on share cropping basis. In Alappuzha, nearly 25 per cent leases were on

Table 11.3: Average Area, Yields and Returns of Crops in Land Leased by Group, Individual and Ownership Cultivation in Kerala

District	*Crop*	*Average yield (₹/acre)*			*Average returns (₹/acre)*		
		Group leased land by women	*Individually leased land*	*Individually own self cultivated land*	*Group leased land by women*	*Individual leased land*	*Individually own and self cultivated land*
Thiruvananthapuram	Banana	90.00	87.29	82.59	85000	40000	55000
	Paddy	—	13.63	13.21	—	15000	20000
	Tapioca	95.00	94.71	96.67	9150	8710	10000
	Vegetables	30.00	39.80	43.91	10000	9000	13000
Alappuzha	Banana	83.00	82.00	82.59	45000	35825	37756
	Flower	—	3.60	3.59	—	15000	20000
	Green gram	3.00	—	—	3500	—	—
	Paddy	23.13	18.73	19.37	18000	15241	17728
	Spices	—	—	0.59	—	—	12000
	Tapioca	60.00	40.00	—	10000	8000	—
	Vegetables	35.00	31.67	31.08	10000	9200	8550
Ernakulam	Banana	85.00	75.05	71.85	58000	56000	57000
	Coconut	—	—	228.57	—	—	10000
	Paddy	22.00	20.88	19.60	8000	12000	15000
	Pineapple	95.00	63.57	75.12	60000	70000	100000
	Tapioca	85.00	63.33	85.71	9000	10000	13000
	Vegetables	—	49.22	75.12	—	10000	14000

Source: Field Survey.

Table 11.4: Ownership Pattern of the Leased Land in Kerala

District	*Total No. of Groups*	*Ownership of leased land*					
		Group Members		*Private Land Owner*		*Private land owner + Group Member*	
		Number	*%age*	*Number*	*%ge*	*Number*	*%age*
Thiruvananthapuram	19	5	26.32	13	68.42	1	5.26
Alappuzha	12	4	33.33	7	58.33	1	8.33
Ernakulam	19	0	0.00	18	94.74	1	5.26
Total	50	9	18.00	38	76.00	3	6.00

Source: Field Survey.

Table 11.5: Type of Lease Agreement and Terms of Lease of Group Leased Land in Kerala

		Districts	*Thiruvanantha-puram*	*Alappuzha*	*Ernakulam*	*Total*
Total No. of Groups			19	12	19	50
Types of lease agreement	Written	Number	14	2	14	30
		Percentage	73.68	16.67	73.68	60.00
	Registered	Number	4	1	1	6
		Percentage	21.05	8.33	5.26	12.00
	Oral	Number	1	9	4	14
		Percentage	5.26	75.00	21.05	28.00
Terms of lease	Fixed Cost	Number	16	5	17	38
		Percentage	84.21	41.67	89.47	76.00
	Share Cropping	Number	0	3	2	5
		Percentage	0.00	25.00	10.53	10.00
	Not Charging	Number	3	4	0	7
		Percentage	15.79	33.33	0.00	14.00

Source: Field Survey.

share cropping basis and in 33 per cent cases, no rent was charged, as the land was owned by group members (Table 11.5). About 44 per cent of the groups reported that they were cultivating the same leased land for the past five years, while 30 per cent groups were cultivating the leased land for the first time in 2011-12 and 26 per cent group reported that they leased in different plots from time to time. In Ernakulam, about 68.4 per cent groups reported leasing and cultivating the same plots, while in Thiruvananthapuram, only 10.5 per cent groups continued to lease in and cultivating the same plots (Table 11.6).

Table 11.6: Tenure Status of Group Leased Land in Kerala

District	*Total No. of Groups*	*Per cent of lessees leasing in the same land*		*Per cent of lessees leasing another land*		*Lessees for the first time*	
		Number	*%age*	*Number*	*%age*	*Number*	*%age*
Thiruvananthapuram	19	2	10.53	6	31.58	11	57.89
Alappuzha	12	7	58.33	1	8.33	4	33.33
Ernakulam	19	13	68.42	6	31.58	0	0.00
Total	50	22	44.00	13	26.00	15	30.00

Source: Field Survey.

Individual Lease Farming in Kerala

In the case of individual land leasing, most of the lessees in the study areas were owner-cum-tenants (Table 11.1). About 88.6 of the lessors were small and marginal landowners and only 3.5 per cent of them were large farmers and 8.0 per cent were medium land owners. In Thiruvananthapuram, 90.8 per cent of the lessors were small landowners and 4.6 per cent were marginal land owners. In Alappuzha district, however, majority of the lessors were marginal landowners–nearly 91.9 per cent, while in Ernakulam district small landowners accounted for as much as 56.5 per cent of the total lessors (Table 11.7). About 100.0 per cent lease agreements in Alappuzha and 53.2 per cent in Ernakulam were oral/informal, while in Thiruvananthapuram 87.7 per cent individual lease agreements were written on white paper but not registered (Table 11.8).

Table 11.7: Distribution of Lessors by Size Class of Land in Kerala

Type of land ownership/ farmer	*Districts*	*Thiruvanantha-puram*	*Alappuzha*	*Ernakulam*	*Total*
Large	Number	2	0	5	7
	%	3.1	0.0	8.1	3.5
Medium	Number	1	3	12	16
	%	1.5	4.1	19.4	8.0
Marginal	Number	3	68	10	81
	%	4.6	91.9	16.1	40.3
Small	Number	59	3	35	97
	%	90.8	4.1	56.5	48.3
Total	Number	65	74	62	201
	%	100	100	100	100

Source: Field Survey.

Table 11.8: Nature of Individual Lease Contract in Kerala

Districts	Total No. of Lessees	Type of contract					
		Verbal		Written on White Paper		Written on Stamp Paper	
		Number	%age	Number	%age	Number	%age
Thiruvananthapuram	65	8	12.31	57	87.69	0	0.00
Alappuzha	74	74	100.00	0	0.00	0	0.0
Ernakulam	62	33	53.23	26	41.94	3	4.8
Total	201	115	57.21	83	41.29	3	1.5

Source: Field Survey.

Further, at the aggregate level, about 97.5 per cent leases were on fixed cash basis, and only 2.5 per cent was on sharecropping basis. However, in Ernakulam and Alappuzha, about 3.2 per cent and 2.7 per cent leases respectively were on sharecropping basis and the rest on fixed cash basis (Table 11.9). About 100 per cent lessees in Thiruvananthapuram reported the need for additional income as the main reason for leasing in land, while in Alappuzha 54.1 per cent and in Ernakulam nearly 27.4 per cent of them reported additional income earning as the main reason. The cent per cent tenant farmers felt that they could utilize their available family labour for lease farming and earn additional income for family welfare (Table 11.10).

Table 11.9: Terms of Individual Lease Agreement in Kerala

District	Total No. of Lessees	Terms of lease (cost)			
		Fixed Cash		Share cropping	
		Number	%age	Number	%age
Thiruvananthapuram	65	64	98.46	1	1.54
Alappuzha	74	72	97.30	2	2.70
Ernakulam	62	60	96.77	2	3.23
Total	201	196	97.51	5	2.49

Source: Field Survey.

Nearly 93.8 per cent lessees in Thiruvananthapuram, 98.6 per cent in Alappuzha and 74.2 per cent in Ernakulam felt that the land leasing policy in the State should be revised for legalization of leasing and allowing leasing of land on long term basis. The cent per cent lessees in Alappuzha and Ernakulam districts felt that size of the land in lease market would increase if land leasing becomes legal.

Table 11.10: Output-Input Ratio in Group Leased, Individually leased and Self-operated Land

Districts	*Output-Input Ratio*		
	Individual Lessee	*Owner and doing Self Cultivation*	*Group lessees*
Thiruvananthapuram	1.15	1.16	1.59
Eranakulam	1.42	1.45	2.45
Alappuzha	1.99	2.03	2.44
Kerala Average	1.37	1.40	1.90

Source: Field Survey.

The Lessons Learned

There are several lessons that can be learned from the group lease farming experiences in Kerala. First, due to legal restrictions, agriculture land leasing is mostly informal and insecure, even though State governments have tried to give some recognition and also encourage lease cultivation by women's groups. But insecurity of tenure continues. Second if the women's groups are socio-economically homogeneous in nature and small in size, there is greater co-operation, transparency and efficiency. Third, the initial albeit proper handholding support by the government is critical for adoption of group lease farming by women. Poor women were able to make land productive only in cases where they received Government or NGO support (Rao, 2005). Fourth, group leasing on the pattern of JLGs in Kerala was as efficient as individual lease farming or individually owned self-operated farming or even more efficient in some circumstances. Fifth, lease farming by poor and marginalized women can be an important source of livelihood or additional income for them if land leasing is made legal and consequently more land becomes available for leasing through an active land lease market. It should be remembered in this context that poor women can hardly afford to purchase land as of now, because of high and rising land prices, unless their increased income by way of lease farming as well as wage income through MGNREGS and other work help them purchase land and become land owners. Thus land leasing can be a step on the path to land ownership. Sixth, lease farming, if encouraged and supported can be instrumental in providing some level of food security for the rural poor households, especially women. Seventh, with proper leadership training and entrepreneurship skills, the poor landless women engaged in lease farming and other activities, could overcome the poverty trap and be on the growth path. In fact, there is need for an appropriate, albeit in-built capacity building programme for this. Eighth, lease farming by SHG/JLG women can create a great sense of security among them to prevent physical violence and exploitation by people at home and outside. They can prevent injustice to them through their joint and concerted actions.

References

Cheriyan, Omana (2003), 'Changes in the Mode of Labour use to Shift in the Land Use Pattern, Discussion Paper No.81, Centre for Development Studies, Thiruvanthapuram.

Government of India (2010), 'Employment and Unemployment Situation in India', NSS 64th Round, NSSO, New Delhi, Report No: 531 (64/10.2/1).

Government of India (2007), 59th Round of NSSO on Distribution of Ownership Holdings (as of 2003).

Government of India, 'Eleventh Five Year Plan (2007-2012), Planning Commission, New Delhi.

Haque, Hina (2012), 'Empowering Landless and Voiceless Women in Rural India' in Land Policies for Inclusive Growth' edited by T. Haque, Concept Publishing Co.Pvt. Ltd., New Delhi.

Haque, T. (2001), Impact of Tenancy Reform on Agricultural Productivity and Socio Economic Status of Tenants Policy paper: National Centre for Agricultural Economics and Policy Research, New Delhi.

John, K.K. (2004), 'Crop Rotation in Kerala: A Case Study of Kaduthuruthy Block, Discussion Paper No. 94', Centre for Development Studies, Thiruvananthapuram.

Nair, K.N. and Vineetha Menon (2006), 'Lease Farming in Kerala–Findings from Micro Level Studies', *Economic and Political Weekly*, June 30.

Rawal, Vikas (2008), 'Ownership Holdings of Land in Rural India: Putting the Record Straight: *Economic and Political Weekly*, March 8.

Revati, E. (2012), A Study of Andhra Pradesh Licensed Cultivators' Act–Unpublished Report, Rural Development Institute, New Delhi.

Saradamoni, K. (1983), 'Changing Land Relations and Women: A Case Study of Palghat District, Kerala in Vina Mazumdar (ed.), *Women and Rural Transformation*, Concept Publishing Co. Pvt. Ltd., New Delhi.

12

Women Farmers and Gender Disparities

The Long Journey for Identity, Citizenship and Entitlements

Subhalakshmi Nandi

The Context

Women farmers play a significant role in India's economy and around 79 per cent of the rural women workers are in agriculture. As per a 2012 UN Women Report[1], it has been said that rural women play a key role in supporting their households and communities in achieving food and nutrition security, generating income, and improving rural livelihoods and overall well-being. They contribute to agriculture and rural enterprises and fuel local and global economies. As such, they are active players in achieving the MDGs. Yet, everyday, around the world, rural women and girls face persistent structural constraints that prevent them from fully enjoying their human rights and hamper their efforts to improve their lives as well as those of others around them[2].

For an analysis of the Indian context, let us begin with the 2007 National Policy on Farmers definition. A farmer refers to "*a person actively engaged in the economic and/or livelihood activity of growing crops and producing other primary agricultural commodities and will include all agricultural operational holders, cultivators, agricultural labourers, sharecroppers, tenants, poultry and livestock rearers, fishers, beekeepers, gardeners, pastoralists, non-corporate planters and planting labourers, as well as persons engaged in various farming related occupations such as sericulture, vermiculture, and agro-forestry. The term will also include tribal families/persons engaged in shifting cultivation and in the collection, use and sale of minor and non-timber forest produce.*"

This all-encompassing definition of farmers shows a very progressive shift in policymaking. Not only has it provided a very comprehensive framework for subsequent policies and programmes, it has also created the impetus for organising farmers in many parts of the country. But it would be worthwhile asking ourselves whether the impacts of these shifts have been the same for women farmers as they have been for men. Professor M.S. Swaminathan has pointed out that nearly 40 crore women out of the total of 60 crore female population depend upon crop and animal husbandry, fisheries, forestry, agro processing and agri-business for their livelihood, yet are held back by their inability to obtain equal access to natural resources such as land and water because of male-biased laws. Therefore, it is exceedingly important that we re-examine the current status of women's empowerment in the field of farming[3].

A Framework for Gender Analysis

This gender analysis in this article stems from global and constitutional normative frameworks that define substantive equality, non-discrimination and justice as key guiding principles. Here it also draws upon UN Women's framework for action on women's empowerment, which is grounded in a human rights and human development approach. The human rights approach calls for critical analysis of asymmetrical power relations, political processes and institutions that reinforce these relations. The human development approach is premised on the concepts of wellbeing, empowerment and agency and justice encompassing the recognition for human rights.

Within this framework, UN Women conceives ***women's economic empowerment*** as "increasing the ability of women to bring about change that drives valuable outcomes as a result of their increased economic capabilities and agency, i.e., their ability to function effectively in the economy; to participate in labour and product markets on equal terms, to shape the gender division of labour; to accumulate assets, to shape the relationship between markets and the State, and to influence the institutions and processes that determine growth and sustainable development[4]." This requires the realization of women's ***rights to livelihoods*** operating in a violent free and enabling environment which is a prerequisite in ensuring women's enhanced capabilities and agency.

Therefore, in this article, the first aspect that I will highlight is the issue of women's ***identity and citizenship***; the second is that of ***women's work*** and the third, of ***women's voice and agency***. Over the years, UN Women has learnt from its work in the field that these are critical issues if we are to address rights of women farmers. Women farmers' right to resources, such as land, water, forests, finance, and to training and skills are equally important, but I will not dwell much upon that because there is a lot of research and existing literature on these issues. I would like to focus a little more on our shared understanding of gender inequalities in the context of women's identity and citizenship, women's work as farmers, as well as their individual and collective voice and agency.

Women's Identity and Citizenship

At the global level, it is a welcome move that there is growing attention being given to farming and agriculture. The year 2014 has in fact been identified as the 'Year of Family Farming'.Our own Plan documents (in the Eleventh and Twelfth Plans) have clear directives to focus on addressing the 'feminisation of agriculture'. And yet, despite the rhetoric, the focus of policy design and delivery has primarily been, and continues to be the 'farming family', as opposed to 'farming women'. For years, women's rights organisations have tried to draw attention to the fact that the family does mediate women's rights as economic agents–this could be in positive as well as negative ways. There are informal barriers that women face for instance in inheriting land. Last year at UN Women we partnered with Landesa on a study examining some of these informal and formal barriers, and one of the findings that struck us all was the fact that women themselves do not ask for their share in ancestral property for fear of being deserted and of facing violence at home. This finding is a clear indication of women's status when it comes to negotiating rights at the intra-household level. It also shows how deep-rooted the inequalities are in that women have internalised and subsumed their own identities, their sense of citizenship and entitlement, in favour of the household or family. If policies and programmes could acknowledge women as individual economic agents, instead of only as members of 'farming families', they could go a long way in strengthening women's identity and citizenship rights. Some examples are given below.

Based on UN Women's field programmes in Andhra Pradesh and Uttar Pradesh (UP) with a civil society organisation Gender at Work and its local partners, we advocated for individual entitlement even under the NREGA (National Rural Employment Guarantee Act), to ensure 100 days each for all women and men above 18 years of age. In UP we had found that women were not being allowed to work on NREGA worksites because they were told to 'bring the man along'. In response to these challenges, UN Women supported an all-women worksite, supported the training of *dalit* women as worksite supervisors (or 'mates') and helped to organise *dalit* women, including Musahar women, as well as Muslim women, and Sahariyas (a particularly vulnerable tribal group) to assert their identities as women workers, as citizens, and be included in NREGA. In a State like UP where women's participation is 19 per cent only, we managed to ensure a 35 per cent increase in participation of women in our project areas. With pushing for individual bank accounts, we also helped women to control their earnings better[5].

Census 2011 tells us that there are large numbers of women headed households–11 per cent nationally, but it is much higher in some States. I do not need to stress more on the feminised nature of agriculture and farming. In such a situation, focusing on a campaign to ensure even basic individual entitlements such as Kisan Credit Cards for all farming women, to ensure access to subsidised credit and other services, by recognising them as heads of household, without complicated procedural hassles and the burden of producing documentation proof, can go a long way in building women's identity and citizenship as farmers, and enhance their access to entitlements.

According to the Planning Commission[6], women in India own only 11 per cent of the total deposits in banks. There is, however, no disaggregated data on women's individual and group accounts; they are all clubbed together. Moreover, there is an overwhelming focus on credit products, as opposed to more comprehensive financial services. When it comes to women farmers, there are limited policies on creating savings, seed capital, crop insurance and other financial products for livelihoods. These are absolutely critical for women in farming but are currently unaddressed in policies and programmes.

While individual identity is one aspect, the collective identity of farming women, indeed of all women, is also critical for their empowerment. In India and in many parts of the global South, an approach that has been adopted in policy and programme is to target women farmers through the group approach–mostly in the form of Self-Help Groups (SHGs), to enable women to access some of the entitlements like land, credit, training and market linkage. Through research and documentation, at UN Women we have found that this has been an effective strategy in the context of accessing resources, such as the experience of joint land leasing that we have studied in States like Kerala and Andhra Pradesh. We find that institutional linkages between leasing land to groups and linking it to land development work under MGNREGA, has gone a long way in ensuring food security and livelihoods support, as well as in building solidarities of farming women, and that there should be longer term leases of this kind.

On the flip side, at the level of discourse, the phenomenon of SHGs has also created a particular identity and citizenship for women that has been criticised from a feminist perspective. A study by Nirantar (2007)[7] says that the 'logic of microcredit'is the gendered construction of the identity of the 'good woman', one who saves regularly, repays regularly, sacrifices her own needs in the interest of the family, and takes on community work. The critique is also rooted in the fact that women's savings, time and labour subsidises many of the essential services that the State is meant to provide. From a gender perspective, this is not considered empowering from women, as women internalise this identity and their claim to citizenship is driven by the gendered notion of the 'good woman'.

A further question on citizenship and identity is also whether this benefit is reaching the most marginalised such as the *dalit* and tribal women farmers, who, according to a ILO study, comprise 81 per cent of farming women[8]. At UN Women, we advocate for a deeper understanding of that fact that 'woman' is not a homogeneous category, and there are some groups and communities that require more immediate and urgent attention in policy and action—*dalit* women, tribal women, single women, women with disability, migrating women, women living in the north-eastern States of India, etc. Working with these groups is also a matter of strengthening farming women's identity, citizenship and entitlement.

Women's Work

There is enough evidence to show that women do more than 60 per cent of the work in farming. They work as unpaid family labour, they work as wage labourers, and they also perform household chores and engage in subsistence work to feed the family and livestock. Not only is the proportion of women's unpaid work really high—it is 51 per cent as per a 1998 Time Use survey done across 6 States of India; but the nature of the work is also full of drudgery. Much of the work does not even get counted as 'economic activities' in mainstream labour surveys. So, besides establishing their identity and citizenship as farmers, women also struggle to get their work recognised. Here, too, it is not surprising that women see the burden of their work as a 'given', and have internalised the gendered division of labour in their homes, farms, and forests as well as in the markets. Even mainstream programmes that target women farmers, somehow fail to account for the support services required by women farmers to reduce their drudgery. MKSP for instance, does talk of 'drudgery reduction' in the context of introducing enabling technologies for women to ease their burden, but has so far not taken on board women's unpaid and subsistence work.

Over the years, UN Women has advocated for Time Use surveys at national, regional and global levels, to make data systems and policymakers more responsive to women's unpaid work, so that appropriate policy responses can be framed to address them. If women are spending more than half their days in collection of water, fuel, fodder and growing food to feed the family, then it is unlikely that they will have time to join agriculture extension programmes. What they need more critically perhaps is accessible, affordable and quality water supply, electricity and a strong Public Distribution System to address their food security needs. In light of women's unpaid work, UN Women advocates for 'recognition, reduction and redistribution' of women's unpaid work as a proposed policy framework and for action. This framework has been promoted by feminist economists in India and the world over. In India, a Time Use pilot is currently on in two States, but it still needs to be seen whether the learnings will feed into the mainstream labour surveys on a nationwide scale.

Another issue related to women's work is the absence of adequate and appropriate rural employment. NREGA has of course changed the rural landscape in significant ways by making one kind of wage employment available for at least 100 days of guaranteed employment. But rural employment generation probably needs greater attention in the coming years.The Millennium Development Goals (MDGs) currently aim for increasing women's employment in the non-agriculture sector, but with policy changes and new legislations in India, there is a huge scope of generating rural employment and decent work for farming women as well. For instance, with the new National Food Security Act, can we think of linking the Anganwadi centres of the ICDS programme with groups of farming women at the local level to produce the supplementary nutrition that is required daily at the centres for children, adolescent girls and pregnant and lactating women? Can we think of women producers supplying raw materials to midday meal schemes; can we think of women farmers more proactively in food processing? This has already been tried in small pockets in the country, and can be replicated on a larger scale if we think a little 'out-of-the-box' and are seriously committed to empowering rural women.

Women's Voice and Agency

The final piece that I would like to cover is that of building women's voice and agency—as individuals in their own right, and also as larger collectives of women farmers. In the long journey of empowering women farmers, they must be brought centre-stage in decision-making processes, and in informing and shaping the policy and programme agendas that are set. Therefore, supporting collectives of farming women, and bringing them to decision-making and agenda-setting platforms is for us a critical strategy for empowerment. Over the years, we have worked with partners on the ground such as SEWA, PRADAN, Gender at Work and its local partners, and other civil society organisations, to build, support and strengthen membership-based organisations of farming women by organising them, and building solidarities, around their identities as women, as citizens, as workers, as economic actors.

Women farmers are also keepers of indigenous knowledge. At UN Women, we are working closely with the Ministry of Rural Development (MoRD) at national and State levels, in order to make the implementation of the Mahila Kisan Sashaktikaran Pariyojana (MKSP) of the National Rural Livelihoods Mission (NRLM) more gender-responsive. As part of this, we are in the process of establishing a cadre of Women Master Farmers in two States—Bihar and Madhya Pradesh (MP)—to support in the visioning around MKSP. Last year we partnered with Landesa to document the successful models from Andhra and Kerala, of women farmers as resource persons, as part of a decentralised agricultural extension service, and as owners and users of technology. This year we are partnering with MoRD and a women's rights organisation ANANDI, to build capacities of frontline functionaries implementing MKSP in Bihar and MP to highlight and develop Gender Action Plans to begin addressing all the above issues related to identity, citizenship, work and voice and agency of women farmers. Our learning has been that it is not enough to engage only with women farmers directly, but also to work with people who work with women farmers and enhance their capacities to undertake gender analysis and gender related programming.

Sometimes the gender barriers are not 'out there'; rather, they are inside us all.

Conclusion

While we have seen huge mobilisation on the ground in India and globally of farmers and those working on land rights, and of women workers in other sectors, unfortunately, there are very few mass organisations or networks of women farmers, as they seem to be subsumed either within the household, or within the SHG movement. As a question of identity, citizenship and building voice and agency of women farmers, we have reflected on this, and find the need to ensure that such organising receives greater attention in future.

Notes

1 http://www.unwomensouthasia.org/assets/UN_Women_Land_Agriculture_in_Rural_India.pdf
2. UN (2012)–Rural Women and the MDGs; http://www.un.org/womenwatch/feature/ruralwomen/facts-figures.html
3. Swaminathan, M.S. (2013), Empowering Women in Agriculture; http://www.thehindubusinessline.com/opinion/empowering-women-in-agriculture/article4393917.ece
4. UN Women (2012), Concept Note on Women's Economic Empowerment.
5. Patel, Leena, Subhalakshmi Nandi and Suhela Khan (2013), Making the NREGA more Gender Responsive: Reflections from the Field.
6. Planning Commission (2012), Report of the Working Group on Women's Agency and Empowerment for the Twelfth Plan.
7. Nirantar (2007), Examining Poverty Alleviation and Women's Empowerment through Self-Help Groups (SHGs): A Qualitative Study.
8. ILO (2010), Women Workers in Agriculture: Expanding Responsibilities and Shrinking Opportunities, authored by Aruna Kanchi.

Part – III
Women's Health, Education and Employment, including Migration

13

Access to Health and Education for Women in Rural Mewat, Haryana (India)

Anjali Godyal and *Anjali Makhija*

Introduction

Women empowerment is an indicator of well-being of any society. Gender equality perpetuates economic growth, promotes harmony and basic dignity of human life. In India, the principle of gender equality is enshrined in our Constitution. The National Policy for Empowerment of Women has a prime objective of 'creating an environment through social and economic policies for full development of women to enable them to realize their full potential.' It calls for equal access for women and girls to education and a holistic approach to women's health. This chapter explores the concerns of women in accessing education and health care in Mewat District of Haryana, and the initiatives of Institute of Rural Research and Development (IRRAD), a civil society organization, in building capacities of women to access health and education services. Towards the end, the chapter recommends actions to improve access to and quality of education, health and healthcare in rural areas.

Status of Access to Education and Health Services for Women in Mewat

Mewat is a district in Haryana inhabited by Meo-Muslims whose origins can be traced back to the early Aryan invasion of Northern India when they called themselves Kshatriyas. During the invasion of the Tughlak dynasty in the fourteenth century, they embraced Islam. However they preserved their social and cultural traits and, as a result, possess a distinct ethno-cultural identity influenced by both Hinduism and Islam (Mewat Profile). Mewat has a total population of 10 lakhs.

Education

The average literacy rate in Mewat is 56 per cent, female literacy being 38 per cent (2011 Census, GoI). The sex ratio of children attending school in the age group of 6-17 years is 720 girls per 1,000 boys in Mewat ("*Mewat At A Glance*", Mewat Development Agency) as compared to the national average of 889 girls per 1,000 boys (Kishore and Gupta 19). This suggests that girls do not have equal access to education. Mewat is a patriarchal society and role of women and girls in the society is limited to their households and women are generally identified with their reproductive roles and not productive roles. In a survey conducted by IRRAD to analyze gender segregation in Mewat, the majority of the respondents stated, "Looking after children and the household are the prime responsibilities of women and hence it is more important for a girl to be adept in household chores than education" (Godyal, *et al.*, 14). Educating a girl is generally considered a waste of time and money, as eventually the girl has to get married and take care of her husband's household.

In addition, the lack of infrastructure and services in schools further deter parents from sending their girls to schools. According to "An Assessment of Convergence of Sarva Shiksha Abhiyaan with Selected Central and State Government Schemes", a collaborative research study by IRRAD and National Resource Centre for Women, Ministry of Women and Child Development; "The dilapidated condition of toilets result in drop out or absenteeism especially among girls. The dearth of female teachers is widespread. While there are sanctioned positions, the under representation is due to absence of qualified teachers. This has resulted in many parents pulling their girl children out of school which is sharply evident after they attain puberty" *(Saxena N., et al., 48).*

Health

Accessing health care is also an uphill task for women in Mewat. While analyzing the gender segregation in Mewat, we also asked the respondents about access to healthcare services by women. Most of the respondents felt that if a health sub-centre is within the village the women can easily access it. However, if women need to go out of the village for seeking health care, then they must be accompanied by a male family member. In Mewat, only 84 villages out of 431 have a health sub-centre. Lack of healthcare facilities within the villages and the social restrictions placed on women's mobility makes them dependent on their male counterparts for seeking health care. As a result, women tend to neglect or ignore their health issues, particularly related to reproductive health, out of shyness and also to avoid inconveniencing others.

The health statistics of Mewat provide testimony to the above mentioned state of neglect for women's health. The Maternal Mortality Rate in Mewat is 275 as compared to 212 in India (SRS, GoI). Similarly, 85 per cent deliveries takes place at home in Mewat as compared to 53 per cent in India (DLHS 3, GoI). Further only 16.4 per cent mothers registered themselves in the first trimester, 15.3 per cent had three ante-natal checkups and 50.4 per cent got at least one Tetanus Toxoid (TT) injection during pregnancy. The percentage of children (12-23 months) fully immunized was 12.2 per cent (*ibid*). Out of the 12 Primary Health Centres (PHCs) in Mewat, only one has Lady Medical Officer.

Another area which impacts a woman's health is sanitation and access to water. About 88 per cent of people in rural Mewat do not have access to toilet facility and only 32 per cent have piped water supply according to the District Level Health and Facility Survey, conducted in 2007-08 (DLHS 3, GoI). Poor water and sanitation facilities in villages pose a serious threat to the health of the community and spread of water borne diseases. Absence of household toilets is also a matter of everyday inconvenience, especially for the elderly, disabled and women. For women and girls, the problem gets compounded as it relates to their dignity and safety. In the absence of toilets, women are the worst sufferers as they either have to go early morning or wait for nightfall to relieve themselves, which is not always a safe proposition. This also causes serious health problems like urinary tract infection and constipation among women. During menstruation, their plight becomes even worse. Also, there is a constant fear of sexual exposure, harassment and assault. Lack of household toilets affect women's health adversely and forces them to live with a constant sense of insecurity.

Promoting Women's Health and Education in Mewat: Initiatives of IRRAD

IRRAD has been working in Mewat for the past 10 years to bring about a positive change in the lives of people. One of the goals of IRRAD is to improve access to health and education for women. We believe that providing quality healthcare and education services are the primary responsibility of the government. IRRAD has a catalytic role to play wherein we build capacities of the community to demand for these services and make the government accountable.

In 2011, a group of villagers from Kharkhari Village in Mewat District who participated in GGN trainings found out that their village has an Aanganwadi Centre since 1975. Upon further enquiry, they realized that the Aanganwadi Worker was operating the Centre from her home and its functioning was mostly on paper.

One of the villagers, Aashu, filed a complaint with the ICDS Programme Officer about this dysfunctional Aanganwadi Centre. However, even after 10 days no action was taken on the complaint. Subsequently, Aashu filed a Right to Information application. The very next day, a Block level ICDS official came and visited Aashu and requested him to withdraw the application. Aashu did not budge from his stand and categorically conveyed to them that he will not withdraw his application unless the Aanganwadi Centre is made functional. Finally the Aanganwadi Centre was shifted to the government primary school in the village and is functioning smoothly now.

IRRAD's Good Village Governance initiative strengthens the ability of villagers to claim their rights and entitlements provided by the government through an initiative called Good Governance Now (GGN), as well as builds capacities of village level institutions (VLIs) to function effectively and deliver basic services, such as health, education and other public services related to village development. As part of this initiative we undertake training sessions with women at the village level to raise awareness about government programmes and schemes on health and education. We also train women on monitoring compliance by educating them about Right to Information and other grievance redressal mechanisms. In addition we build capacities of women who are members of a village level institution, such as the School Management Committee; Village Health, Sanitation and Nutrition Committee (VHSNC); and Gram Panchayat (village council).

Jatka is a village in Mewat District with a population of 1362. We started working with VHSNC of Jatka in the year 2011. With our support, VHSNC and Panchayat of this village leveraged ₹2 million from the government and undertook activities such as construction of paved village lanes, waste-water disposal systems, provision of drinking water in schools, distribution of mosquito nets to pregnant women and construction of household toilets for BPL families. The village is now cleaner and there are fewer incidences of water-borne diseases. Provision of household toilets has particularly benefited the women. In the absence of toilets they had to wait for dawn or nightfall to relieve themselves, which was not good for their health. Better roads have improved accessibility. Availability of drinking water at school during school hours has improved children's attendance. The VHSNC and Panchayat have become confident and are seeking more funds from the government for village development. Furthermore, the accountability of these institutions towards the community has increased and the villagers now expect them to carry out development works.

Promoting Access to Health and Healthcare Services

Our major focus in health is to make the government healthcare services functional and expand *the coverage of National Rural Health Mission in villages. We educate women about various schemes under National Rural Livelihoods Mission and Department of Women and Child Development.* In addition, we support women for availing these benefits and services. We work with village Panchayats and District Health Department to improve the conditions of village health sub-centres, which are the primary unit of government healthcare services.

Water and health are directly related and impact women. IRRAD's Water Management programme aims to address the problem of inadequate water quality and insufficient water availability. Through activities such as installation of rain water harvesting structures, promotion of bio sand filters for clean drinking water, taps and stand posts, the programme aims to improve well being of women.

Promoting Access to Education

To promote access to education, particularly among girls, we work towards increasing the community participation in the government education process by building the capacity of school management committee members regarding their roles and responsibilities and making them accountable to the community. We also undertake awareness drives in the community to raise awareness about Right to Education. To promote the enrolment of girls in schools we carry out enrolment drives and visit every household to motivate parents to send their daughters to school. We advocate with School Management Committees (SMCs) to demand for lady teachers as absence of them is a major cause for low retention of girls in schools. We facilitate development of school development plans so that some of the basic amenities such as water and provision of toilet reaches the school.

Promoting Health and Education among Rural Women using ICT

"NGOs in India are proactively piloting new ICTs in rural communities while at the same time advocating for and staying alert to emerging government ICT efforts. Under the Universal Service Obligation, the Government of India is obliged to provide access to telecommunications services to people in rural and remote parts of the country at reasonable and affordable prices. The Universal Service Obligation fund has taken gender-specific initiatives in compliance with the requirement of gender responsive budgeting" (Schukoske J.). At IRRAD, Community radio is used as a ICT tool for dissemination of information on various themes. The radio station Alfaz-e-Mewat, FM 107.8, broadcasts from IRRAD's community centre in Mewat District, "Caller records indicate that listeners hail from 183 villages in Mewat district of Haryana and 10 villages in Alwar district, Rajasthan", *ibid.* The community radio has specific programmes designed for women and children including panel discussions, phone in programme, experts' comments, and many others. This tool provides a comprehensive mode to disseminate messages on a wider scale and is a mode of entertainment, especially among rural women. It also provides a platform for promotion of women role models, which are very few in Mewat. It is an important tool to educate and sensitize men on gender equality as their use of this medium is more as compared to women.

Challenges in Implementation

IRRAD had taken small steps to address the education and health needs of women in Mewat. This has given us an understanding that there are a wide range of factors hampering the progress of women.

Firstly, religion is an important aspect as it shapes the belief system and impacts the society. The sayings from religious books or leaders referring to role of women can both augment or dampen women's pace of development. In Mewat too the participation of women at various platforms gets affected due to religious sentiments. It is often used as a pretext to justify the patriarchal norms.

Secondly, the society at large perceives men to be the head of families and this continues in the area of governance where they take on leadership roles. The perspectives and needs of women are often not a priority for these men folk. Voices of women do not reach them and they often plan activities according to their own interests. Initiatives such as toilets, drinking water, education of girl child and reproductive and child health often do not find a mention in the village plans.

Thirdly, the dismal and resigned attitude of the government officials is an important factor contributing towards inertia in women's development. Their inclination and proactiveness, or the lack of it, impacts women's participation in governance. For example they openly accept the participation of male proxy Sarpanches and are many times, more comfortable working with them as they have willingly accepted it as a continued social and political custom.

Lastly, poor convergence between the departments of health, education and Panchayats leads to a silo effect. The Panchayat is responsible to prepare the overall village plan. The committees on health and education, which are Village Health Sanitation and Nutrition Committees (VHSNCs) and School Management Committees (SMCs), work in isolation and the village head often does not include their aspects in the village plans, unless the village is headed by a woman.

Conclusion

A wide range of measures are required to improve the access to and quality of healthcare and education for women. According to Iqbal Qureshi, "Muslim women must be encouraged and given means to educate themselves and others and to define their own identities as autonomous spiritual and intellectual beings"—these thoughts are shared by many intellectuals, academicians and practitioners (Ch. 11). Aspects of religion which promotes gender equity needs to be tapped to augment the progress made for active participation of women.

The government has a diverse range of programmes for women on health and education, however, the programmes are generally not able to reach the intended beneficiaries because of poor implementation. For these programmes to have wider reach it is imperative to have a strategy for raising awareness among women about the programme. Restricted mobility and lack of education makes it difficult for women to be aware of various government programmes. Hence, a targeted approach is required to reach out to maximum women and educate them about government programmes. Various modes of Information Education Communication (IEC) are required to create mass awareness and mobilize masses, particularly among women to take care of their education and health needs. This also includes use of ICT. Various pilot projects have been tested, such as mobile based technologies, village based kiosks, helpline numbers, etc. However, the challenge is to select the appropriate technology and take it to scale.

In addition, a strong advocacy with men folk, especially the youth, is required for their cooperation and understanding to promote gender equity. In addition, there is a need for more proactive approaches to bring women in the forefront of governance process so that they are involved in the decision making. It is further essential to build their capacities so that they become informed citizens. They need to be educated, inspired and enrolled and given a legitimate space for planning and execution of health and education domain.

India Human Development Report 2011 quotes, "inclusive development cannot be attained unless women participate equally in the development process" (Ch. 2). S. Prasanarajan has pointed out that India's "record in social sector pertaining to health care, education and gender justice is dismal." He has further said that what is required is renewed focus on primary health centres, village level health workers and need for public involvement in preventive health measures. Furthermore, Sunil Jain states, "Health, education, sharing of social opportunities, a more equal deal for women, and other such 'social' factors are not only crucial for quality of life, they are also important aspects of shared economic development".

For India to gain prosperity, it is important to address economic development and social backwardness simultaneously. These are two pillars on which the overall pace of development rests. To reap long term benefit of growth, we must focus on equal participation of women in all spheres of life so that they contribute gainfully and holistically in their progress as well as the development of the nation.

References

Godyal, A.; P. Sahu; M. Oberoi. (2011), "Capacity Building Needs: Village level Committee-cum-Village Health and Sanitation Committee." Technical Paper-2. Gurgaon. Institute of Rural Research and Development.

Godyal, A.; A. Makhija; M. Oberoi. (2010), "Need Analysis for Gender Equity Training." Technical Paper-4, Gurgaon. Institute of Rural Research and Development.

Godyal, A.; A. Makhija. (2012), "Empowering Rural Meo-Muslim Women in Mewat: Experiences and Challenges." *Women's Link*, Volume 18, Number 1 (Jan-March): Prin.

Government of India. (2001), "National Policy for the Empowerment of Women." Internet. Available: http://wcd.nic.in/empwomen.htm. August 2011.GoI.

Government of India. Ministry of Health and Family Welfare. *District Level Household and Facility Survey 2007-2008.*DLHS-3 Fact Sheets. Mumbai: International Institute for Population Sciences.

"India Human Development Report: Towards Social Inclusion." Institute of Applied Manpower Research, Planning Commission, Government of India, 2011.

Jain, S. (2013), "Improve Social Services." Internet (July 4, 2013) Available: http://indiatoday.intoday.in/story/improve-social-services-amartya-sen/1/286846.html. July.

Mewat At A Glance. Mewat Development Agency, Nuh. Internet. Available: http://mda.nic.in/Mewat-Glance.htm August 2011.

Prasannarajan, S. (2013), "Unequal India." Internet (July 15, 2013) Available: http://indiatoday.intoday.in/story/india-economic-growth-human-development-amartya-sen-jean-dreze/1/287087.html. July.

Qureshi, Iqbal. "Islamic Higher Learning in Muslim Women." In *Women and Islam.* Ed. New Delhi: Saurabh Publishing House, 2007, 204-220.

Saxena, N.; Mehta, P. (2012), "An Assessment of Convergence of Sarva Shiksha Abhiyaan with Selected Central and State Government Schemes." A collaborative research study by Institute of Rural Research and Development, Gurgaon and National Resource Centre for Women, Ministry of Women and Child Development.

Scukoske, J. (2013), *Role of NGOs in Empowerment of Rural Women Through ICT.*

14

Driving Demand and Increasing Access to Health and Education in Maharashtra (India)

The Experience of *Swayam Shikshan Prayog*

Naseem Shaikh

Background

Most of the families in rural Maharashtra spend approximately a fourth of their monthly income on health care. They suffer from an alarmingly high rate of various morbidities that are mainly due to poor sanitation, inadequate diet and lack of health awareness and services. The government has provided Primary Health Centres (PHC) that are designed to serve a population of 30,000 with one medical officer and two health assistants and Sub-centres with one female and one male multipurpose health worker for a population of 5,000. However, PHCs are often poorly equipped and doctors are absent for long stretches of time. Rural communities mistrust PHCs and prefer more expensive private practitioners who are not necessarily more competent. Often the poor, particularly women, avoid seeking medical care altogether since these private facilities are too costly.

Swayam Shikshan Prayog (SSP) is a learning and development organization based in Mumbai (India), whose goal is to move poor women and communities from the margin to the mainstream of development. It began its work after the destructive earthquakes in Maharashtra (1993) and Gujarat (2001) and tsunami in Tamil Nadu (2004). Today, SSP's combined operations reach out to over 300,000 families in ten districts of these States. SSP mobilized grassroots women as Self Help Groups

(SHGs) around reconstruction and local governance issues. Ever since, SSP has worked with these SHGs to build the capacities of women as grassroots advocates to engage with the government service providers and ensure accountability. SSP facilitated the creation of an active working partnership between grassroots women, district level health officials and health service providers to ensure better access to healthcare services for the poor.

From 'Beneficiaries' to 'Partners'

In 2003, SSP piloted their community health programme in Maharashtra by raising awareness of women on how to access available resources and educating the community on hygiene and nutrition to prevent common illnesses. Through initial facilitation, women met the service providers to gain more information on health, including information on how to access existing programmes and facilities. Empowered with such information and increased capacity to voice their needs, the women soon started demanding better services. Such interactions also focused on building relationships with government health service providers, particularly PHCs, as they are necessary for both improving community health and reducing health related expenditure. To further strengthen the collaboration, a district workshop was organized through which 300 SHG women learnt from the district officer of the range of services offered and means to access them. This knowledge was, in turn, disseminated across the community through SHG meetings. The workshop helped to build SHG capacities to act as pressure groups for local government to ensure reliable PHC services. Consequently, SHGs launched a campaign to promote PHC services. The women were recognized as community monitors and were given identity cards by the government, who got regular reports from them if the PHC staff failed to deliver services or if the communities ceased to access them. Regular dialogues and workshops strengthened the relationship between the grassroots communities and government representatives like PHC doctors and district health officers.

SSP started building community ownership by training the community monitors and some SHG women as health educators, called *Arogya Sakhis* who provide basic health education and services, follow up visits and act as referrals. They have developed a relationship with the PHCs, as well as district level health officials which allows them to stay informed of government schemes, programmes, and public health concerns. Using the same peer education method and by strengthening existing channels of communication, information is spread by these health educators to the community through SHGs.

When the epidemic of Chickungunya spread in Osmanabad district of Maharashtra, the government trained 150 *Arogya Sakhis* to disseminate information on prevention and treatment of Chickungunya to the community. Along with village health officials, the *Arogya Sakhis* organized meetings to educate villagers on the disease and encouraged them to use PHCs instead of private doctors. They also arranged health camps where villagers could receive treatment at subsidized rates. Within a month and half, there was a noticeable decrease in new cases and the epidemic began to subside.

One objective of the government's National Rural Health Mission (NRHM) is to identify and train community health leaders at the village level. Grassroots women can apply to become government sponsored community health leaders through their *Gram Panchayat* (local level government), which appoints leaders based on a specific set of criteria such as education, family support and experience of working in health. Fifty of the eighty five *Arogya Sakhis* in Osmanabad are now government sponsored community health leaders who receive free government training and an identity card that gives them recognition at local hospitals. They also receive some honorarium for each of the service they render to the community.

Forming Health Governance Groups

In 2005, SSP organized an exposure visit of SHGs in Maharashtra to meet the women in Tamil Nadu who were affected by the tsunami to learn about the effectiveness of working as a health collective to lobby local authorities to meet community needs. Women's Federation of SHGs have formed health collectives called Health Governance Groups (HGGs) each consisting of 15-20 women. HGGs aim at linking the communities to government programmes, as well as, building accountability of the service providers. In July 2008, the SHGs of Osmanabad decided to adopt some aspects of the HGGs model and have since formed 100 HGGs.

Role of Health Governance Groups

In Maharashtra, HGGs play the following roles:

- Strengthen partnerships with village PHCs.

- Handle the administrative responsibilities of community based Health Mutual Fund (which is explained subsequently).
- Organize regular village health check-up, camps and hospital referrals.
- Conduct workshops on nutrition and healthy living involving all members of the community.
- Work with government officials to effectively implement government health programmes.
- Encourage institutional delivery for women and immunization.
- Implement community 'trainers team' to transfer knowledge and skills of HGGs.
- Maintain village cleanliness and encourage waste segregation and disposal.

Representatives of HGGs attend weekly PHC planning meetings through which they raise awareness on government health schemes in their communities. PHCs use datasheets prepared by HGGs on common illnesses in the village to plan their interventions. Interactions with PHCs have helped disseminate information on government subsidies on toilets, the schedule of PHC activities like village visits of nurses and health workers and also the government mandated role of the PHCs. ASHAA members work with village health nurses on pregnancy related issues and accompany them on their visits which resulted in increased institutional deliveries.

SHGs are traditionally seen as microcredit groups. However, with the formation of HGGs, the community has started recognizing them as groups devoted to community welfare. HGGs are better positioned to meet community health demands, expand on the work of the Arogya Sakhis as a group and have the kind of outreach and impact that a single individual alone cannot achieve. HGGs organize community health check-up camps at the PHCs and community centres which are attended by a doctor, laboratory staff and assistant. Women have taken the initiative and negotiated subsidized fees with the doctor and staff to make the camps affordable.

Insuring Community Health

SHG women often access loans mainly for health related expenditure. Despite several interventions, many households still bear the burden of expensive treatment. In February 2006, the Sakhi Mutual Fund was launched to protect rural communities from unexpected health expenditures. The SHG Federations have tied up with a network of hospitals and clinics to ensure accessible and affordable treatment for all. Private hospitals are also included in the hospital network of Sakhi Health Mutual Fund to maximize convenience in emergencies. However, special incentives to use government health facilities were designed wherever possible.

Impact

In Maharashtra, through the network of 5,500 SHGs, SSP's Community Health Programme with strength of over 72,000 grassroots women has empowered them to demand better health, water and sanitation and make the public health system more accountable. Women act as planners and monitors, assuming responsibility for the effectiveness of local facilities. They are instrumental in establishing and maintaining a relationship with service providers and the communities.

The Importance of Awareness Camps: The Story of Sajeda

Sajeda, a peer educator in Lohara Block, Osmanabad, trains women on the transmission of HIV/AIDS and motivates them, especially pregnant women, to get tested for the virus. Sajeda is aware that local women are generally hesitant to openly discuss the disease. She has found a way to encourage pregnant women to undergo an HIV test, who are usually reluctant to get tested for HIV. She says, "When I visit these women, I talk about the government schemes for pregnant women, the care available to them and incentives offered for institutional delivery. This gets them interested. Then I introduce HIV as being part of the routine tests for pregnant women, emphasizing the importance of knowing one's status of the disease, the risk of transmission and the positive effects of anti-retroviral treatment. Sajeda organizes several HIV testing camps for all women including pregnant women in Lohara Block, a process which has helped strengthen her relationship with local doctors and rural hospitals. "They now think of me as a member of their staff!" Sajeda laughs.

New avenues of partnership between the community and local government have opened up. SHGs have partnered with village governments to stop open defecation, a prevalent practice leading to poor health in India. They design community plans for safe drinking water and sanitation, actively mobilize resources and lobby the *Gram Panchayat* to include women in the Village Water and Sanitation committees and see these plans are implemented. This has already influenced the lives of more than 300,000 households in Maharashtra. The HGGs disseminate information to community members in *Gram Sabhas* (Village level meetings with Gram Panchayat) on all activities, important decisions taken, health and sanitation. This process increases the demand for better health services.

Partnerships were sought at every level, including *Anganwadis* (government child care centres), responsible for maternal and child health. Community women acting as peer educators collaborated with them to identify HIV infected pregnant women and access HIV care services. They follow on the advice given by doctors on family planning, nutrition, formula feeding and also provide them with counselling.

Making PHCs More Effective

Katgoan is a large village, with a population of over 10,000 inhabitants. The facilities at the village PHC were inadequate—the appointed doctor was not active and unpaid electricity bills led to the power supply being cut off. With no government health services, people were forced to seek medical treatment in Solapur, which is 30 kilometres away. The village Arogya Sakhi group and the Gram Panchayat appealed to the District Health Official to invest in the facilities. Through the National Rural Health Mission (NRHM) ₹ 20,00,000 was accessed for the construction of a new PHC building in the centre of the village on the land generously donated by a local farmer.

Lessons Learnt on Service Delivery and Decentralization

Health awareness camps are cost-effective and have succeeded in effective outreach to communities on government health schemes. Over the years, SSP has recognized the significance of partnerships with government officials for accessing critical information.

Decentralization has opened up avenues for women's participation in local development. Prior to decentralization, community participation was taking place in a vacuum. Decentralization has given meaning to citizens, especially women; to act as part of the community, part of decision making bodies and as resources.

In India, policies and programmes have devolved resources and decentralized management to the local level, including the provision of basic services. Over time, greater decentralization of decision making has taken place, but not so with the devolution of resources. Today, there is a framework and institutional system for decentralization. Women have benefited from decentralization more in the form of participation, especially locally. Leakages are monitored.

Women can be effective if they are on agenda making committees, provided they are also part of organized women's groups. Yet, the role of women's groups in the agenda setting committees is not formalized nor are their roles as key leaders recognized. Being part of a SHG, has helped women to spot avenues for participation and capitalize on these opportunities to access basic services. However, their role in the public arena as of now remains undefined. Therefore, till such participation is formalized, SHGs cannot easily act as resources. As seen in Osmanabad, SHGs and women's groups like HGGs were able to develop innovative solutions to solve local problems as certain preconditions were in place, namely partnerships with local governments and access to resources. It is important for women to be paid for their efforts, like the *Arogya Sakhis* who were sponsored by government as Community Health workers, without which these women are further burdened with the development work of the community. Since grassroots women have strong relations based on trust with the community, they are able to deliver services and can act as resources. Just as the private sector has recognized this and entered into collaboration with SHGs from SSP, it is equally important that advocates of decentralized governance recognize the key role women can play in service delivery.

15

Status of Rural Female Employment in India

Mondira Bhattacharya

Introduction

Women's access to economic and financial resources is necessary for their empowerment. Employment of women increases the family income, increases their say in household decision-making, and also enhances their status in the society, thereby leading to their empowerment. While India's economy has grown at increasingly high rates over the past decades, the female work force participation rate has increased only since the start of the twentyfirst century. However, it has also declined in recent years and in 2012 Indian women comprised 27.37 per cent of the economically active population. Out of these economically active women, 60 per cent worked in agriculture, accounting for 35 per cent of the agricultural labour force. The contribution of women in the farm production is estimated at 55 to 66 per cent of the total labour (Gender and Land Rights Database–FAO). Women by nature take on household responsibilities, child care, taking care of the sick and even attending to extra work like fetching fuelwood etc., but such gender roles limit rural women's participation in labour markets and confine them to lower paid and more precarious employment conditions. Women farmers face discrimination in access to resources and services needed to improve their productivity, such as credit, secure land titles and education (FAO). Had women enjoyed the same access to productive resources as men, they could boost farm productivity significantly.

The falling female work force participation rate in India could be due to increased educational enrolment, income effect (as household incomes rise, women are withdrawing from agricultural activities), lack of job opportunities, and also measurement as it is difficult to measure the participation of women in work, because of the nature of the jobs they do (home-based work, subsistence agriculture, etc). Against this backdrop, the objective of this chapter is to examine trends and drivers of female work force participation in rural India, captured through the lens of land rights, migration, education, agricultural income and wages. This chapter is based on data from NSSO quinquennial rounds, including the few recently released reports of the 68th round (July 2010–June 2012) as well as data from the Census of India and Agricultural Census 2010.

Trends in Rural Female Occupation Structure

The shares of males and females in total rural workforce shows that, the share of female workforce is much lower than males and their shares started to decline since the 61st round (July 2004–June 2005) from 36 per cent to 31.10 per cent in the 66th round (July 2009-June 2010) to 30.24 per cent in the 68th round (July 2010-June 2012) (Figure 15.1).

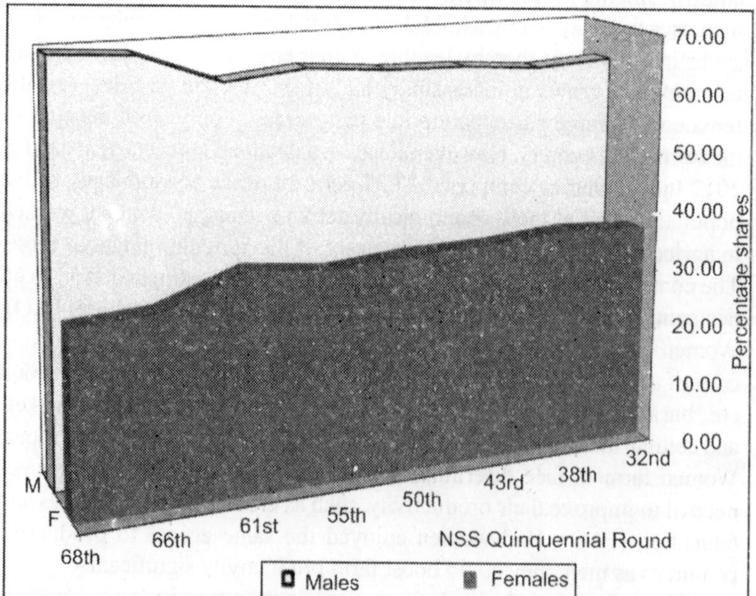

Source: Calculated from NSSO Quinquennial Rounds

Fig. 15.1: Share of Males and Females in Total Rural Workforce (%)

The workforce participation rate which is defined as the share of employed persons to total population has also shown a decline, especially for females (Table 15.1). As per the NSSO 68th round (July 2010-June 2012), female worker population was highest in the States of Himachal Pradesh (524), Sikkim (487) and Andhra Pradesh (445) and lowest in the States of Bihar (53), Assam (122) and Delhi (146).

Table 15.1: Workforce Participation Rate (per 1000) for All Persons according to Usual Status (PS+SS)

NSSO Quinquennial Rounds	*Rural Females*	*Rural Males*
32 (July 1977-June 1978)	331	552
38 (January-December 1983)	340	547
43 (July 1987-June 1988)	323	539
50 (July 1993-June 1994)	328	553
55 (July 1999-June 2000)	299	531
61 (July 2004-June 2005)	327	546
66 (July 2009-June 2010)	261	547
68 (July 2010-June 2012)	248	543

Industrial Classification of Rural Female Workers

Table 15.2 shows the share of male and female workers according to industry categories in rural areas. It is seen that out of total female workers in rural areas the share of those engaged in the primary (agriculture) sector has been the highest (around 80%) and this is higher than the share of male primary workers (around 70%). The share of female workers in secondary and tertiary sectors is lower than that of males. In the latest round of NSSO (68th Round) it is seen that in rural areas, 59.4 per cent of the usual status (PS+SS) male workers and 74.9 per cent of the female workers were engaged in the agricultural sector. Among the male workers, 21.8 per cent and 18.8 per cent were engaged in secondary and tertiary sectors. The corresponding proportions for female workers were 16.7 per cent and 8.7 per cent, respectively.

Further, the shares of primary workers for both males and females have been declining over the years, while that of secondary and tertiary workers are increasing. This improvement in rural work force participation since 2004, especially in the secondary sector could be attributed to MNREGA, which mandates that at least one-third of the beneficiaries should be women, and that men and women should be paid equally (Desai 2013). But despite opportunities in MNREGA, the shares of rural women

Table 15.2: Percentage Distribution of Usual Status (PS+SS) Workers of all Ages by Industry of Work in Rural Areas

NSSO Quinquennial Rounds	*Rural Females*			*Rural Males*		
	Primary	*Secondary*	*Tertiary*	*Primary*	*Secondary*	*Tertiary*
32 (July 1977-June 1978)	88.21	6.65	5.14	80.70	8.79	10.51
38 (Jan-Dec 1983)	87.72	7.41	4.87	77.71	10.04	12.26
43 (July 1987-June 1988)	84.73	10.00	5.27	74.51	12.08	13.41
50 (July 1993-June 1994)	86.16	8.30	5.53	74.11	11.19	14.70
55 (July 1999-June 2000)	85.43	8.89	5.68	71.40	12.59	16.01
61 (July 2004-June 2005)	83.24	10.15	6.61	66.50	15.49	18.01
66 (July 2009-June 2010)	79.37	12.99	7.64	62.89	19.31	17.80
68 (July 2010-June 2012)	74.90	16.89	8.20	59.41	21.76	18.83

Source: Calculated from NSSO Quinquennial Rounds.

in secondary and tertiary sectors (non-farm occupations) is lower than that of men, indicating a crowding out of female by male workers in these sectors. The exclusion of women from rural labour markets and feminization of the agricultural workforce is a potential concern.

As regards type of female workers in rural areas, the share of cultivators and agricultural labourers is the largest (Table 15.3). In the recent census, the share of female cultivators both main and marginal is seen to be declining while that of agricultural labourers is increasing.

Table 15.3: Share of Female Cultivators and Agricultural Labourers in Total Female Workers in Rural Areas (%)

Census Years	*Cultivators (Main)*	*Agricultural Labourers (Main)*
1991	38.92	48.49
2001	41.53	35.66
2011	32.88	43.30
Census Years	*Cultivators (Marginal)*	*Agricultural Labourers (Marginal)*
2001	31.99	51.58
2011	23.76	54.96

Source: Census of India.

According to the National Industrial Classification 2008, just as national figures suggest, majority of rural women in most States are engaged in agriculture and allied activities (74.9%) followed by secondary (16.89%) and then tertiary activities (8.20%) (Table 15.4). Within the secondary sector most women are engaged in manufacturing (9.79%) followed by construction (6.39%) activities. However, in States such as Goa, Manipur and Tripura, a high proportion of rural women are engaged in the secondary sector, mainly in manufacturing and construction. In Delhi a high proportion of rural women are engaged in wholesale and retail trade and repair of motor vehicles and motorcycles (37.45%). In Chandigarh a high proportion of rural women are engaged in activities of households as employers (40.14%), while in Daman & Diu 60 per cent of women are engaged in public administration. But still, the overall movement of women into better formal jobs like professional, scientific and technical activities is weak.

Role of Migration in Rural Occupational Structure

It is important to understand patterns to migration to explain occupational structure of male and female workers in rural areas. Overall, rural female

Table 15.4: Share of Rural Female Workers according to Usual Status (PS+SS) by Industry Sections of NIC-2008 for each State/UT (%)

States	A	B	C	D	E	F	G	H	I	J	K	L	M	N	O	P	Q	R	S	T	U
Andhra Pradesh	76.66	0.67	8.81	0.01	0.00	5.20	3.45	0.04	1.09	0.14	0.01	0.00	0.00	0.01	0.23	1.62	0.49	0.00	1.46	0.12	0.00
Arunachal Pradesh	90.37	0.00	0.04	0.00	0.00	1.38	1.46	0.26	0.17	0.06	0.00	0.00	0.23	0.17	1.54	1.28	1.10	0.00	1.02	0.91	0.00
Assam	79.04	0.25	3.40	0.00	0.00	3.13	3.01	0.06	0.79	0.29	0.00	0.00	0.51	0.04	0.17	5.04	1.13	0.00	0.51	2.62	0.00
Bihar	76.84	0.00	8.23	0.00	0.00	2.87	3.92	0.04	0.17	0.00	0.05	0.00	0.00	0.00	0.12	6.75	0.20	0.00	0.79	0.03	0.00
Chhattisgarh	90.19	0.32	2.48	0.00	0.00	3.02	1.28	0.08	0.05	0.00	0.00	0.00	0.00	0.00	0.06	0.68	1.30	0.25	0.09	0.19	0.00
Delhi	0.00	0.00	0.03	0.00	0.00	0.00	37.45	0.00	0.00	22.63	0.00	0.00	0.00	0.00	8.93	28.37	1.57	0.00	0.00	1.02	0.00
Goa	7.07	0.38	27.06	0.00	0.00	6.04	14.50	0.91	0.11	0.64	10.69	0.00	6.05	0.00	1.14	4.48	0.52	0.00	14.98	5.41	0.00
Gujarat	85.55	0.78	5.08	0.00	0.00	2.84	1.59	0.00	0.09	0.00	0.05	0.00	0.00	0.00	0.18	2.02	0.50	0.00	0.75	0.56	0.00
Haryana	86.02	0.00	3.98	0.00	0.04	4.40	0.16	0.37	0.09	0.00	0.00	0.00	0.00	0.00	0.14	3.26	0.69	0.00	0.86	0.00	0.00
Himachal Pradesh	86.98	0.00	0.94	0.28	0.01	5.36	0.82	0.20	0.06	0.01	0.14	0.00	0.03	0.00	0.60	3.95	0.24	0.00	0.38	0.02	0.00
Jammu & Kashmir	85.05	0.00	5.79	0.00	0.00	3.51	0.23	0.00	0.08	0.01	0.02	0.00	0.00	0.00	0.20	3.06	1.03	0.00	0.60	0.41	0.00
Jharkhand	84.44	0.99	7.00	0.00	0.00	2.55	2.41	0.01	0.29	0.00	0.08	0.00	0.00	0.00	0.16	1.29	0.31	0.00	0.38	0.10	0.00
Karnataka	79.37	0.22	10.00	0.04	0.00	1.14	3.45	0.15	1.07	0.03	0.34	0.00	0.02	0.00	0.98	2.40	0.41	0.00	0.20	0.19	0.00
Kerala	38.69	0.09	18.01	0.00	0.11	13.04	4.75	0.62	1.31	0.31	2.28	0.01	0.24	1.55	1.19	7.96	5.92	0.04	2.17	1.69	0.00
Madhya Pradesh	80.02	0.02	5.10	0.00	0.00	10.36	1.99	0.01	0.05	0.00	0.00	0.00	0.00	0.01	0.16	1.50	0.36	0.03	0.12	0.27	0.00
Maharashtra	89.12	0.01	3.10	0.00	0.00	2.26	2.28	0.07	0.16	0.00	0.00	0.00	0.01	0.00	0.12	2.01	0.30	0.00	0.23	0.33	0.00
Manipur	24.12	0.45	17.36	0.00	0.69	40.52	9.67	0.04	1.55	0.00	0.00	0.00	0.00	0.00	1.21	3.26	0.49	0.00	0.63	0.00	0.00
Meghalaya	73.62	0.96	1.81	0.05	0.00	3.49	7.90	0.09	3.02	0.00	0.00	0.11	0.00	0.00	2.34	4.83	1.30	0.00	0.37	0.10	0.00
Mizoram	74.69	0.62	0.20	0.00	0.10	13.24	6.29	0.00	0.73	0.00	0.00	0.00	0.00	0.00	0.85	2.27	0.56	0.00	0.44	0.00	0.00
Nagaland	90.17	0.00	1.24	0.02	0.00	2.57	3.19	0.00	0.25	0.15	0.00	0.00	0.00	0.00	0.75	0.88	0.79	0.00	0.00	0.00	0.00
Odisha	69.31	0.69	14.50	0.00	0.00	7.77	2.07	0.57	0.26	0.00	0.01	0.00	0.00	0.00	0.12	2.49	0.40	0.00	1.76	0.05	0.00
Punjab	75.40	0.00	10.70	0.00	0.18	0.88	1.67	0.03	0.04	0.00	0.09	0.00	0.00	0.00	0.06	4.47	0.67	0.00	5.37	0.43	0.00
Rajasthan	77.39	0.03	2.29	0.00	0.10	14.98	1.43	0.22	0.03	0.00	0.00	0.00	0.00	0.00	0.60	1.52	0.71	0.04	0.26	0.40	0.00
Sikkim	85.64	0.00	1.44	0.20	0.00	3.44	3.53	0.12	0.19	0.01	0.06	0.00	0.00	0.04	0.73	3.00	0.94	0.00	0.62	0.04	0.00
Tamil Nadu	50.59	0.36	16.77	0.03	0.30	22.01	3.90	0.01	1.14	0.03	0.23	0.00	0.05	0.00	0.17	2.73	0.47	0.03	0.83	0.36	0.00
Tripura	19.12	0.00	10.16	0.00	0.00	60.29	1.21	0.04	0.24	0.00	0.01	0.00	0.00	0.00	0.19	5.68	0.51	0.00	0.00	2.54	0.00
Uttarakhand	90.25	0.00	4.77	0.03	0.00	1.03	1.27	0.00	0.00	0.00	0.00	0.00	0.00	0.10	0.00	1.61	0.32	0.00	0.57	0.06	0.00
Uttar Pradesh	82.61	0.40	8.48	0.00	0.13	2.17	1.52	0.00	0.41	0.00	0.00	0.00	0.00	0.00	0.08	2.65	0.21	0.00	1.20	0.14	0.00
West Bengal	41.69	0.00	42.24	0.01	0.00	2.89	2.27	0.15	0.55	0.00	0.04	0.02	0.15	0.00	0.21	4.78	1.04	0.30	0.32	3.32	0.00
A & N Islands	41.61	0.00	0.41	1.45	0.00	10.21	9.10	2.45	2.05	0.00	3.32	0.00	0.00	0.53	3.04	16.06	5.39	0.00	0.00	4.39	0.00
Chandigarh	12.19	0.00	14.29	0.00	0.00	0.00	5.55	0.00	0.00	0.00	0.00	0.00	0.00	5.55	0.00	7.08	15.19	0.00	0.00	40.14	0.00

(Contd.)

Table 15.4 (*Contd.*)

States	A	B	C	D	E	F	G	H	I	J	K	L	M	N	O	P	Q	R	S	T	U
Dadra & Nagar Haveli	54.14	0.00	29.49	0.00	0.00	5.40	0.47	0.00	0.00	0.00	0.00	0.00	0.00	0.00	0.00	9.67	0.00	0.84	0.00	0.00	0.00
Daman & Diu	10.34	0.00	29.15	0.00	0.00	0.00	0.34	0.00	0.00	0.00	0.00	0.00	0.00	0.00	60.17	0.00	0.00	0.00	0.00	0.00	0.00
Lakshadweep	39.73	0.00	11.90	0.00	0.00	10.96	0.00	0.00	0.00	0.00	14.85	0.00	0.00	0.00	0.00	20.98	1.59	0.00	0.00	0.00	0.00
Puducherry	44.94	0.00	16.19	0.00	0.00	13.59	9.12	0.00	7.54	0.10	3.23	0.00	0.07	0.00	0.00	4.97	0.00	0.00	0.26	0.00	0.00
All-India	74.94	0.29	9.79	0.01	0.06	6.59	2.45	0.11	0.50	0.05	0.13	0.00	0.03	0.05	0.29	2.64	0.67	0.04	0.85	0.51	0.00

Source: NSSO 68th Round (July 2010-June 2012)

Notes: Agriculture Sector: Section A; Secondary Sector: Sections B to F; Tertiary Sector: Sectors G to U.

NOTES: Descriptions of the Sections of NIC 2008

Section A: Agriculture, forestry and fishing
Section B: Mining and quarrying
Section C: Manufacturing
Section D: Electricity, gas, steam and air conditioning supply
Section E: Water supply; sewerage, waste management and remediation activities
Section F: Construction
Section G: Wholesale and retail trade; repair of motor vehicles and motorcycles
Section H: Transportation and storage
Section I: Accomodation and Food service activities
Section J: Information and communication
Section K: Financial and insurance activities
Section L: Real estate activities
Section M: Professional, scientific and technical activities
Section N: Administrative and support service activities
Section O: Public administration and defence; compulsory social security
Section P: Education
Section Q: Human health and social work activities
Section R: Arts, entertainment and recreation
Section S: Other service activities
Section T: Activities of households as employers; undifferentiated goods and services producing activities of households for own use
Section U: Activities of extraterritorial organizations and bodies

migration in India has been much higher than males. As per the 64th round (July 2007 to January 2008), 477 women per 1000 persons migrated from rural areas as compared to 54 men per 1000 persons. Rural female migration has also been increasing over the years, while rural male migration has shown a declining trend. As per the Census of India, female migration was highest in the rural to rural stream (63.78%) followed by the rural to urban stream (16.72%) (Table 15.5). Recent NSSO data in Table 6 shows that in the latest round (64th round—2007/08) female rural to rural migration was 59.6 per cent while for males it was 27.5 per cent. On the other hand, rural to urban migrations have been higher for males (33.9%) compared to females (18%). It is also seen that rural to rural migrations have declined for both sexes and rural to urban migrations have increased for both sexes over the two time periods, although the change is insignificant for females. Perhaps creation of employment in rural areas through MNREGA is reducing rural to rural flow by mitigating distress/seasonal migration. Female migrants in the rural to urban stream largely worked as domestic workers (Mahapatro, 2010).

Table 15.5: Percentage Distribution of Migrants by Sex and Migration Streams (Duration of Residence < 5 years)

Migration Streams	*Males*				*Females*			
	1971	*1981*	*1991*	*2001*	*1971*	*1981*	*1991*	*2001*
Rural to Rural	27.36	44.97	42.26	40.12	36.30	62.92	63.36	63.78
Rural to Urban	28.91	25.80	28.82	30.73	21.42	15.65	16.65	16.72
Urban to Rural	12.25	10.13	9.72	8.81	10.82	7.82	7.39	6.39
Urban to Urban	31.48	19.09	19.20	20.34	31.46	13.59	12.60	13.11

Source: Mahapatro, 2010.

Table 15.6: Percentage Distribution of Migrants by Sex and Migration Streams (Duration <5 years)

Migration Streams	*Males*		*Females*	
	55th Round (1999/00)	*64th Round (2007/08)*	*55th Round (1999/00)*	*64th Round (2007/08)*
Rural to Rural	32.1	27.5	60.5	59.6
Rural to Urban	29.8	33.9	16.5	18
Urban to Rural	13.1	12.1	8.3	6.8
Urban to Urban	25.1	26.5	14.7	15.6

Source: Mahapatro, 2010.

As regards reasons for rural migration, it is seen that 78.14 per cent rural female migrations have been due to marriage (Table 15.7). Only 1.78 per cent migrations have been due to employment and 2.78 per cent have been due to education (Mahapatro, 2010). This is in stark contrast to rural male migrations, which have been mainly due to employment (29.67%) and education (23.12%). However, migration for employment is seen to be reducing in both sexes. It is also seen that migration for education is increasing, though it is much higher for males compared to females, but still it is a movement in the right direction.

Table 15.7: Reasons for Rural Migration by Sex (Duration <5 year) (%)

Reasons	*Males*		*Females*	
	55th Round (1999/00)	*64th Round (2007/08)*	*55th Round (1999/00)*	*64th Round (2007/08)*
Employment	30.92	29.67	2.06	1.78
Education	11.42	23.12	1.49	2.78
Marriage	4.8	3.59	76.53	78.14
Family	25.76	20.03	12.71	10.32
Others	27.09	23.6	7.21	6.99

Source: Mahapatro, 2010.

Thus, the occupational shift in male and female workers in rural areas shows that, male workers have steadily moved out of agriculture (and also out of rural areas) while for women workers, this movement has been extremely slow. This is because; men have entered into more diversified occupations in non-agriculture, while women have tended to remain in the largely stagnant agriculture.

Women's Land Rights

In India majority women still do not have ownership or control over land resources. Agricultural census provides information on operational (agricultural) holdings operated and by men and women, irrespective of their ownership status. According to the latest Agricultural Census 2010-11, only 12.79 per cent of agricultural landholdings, covering 10.36 per cent area, were operated by women (Table 15.8). These proportions have increased only marginally over the last Agricultural Census of 2001-02. In 2001-02, women operated only 11.6 per cent of cultivated agricultural landholdings, covering 9.1 per cent area. Further, there is an inverse relationship between the size of landholdings and the percentage of landholdings and area operated by women. In marginal holdings, the percentage of landholdings operated by women was 13.66 whereas the area operated by them was 12.82 per cent. In large holdings, the corresponding percentages declined to 7 and 6.34, respectively. These figures could partly be explained by the pattern of outmigration as male outmigration was likely to be higher in smaller landholdings. However, cultural and social factors in India are also responsible for lesser control of women on a critical resource such as land (Srivastava and Srivastava, 2010).

Table 15.8: Share of Number and Area of Operational Holdings by Size Classes (%)

Size Class (in ha)	*Gender*	*Share of No. of Operational Holdings*			*Share of Area Operated*		
		Individual	*Joint*	*Total*	*Individual*	*Joint*	*Total*
Marginal	Male	85.54	91.28	86.19	86.50	91.29	87.05
	Female	14.46	8.72	13.66	13.50	8.71	12.82
Small	Male	87.30	91.36	87.72	87.50	91.31	87.89
	Female	12.71	8.66	12.14	12.50	8.69	11.97
Semi Medium	Male	89.30	91.16	89.41	89.52	91.16	89.61
	Female	10.70	8.84	10.39	10.48	8.84	10.19
Medium	Male	91.43	91.79	91.15	91.56	91.87	91.26
	Female	8.55	8.21	8.45	8.44	8.13	8.34
Large	Male	92.80	93.04	91.10	92.90	93.85	86.73
	Female	7.20	6.59	7.00	7.10	6.15	6.34
All Classes	Male	**86.51**	**91.34**	**87.04**	**89.06**	**91.88**	**88.70**
	Female	**13.49**	**8.66**	**12.79**	**10.94**	**8.12**	**10.36**

Source: Agricultural Census, 2010.

The regional patterns of women's control over landholdings show them to be much higher in the Southern States (Table 15.9). In Andhra Pradesh, women operated 25.40 per cent of landholdings and 22 per cent of area. In Kerala, the corresponding figures were 19.62 per cent and 13.9 per cent respectively while in Tamil Nadu, they were 19.11 per cent and 16.28 per cent respectively. In the absence of land titles, women farmers tend to have lesser access to institutional credit and institutional support compared to male farmers (L. Srivastava and Srivastava, 2010).

Employment and Agricultural Income

As GDP from agriculture increases, rural female workforce participation rate (WPR) is seen to decline (Figure 15.2). It is also seen that the trend

Table 15.9: Statewise Share of Women's Operational Holdings

States	*Number ('000)*	*Area ('000 Hec)*	*States*	*Number ('000)*	*Area ('000 Hec)*
A & N Islands	25.00	27.27	Lakshadweep	40.00	33.33
Andhra Pradesh	25.40	22.00	Madhya Pradesh	9.64	7.60
Arunachal Pradesh	10.09	8.07	Maharashtra	14.99	13.07
Assam	2.13	2.37	Manipur	3.31	2.91
Bihar	14.06	13.29	Meghalaya	26.32	27.18
Chandigarh	0.00	0.00	Mizoram	10.87	9.52
Chhattisgarh	12.60	9.89	Nagaland	10.11	8.54
D & N Haveli	13.33	15.00	Odisha	3.30	3.04
Daman & Diu	25.00	33.33	Puducherry	21.21	13.64
Delhi	10.00	6.67	Punjab	0.95	0.66
Goa	25.86	16.98	Rajasthan	7.93	6.29
Gujarat	14.06	13.09	Sikkim	4.00	3.74
Haryana	12.06	11.11	Tamil Nadu	19.11	16.28
Himachal Pradesh	7.08	4.71	Tripura	10.87	8.74
Jammu & Kashmir	7.32	5.36	Uttar Pradesh	6.99	5.51
Jharkhand	10.96	8.18	Uttarakhand	9.86	8.33
Karnataka	18.97	15.61	West Bengal	3.50	2.00
Kerala	19.62	13.90	India	12.79	10.36

Source: Agricultural Census, 2010.

shares of self employed rural women is similar to the trend of rural female WPR, i.e., they both show a decline as agriculture income increases, but only till the 66th round. They are seen to diverge a little in the 68th round. The shares of self employed women is the highest followed by casual workers and then regular workers. It is further seen that, the share of self employed women in the total rural female work force is increasing in the recent NSS round compared to the last round,and this is followed by an increase in regular salaried workers. The share of female casual workers is seen to be declining. Here it would be interesting to understand the nature of self employment in women. As per NSSO definition of self employed persons, women are self employed in households enterprises mainly land, as own account workers, employers or as helpers[1]. Thus it may be assumed that in India, if majority of the rural women are engaged in agriculture[2], are mostly self employed, having a lower proportion of landholdings operated by them[3], then it would mean that most of these women are engaged as 'helpers' in the work force. It is to be noted that women self employed as helpers usually did not receive any regular salary or wages in return for the work performed.

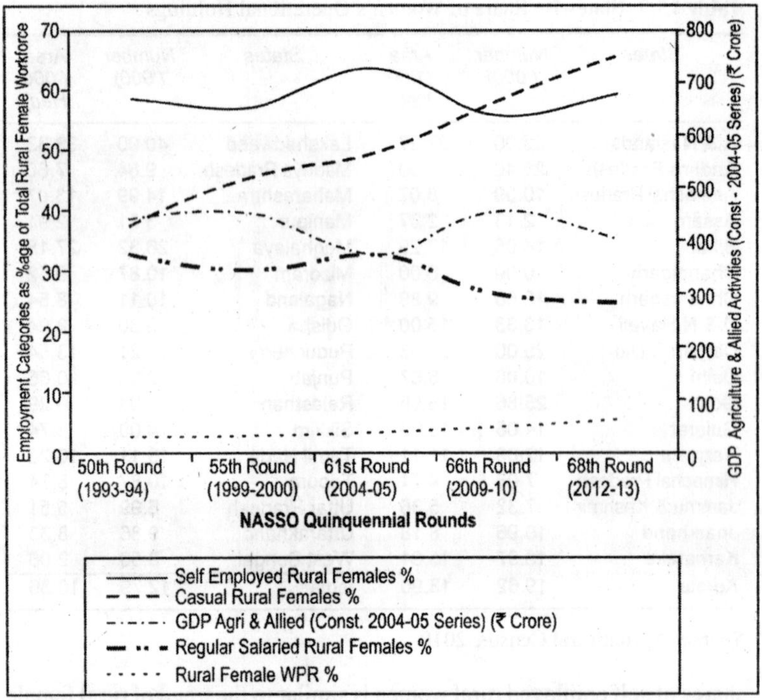

Source: Calculated from NSSO Quinquennial Rounds and Planning Commission Data

Fig. 15.2: Relation between Agricultural Income and Broad Employment Categories

Further, Figure 15.3 also shows that when GDP from agriculture grew at a slower rate between 1999-2000 and 2004-05, there was a steep increase in self-employed women as well as the overall female WPR in rural areas. The slow growth in agricultural income had led to shrinking availability of wage work and compelled workers to eke out subsistence from self-employment. It is argued that rural women had entered self employment ventures to supplement the low household incomes, in response to distress conditions in rural areas (Srivastava and Srivastava, 2010). Just as the steep rise in female agricultural employment during the first half of the 2000s was linked to rural distress, its equally steep decline during the second half of the 2000s was likely to be associated with some improvement in agricultural incomes (Thomas, 2012). However, in the 68th round, women's self employment is seen to be rising in spite of growing agricultural incomes. The reason could be that women find work conditions unsafe or unsuitable and hence feel better if self employed. Further, higher incidences of self employment in the north-eastern and northern hill States also generated an overall increase in self-employed persons especially females in recent years (Figure 15.3).

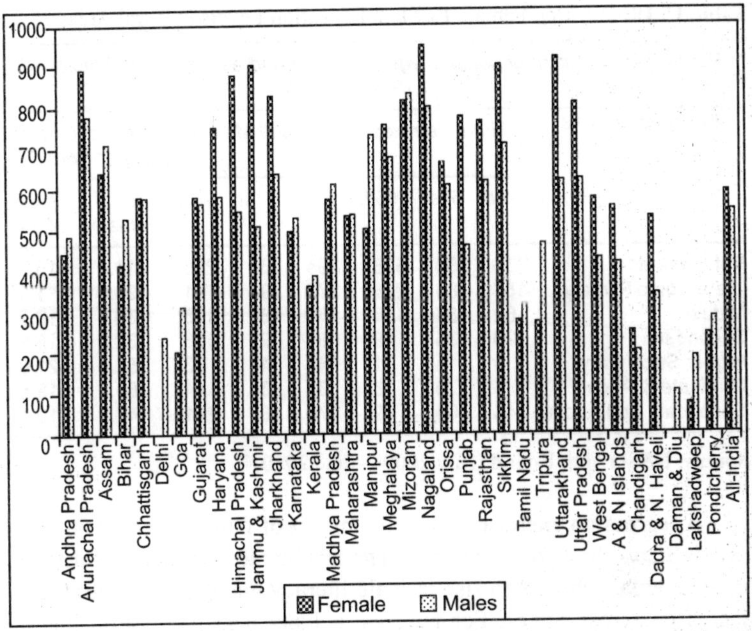

Source: NSSO 68th Round (July 2010-June 2012)
Fig. 15.3: Self Employed Persons per 1000 Population

Education and Workforce Participation Rate

Rural female literacy rate increased from 30.62 per cent in the 1991 Census to 46.14 per cent in 2001 to 58.75 per cent in the 2011 Census. The gender gap also showed a decline over the years. Table 15.10 shows distribution of rural workers across various education levels over several NSS rounds. It is seen that the shares of illiterate working women is the highest among all education levels, but it is declining. The shares of working women in all other education levels are increasing, and the rate of increase per round is seen to be greater than males, though the shares of educated males are much greater than women.

However, despite working women shares in higher education levels (especially secondary and above) increasing, the overall rural work force participation is declining. Further, most of the rural female workforce is either illiterate or having just primary and middle education, which means that there is a preponderance of low skilled women in the rural work force and that is not a good development.

Table 15.10: Working Female *Vs* Male Education Levels in Rural Areas

Per 1000 distribution of persons aged 15 years and above usually employed (PS+SS)

Education Levels	*Rural Females*			*Rural Males*			*Rate of Growth per Round*	
	55th	*61st*	*66th*	*55th*	*61st*	*66th*	*Rural Females*	*Rural Males*
Not Literate	736	664	578	394	338	280	–11.4	–15.7
Literate upto Primary	157	184	226	273	294	281	20.0	1.5
Middle	62	87	106	163	181	198	30.8	10.2
Secondary	28	36	49	94	93	126	32.3	15.8
Higher Secondary	9	14	21	43	46	63	52.8	21.0
Graduate & Above	6	9	16	33	38	44	63.3	15.5
Secondary and Above	44	64	89	170	187	241	42.2	19.1

Source: NSSO 66th Round (July 2009—June 2010)

A regression exercise to see the impact of female literacy on WPR across States shows that, with rise in female literacy female WPR declines in rural areas while with rise in male literacy male WPR in rural areas increases across States. For females, a 1 per cent increase in literacy leads to 0.76 per cent reduction in female work participation that is statistically significant at 10 per cent levels of significance, while a 1 per cent increase in male literacy leads to 0.31 per cent increase in work force participation that is statistically significant at 5 per cent levels of significance (Table 15.11).

From Figure 15.4 it is seen that in case of females, higher literacy in certain States like Kerala (90.80%) did not show high WPR of women. It was a meagre 20.24 per cent. Similarly the lowest rural female workforce participation was recorded in Delhi (9.72%) despite a high literacy rate of 73.10 per cent. However, some states like Nagaland, Chattisgarh, Andhra Pradesh and Himachal Pradesh did show high WPR along with high literacy.

Further, as female literacy rate increases female self employment across States is seen to decline and the relationship is statistically significant at 1 per cent levels of significance. As female literacy rate

Table 15.11: Regression of Male and Female Literacy Rates on WPR across States

Regression of Female Literacy Rate or WPR						*Regression of Male Literacy Rate on RTR*					
Multiple R	0.31					Multiple R	0.35				
R Square	0.10					R Square	0.12				
Adjusted R Square	0.07					Adjusted R Square	0.10				
Standard Error	0.43					Standard Error	0.03				
Observations	35.00					Observations	35.00				
ANOVA						ANOVA					
	df	*SS*	*MS*	*F*	*Significance*		*df*	*SS*	*MS*	*F*	*Significance*
Regression	1.00	0.66	0.66	3.57	0.07	Regression	1.00	0.03	0.03	4.68	0.04
Residual	33.00	6.08	0.18			Residual	33.00	0.20	0.01		
Total	34.00	6.74				Total	34.00	0.23			
	Coefficient	*Standard*	*t-Stat*	*P-value*			*Coefficients*	*Standard*	*t Stat*	*P-value*	
Intercept	6.50	1.68	3.86	0.00		Intercept	2.62	0.64	4.12	0.00	
Literacy Rate (2011 Census)	–0.76	0.40	–1.89	0.07		Literacy rate (2011 Census)	031	0.14	2.16	0.04	

Regressions based on 2011 Census.

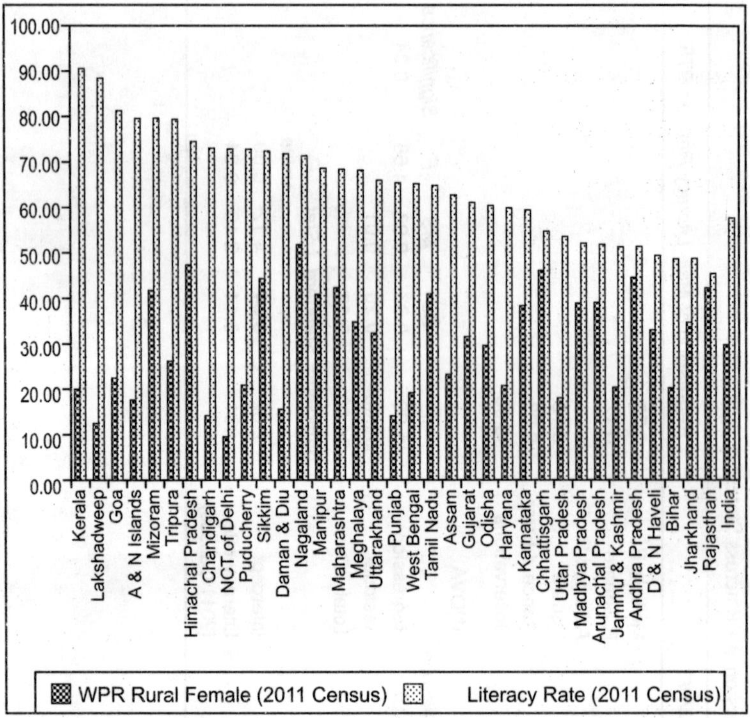

Source: Census of India (2011).

Fig. 15.4: Rural Female WPR and Literacy Rates (%)

increases females engaged in regular salaried jobs across States also increase and this is statistically significant at 1 per cent levels of significance. However female casual labour decreases with rise in literacy across States though the relationship is not statistically significant (Table 15.12).

The inverse relationship between literacy/education levels and female workforce participation rate can be explained by two reasons. The optimistic explanation is that more women are choosing study over work compared to men in rural areas. This is brought out by the fact that in recent years rural women have been migrating for educational purposes, though the proportions are very less compared to males. Secondly there has also been a high rate of growth in various levels of education among rural women compared to men. At the same time it is also important to note that, though a shift to education among the rural women is a positive development, but that does not by itself explain the decline of the work force participation rate. Hence the pessimistic

Table 15.12: Regression of Female Literacy Rate on Self Employment, Regular Salaried Employment and Casual Employment across States

Regression of Female Literacy on Self Employment

Multiple R	0.45				
R Square	0.21				
Adjusted R Square	0.18				
Standard Error	0.51				
Observations	33.00				
ANOVA	*df*	*SS*	*MS*	*F*	*Significance F*
Regression	1.00	2.10	2.10	8.03	0.01
Residual	31.00	8.10	0.26		
Total	32.00	10.19			
	Co-efficients	*Standard Error*	*t Stat*	*P-value*	
Intercept	12.02	2.03	5.92	0.00	
Literacy Rate (2001 Census)	–1.38	0.49	–2.83	0.008	

Regression of Female Literacy on Regular Salaried Employment

Multiple R	0.51				
R Square	0.26				
Adjusted R Square	024				
Standard Error	0.97				
Observation	35.00				
ANOVA	*df*	*SS*	*MS*	*F*	*Significance F*
Regression	1.00	11.10	11.10	11.70	0.002
Residual	33.00	31.30	0.95		
Total	34.00	42.40			
	Co-efficients	*Standard Error*	*t Stat*	*P-value*	
Intercept	-8.59	3.82	-2.25	0.03	
Literacy Rate (2001	3.14	0.92	3.42	0.002	

Regression of Female Literacy on Casual Employment

Multiple R	0.02				
R Square	0.00				
Adjusted R Square	–0.03				
Standard Error	1.21				
Observations	34.00				
ANOVA	*df*	*SS*	*MS*	*F*	*Significance F*
Regression	1.00	0.02	0.02	0.01	0.92
Residual	32.00	46.87	1.46		
Total	33.00	46.89			
	Co-efficients	*Standard Error*	*t Stat*	*P-value*	
Intercept	5.64	4.78	1.18	0.25	
Literacy Rate (2001 Census)	–0.12	1.15	–0.10	0.92	

Regressions based on 2011 Census

explanation is that women find work conditions unsafe or unsuitable. Unemployment rates for both men and women in rural areas increased to 1.7 per cent in the the 68th NSS round. But an alternative data source, i.e., the second employment and unemployment survey conducted by the Labour Bureau at the same time as the 68th round found the unemployment rate for rural women (4.1%) to be nearly double that for men (2.4%), thereby lending credence to the pessimistic explanation.

Further, being literate may not positively influence a woman's participation in work, but for women who are in the workforce, literacy and education is the most important determinant of better quality and better paid work, especially non-agricultural work. As seen in Table 15.13, women with higher education levels get paid better, especially in non-agricultural work compared to women with lower education levels.

Female Wages and Workforce Participation Rate

Wage rates are increasing over the years for both males and females, however male wages have been consistently higher than female wages for both regular and casual work (Table 15.14). The difference in male wages over female wages has been highest for regular employees (nearly 60%) over the years. This is followed by casual labour in works other

Table 15.13: Average Wage Earnings (Rs) Per Day received by Regular Rural Female Wage Employees of Age 15-59 Years by Industry of Work and Broad Education Category

Sector of Work	*Not Literate*	*Literate and up to Middle*	*Secondary and Higher Secondary*	*Diploma/ Certificate*	*Graduate and Above*
Agriculture	71.63	65.02	134.15	821.43	145.21
Mining and Quarrying	219.85	47.40	348.84	—	—
Manufacturing 1	50.65	61.47	102.62	—	281.47
Manufacturing 2	71.55	89.53	119.31	61.14	392.57
Electricity, Gas and Water	142.86	417.90	337.17	336.89	568.72
Construction	147.85	101.41	278.39	357.14	717.14
Trade	33.77	74.49	61.08	69.56	83.15
Transport and Storage etc.	130.22	143.41	133.44	614.72	349.74
Services 1	428.57	218.49	186.76	144.30	207.48
Services 2	66.09	84.38	159.76	310.82	288.52
Private HHs. with emp persons	55.35	75.37	82.79	—	96.47
Others	—	—	43.43	—	—
All	**65.47**	**80.32**	**151.54**	**291.01**	**285.98**

Source: NSSO 66th Round (July 2009 to June 2010).

Table 15.14: Daily Wages Received by Casual Labourers and Regular Wage/Salaried Employees of Age 15-59 Years in Rural Areas

(in rupees)

NSSO Quinquennial Rounds	*Regular Wage/ Salaried Employees*		*Casual Labour in Works other than Public Works*		*Casual Labour in Public Works other than MNREGA Public Works*		*Casual Labour in MNREGA Public Works*	
	Males	*Females*	*Males*	*Females*	*Males*	*Females*	*Males*	*Females*
50 (July 1993-June 1994)	58.48	34.89	23.18	15.33	24.65	18.52	—	—
55 (July 1999-June 2000)	127.32	114.01	45.48	29.39	49.04	39.48	—	—
61 (July 2004-June 2005)	144.93	85.53	55.03	34.94	65.33	49.19	—	—
66 (July 2009-June 2010)	249.15	155.87	101.53	68.94	98.33	86.11	90.93	87.20
68 (July 2010–June 2012)	322.28	201.56	149.32	103.28	127.39	110.62	112.46	101.97

Source: NSSO Quinquennial Rounds

than public works, where the differential is about 50 per cent. The wage differentials have been around 21 per cent in case of casual labour in public works other than MNREGA public works, followed by around 7 per cent wage differential in casual labour in MNREGA public works. Further the wages of regular salaried workers (average of males and females) is the highest (nearly ₹ 261.92) while that in MNREGS is the lowest (nearly ₹ 107.21). Thus, contrary to popular perception, the employment guarantee scheme (MNREGA) has not been the key driver of higher wages (Aiyar, 2012).

Table 15.15: Average Daily Wage Rate Differentials for Agricultural and Non-Agricultural Occupations in Rural Areas during September 2012 across States and Sex

(in rupees)

States	*Agriculture*			*Non-Agriculture*		
	Males	*Females*	*% Difference (Males over Females)*	*Males*	*Females*	*% Difference (Males over Females)*
Andhra Pradesh	179.24	136.13	31.67	194.20	123.03	57.85
Assam	140.22	121.82	15.11	191.93	110.77	73.27
Bihar	134.73	117.17	14.98	171.04	123.03	39.02
Gujarat	132.79	117.32	13.18	194.75	104.71	85.99
Haryana	225.88	214.82	5.15	266.23	222.20	19.82
Karnataka	169.96	110.16	54.29	174.38	89.33	95.21
Kerala	465.51	267.83	73.81	473.62	266.00	78.05
Madhya Pradesh	120.83	105.98	14.01	137.01	89.63	52.87
Maharashtra	180.10	118.74	51.67	192.25	92.02	108.92
Manipur	174.50	160.06	9.02	210.48	125.56	67.63
Meghalaya	135.85	91.11	49.11	170.80	91.67	86.32
Orissa	148.78	131.58	13.07	181.43	128.07	41.67
Rajasthan	213.03	169.72	25.51	268.20	205.00	30.83
Tamil Nadu	231.36	139.36	66.02	332.34	159.76	108.02
Uttar Pradesh	146.20	126.26	15.80	206.55	122.31	68.87
West Bengal	175.53	147.46	19.03	174.69	126.23	38.39
All India	**167.87**	**128.94**	**30.19**	**193.82**	**112.72**	**71.96**

Source: Wage Rates in Rural India (http://labourbureau.gov.in/Wage_Rate_Sept2012.pdf)

The average daily wage rates are much lower for females compared to males when both agricultural and non-agricultural occupations are compared (Table 15.15). It may be assumed that as proportion of illiterate women in the rural workforce is very high compared to men and the share of better educated men in the rural workforce is much higher than women[4], hence low female wages could also indicate that women in rural areas are subject to discrimination, including job-typing that pushes them into low-paying jobs in both agricultural and non-agricultural sectors.

At the all India level, for all agricultural operations average male daily wages were higher than their female counterparts by 30.19 per cent (Table 15.15). Across States it is seen that the highest wage differential is in Kerala (73.81%) followed by Tamil Nadu (66.02%) and Karnataka (54.29%). The lowest wage differential is seen in Haryana (5.15%) followed by Manipur (9.02%) and Madhya Pradesh (14.01%). In case of non-agricultural operations average male daily wages were higher than their female counterparts by 71.96 per cent. Across States it is seen that the highest wage differential is in Maharashtra (108.92%) followed closely by Tamil Nadu (108.02%) and Karnataka (95.21%). The lowest wage differential is seen in Haryana (19.82%) followed by Rajasthan (30.83%) and West Bengal (38.39%). Further, it is also seen that male non-agricultural wages are greater than their agricultural wages by 15.46 per cent. The former was higher in all the States. However, female non-agricultural wages are lesser than their agricultural wages by 12.58 per cent. The former are lesser than the latter in all the States excepting Bihar, Haryana, Rajasthan and Tamil Nadu.

Surprisingly, higher rural wages does not seem to be attracting more women into the workforce. As observed from Table 15.16, a 1 per cent increase in daily wages across States leads to 0.41 per cent reduction in female work, while a 1 per cent increase in male daily wages across States leads to a 0.02 per cent increase in their work force participation. However both types of relationships are not statistically significant.

Thus, the biggest problem derived from the study appears to be the lack of adequate working women in rural areas. As said earlier the optimistic explanation is that rural women are gradually choosing to study instead of working. The pessimistic explanation, as high unemployment rates among women suggests is that, women find work conditions unsafe or unsuitable. However, further research needs to be done on some of the assumptions used in this study, such as the nature of self employment, job types and also the availability (number) of jobs for rural women.

Table 15.16: Regression of Male and Female Agriculture Wages on their WPR across States

Regression of Female Agriculture Wages on WPR

Multiple R	0.33				
R Square	0.11				
Adjusted R Square	0.04				
Standard Error	0.33				
Observations	16.00				
ANOVA	df	SS	*MS*	*F*	*Significance F*
Regression	1.00	0.18	0.18	1.68	0.22
Residual	14.00	1.53	0.11		
Total	15.00	1.71			
	Coefficients	*Standard Error*	*t Stat*	*P-value*	
Intercept	5.42	1.55	3.-19	0.00	
Fem Agr Wages	–0.41	0.31	–1.30	0.22	

Regression of Male Agriculture Wages on WPR

Multiple R	0.09				
R Square	0.01				
Adjusted R Square	–0.05				
Standard Error	0.09				
Observations	20.00				
ANOVA	*df*	SS	*MS*	*F*	*Significance F*
Regression	1.00	0.00	0.00	0.13	0.72
Residual	18.00	0.14	0.01		
Total	19.00	0.14			
	Coefficients	*Standard Error*	*t Stat*	*P-value*	
Intercept	3.87	0.32	12.02	0.00	
Male Agr Wages	0.02	0.06	0.37	0.72	

Note: Regressions based on 2011 Census and Labour Bureau data.

Conclusion

The main conclusions that emerge from this study are that India boasts of rapid rural economic growth, but women's participation in the rural workforce is on the decline. Share of women workers in agriculture is higher compared to men, though the shares are declining gradually and moving towards non-farm activities too. However, non-farm employment in rural areas is still heavily biased towards male workers. The declining female work force participation in agriculture is an indication of economic growth, as with economic growth, one would expect a shift in employment from agriculture to other sectors. However the low share of women in secondary and tertiary sectors and the feminization of the agricultural workforce, with a preponderance of low skilled women inspite of implementation of MNREGA is a negative sign. Further, even within other sectors most rural women are engaged in manufacturing and construction activities and movement of women into better formal jobs like professional, scientific and technical activities is weak.

Most female migration in India is within the rural to rural stream and is driven mainly by marriage though latest data shows that rural women are also migrating for educational purposes (though the proportions are very less), and this is a welcome step.

In India majority women still do not have ownership or control over land resources and the control is inversely related to land size, which means that women's control over land decrease as landholding size increase. This inverse relationship could be because in small and marginal holdings men tend to outmigrate more leaving the women folk behind to operate the land. However, cultural and social factors in India are also responsible for lesser control of women on land.

Women are still largely self-employed and to some extent are employed as casual labour in agriculture. There seems to be a direct relationship between rural distress and female self employment as well as the overall female WPR, which means that rural women tend to work under distress conditions. However, in the recent years, women's self employment is seen to be rising in spite of growing agricultural incomes. The reason could be that women find work conditions unsafe or unsuitable and hence feel better if self employed.

Rural female literacy rates and education levels have been rising over the years, but it does not seem to have a direct relationship with female work force participation, however, educated women tend to work in better paid non-agricultural work.

Rural wages have been increasing over the years, though female wages have been consistently lower than male wages both in agriculture and non-agriculture. Lower female wages compared to men could indicate discrimination and employment in low paid jobs. Regular salaried wages have been the key driver of higher wages in rural areas and not MNREGA. Despite rising wages rural women are not attracted to the workforce.

Female workforce participation rate is declining possibly because rural women tend to work only during distress conditions, or may be they are gradually choosing study over work, or women are finding work conditions unsafe or unsuitable which is a matter of grave concern. The primary focus should, therefore, be to create jobs that would enable women to join the work force. Jobs should be created such that they promote economic growth and at the same time provide work-life balance, maternity protection, flexible working arrangements and better access to credit and skill development. Ultimately, the goal is not merely to increase female work force participation, but to provide opportunities for decent work that will, in turn, contribute to the economic empowerment of women.

Notes

1. Categories of self-employed persons as defined by NSSO are as follows:
   (i) **Own-account workers**: Those self-employed persons who operated their enterprises on their own account or with one or a few partners and who, during the reference period, by and large, ran their enterprise without hiring any labour. They could, however, have had unpaid helpers to assist them in the activity of the enterprise;
   (ii) **Employers:** Those self-employed persons who worked on their own account or with one or a few partners and, who, by and large, ran their enterprise by hiring labour; and
   (iii) **Helpers in household enterprise:** Those self-employed persons (mostly family members) who were engaged in their household enterprises, working full or part time and did not receive any regular salary or wages in return for the work performed. They did not run the household enterprise on their own but assisted the related person living in the same household in running the household enterprise.
2. See Table 15.2.
3. See Table 15.8.
4. See Table 15.10.

References

Aiyar, Swaminathan A. (2013): 'Rising Rural Wage May Boost UPA's Chances', *Economic Times*, 7th July 2013.

GoI (1991, 2001, 2011): Census of India, Ministry of Home Affairs, Office of the Registrar General and Census Commissioner, India.

GoI (2012): 'Report on Employment and Unemployment Survey 2011-12', Labour Bureau, Ministry of Labour and Employment, Chandigarh.

GoI, Labour Bureau http://labourbureau.gov.in

GoI, Planning Commission http://planningcommission.gov.in

FAO–Gender and Land Rights Database http://www.fao.org/gender/landrights/en/

FAO (2011): 'Women in Agriculture–Closing the Gender Gap for Development', *The State of Food and Agriculture 2010-2011*.

Desai, Sonalde Desai (2013): 'When Incomes Grow, But Jobs Elude', *Indian Express*, 3rd July 2013.

Himanshu (2011): 'Employment Trends in India–A Re-examination', *Economic and Political Weekly*, September 10, Vol. XLVI, No. 37.

Jha, Brajesh (2005): 'Employment, Wages and Productivity in Indian Agriculture', *Institute of Economic Growth*, Delhi.

Mahapatro, Sandhya Rani (2010): 'The Changing Pattern of Internal Migration in India Issues and Challenges', *Working Paper, Institute of Social and Economic Change*, Bangalore.

National Sample Survey Organisation, Various Quinquennial Rounds.

Srivastava, Nisha and Ravi Srivastava (2009): 'Women, Work and Employment Outcomes in Rural India', *Economic and Political Weekly*, July 28, Vol. XLV, No. 28.

Thomas, Jayan Jose (2012): 'India's Labour Market during the 2000s—Surveying the Changes', *Economic and Political Weekly*, December 22, Vol. XLVII, No. 51.

16

Socio-Economic Impacts of Migration on Women

A Case Study of Odisha (India)

Padmaja Mishra

I

Introduction

Migration is a necessary associate of urbanization, industrialization and economic development. Migration is a social process and gender is a social construct. Individuals are defined largely by their gender roles and take up tasks and responsibilities accordingly in the society. Male and female migration are structured according to their gendered positions and the impacts are also different. A gender perspective on migration is essential to understand these impacts. But, unfortunately, the main theories of migration available in the literature though seemingly gender neutral have focused mostly on male experiences and this neglect of women issues has been reflected in migration policies also. With this background, the following part of this chapter is arranged in four sections. Section 2 gives a brief theoretical exposition of migration literature with special emphasis on gender concerns. Section 3 gives a picture of migration in India and brings out the extent of female migration. Section 4 discusses an empirical study undertaken and lists the major findings and section 5 brings out the concluding observations.

II

A Brief Theoretical Review

Gender insensitiveness in migration literature has led to policy insensitiveness and lack of focus on women migrants' problems and prospects. A theoretical review of migration literature clearly indicates that gender unawareness or insensitiveness can be traced back to historical development of migration models. The push-pull models of migration (Lee; 1966, Thadani and Todaro; 1984) explored both social and economic determinants of migration decisions and had been individualistic and behavioural models. These models predominantly assume that individual migrants act rationally out of economic self interest and migrate in response to higher expected economic benefits. It may be the push of the origin or the pull of the destination. But, the Marxists challenge the individualistic approach and emphasized the structural reasons given by political and other institutions. They emphasized on labour migration as an inevitable consequence of capitalism. With a different sociological and cultural perspective, some theories look into cultural factors behind migration. Recent theories combine both individual motives and the structural factors and describe migration as the result of capital's supremacy over labour and migration as the only option—not a choice of the poor. Unfortunately, these theories lacked any specific focus on women migration as different from male migration experiences and all of these considered migrants as a homogeneous group.

Research in the 1970s exhibited emergence of an inter-disciplinary synthetic framework but carried the legacy of gender unawareness in migration theory. There was a growing ascendancy of a structural perspective which included world systems approach and dual labour market theory approach. These theories in 1980s and 1990s started including women into migration analysis, but as an extra variable only, not as a core issue. Focus on the relations of production ignored gender differentials in migratory behaviour (Chant, 1992; Ellis, *et al.*, 1996). Migration was still looked as sex undifferentiated response to capitalistic developments. Also, women's presumed passivity has led to their near invisibility in migration theory and statistics. Gender as a core organizing principle underlying the process and product of migration is considered only recently when women migrants occupied an increased share in international migration. Recent migration statistics and research literature recognizes women migrants as they are now an important component of international migration representing nearly half of the total migrants (Joly, *et al.*, 2003; UN, 1998). Gender analysis in migration studies cuts across all disciplines and is seen as 'an essential tool for unpicking the migration process' (Wright, 1995; Sinclair, 1998).

Accordingly ILO recognizes (2001),

> 'It is the gender segregated labour market as well as sexual division of labour in the household that determine gender-selective migration flows. Stated simply, men and women follow different migration patterns (e.g., they migrate for different reasons) because they do different things....".

Though for a long time, individuals were considered as the only relevant units for migration analysis, the new economics of migration emphasizes family (household) as the appropriate unit of analysis. According to Stark, 'even though the entities that engage in migration are often individual agents, there is more to labour migration than an individual optimizing behaviour. Migration by one person can be due to, fully consistent with, or undertaken by a group of persons, such as the family' (Stark; 1991). Migration is, therefore, viewed as a form of portfolio diversification by the families and the costs and benefits are shared by the family members. However, the ability to migrate in the first place and the ability to cope with after-migration situation and to use it as a livelihood strategy is affected by the degree of social and economic inclusion or exclusion. Women's exclusion is multidimensional as their subordinated gender position is associated with low income, low political presence and so on, which cuts across class and caste. The pattern of land holding, land rights, access to all kinds of resources including access to rural labour market, etc., are extremely important for determining women's position as potential migrants or as actual migrants—active or passive. As there is huge gender gap in the inclusion/ exclusion dimensions, socio-economic impacts of migration on women is different from that on men. Therefore, the following three interactive facts (Radcliff, S., 1991) are crucial in understanding women issues in migration:

1. There is gender differentiated access to resources,
2. Households have a crucial role to play in the process of negotiating resources and migration decisions, and
3. Within the households domain, gender interacts with other dimensions of inequality and identity such as age, marital status

to create conditions which directly and indirectly influence mobility and movement.

The studies available on female migration have discussed both the positive and negative impacts of out migration on women. According to some studies, increasing availability of opportunities for women migrants in labour market has resulted in their deskilling and devaluation of women labour in general (Connel, *et al.*, 1976; Fernandez-Kelly, 1983; Khoo, 1984; Rao, 1986). In this context, the oppressive situation at the destination place has been highlighted in the literature (Morokvasic, 1983; Phizlackea, 1996, Andal; 2000). Morokvasik (1983), discusses four levels of oppression of migrant women on the basis of (i) working class, (ii) gender,(iii) migrant minority group, and (iv) accepting oppression as their fate. The main reasons cited are given as women labour belonging to working class and available as cheaper labour with less bargaining power. The main reasons cited are given as women labour belonging to working class and available as cheaper labour with less bargaining power. On the other hand, positive impacts are also noted in many studies in context of female migration in South Asia, Thailand and China where women gain more than the risk and loss involved (Kabeer, 2000; Chantavanich, 2001; Gamburd, 200; and Hugo, 1993).

III

Female Migration in India

Female migrants constitute 218 million while there are 91 million male migrants in India according to 2001 Census. While migrants constitute around 30 per cent of the total population, out of the total female population, 45 per cent are migrants (corresponding figure for male is 18%). While male migration is reported to be mostly motivated by economic opportunities, female migration is considered to have been provoked more by social: such as marriage and other family related reasons, rather than economic opportunities (Bose, 1973; Nangia *et al.*, 1990). According to NSS survey on Migration in India (2007-08, 64th Round) 91 per cent of rural migrants have "marriage' as the main reason and the corresponding figure for urban females is 61 per cent. Liberalisation and globalization have added more of economic dimensions to female migration due to changes in labour market structure, segmentation and new opportunities. Increased rural-urban disparities and emergence of different kinds of gender segregated labour markets have changed the notion of women as dependent passive migrants. In this context, Table 16.5 hints at the feminization of internal migration in India.

Table 16.1: Internal Migration in India (1971-2001)

Census Year	*No. of migrants (in million)*		
	M	*F*	*T*
1971	49.6 (19)	110 (43.1)	159.6 (30.6)
1981	59.2 (17.6)	142.4 (43.9)	201.6 (30.3)
1991	61.1 (14.6)	164.8 (41.2)	225.9(27.4)
2001	90.7(17.5)	218.7 (44.6)	309.4 (30.6)

Note: The figures in the parentheses shows the percentage of migrants to their respective total population.

Source: Census of India (1971 to 2001).

The various factors responsible for increasing feminization of migration have been ascribed to changes in labour market due to globalisation, increase in rural poverty and agrarian crisis, etc. (Sundari, 2004; Arya, *et al*., 2005). However, gender insensitive methodology of collecting and presenting migration statistics, either by Census or by NSS surveys do not yield much specific information women specific issues. A literature survey shows various reasons varying from economic, to cultural to social to structural/environmental reasons and many more. In case of female migrants, though marriage still remains the single most important (socio-cultural) reason for migration, economic factors are also increasingly contributing (Shanti, 1991; Sundari and Rukmini, 1998; Ghosh, 2002).

Table 16.2 below gives the all-India scenario of the percentage distribution of migration by reasons and shows the male female differences.It shows that while marriage is still the single most important reason behind female migration, employment reasons are gaining strength.

IV

Some Micro Level Observations

The feminist view on gender issues in migration has raised questions relating to patriarchy and its continuity before and after women migration?

Table 16.2: Percentage Distribution of Migrations by Reason in India (1991-2001)

Reasons for migration	*Male*		*Female*	
	1991	*2001*	*1991*	*2001*
Employment	30.00	36.78	3.67	4.19
Business	6.33	2.55	0.98	0.33
Education	11.31	8.49	2.54	2.16
Marriage	2.20	1.66	59.76	58.80
Natural calamities	0.80	N.A.	0.33	N.A.
Moved with household	29.98	16.97	21.64	21.50
Others	19.38	16.97	11.08	8.22

Source: Census of India—1991 and 2001.

How does patriarchy shape women's ability to migrate, the timing and destination and how does patriarchy reconstructs itself after migration are some of the valid questions to be answered as it helps to understand the socio-economic impacts of migration on women. It can be argued that for women migrants both the causes and the consequence are to be considered at three levels–individual, familial and societal.

Does outmigration expand women's capabilities, freedom, entitlements and well-being? Does it empower women by enhancing their active agency in participating in the society and as well as in economic arena? Some empirical micro level observations have been made as a part of the present study to find an answer.

The empirical study has been undertaken in the State of Odisha where rural-urban differences in per capita income are high with 49 per cent people in rural Odisha being poor. For the study, two different sample studies have been undertaken. One Block (Sorada) in the Ganjam district has been selected to study the impact of male migration on female members of the family back home and the capital city of Bhubaneswar has been chosen to study the condition female migrants from different villages. Ganjam is selected because of maximum male outmigration from the district and Bhubaneswar is selected for being the city having maximum intra State migrants. Total 200 number of women have been selected for the study equally divided in both the categories.

The first sample study on impacts of male outmigration on women has been carried out in Sorada Block of Ganjam district. The district is well known for maximum male outmigration in the State and most people go to Surat, Ahmedabad as industrial workers and also go to Kerala as construction workers. Some of them also go to Gulf countries. The obvious reason is economic pull of the destinations and huge expected earning differential between the home villages and the destinations. The families left behind are mostly *de facto* female headed.

The second sample consists of 100 women migrants selected from two major slum areas of Bhubaneswar. 91 of the women interviewed are married and 9 are unmarried. The median age group is 30-40. 51 of them belong to scheduled caste, 30 belong to scheduled tribe, 11 belong to OBC and the rest 8 respondents belong to general caste. It is observed that almost all of them are illitearte with only 5 per cent having some schooling. Many studies point out that female migrants are from poorest section with low level of education and 2001 Census shows that around 50 per cent of rural women migrants are illiterate. Those illiterate and unskilled women actually take up any employment available in the cities and the probability of getting employment in feminized jobs in domestic sector and other informal sector is quite high. Out of the total 50 women interviewed 32 are found working in households and 14 are in construction sector and 4 are engaged in other service sector such as in crèches/schools and in offices as sweepers.

It seems that migration has moderated and mediated their movement to a higher socio-economic position. Their economic condition has improved and they gain economic independence with 'cash-in-hand'. However, the social costs associated with the gain are also many. What is worrying about their life in the city is lack of access to civic amenities. There is no easy access to safe drinking water, sanitation, cooking fuel, electricity and above all, a secured roof on their head! Out migration has had its repercussions on the labour market outcomes, access to both government and other institutional support networks, access to health and education services, asset accumulation and a whole range of social opportunities. They do not belong to any close knit society any more and have a smaller social circle.

Women migrating for economic reasons expect lower unemployment rate and higher income. However, socio-economic conditions go much beyond employment and earning. The quality of employment and the quality of social life need to be captured as multidimensional concepts. Migration might have determined the dynamics of change in their socio-economic status through factors like asset base, earnings and remittances, networks and institutional support. Individual cases confirm that the means, motivations and the migration strategy adopted make a lot of difference. If women migration is seen as a traditional modernity continuum, then women are supposed to break free from their traditional gender roles and move to emancipation and empowerment. This has actually happened to some extent as evident from the sample studies, but combined with some losses in socio-cultural capital they had at their origin along with some other new risks and responsibilities.

The major findings derived from the study can be summarised as follows:

1. Male outmigration has mostly resulted in female headed households in rural areas. The economic benefits of male outmigration on female family members completely depends on the amount, frequency and mode of remittances. If the *de facto* female household head receives the remittances and has the authority over that a huge amount of socio-economic benefit is derived. The women feel empowered and the expenditure on food and on children's health and education improved. However, the amount of remittances are found to have been not very high in our sample study and also irregular in frequency which leaves the women disempowered with insecurity and burden of poverty.
2. The sample findings show that for households with remittances (average ₹ 3,000 per month) socio-economic conditions have improved with savings and asset creations such as consumer durables like two wheelers, TV, cell phones, etc. House repair and maintenance have also improved. But, the responsibilities of the women have increased manifold with children and old people left behind with them. In households with meagre and infrequent remittances, work burden of women have increased to make both ends meet.
3. On the other hand, the women migrants in the city find themselves economically empowered if they are employed. Most of the respondents say that their economic condition has improved and they gain economic independence with 'cash-in-hand'. Expenditure on health and education is found to have increased due to increase in women's earnings.
4. There has been some amount of skill underutilisation by female migration. The female skills acquired in forestry, fishery, animal husbandry and agriculture back home are underutilized. Though there has been some gain in their capabilities due to urban

exposure, skill addition has been an increasing function of the level of education of the women. Most of the women migrants being uneducated, get employed in domestic and construction sector as unskilled daily wagers.

5. The social costs associated with the gain are too many. The period of adjustment at the place of destination has been loaded with lots of stress for the women. Vulneraibility of the women migrants is found to have increased with less of entitlements. Unregulated work conditions in informal sectors have added insecurity to their lives. Debt burden is found to have increased with no credit assurance leading to debt traps. Therefore, exploitation of female migrants is found to be rampant by the employers.

V

Concluding Observations

The above findings leads to the following suggestions for a gender sensitive migration policy to minimize the adverse impacts of migration on women.

1. A proper data/information base be created with a gender oriented design of migration census which has so far been inadequate to capture women experiences.
2. Access to legal rights, public services and social institutions need to be assured as per both practical and strategic gender needs to protect women migrants from socio-political alienation and economic exploitation in insecured, hazardous and low paid jobs.
3. Land rights for women remains a serious concern. Most of the rural women who migrate are found to be landless. The issue need to be tackled both in rural and urban areas.
4. Urban development policies must include rehabilitation policy for migrants. Provision of safety nets in the form of social security must be assured.
5. Informal job markets are to be regulated with pro-women provisions to save them from exploitation by improving their bargaining strength.
6. Women migrants' awareness on their rights, labour laws and training facilities are to be enhanced.

7. Health, sanitation, education and training, child care and old age care facilities are to be, made available and accessible as a part of human rights.
8. More importantly, well designed skill formation among migrant women can help them empowering themselves and deriving sustainable benefits of migration.
9. Government policies for rural development should be more focused towards suitable employment assurance. NREGS has not solved the purpose due to many inherent problems, particularly for women. Agricultural development and related non farm activities require a huge boost in our villages where the women can actually benefit with active economic participation.
10. To sum up, a migration policy integrated into developmental framework is needed for a holistic empowerment of women.

In conclusion, it can be said that migration, especially female migration, is not a social evil as usually perceived. Women will move over geographical space as their mobility increases due to increase in their capabilities. What is needed is a healthy, safe and empowered migration for women for maximizing the potential gains for individuals and the communities. Skill formation and capacity creation among women can place them at a better socio-economic plateau and proactive gender sensitive migration policies can add to that dimension. However, heavy migration out of rural areas due to extreme poverty and lack of economic opportunities are to be redressed by appropriate rural development policies which will bridge the rural-rural and rural-urban gaps. Reducing social and economic vulnerability and enhancing capability for women will reduce forced undesirable migration and will strengthen healthy migration.

References

Arya, S. and A. Roy (2006): *Poverty, Gender and Migration*, New Delhi, Sage Publications.

Bose, Ashish (1973): *Studies in India's Urbanisation, 1901-1971*, New Delhi, Tata McGrw Hill.

Castle, S. and M. Miller (1993): *The Age of Migration*, New York, Guilford Press.

Chant, S. (1997): "Women headed Households", in *Diversity and Dynamics in the Developing World*, Macmillan.

Chant, S. and S. Radcliff (1992): "Migration and Development: The importance of Gender", in Gender and Migration in Developing Countries (ed.), S. Chant, Bellhaven Press, London and New York.

Connel, John (1984): "Studies in Subjugal Women—Migration and Development in the South Pacific", *International Migration Review*, 18(4), 966.

De Haan (2006): "Migration, Gender, Poverty: Family as the Missing Link?' in Arya, S. and A. Roy (eds), Poverty, Gender and Migration, New Delhi, Sage Publications.

Deshinger, P. and Grim, S. (2004): *Voluntary Internal Migration: An Update*, Overseas Development Institute, London.

Ellis, M. *et al.* (1996): "The circular Migration of Pureto Rican Women: Towards a Gendered Explanation" International Migration, 34, 31-64.

Epstein, *et al.* (1998): *Village Voices: Forty Years of Rural Transformation in South India*, New Delhi, Sage Publications.

Fawcett, J. (1989): "Networks, Linkages and Migration Systems", *International Migration Review*, 23, 671-680.

Folbre, N. (1986): "Cleaning House; New Perspective on Household and Development", *Journal of Development Economics*, 22, 5-40.

Garcia, B. (2000): *Women, Poverty and Demographic Change*, New York, Oxford University Press.

Gos, J. and B. Linquist (1995): "Conceptualising International Migration: A Structurist Perspective", *International Migration Review*, 29, 317-351.

Gurreo Sylvia *et al.* (2001): "Women, Gender in Population and Development", Quezon City.

Hugo, G.J. (1993): "Migrant Women in Developing Countries", in Internal Migration of Women in Developing Countries, Proceedings of United Nations.

Kundu, A. (2002): *Globalisation, Inequality and Mobility in Population in India.*

Lee, S. (1966): "A Theory of Migration", *Demography*, 3,47-57.

Lingam, L. (1998): "Locating Women in Migration Studies: An Overview", *The Indian Journal of Social Work*, 59(2): 715-727.

Morokvasic, M. (1983): "Women in Migration: beyond the Reductionist Outlook", in *One Way Ticket: Migration and Female Labour* (ed) A. Phizacklea, Routledge, London, 13-31.

Nagia, S. and Praveen Nangial (1990): "Work Pattern of Female Migrants in Metropolitan cities of India:, *Demography India*, 19 (1): 109-119.

Oishi, N. (2002): *Gender and Migration: An Integrative Approach*, Working Paper No.49, Centre for Comparative Immigration Studies, University of California.

Pandey, D. (1998): "Labour, Employment and Gender Dimensions", *The Indian Journal of Social Work*, 62(1).

Premi, M.K. (1979): "Patterns of Internal Migration of Females in India", Centre for Study of Regional Development, Occasional Paper No. 15, New Delhi.

Radcliff, S.(1986): "Gender Relations, Peasant Livelihood Strategies and

Migration: A Case Study from Cuzco, Peru", *Bulletin of Latin American Research*, Vol. 5 No. 2, pp. 29-47.

Rafiq, A. (2003): "Internal Seasonal Migration, Livelihood and Vulnerability in India", Conference on Migration, Development, Pro-Poor choices in Asia.

Saradamoni, K. (1985): *Crisis in Fishing Industry and Women's Migration: The case of Kerala, in Women and Seasonal Labour Migration*, New Delhi, Sage Publications.

Shanti, K. (1991): "Issues relating to economic Migration of females", *The Indian Journal of Labour Economics*, 34(4), 335-46.

______(2006): "Female Labour Migration in India: Insights from NSSO data, Working Paper No. 4. http:/www.mse.ac.in.

Sharma, U. (1986): *Women's Work, Class and the Urban Household: A Study of Shimla, North India*, New York, Tavistock Publications.

Stark, O. and D. Levhari (1982): "On Migration and Risk in LDCs", *Economic Development and Cultural Change*, 31, 191-196.

UN (1994): "The Migration of Women: Methodological Issue in the Measurement and Analysis of Internal and International Migration," Santo Domingo, Dominican Republic.

17

Socio-Economic Impacts of Outmigration

Susamma Varghese

Introduction

Migration of persons within national borders is far greater in magnitude than migration across international borders. Further migration from rural to urban and semi-urban area is still greater yielding to economic prosperity. Internal migration seems to be increasingly accepted and inevitable in the context of socio-economic growth of individuals and communities and States in general. Therefore, it is absolutely necessary to promote safe migration especially in cases when large numbers of youth, women and other vulnerable groups also have opted to migrate in search of employment opportunities.

The International Labour Organization (ILO) has been dealing with labour migration issues since its inception in ·1919. It has pioneered international Conventions to guide migration policy and protection of migrant workers. (Convention No. 97—Migration for Employment Convention (1949); Convention No. 143—Migrant Workers Convention (1975). All major sectors of the ILO—standards, employment, social protection and social dialogue—work on labour migration within its overarching framework of Decent Work for All. The ILO adopts a rights-based approach to labour migration and promotes tripartite participation in migration policy.

In 2006, the ILO Multilateral Framework on Labour Migration was adopted by the ILO constituents. These non-binding principles and guidelines are a response to widespread demands for practical guidance and action with a view to maximizing the benefits of labour migration for all parties.

Some Statistics on Outmigration

In the Constitution of India the Article (19) gives right to all the citizens to move freely throughout the territory of India; to reside and settle in any part of the territory of India.

- Internal migrants in India constitute a large population.
- 326 million or 28.5 per cent of the population (NSSO 2007-2008).
- This far exceeds the estimates of Indian emigrants (11.4 million) (WB 2011).

Types of Migration: Migration in India is of Two Types

- Long term (permanently migrating for work or living in another place.
- Short term (seasonal/circular–1 to 6 months)/back and forth movement between source and destination.
- Estimates of short term migrants vary from 15 million to 100 million (NSSO 2007-2008.
- Short term migrants generally belong to scheduled caste, scheduled tribe, other backward class, socio-economically deprived groups such as having negligible educational attainment, limited assets and resource deficits.
- Out of total internal migrants 70.7 per cent are women (Census India 2001).
- Marriage is given as the prominent reason for female migration in both the rural and urban areas—91 per cent rural and 61 per cent urban.
- Employment related reasons is given as the prominent reason for male migration in both rural and urban areas—29 per cent rural and 56 per cent urban.
- Although no clear data is available there are about 15 million child migrants in India.
- Source States being Uttar Pradesh, Bihar, Rajasthan, Madhya Pradesh, Andhra Pradesh, Chhattisgarh,. Jharkhand, Orissa, Uttarakhand and Tamil Nadu.
- Destination States: Delhi, Maharashtra, Gujarat, Haryana, Punjab and Karnataka.
- Sectors: Construction, domestic work, textile, brick kilns,

transportation, mines, quarries agriculture, hotel and service sector.

- Remittances have been among the most important impacts of migration in India. There is increasing evidence about the amounts that migrants send home and their effect clearly visible in States like Kerala.
- International migrants on an average send back INR 52,000 and migrants within India remit INR 13,000 monthly.

Impacts of Migration

- Women migrants tend to remit to their home destinations more than men.
- Migration provides an opportunity to escape caste division and restrictive social norms and increased economic opportunities in cities.
- In case of male migration women are empowered and competent with increased interaction in society, including their participation as workers and decision makers of households and also of communities.
- Women become the decision makers on day to day affairs and also on other aspects which otherwise would be the responsibility of male member of the family.
- Handling cash and managing cash itself is a major responsibility taken up by the women, money brings power, respect and self confidence in one's self.
- Women are directly consulted for family matters as well as community issues giving them a separate recognition in the society.
- Migrant men and women bring back to their source areas a variety of skills, innovations and knowledge, known as social remittances, including change in tastes, perception, attitudes, etiquettes along with other serious issues like non-acceptance of low wages and improved knowledge and awareness about workers' rights.
- Evidences reveal that with rising incomes, migrant remittances can encourage investment in human capital formation with increased expenditure on health and education.
- However, some studies point out that some 90 per cent of income

is spent on household consumption goods that shows that remittances lead to limited investments.

- Also some studies reveal that a small share of remittance in rural areas was used for debt repayment as compared to urban areas where savings and investments were a common way of utilizing remittances.

Challenges

In India most of our policies and programmes do not include migration or internal migration as an area of concern. Policies have largely failed in providing any forum of legal or social protection to this vulnerable group of the migrants.

- There is also lack of coherent policy framework, proper enforcement mechanisms, decent working conditions, labour arrangements, has led to inhuman working conditions.
- In cases where the families move as unit along with all the family members and the children the biggest obstacle is access to basic shelter, food, water, health care, education facilities and subsidised food.
- There is a huge proportion of young workers migrating in search of employment and these workers face great difficulties in getting themselves into the mainstream of the local areas and communities.
- Language barrier and other living conditions, life styles in the initial years is very challenging for the migration population.
- At the same time, many migrant labour have no option but to bring their children along thus contributing to child labour and gaps in education and thus possibly further transmitting poverty across generations.
- Lack of inter-State cooperation on migration workers.
- There is a serious data gap on internal migration.
- Harassment of migrant workers is becoming a serious issue, e.g., in Kerala State, now any migrant worker has to get registered with the local police station and migrants feel as if they are looked down on as criminals.
- Migrants have very little or no access to social security/social protection programmes in their destinations States as they are

generally not able to provide the required documents to prove their permanent address and establish their local identity.

- In some instances, migrants may have to return without savings and remitting and even be unable to earn back the investment.
- Banks and access to local banking facility is again a Herculean task for many migrants.
- Migrants are often treated as second class citizen in destination countries with very little or no access to legal rights, public services, lack of political representation.
- Inadequate housing and lack of formal residency rights, low paid, insecure or hazardous work, limited access to State provided facilities like health, education and discrimination.
- Lack of information prior to departure from source and also no support or assistance on arrival at destination.

Steps to be Taken to Make Out Migration Work Beneficial

1. Develop coherent legal and policy framework on migration.
2. Mainstream migration in national development plans and policy documents.
3. Develop universal national minimum social security package covering minimum wage, labour standards and incorporating benefits of social protection and public services for migrant workers.
4. Set up prior and after trainings/briefing sessions/knowledge sharing for migrants to be able to cope with and acclimatize themselves with the demands of the new location and setup.
5. Revise the Inter-State Migrant Workers Act 1979.
6. Conduct detailed country wide mapping of internal migration with local Panchayat.
7. Encourage State-level research institutions.
8. Increase research on sector-wise contribution of migrants in different industries of the economy, including their contribution to GDP and domestic remittances.
9. Create inter-district and inter-State coordination committees.
10. Ensure access to formal banking facilities for migrants to include safe and secure transfer of remittances.

The ILO through some concrete initiatives has assisted the rural migration workers by bringing them into the mainstream of the local communities and system. Some of these initiatives are:

1. **Developing support systems at the source and destination areas for migrant workers through Workers' Information Centres (WICs):**
   Prior to migration the workers are oriented by the trade union organizations and also enrolled as paid members into the trade unions. Further the WIC also provides information and all technical assistance to the workers to be able to access the various social security/protection benefits entitled to them as workers. The Unions provide assistance in linking the paid members into the State run welfare boards. They receive identity cards from the union as well as the State government. Once the workers are enrolled into the welfare boards they are eligible to receive various benefits some of which are as follows: marriage, maternity, child birth, abortion, accident, accident death, natural death, pension, education and higher education schemes, etc. The union basically plays a catalyst role between the workers, the State and the local government in order to assist the migrant workers to be able to access various social protection and welfare schemes. Many a time it so happens that either the male or female worker of the household has migrated from the rural areas to a city or semi-urban sites in search of work, and their children who are back home through the union efforts are able to receive the benefits under the social security schemes through education grant, etc. There have been incidents where the children of migrant workers have applied for higher education like the IAS examinations, engineering and such other courses through the assistance they receive from the various government schemes. Today through the project assistance, the workers have accessed INR 4,20,53,210/-(USD 6,95,325) through social security programmes.
2. **Access to insurance schemes**:
   The migrant workers also through the union receive assistance on group insurance, health insurance and other such insurances which takes care of the health and business aspects, e.g., insurance for agriculture land and crops as a whole, here again the union facilitates by assisting the workers and their families to gather information and follow up on the various insurance

schemes which are useful specially in the event if there is a drought, flood, etc.

3. **Collective group actions for empowerment:**
   The trade unions also facilitate the migrant workers to form collective groups for effective actions. In the village generally the women who are left behind by their spouses are motivated to join self help groups/pressure groups who are on a regular basis trained on various subjects relevant to their day to day affairs and thus motivated to take the lead role in addressing individual and community issues. These issues vary from access to basic amenities like electricity, roads, housing to issues related to minimum wages, MGNREGA, mid day meals, PDS, etc. Savings also has been one of the focus areas of the SHGs. The project facilitated 1,310 groups in accessing INR 1,75,66,100 (USD 2,90,445) amount of loans through various banks and financial institutions. Through the SHG/pressure group activity the women also initiated income generation activities which are taken up as a part time activity done in their spare time but it yielded great benefits both in terms of social and economic gains.

4. **Skills upgradation training:**
   Empowering rural youth youngsters through skills development and skills upgradation who are potential migrants: 343 youth candidates (163 female and 180 male candidates) were enrolled into various short term skills upgrading and training courses, viz., Spinning Tenter-Sider, Computer, Cell Phone repair and service, Electrician, Turner, Mechanic, Driving, A/C Mechanic, and Tailoring and Embroidery. These trainings were undertaken with the support of public/private skills training institutions in the project districts. Providing upgraded skills and government certified degrees has facilitated the rural youth in negotiating better wages and resulting in drawing better incomes.

5. **Ratification of the ILO Core Conventions and the ILO Conventions on Migrant Workers (C97 and C143)**
   The ILO being a standards setting organization has a mandate to ensure the ratification and proper application of what is known as core labour standards which embodies fundamental principles and rights at work to promote decent work. At the same time, there are ILO standards that also aim to serve as basic rights for migrant workers (C97 and C143). ILO member-states have an obligation to respect and adhere to these standards by an act of

ratification and application in national legislation. Employers and workers organizations, being part of the ILO's tripartite structure are encouraged to impress upon their respective governments to honour their commitments towards proper implementation and enforcement of these standards.

Thank you very much for this opportunity and I hope my discussion this morning can contribute to the debates and discussions in this conference.

18

The "Invisible" Workers and their "Needs' Politicisation"

Subsuming Women Home-based Workers' Contribution in the Global Chain of Production

Anamika Priyadarshini

Introduction

UNDP's Human Development Report of 1995, titled "Gender and Development"[1], estimated that 53 per cent of the total working hours in developing countries represented women's contribution. This rate was 51 per cent in industrial countries. Yet, the report noted, women consisted 73 per cent of world's total population living in poverty. Until the 1995's UN Conference on women, held at Beijing, mapping non-monetized contribution of women in the total global output had not emerged as an international concern. This report was an outcome of the first global attempt of recognizing women's non-monetized contributions in the total global output. The Beijing Conference was also an indication of the changing dynamics of post-USSR global economy, committed for an insatiable desire for profit maximization which also implies minimization of production cost and increasing population of surplus labour. One common approach opted for mounting surplus labour production is reconstructing gender identity of the workforce according to the needs of market. Representation of masculinity as "the" worker and femininity as the sub-worker, fit for labour intensive but insignificant work, had been pertinent even in the pre-capitalist context. Various forms of femininities have always symbolized cheap and submissive labour. What distinguishes the post-World War II representation of femininities is its swift dismentalisation and reconstruction as per market needs. Researchers like Leslie Salzinger and Naila Kabeer have made an effort to closely examine these processes of rupturing and reinventing gender identities, orchestrated for increasing profit by demeaning labour and its price. Declining negotiation capacity of labour makes it further susceptible and leaves it with no option but to be subsumed into the grand narrative of the global chain of production. This, in turn, also facilitates concentrated accumulation of capital and power.

Changing global dynamics have had some profound impacts on women workers. In many cases, it challenged traditional patriarchal norms and facilitated women in accessing the world beyond home. Naila Kabeer finds in her study of Bangladeshi factory workers that opportunity to work for a factory allows women workers, whom she calls the "weak winners", to savour the monetary reward of their labour (2000). However, in most of the cases, these "weak winners" reach to the stage of becoming paid labourer after being dispossessed from their traditional means of subsistence, already jeopardized by the global trade policies (Gore, 2000: 791). The traditional sector seldom acknowledges women's contribution in the economy. Nonetheless, it is usually not inspired by Fordist[2] definition of gender roles that recognizes man as the breadwinner and women as the homemaker. In the traditional sector, women play a crucial role in production processes along with their children and male counterparts. Despite past five-six hundred years' experience of rapid progression through colonization, modernization and development, majority of the global workforce still belong to the traditional sector, also synonymous to informal and unorganized sector in most of the cases.

One of the groups of informal sector workers is home-based workers who were often referred as "invisible" workers until the turn of the millennium. They work in the global chain of production without being part of any factory, swetshop or free trade zone. They work at home. Unlike domestic workers, homemakers/housewives and other groups working at home, home-based workers produce marketable or saleable goods. Their skill as manufacturers makes them more prepared and desirable for the corporations interested in skilled manufacturer who could work at home without being on company's payroll. This article is about home-based workers. The article, by referring the example of Bhagalpur's silk spinners, a group of home-based women workers in India, intends to analyse the challenges faced by women workers' organisation in underscoring the contributions of "invisiblised" workers. The article also attempts to explore the factors that might have obstructed Indian women workers' movement in conducting a national level campaign for home-based workers' mapping, a basic step to recognize this "invisible" part of the workforce. This project becomes specially crucial in the backdrop of International Labour Organization's (ILO) finding that labour force participation rate for women fell from over 37 per cent in 2004-05 to 29 per cent in 2009-10 in India (ILO, 2013). There are ample evidences that establish Indian women's active engagement in both farm and non-farm production processes and they bear larger burden of work than man. Nevertheless, the official statistics reflect a contradictory picture. An important research question in this context could be what obstructed the official statistical mechanism and the women workers' organizations, which seemed to be determined to "visibilise" the "invisible" labour force at the turn of the millennium, in underscoring the size of these workers? The article, by using a case study of Bhagalpur's silk spinners, who were participants of my Masters thesis, and the concept of "three discourse" suggested by Nancy Fraser, attempts to understand the challenges of women's organizations working with home-based workers (Fraser, 2008).

The Invisible Silk Spinners of the Silk City

The silk spinners of Bhagalpur, also known as the silk city of India, are crucial for many reasons. They are women home-based workers from a minority community living below the poverty line in the impoverished State of Bihar. All these identities represent layers of subjugation, which manifest their status as a marginalized group of home-based workers. This article unravels how home-based women workers are not only "invisible" from the statistics of workers but also from the common perception of workforce. This section reflects Bhagalpur silk spinners' gradual marginalisation and "invisiblisation" from the economy and society. I conducted my research with silk spinners of Bhagalpur in the summer of 2005 and revisited the research participants in 2006, 2009 and 2012[3]. Situation of silk weavers was an important issue of concern and stories of their vulnerable condition were quite apparent in the local newspaper of Bhagalpur. However, it was difficult to find any specific news on the spinners. Spinners' striking absence in the neighbourhoods where I used to work with them in early 2000s was a crucial finding of my Masters' thesis. Things seemed to have drastically changed since the last decade of twentieth century, especially after the turn of the millennium. This preliminary work of silk production was becoming more and more uncommon in the city. Spinning was now mainly done in the villages by the wives of the weavers and their contribution was concealed as an unaccounted part of weaving process. Even in the villages, the wives of some weavers made threads for weaving and they did it during "free time" so they did not considered it a "work" done for living. The word "spinner" has become a silent letter in the production of silk clothes. Though preliminary work of spinning was never considered important, it was not an unfamiliar work. The subsequent section attempts to explore how this work, which once was recognized by Gandhi as a tool to promote self-dependence among Indians, became "invisible."

Spinners, who were participants of my research, identified development projects and modernization as crucial factors behind their economic deterioration. Deforestation, which made cocoon rearing difficult, was registered as the first devastating influence of development by my research participants. Businessmen purchased good cocoons at a cheaper rate from the neighbouring States whereas poor weavers and spinners could not afford to buy good cocoons. The second setback for the spinners came with the liberalization of Indian economy in 1990. The impact of the liberalization and the Uruguay Round (1986-94), which led to the removal of import restrictions on many commodities including textiles, are visible on the lives of the participants (Chatterjee and Mohan, 1993: 96-99). According to an agreement with the World Trade Organization, India had to remove restrictions for a large number of silk and textile products after 1990 (Ministry of Textile, Government of India, 1991). This led to an inflow of silk yarn and clothing from other Asian countries, especially China and Korea. Now all one needed to buy imported yarn was money and a licence. But poor spinners, who were not able to rear cocoons because of deforestation, were also not able to afford the application fees required for getting the licence. Besides, many of them found it difficult to deal with the official procedure of getting licence. Consequently, they lost access to raw material. There was a steep decline in the demand of hand spun yarn as the imported yarn was cheaper and more durable[4]. Silk spinners were finding it difficult to survive by depending on their traditional skill. It was difficult to find spinners in the city in 2005, during my field research, whereas only five-six years ago they were visible in some pockets of the city. Decrease in the demand for hand spun silk led the spinners to seek for other livelihood opportunities. However, those who had no other skill or option than spinning had to settle for an extremely low wage and vulnerable working conditions.

There were also independent units of finishing and dyeing in the city. It was in the form of small scale and cottage industry. Slowly the whole process of silk making shifted in the hands of a few businessmen who could afford to establish a complete unit of silk production. Rich businessmen usually purchase bulks of good cocoon from the neighbouring States of Madhya Pradesh and Jharkhand where it is cheaper. Spinners and weavers get wages for spinning and weaving. The silk business is being centralized and monopolized. Spinners, weavers and small businessmen believe that things changed drastically after the 1990. Many of my research participants consider communal riot as an important reason whereas all of them viewed influx of imported silk as the most important reason that helped powerful businessmen to capture the market. Rich businessmen were able to expand their production units in Bhagalpur and even outside. Some of them had dyeing and polishing units in NOIDA (Uttar Pradesh), which is close to the international airport of New Delhi and also to the main market of India. This enables them in responding to the demand of national and international markets and thereby also in occupying maximum space in the industry. On the contrary, the share of small businessmen, dyers, weavers and spinners is diminishing and they are left with no other option but to work for the powerful businessmen. In this situation, it is difficult for the feminine work of spinning to secure space in the market and maintain its identity as a work.

Needs Politicization in the Colonial Context

Nancy Fraser, in her article "Struggle over Needs: Outline of a Socialist-Feminist Critical Theory of Late Capitalist Political Culture" (1998), proposes a framework of three discourses for classifying the "needs talk" in contemporary societies. Fraser's first discourse is "Oppositional discourse" in which needs are politicized "from below". The second refers to the response of rearticulating, reframing and legitimizing the oppositional needs. Fraser calls it "reprivatisation discourse". The third discourse, the "expert discourses", which links popular movements to the State, emerges from the "oppositional" and "reprivatisational" discourse. I could not find a better way than to refer to Fraser's model for understanding the limitations of Indian women workers' movement in underscoring home-based workers and to analyze the significance of these workers' "invisibility" in the contemporary world order (1998: 10). The sequel progression of the "three needs discourse" also offers an opportunity to understand the significance of historicity for a group that is not only going through a process of "ahistoricisation" but also being alienated from their existential reality as workers.

Operational discourse that refers to needs' politicization from the "below", is the first in the list of three discourses of Fraser's model. In India, women's needs were first politicized during the colonial regime. Women's issues, like, *Sati*[5], girls education, child marriage, widow remarriage, etc., got momentum during India's first national movement, the *Punarjagaran* (reawakening) movement. However, customary norms like *purdah* (veil) restricted women to participate in this nineteenth century movement. The main paradox of *Punarjagaran* movement in the context of Nancy Fraser's theory of "need politicization" is that women's needs were being politicized by upper caste men with an objective to counter colonizers' condescending approach towards Indian culture and, therefore, it was not an organic process of needs' politicization from the below. Although it was not women but the culture which was at stake, women's vulnerable condition emerged as the central theme of *Punarjagaran* movement (Mani, 1990: 122-24). The first discourse of Fraser's model does not seem to be applicable in a context where feudal system was not replaced through a process of industrial revolution but through imposed modernization, orchestrated by alien colonial agencies.

Women's groups, which were already visible by late nineteenth century, started formally organizing, discussing, writing[6] and advocating for their issues in early twentieth century (Forbes, 1996: 12-15). However, the "larger struggle" for freedom from colonial rule easily marginalised not so important question of women. In sum, women could not articulate themselves in the two major national movements of colonial India.

Women Workers' Movement and Challenges of Needs Politicization from the Below

Women were never seen as a major group of voters in world's largest secular democracy, which was defined and interpreted by elite men. Issues like marriage, property and inheritance are dealt in the country by the patriarchal religious law boards or the personal law boards as these issues are considered "personal and family matter". Religious leaders, with a stronghold on the vote bank, play a crucial role in Indian electoral politics and challenging patriarchal laws or fundamental norms/practices has been a major challenge in the construction of a truly secular and democratic nation-state of India. The architects of independent India failed to ensure women's participation in the formulation of the Constitution of India and women's issues were legalized and formalized by the political and religious leaders of the country. Absence of a uniform civil code ingrained possibilities of women's subjugation and added challenges for women's organizations in independent India.

Reference of development discourse is also crucial for this article. Considering development's market driven progression and our dependence on this discourse I think different stages of development/progression have to play a significant role in women's economic independence. In a colonial context, modernization and industrialization always remained processes introduced and implemented by foreign authorities that detested native culture as rude and "traditional" and subsequently also generated conflict between the traditional patriarchal norms and modernity. Women are the hardest hit in such conflicts. Colonized women's objectification as victims of barbaric traditional patriarchy has a long history. Historians have widely discussed the nationalist effort of glorifying and veiling women simultaneously in response to their proliferation as victims of barbaric native culture and impact of conflict between the colonial and nationalists' standpoint on colonized women (Sanghari and Vaid, 1990). This tension perplexed women's space in a colonized context where they were expected to be modern while bearing the burden of preserving their tradition and culture in the wake of modernization, industrialization and development. While this tension created scope for few women's, mostly privileged, progression as modern educated professionals, it veiled majority of women's contribution by refraining their labour from being monetized. In a context where a human's worth is mainly determined by her contribution into the [market] economy, engaging women into non-monetized production and services and seizing their access and control over market had a severe impact on women's identity as workers. The compulsion of veiling women for preserving culture was so incensed that it almost "invisibilized" women from the public sphere, specially market and economy. This reluctance to envision women as existing human beings whose hard labour makes the society and economy function is a crucial factor that adds to the challenges for Indian women's movement in general and women workers' movement in particular.

Politicization of women's needs "from below" actually started in independent India. Independent India (post 1947) witnessed this form of politicization during the 1960s when women's groups organized and started struggling for their rights (Kishwar, 1999: 15, 20). The 1970s and

1980s was the era of active protest. It was the most vivacious period of women's movement in India. 1980s was a sort of climax of anti-dowry and anti-rape protests, started in the 1970s (Sirohi, 2003: 19). Women started contesting their domestic boundaries and publicizing their exploitation as the "second sex" and their status as "invisible workers". As Fraser argues "politicization of needs in oppositional discourse does not go uncontested", the women's groups had to face strong resistance not only from men in general, but also from institutionalized forms of patriarchal mind set, ranging from State to political Right and even Left. For example the founder of SEWA and trade union leader Ila Bhatt's demand for separate trade union for women home-based workers was opposed by her male colleagues who argued that self employed women are not part of any factory or work place and hence they cannot be the members of a trade union (Nussabaum, 2000: 44). However, Ila Bhatt and her organisation succeeded in establishing the Self Employed Women's Association (SEWA) in 1972 as the first registered trade union of self-employed women (Rose, 1992). This union struggled for underscoring home-based workers' existence in the economy and played a crucial role in the adoption of the convention of home-based workers by ILO in 1996. However, formulation of strong laws for women and registration of women workers' organizations along with a world famous trade union also implied transition of "oppositional discourse", which started in the 1960s, into "reprivatization discourse" in the 1980s. Independent India, especially during and after 1960s, witnessed emergence of women's organizations, professional social workers and activists who played a crucial role in transforming women related policies and laws. Fraser claims that "repoliticization" of discourse blends the old and new. This was evident in the transition period of 1980s. The protests of 1970s and 1980s captured the attention of the State and experts and "needs were transformed into object of yet another group of discourse" (Fraser, 2008: 11). Now the needs were becoming the agenda of experts and policy makers.

Experts Representation of Needs

The last two decades of twentieth century became an era of "experts" and "specialists" on Indian working class needs (Roy, 2001). Expert discourse appears as a "problem solving discourse" and this also works as a bridge that loosely links organized social movements with the State (Fraser, 2008: 162). In the context of women's movement in India, the "expert discourse" implied NGOisation of women's issues; articulation of their needs by the "experts" and "professional consultants"; and implications of "donor-driven" agenda in the women's organizations and their movement (Sirohi, 2003: 32). Fraser registers that social movements followed by "expert discourse", creates complex struggle within the praxis of development. This complexity emerges from the paradox of development as well. The concept of development is probably the most controversial and yet essential discourse of our time. The dependency on development and ideological conflict with developmentalism further complicates social organizations' struggle by jeopardizing their stand/ position in relation to the State. Though these organizations often disagree with the interpretation of people's needs by the expert advisers of State, they seek State's support for addressing people's needs. These interpretations also represent the influence of market oriented global policies on the nation-state. Most of the social movements, emerging from marginalised people's initiation of politicizing their needs, followed by an organisational effort of reprivatisation and finally high jacked by "experts", often face a downward mobility (Baneria, 2003: 49-54). The women's movement in India is also suffering from the process of "expertisation." The established organizations are those where trained social workers, management graduates and experts work with the activists. Some of the established Indian women workers' organizations are globally known and have played a crucial role in raising the issues of informal women workers. However, these well known organizations could not persuade the State to incorporate the contribution of over 90 per cent of the total workforce in official statistics and monetize informal women workers' contribution.

The rapidly growing population of home-based workers in remote areas of the country is still "invisible" and struggling for survival. In fact labour force participation rate for women in India has declined from over 37 per cent in 2004-05 to 29 per cent in 2009-10 (ILO, 2013). This indicates further intensification of those processes that invisibilise women's labour. Ironically, this statistics emerged when women workers' globally known organizations and the State seemed to be concerned for mapping the informal sector workers. In many cases it is becoming almost impossible for home-based workers to survive in the liberalized Indian economy. The group of silk spinners from Bhagalpur is one of them.

Local Organizations and Repossession of "Needs Politicization" Process

Human's dependence on the market for livelihood has allowed pro-market agendas to be the dominant discourse of the Euro-American centric world system (Polayni, 1944: 83). The social organizations working within this world system could seldom manage to sustain while sticking to their pro-poor agendas that hardly align with the market interest. The greatest challenge for social organizations working to counter market's agendas of dispossessing people from their means of subsistence, often carried in the name of development, is to disengage itself from pro-market discourses (Priyadarshini, 2011: 78). It is this context that makes small local level organizations relevant for representing women's needs. The main comparative advantage of small local organizations is their proximity to women home-based workers that facilitates them in representing and politicizing workers' needs. Furthermore, limited operations and lower fund requirements of local organizations allow them to function with lesser fear of being subsumed by the market.

Silk business in Bhagalpur is shrinking in the hands of a few businessmen and spinners have to compromise on very low wages. The unpredictable moves of the policies of contemporary world order believe in performance (Gore, 2000: 789). The one who fails to succeed in the performance competition is thrown out of the game. This could be an individual, a firm, a group of workers, and even a whole nation. Unfortunately, the market hardly leaves any options for failure. An increase in the population of unemployed youth and refugees; rate of informalisation and feminisation of labour; suicidal rate among peasants and home-based workers; death because of hunger; poverty and curable diseases are some of the outcomes of this output oriented market (Jameson, 1998: 55). The unorganized and unregistered groups of home-based workers, who do not have the support of established organizations, are also the groups that failed in this "performance competition". They do not have any other option than to live an almost "invisible" life and, in many cases, gradually move towards the verge of extinction.

The role of State has also drastically transformed. Now the State is expected to act as a tool/implementer of the market-driven agendas. The role of a welfare State is much needed in a nation like India and especially in a State like Bihar where development indicators are extremely poor. It is difficult to propose a long term solution for a group of marginalised home-based workers, who happen to be the residents of Bihar in the contemporary world order, being driven by the philosophy of accumulation by dispossession and differentiation. However, I cannot think of any other option then to counter this philosophy by reclaiming dispossessed people's possession and working for equitable distribution of resources.

One way to initiate such project of reclaiming resources and means of subsistence could be to research the needs of women home-based workers, working in extremely poor conditions. It is also necessary to facilitate them in accessing education, especially about their bodies and rights, and ensure their participation in policy formulation. Home-based workers must be aware of their space in the global chain of production that is thriving by minimizing their wages. These workers are being marginalised from the production process and gradually becoming less and less visible. This invisible form of workforce is desirable for the market that has been dissuading the State and experts from working on formulation of policies to incorporate home-based workers in the mainstream labour force. The women home-based workers and their local organizations need to take up the responsibility of their own representation and dissuade "expert" advocates and agencies from trapping women workers in alien agendas and languages. As Chandra Talpade Mohanty says in her famous article "Under the Western Eyes", ""we as women, need to move beyond Marx's assumption that women "cannot represent themselves; and they must be represented" (Mohanty, 2003: 42).

Women workers and their local organizations must prepare themselves for this role and here I find Rankin's suggestion very significant (Rankin, 2001: 33). Rankin recognizes ethnography as a feasible and remarkable approach for understanding challenges faced by those women who are either marginalized or targeted by joint projects of the nation-state and its dominant global partners. I think her suggestion is a promising and effective empirical approach for understanding the impact of global policies on the real lives and bodies, where these policies, often determined by market interests, materialise in its crudest form. The experience of these bodies enables them to offer some real, practical and feasible solution. If we, the subjects, are really interested in exploring ways to protect our world from the precarious circle of pro-market global policies, which is also dragging the world towards a "self-destructive discourse", we will have to understand the standpoint of the objects—the hardest hit by the corporate globalization (Rankin, 2001: 30-3; Baudrillard, 2003: 5-6).

Notes

1. UNDP's Human Development Report of 1995, titled "Gender and Development", is recognized as a landmark UN report instrumental in engendering global policies.
2. Fordist theories identified factory as the production centre, man as the bread earner/worker and woman as homemaker. These fixed identities of worker and workplace became more fluid and flexible in the post-Fordist era. Post-Fordist era refers to the era of corporate globalization. (Prugl, 1999: 103-6).
3. I lived in the hamlets of silk weavers while conducting my ethnographic study with the silk spinners during 2005. But next 3 visits were casual visits for refreshing my association with the research participants. I had worked as a development professional with the research participants for over two years. Another crucial association with my research participants is that my ancestral home is in Bhagalpur.
4. See Monthly News Letters (August, 1999) of the Ministry of Textile, Government of India, 1 (8)
5. *Sati* is a Hindu custom, in which women used to immolate themselves on their dead husband's funeral pyre.
6. Women's issues were discussed by women authors in some of the early nineteenth century periodicals like *Stri Darpan*, Women's Mirror (1909-28); *Grihalakshmi*, *Lakshmi* (Goddess of wealth) of the Home (1909-29); *Arya Mahila*, *Arya* Woman (1917-1940s); *Madhuri*, Sweetness (1922-50); *Chand*, Moon (1922-40s), etc. Shobna Nijhawan discusses these periodicals and its role in projecting women's issues in colonial North India in her book "Women and Girls in the Hindi Public Sphere: Periodical Literature in Colonial North India" (2012).

References

Baneria, L. (2003). *Gender, Development, and Globalization: Economics as if All People Mattered.* New York: Routledge.

Baudrillard, J. (2003). *The Spirit of Terrorism.* New York: Verso.

Brass, P.R. (1991). *Ethnicity and Nationalism: Theory and Comparison.* London: Sage Publications.

Buchanan, D.H. (1934). *The Development of Capitalistic Enterprise in India.* New York: Macmillan Company.

Carr, M., Chen, M. and Tate, J. (2000). Globalization and home-based workers. In *Feminist Economics*, 6 (3), 123-142.

Chatterjee, S. and Mohan, R. (1993). India's garment export. In *Economic and Political Weekly*, 28 (35), 95-119.

Dussel, E. (1998). Beyond Eurocentrism: The World-System and the limits of modernity. In Fredric Jameson and Masao Miyoshi (Ed.) *The Cultures of Globalization*, (pp. 3-31). Durham: Duke University Press.

Forbes, G. (2007). *Women in Modern India.* Cambridge: Cambridge University Press.

Fraser, N. (2008). *Unruly Practices: Power, Discourse and Gender in Contemporary Social Theory.* Minneapolis: University of Minnesota Press and Polity Press.

Gore, C. (2000). The rise and fall of Washington Consensus as a paradigm for developing countries. In *World Development*, 28 (5), 789-804.

Grewal, I. and Kaplan, C. (1994). Introduction: Transnational Feminist Practices and Questions of Postmodernity. In *Scattered Hegemonies: Postmodernity and Transnational Feminist Practices.* Minneapolis: University of Minnesota Press.

Harvey, D. (2007). *A Brief History of Neoliberalism.* New York: Oxford University Press.

Hennessy, R. (2000). *Profit and Pleasure: Sexual Identities in Late Capitalism.* New York: Routledge.

Human Development Report (1995). New York: Oxford University Press. (http://hdr.undp.org/en/media/hdr_1995_en_complete_nostats.pdf)

Hunter, W.W. (1878). *A Statistical Report on Bengal.* Calcutta: Government of Bengal.

International Labour Organisation (2007). *Women and Men in the Informal Economy: A Statistical Picture.* Retrieved July 4, 2011, from http://wiego.org/publications/women%20and%20men%20in%20the%20informal%20economy.pdf

International Labour Organisation (2013). *Global Employment Trends Report for 2013.* Retrieved June 10, 2013, from http://www.ilo.org/wcmsp5/groups/public/—dgreports/—dcomm/—publ/documents/publication/wcms_202215.pdf

Kabeer, N. (2000). *The Power to Choose: Bangladeshi Women and Labour Market Decisions in London and Dhaka.* London: Verso Press.

Kishwar, M. (1999). *Off the Beaten Track: Rethinking Gender Justice for Indian Women.* New Delhi: Oxford University Press.

Lacher, H. (1999) "Embedded liberalism, disembedded markets: Reconceptualising the Pax Americana." In *New Political Economy*, 4 (3), 343-360.

Mani, L. (1990). Contentious traditions: The debate on *Sati* in colonial India. In Kumkum Sangari and Sudesh Vaid (Ed.) *Recasting Women: Essays in Colonial History* (pp. 88-126). New Jersey: Rutgers University Press.

Moghadam, V. (2005). *"Globalizing Women: Transnational Feminism Networks."* Baltimore: The John Hopkins University Press.

Mohanty, C.T. (2003). *"Feminism Without Boarders: Decolonizing Theory, Practicing Solidarity."* Durham: Duke University Press.

Morris, W.H. (1971). *"The Government and Politics of India."* London: Hutchinson University Press.

Nijhawan, S. (2012). *Women and Girls in the Hindi Public Sphere: Periodical Literature in Colonial North India*. New Delhi: Oxford University Press.

Nussbaum, M.C. (2000). *Women and Human Development: The Capabilities Approach*. New York: Cambridge University Press.

Polanyi, K. (1944). *The Great Transformation*. Boston: Beacon Press.

Prugl, E. (1999). *The Global Construction of Gender: Home-based Work in the Political Economy of Twentieth Century*. New York: Columbia University Press.

Rankin, K.N., (2001). "Governing development: Neoliberalism, micro credit, and rational economic woman". *In Economy and Societies*, 30 (1), 18-37.

Rose, K. (1992). *Where Women are Leaders: The SEWA Movement in India*. Delhi: Vistaar Press.

Roy, A. (2001). *Power Politics*. Massachusetts: South End Press.

Salzinger, L. (2003). *Genders in Production*. Berkeley: University of California Press.

Selden, Z. (1999). *Economic Sanctions as Instruments of American Foreign Policy*. Oxford: Greenwood Publishing Company.

Sirohi, S. (2003). *Sita's Curse: Stories of Dowry Victims*. New Delhi: Hoppers and Collins and The India Today Group.

Part – IV
Women's Organisations and Institutions

19

Mahila Samakhya for Women's Empowerment

A Quiet Revolution towards Sustained Change in Andhra Pradesh (India)

P. Prasanthi

Women occupy half the sky in the sense that women population is half of the total population. But the same is not true in terms of access to rights or claim to equality. There are often debates and discourses on women's equality at both national and international levels, which bring out all the concerns and framed action points. Nevertheless the progress is still far from real empowerment of women. In this context here this article examines the contrast between power and empowerment and the experience of Mahila Samakhya programme[1] in facilitating women's empowerment.

Background

Way back in 1979, UN adopted 'CEDAW', i.e., Convention on Elimination of Discrimination against Women which is generally termed as the international bill for women's rights. The Convention provides the basis for realizing equality between women and men through ensuring women's equal access to, and equal opportunities in, political and public life—including the right to vote and to stand for election—as well as education, health and employment. The Beijing conference 1995 further laid specific indicators for women's empowerment. All the participating States including India have reaffirmed their commitment to women's equality, the result being introduction of many progressive laws and programmes in the past few years.

Millennium Development Goals (MDGs 2000-2015) is yet another step to address the inequalities in gender, caste, class and race. They also come with a promise to remove all disparities within a time frame with specific reference to education, health and women's empowerment. To realise this, the Indian Government's National Common Minimum Programme laid down specific goals for the country. Despite all these, the human development index report points a further downward trend for India with its rank lowered from 126th to 136th while the gender inequality index rank is at 132 (UNDP, HDI Report, 2013).

A report on Status of Health and Education in India 2007 (Status of Health and Education in India, Some Critical Questions to Nation's Development 2007) reveals alarming facts about the progress of the country in the fields of health and education. While close to 90 per cent children in the 6-11 age group are formally enrolled in primary schools, nearly 27 per cent drop out at the primary stage. The enrolment ratios of Scheduled Caste (SC), Scheduled Tribe (ST) and Muslim children (especially girls) still remain far lower than the national average. Malnutrition, hunger and poor health remain core problems, which comprehensively affect attendance and performance in the class. The added burden of home chores and child labour influence a large number of children, especially girls, to drop out of school.

The health indicators also are no better. 79 per cent of the children between the age of 6-35 months, and more than 50 per cent of women, are anaemic, and 40 per cent of the maternal deaths during pregnancy and child-birth relate to anaemia and under-nutrition. Infant Mortality Rate (IMR) in India was 67.6 in 1998-99 and has come down to 44 in 2011 (Sample Registration System 2011). Maternal Mortality Rate (MMR) is currently 212 deaths per 100,000 live births (Zee News, 03 July 2012). According to a World Bank report it was 200 in 2010. India accounts for a large number of maternal deaths in the world.

When we look at the participation of women in public and political fields, being equal to their male counterparts is still a far cry for Indian women. They seem to be still marginal in numbers even now despite laws and legislations providing them all the opportunities. According to a report by *Times of India*, in 2012, women occupied only eight out of 74 ministerial positions in the Union council of ministers. There were only two women judges out of 26 judges in the Supreme Court, and there were only 54 women judges out of 634 judges in various High Courts (*Times of India.com, India Times* report by Kounteya Sinha, 4 Dec. 2012).

If this is the case for the social indices, India ranks fourth in the world among the most unsecure place for women according to an international survey (source: ETV). The crime records and the recent instances of heinous crimes against women stand proof to this.

At this juncture, we need to ponder upon the basic question–why is this position for women in India? The answer seems evident–the traditional patriarchal value systems still prevailing upon every aspect relating to women's lives from birth to death. This is definitely a debatable point as many would argue that women are equal to men and are enjoying most out of pro-women policies and legislations.

The status report (2007) further makes certain specific recommendations in the context of ensuring equal access to health and education for all—

- Both Health and Education are Rights guaranteed by the Constitution. Hence it is the duty of the government to deliver them to the citizens.
- Education and health are social investments not public expenditure. Hence it is the immediate concern to raise the expenditure on both these.
- The government must prioritize the needs of traditionally marginalised sections—tribes, women, vulnerable groups, minorities in planning.

Thus the contrast is between the policies and implementation, between power and empowerment, providing opportunities *versus* enabling equal access to them. Here, we need to read between the lines and examine the position and condition of women in relation to the present development scenario where government promises of equality to women in all fields and States that sky is the limit.

Given this background, the following pages make an attempt to put before the readers the relevance of programmes like Mahila Samakhya in achieving Equality of women through Education. Education of women leads to their empowerment and in turn allows them to address issues relating to their status, be it social or economical or political. The term empowerment is often understood in a narrow perspective of economic independency but it need to be taken in an integrated sense of physical, social, economical, political and legal.

Education for Women's Equality–Mahila Samakhya Way

Building Women's Agency is a core investment for Mahila Samakhya (MS). The programme has been launched in 1988 in pursuance of the objectives of NPE 1986, wherein it is stated that *"Education will be used as an agent of basic change in the status of woman. In order to neutralise the accumulated distortions of the past, there will be a well-conceived edge in favour of women. The National Education System will play a positive, interventionist role in the empowerment of women. It will foster the development of new values through redesigned curricula, textbooks, the training and orientation of teachers, decision-makers and administrators, and the active involvement of educational institutions. This will be an act of faith and social engineering... "*. (NPE, 1986, GoI)

The critical focus in MS is recognizing the centrality of education in empowering women to achieve equality. To move towards this objective, *MS has adopted an innovative approach that emphasizes the process rather than mere mechanical fulfilment of targets*. Education in MS is understood not merely as acquiring basic literacy skills but as a process of learning to question, critically analyzing issues and problems; and seeking solutions. An environment is created for women to learn at their own pace, set their own priorities and seek knowledge and information to make informed choices. This process enables women to deal with problems of isolation, lack of self-confidence, oppressive social customs and struggle for survival, all of which inhibit their learning.

Recognising that education can be an effective tool for women's empowerment, the parameters laid down by the programme are:

- enhancing self-esteem and self-confidence of women;
- building a positive image of women by recognizing their contribution to the society, polity and the economy;
- developing ability to think critically;
- fostering decision making and action through collective processes;
- enabling women to make informed choices in areas like education, employment and health (especially reproductive health);
- ensuring equal participation in developmental processes;
- providing information, knowledge and skill for economic independence; and
- enhancing access to legal literacy and information relating to their rights and entitlements in society with a view to enhance their participation on an equal footing in all areas.

Coverage

This programme is being implemented in 11 States[2] of the country across 122 districts covering 610 Blocks and 40,275 villages. There are about a million women as members in the Samakhya and 4,95,915 adolescents in the Kishori Sanghas[3]/Bala Sanghas[4]. In AP State the programme covers 14 districts, 124 Mandals and 5,201 villages. 6,392 Sanghas have been formed with a membership of 2,43,559 women, belonging to poor and marginalized sections. Believing that the empowerment process starts at a young age APMSS has been facilitating formation of Bala Sanghas with adolescent girls and boys together to address issues of discrimination, vulnerability and child rights. There are 3,036 Bala Sanghas with a membership of 51,248 girls and 40,242 boys. The average number of villages covered in each district is 250 to form a 'critical mass'.

The regular membership of women in Sanghas ranges from 25–60, which is around 15–30 per cent of the village women population. The figure refers to the women who meet regularly twice in a month. It must be noted that many other women also participate in the activities of the Sangha depending on the nature of issue or activity being addressed. Initially women from the poorer and marginalized section are organized into Sanghas but the recognition and visibility that the Sanghas gained have begun to draw in women from other social groups as well. Thus, the membership is not fixed unlike the thrift and credit groups.

Strategies and Approach

The major strategy towards achieving the objective is organizing women into village level collectives–*the Mahila Sangha.* These are collectives that work towards a common cause, not necessarily homogeneous in nature. These Sanghas thinks, decides, acts and reflects collectively with a thrust on addressing women's issues with social agenda.

From the beginning of the programme, it is clear that the focus would be to reach out to marginalised women and girls. The Mahila Sangha is the focal point in each village that will provide the space where women can meet, be together, and begin the process of reflecting, asking questions, speaking fearlessly, thinking, analysing and above all, feeling confident to articulate their needs through this collective. These groups have provided the collective strength for women, usually from poor and marginalized groups, to overcome barriers to their participation in and access to education and development. It is this process that sets in motion the education.

Being members of the Sangha, women get opportunity to discuss and reflect on their status and critically analyse their situation within the family and the society with regard to their "traditional roles". They are often faced with confrontation from their family members when they raise their voice and question the predominant patriarchal values and norms. However, the collectiveness of the Sangha members gave them strength to withstand the struggle and continue their effort to deal with the power structures within the family and in the society. This enabled them to develop a perspective to understand gender and equity issues and think of appropriate strategies to address the same.

There is a notion that the economic development programmes are the major means to address development issues and women's inequality. But our experience reveals that creating assets on women's name do not necessarily provide neither decisive role to women nor control over it to them. Unless they are educated of their rights and understand about their marginalization within the family and the society which are reinforcing the patriarchal value system; equality and empowerment becomes a question. An important dimension of this process has been enabling the agency of poor women to be heard and to act to bring about changes in their lives as well as the larger community. It is in this process that women become empowered.

In the entire process the programme personnel is guided by the objectives and non-negotiable principles framed for the purpose. It does not specify any one—entry strategy nor is there a set agenda. The issues and needs articulated by the Sanghas becomes the plan of action for the programme. The team is continuously challenged to translate the programme objectives into workable strategies on the ground. This has meant that the programme have a cadre of workers with an in-depth understanding of gender issues, the empowerment process, information at hand and the ability to respond sensitively to the local specific needs of the Sanghas. It essentially involves women from the grassroots, largely from the same social strata, to be part of the process so that they also undergo the process of empowerment while facilitating the same in the Sanghas, thereby making the programme unique in its nature.

Issues of Women's Concern: Agenda for the Programme

In the nascent stages of Sangha formation, women have tended to discuss and act to access services, rights and entitlements like pensions, ration cards, maternity assistance, getting street lights, getting drains cleared, hand-pumps repaired, applying for houses, etc., by interacting with the Block and district administrations. It is in this process that Sanghas have coalesced and learnt their first lessons on how to deal with systemic power structures. This led to building collective strength and cohesiveness among the members of the Sanghas. This has often been the initial experiencing of empowerment, of taking decisions and collectively seeking to resolve their problems.

The *Sangha*s takes up issues according to the needs articulated by women in the villages and in turn they demand for need based information and capacities. The action plans or the agenda raised by them informs the direction of the programme and the processes. This non-negotiable feature of the programme accounts for the sustainability of the Sangha and laying path for women's empowerment.

While no two Sanghas address the same issue at the same time, the programme's response to the needs of the women has been categorized into following five core areas:

- Education of Women and Girls,
- Health with a special focus on women's and adolescents health,
- Women's Participation in Local Governance,
- Access to and Control over Natural Resources and Asset Building, and
- Social and Gender Equity Issues.

All the strategies and interventions are designed around these core areas with the inner connecting thread being the gender perspective. Critical and analytical discussions on each issue in the Sanghas have enabled the Sanghas to take decisions on their work load, literacy status, nutrition, health status and accessing resources, be it land or any government schemes. Also they ponder upon how all these are determined by women's social status, societal attitudes and perceptions. Further the programme developed linkages and convergence with all related departments and various programmes for women and girls in realization of the needs articulated by women. In this process the Sangha women realize the need for literacy and come forward to acquire literacy skills. As the need is created or felt for literacy the women come up with their own plans of literacy interventions which are translated into various short term to long term activities, both residential and non-residential, basing on the time of the Sangha women.

Health being the first concern raised by women in the process of forming collectives the focus of the programme in the initial years was on building knowledge and awareness on women's health, particularly reproductive health and related rights. Realizing that the secondary status of women is making them vulnerable to poor health and lack of timely access to health services the focus was also on building convergence with health care services at various levels. While addressing the concerns of women in health the life cycle approach has been adopted. Demand for basic health services at village level and facilities for maternal health by the Sanghas yielded positive results in ANM visiting them regularly, improved conditions at health institutions, immunization and adolescent health. Simultaneously, the indigenous knowledge of women on using herbs and kitchen ingredients for minor ailments was valued, revived and encouraged to bring it back into practice. This increased the esteem of women in terms of their contribution to the world of knowledge.

Though the Constitution of India provides equal rights to women the strong rooted patriarchal system and the societal norms are contributing to their subordination. Towards addressing the issue a progressive amendment has been made to the constitution providing reservations for women's participation in the governance. Despite this, women remained passive in their participation in Panchayats and taking decisions because of their inability to lock horns with the dominant social and political structures. In this context MS encouraged for their proactive participation in the local governance by building their information and leadership skills. It resulted in multifold increase in the number of women entering into Panchayats in various positions in the MS project area from 63 in 1995 to 4,337 in 2013. Same time the efforts put in equipping them with knowledge on their duties and powers paved way for their effective and informed participation. They could focus on fulfilling the practical gender needs like drinking water, ensuring regularity of Anganwadi Centre, education for children, etc. Solidarity extended by Sangha women and support from MS built their confidence further and enabled them to take appropriate decisions. Majority of these elected women representatives could create a positive environment where they could earn a position for themselves and successfully complete the tenure in the Panchayat.

Rural India being an agrarian society, women play a vital role in agricultural activities, both land based and allied. It includes ensuring food security, managing natural resources and conserving environment. But it was never realized by themselves as well as the society and they continue to remain as consumers rather than producers. This position adds to their secondary status and does not give any scope for ownership on assets or control over resources. It was discussed at length in the Sanghas by critically analyzing the consequences and organsing capacity building sessions. The outcome has been very positive as the women started demanding for equal wages, work sharing, right to property, creation of assets in their name and recognition as women farmers.

Pedagogy

The key strength of MS approach has been its training and pedagogy, with its focus on reflection, analysis and participation (JRM, Mahila Samakhya, 2013). Equipped with information and increased capacities, women collectively and individually developed a sense of social responsibility to address inequalities with respect to women and girls. They are able to articulate their demands clearly and these ranged from effective access to programmes, schemes and entitlements to working against larger social challenges–child marriages, domestic violence, dowry, harassment of women and girls, initiating girls into Jogini[5] cult, etc. Increased mobility, greater community level participation, bargaining/ negotiation for effective service delivery are the achievements of the women's collectives. This is well reflected in MS project areas.

In this process women's literacy coupled with life skill education was given weightage. The issues raised by the Sanghas, the concerns of women and its relation to the larger social context find a prominent place in the content of the literacy programmes. Thus a conscious effort is made to weave strategic gender interests into the practical gender needs. This creates a forum for women to acquire literacy at a greater pace as it comes from their lived realities. The content of all the educational programmes has been developed with active participation of the learners and the facilitators. This is another unique feature of the MS programme that brings in the elements of ownership of women and accountability of the programme functionaries.

All this has not been a linear process of learning and empowerment. There have been many a challenge, ups and downs. Individual women both within the programme and the Sanghas have their complex experiences of passing through difficult times, facing violence from the family and also from outside. But the programme has provided a space for women to reflect upon their situation, gain confidence and relate their personal experiences to the larger women's situation (*personal is political*). It is this process of collective reflection and analysis that keeps the programme dynamic and vibrant.

Autonomy and Sustainability

Over the years a clearer understanding has evolved of the dimensions to the education for empowerment that MS seeks to provide. As the women's collectives and the programme have matured there has been a broader understanding that has unfolded from the initial understanding of enabling women to come together, to be mobile, and find time for themselves to meet and reflect on their lives. This process lead to Sangha emerging as a pressure group at village level in addressing women's concerns ranging from availing infrastructural facilities to accessing their rights and entitlements, to address issues of violence and vulnerability of women and girls. At times, two to three Sanghas of the nearby villages joined hands to address more critical issues like abuse, rape or any sort of violence against women.

Taking this thread along in extending their sphere of influence from the village to the much wider *mandal*, the Sanghas felt the need for a federation[6] at the *mandal* level. This, they felt, enables them emerge into a strong pressure group to address social concerns particularly of the women and the girls. Federations are also facilitated as part of the strategy for sustainability and decentralization. MS believed that this is an integral part of the empowerment process, which would initiate through learning by doing. It is anticipated that these federations would provide solidarity for the Sanghas to work together on social issues, ensuring a learning environment and at the same time respond to the ever changing socio-political environment. It is also envisaged that these federations, as they get stronger and ready to function independently, will emerge as grassroots institutions, often registered as societies. These federations work with social agenda taking forward the issues of women from marginalized sections of the community by building linkages with various government and non-government agencies. These federations also take up the responsibility of coordination, monitoring and management of alternative structures like MSKs[7], Naari Adalats[8] and Sanjeevani Kendras[9] as part of their intervention towards addressing women's issues. This social intermediation distinguishes them from other SHG federations.

The federations are the "exit strategy" for the programme in older areas where they take on the responsibility of continuing the initiatives, giving scope for the programme to move to newer areas. The organic linkage continues as the federations and MS work in partnership with mutual support. This is a major factor for sustainability of the institution even after winding up the direct implementation by MS.

Programme Outcomes

Mahila Samakhya programme was started as a pilot in the Eighth Five Year Plan with a focus on education as a process for women's equality. The journey over two decades has proved it to be a successful programme being facilitated by women for empowerment of women. There has always been a conscious effort from all levels not to dilute the *process* at every step of facilitation leading to qualitative impact in the lives of women—those who are directly part of the process and also women who are connected to them. This impact is clearly visible in their attitudes, increased knowledge levels, abilities to critically analyse, negotiate for their space and demand for their stakes; all of which gives them recognition as equal partners.

When these qualitative outcomes are translated into quantifiable outcomes it reflects in the number of women pursuing their education, members entering political arena and the number of trainers/resource persons reaching out to the larger society not limiting to MS programme area, etc. The following table gives a glimpse of such experience of APMSS:

Sl. No	*Category*	*Number of women*
1.	Attained literacy	63,985
2.	Pursuing Education	7,433
3.	Women in Panchayats	5,119
4.	Para legal volunteers	106
5.	Para medical volunteers (herbal medicine and DOT providers)	530
6.	Grassroots service providers (Asha, AWW, ANM, VVs, ALC teachers)	3,936
7.	Mates in NREGS	2,376
8.	Resource persons/trainers	22,418
9.	Autonomous federations	32

Conclusion

Our Constitution has guaranteed equal rights to all citizens while creating a scope for special interventions for disadvantaged and marginalized sections of the community. For translating it into action, various policies and programmes are created. Many a time these policies, however, dynamic may be, are becoming service delivery and limiting to welfare rather than educating communities on their rights and to access it. Reason could be facilitation for accessing rights requires lot of time and energy.

Another factor could be scale of implementation, which may dilute the spirit of the original design of any programme down the line and limits to fulfilling the needs rather than access to rights.

Strong perspective, political will, rights based orientation with sustained spirit and reflective process, both horizontal and vertical in the administering system, are the core for implementation of rights based programme. There are a few such programmes in our country which demonstrated that when the grassroots communities are educated, power is decentralized and provided scope for them to participate proactively at all levels of implementation, the result will be achieving equality and empowerment of the marginalized.

Mahila Samakhya is one such programme which could demonstrate that sustainable process of grassroots facilitation and decentralization of leadership and power is possible. The unique processes enabled the rural poor women as change agents and icons of democratic leadership. The strength is its replicability and adaptability with contextual modifications. The strategies and the processes followed in the programme are summarized as under for wider application:

- Planning from grassroots–women's needs becoming programme's agenda.
- Interventions–Women centred, knowledge building, participatory, giving the charge to women.
- Facilitating holistic perspective of empowerment–physical, social, economic, political and legal.
- Capacity building–moving from practical gender needs to strategic gender interests and mainstreaming gender into the core areas of implementation.
- Information is power–acquiring knowledge, understanding and making informed choices–taking charge of their lives.
- Greater access to schemes and entitlements–working as pressure groups for effective service delivery and demand driven programmes/interventions.
- Demand for need based educational facilities for women and influencing girls' education.
- Women's collectives emerging as pressure groups for planning and action–evolving into a cadre of activists to address issues of violence against women and girls.
- Distribution of power—decentralised structures at different levels functioning in coordination and partnership.

- Autonomy and sustainability–transfer of power and handholding support in independent functioning.

Notes

1. Mahila Samakhya is a programme of Government of India under the Ministry of Human Resource Development, Department of Secondary Education and Literacy, evolved from the National Policy on Education 1986 and the subsequent Plan of Action 1992.
2. Andhra Pradesh, Assam, Bihar, Chattisgarh, Gujarat, Jharkhand, Karnataka, Kerala, Uttar Pradesh, Uttarakhand and Rajasthan (Newly launched).
3. Facilitating empowerment process from childhood to build a cadre of well informed girls and young women with sensitized leadership was the focus of Kishori Sanghas ('*Cheli Sanghams*'–Girls Collectives in A.P.).
4. Realising the need to address both genders together to address the influences of patriarchal values built through socialization process *Cheli Sanghams* in A.P. transformed into *Bala Sanghams*–village level collectives of Boys and Girls, to facilitate sensitized second generation for advocating Equity and Equality issues collectively.
5. *Jogini* is a practice of dedicating girls to God. This practice is a form of prostitution with religious sanction, similar to the *devadasi* system practised elsewhere in the country. In the initial years of MS in AP this practice was high in some districts like Mahabubnagar, but with rigorous intervention for more than a decade it could be successfully addressed and this practice is no longer in vogue.
6. *Federations* are the confederation of village level Sanghas at Mandal level formed as a part of decentralization process. These federations are autonomous bodies registered under the Societies Registration Act and are envisaged to work as CBOs.
7. Mahila Shikshana Kendra is a year long residential educational programme for adolescent girls and young women to provide life skills education. After completion of the course in MSK the younger girls are mainstreamed into formal schools and the young women continue pursuing their education through open school system.
8. Naari Adalat is an alternative conflict redressal mechanism at village/ Block (Mandal) level. A group of well trained women from Sanghas work as para legals in addressing the cases and offer legal support to the victims of violence. These Naari Adalats work in collaboration with police and judiciary in counselling and resolving cases.
9. Sanjeevani Kendras are herbal medicine centres maintained by trained Sangha women who prepare herbal medicines and make it available to the public.

20

Women Empowerment Programmes

Kudumbashree Experiences in Kerala

Soya Thomas

Launched by the Government of Kerala in 1998 for wiping out absolute poverty from the State through concerted community action under the leadership of Local Self Governments. Today Kudumbashree is the largest women-empowering project in the country. The programme has 40 lakhs members and covers 50 per cent of the households in Kerala.

The economic empowerment initiatives of Kudumbashree have created a range of potential local women entrepreneurs in the State. But sustainable economic independence and empowerment have been hampered, given established patriarchal norms, male-centred knowledge bases and the inaccessibility to constitutional and legal provisions. On the other hand, the conventional indicators of development are highly favourable to women in the State-high literacy rates, good health conditions and above-average employment. But micro statistical reports on female work participation; health and nutritional levels among women; their participation in decision making and governance; and their role in planning, implementation and evaluation of the development process show how they are most often positioned as "beneficiaries". Kudumbashree has provided a space for women to identify the right combinations of collective, monetary and intellectual support that will ensure it succeeds as a poverty eradication programme. This has paved the way to deconstruct strategies and formulate a new methodology for women's empowerment.

The grassroots of Kudumbashree are Neighbourhood Groups (NHG) that send representatives to the Ward level Area Development Societies (ADS). The ADS send representatives to the Community Development Society (CDS), which is unique three-tier structure of Kudumbashree.

Now there are 2,53,197 NHGS, over 19,114 ADSs and 1,072 CDSs in Kudumbashree.

Kudumbashree plays a vital role in enhancing financial status of the less privileged women in the State through its thrift and credit societies. These society facilitate them to save and provide them with cost-effective and easy credit.

In 2007, Kudumbashree devised a special project called the Gender Self Learning Programme (GSLP) that directly caters to women's empowerment. The programme recognises the necessity of understanding the importance of "self learning" and using it to take advantage of the innate potential of women. The GSLP reinterprets the concept of learning by positioning women in multiple roles such as participants, information providers and knowledge creators.

As participants: Women take part in neighbourhood group (NHG)-level discussions on subjects and situations where they believe a disparity in treatment or discrimination against them as a gender exists.

As information providers: Women converse on their rich life experiences (including both discrimination and recognition) and in the process provide valuable pieces of information.

As knowledge creators: A gender-sensitive knowledge base is created at the grass roots that can be recognized as such or contested through participation. At the same time, this knowledge base is integral to the local planning and implementation processes.

In short, the GLSP takes the collectives through all dimensions of discrimination and disparity and shows women how to analyse their plight and raise their voices against everything unjust in it.

The primary objectives of the learning process are:

- To convey the messages of women's status, rights, equality and justice;
- To initiate women to have access to, and control over, assets;
- To widen the platform for participation in local development;
- To analyse gender status on the basis of rich life experiences;
- To equip women against domestic violence; and
- To strengthen the network beyond collectivization,

The details about how to Kudumbashree Mission in Kerala shows the pathway to empowerment of rural women follows, as given in the Kudumbashree Mission statement:

Kudumbashree, conceived poverty as a basket of relative deprivations and vulnerabilities and has developed an innovative methodology to identify the poor using non-economic parameters. The poor thus identified were organised under a well-networked Community Based Organisation (CBO). This methodology has since been incorporated into the policy framework of the State for the identification of the underprivileged.

Structure

Neighbourhood Group (NHG)

The lowest tier constitutes the Neighbourhood Group with 10 to 20 women members selected from economically backward families. Meetings are convened on a weekly basis in the houses of NHG members. In the weekly meeting all members bring their thrift, which will be collected and recycled, to the system by way of sanctioning loans.

Area Development Society (ADS)

The second tier is the Area Development Society which is formed at Ward level by federating all the NHGs in the Ward. The activities and the decision in the ADS are decided by the representatives of the women elected from various NHGs.

Community Development Society (CDS)

At the Panchayat/Municipal level a Community Development Society (CDS), a registered body under the Travancore-Cochin Literacy Scientific and Charitable Societies Act, is formed by federating all ADSs in the local bodies.

CDS

Action Plan

The CDS Action Plan is an annual demand plan. Consolidating development requirements from the NHG to the CDS level. Objectives of the CDS Action Plan are the following:

- Enable participatory, bottom-up consolidation of development demands in the community.
- Provide a tool for the local self government to converge resources for community development and poverty alleviation from various sources.
- Act as the basis for monitoring performance and achievements of the community network and supporting structures.

Economic Empowerment

Kudumbashree considers economic empowerment as one of the three important tools for poverty alleviation. Kudumbashree organised women at the grass root level with the support of local self governments and imparted training to start their own enterprises. Micro finance activities through thrift of credit activities and bank linkage are widespread. Mission provides support to enterprises for business development, bank linkage, capacity building both technical and managerial, as well as market access. Today thousands of small scale enterprises are run successfully in various sectors including IT, hotels, eco friendly products, food products manufacturing, food processing units, readymade dress making units, umbrella, sandals and shoe making, handicraft production dairying, agriculture, carpentry and other household items. The Kudumbashree members take land on lease for collective farming, producing paddy, vegetables and fruits and even to do floriculture.

In the past four years, the Mission has expanded its activities to other income generating and marketing activities, while consolidating the earlier gains made in the micro finance sector.

Micro Finance

Kudumbashree does not consider Microfinance as a one stop solution for poverty alleviation, but considers it an important pre-condition. Kudumbashree has chalked out a comprehensive Financial Literacy Plan in order to provide a platform for the members of NHGs to be aware of the programmes and benefit from formal banking services.

Thrift and Credit

Kudumbashree promotes Neighbourhood Groups (NHGs) of 10-20 poor women members as an interface between poor women, banks and government agencies. NHGs are instrumental in thrift mobilization, encouraging the poor to save and to avail low cost formal credit. They facilitate easy and timely credit to the unreached.

Bank Linkage

NHG-Bank linkage scheme is one of the flagship programmes of Kudumbashree. NABARD SHG-Bank linking grading procedures are applied while selecting eligible NHGs for availing loan. CDS assists NHG in getting graded by the bank. Bank will provide loans to those NHGs who pass 80 per cent of marks in the grading. Loan amount to a NHG is linked to thrift amount mobilized and retained within the group as internal loans. Maximum loan amount possible for a NHG is four times of its thrift. The Bank Linkage programme has helped the NHGs to augment their existing resources mobilized through thrift.

Matching Grant

Matching grant is an incentive provided to NHGs. This grant linked to amount of thrift mobilized, performance of NHG in the Grading and loan availed from banks. An amount of 10 per cent of the savings of the NHG subject to a maximum of ₹ 5,000 is provided as matching grant to each NHG.

Interest Subsidy Scheme

Government have sanctioned the interest subsidy scheme for the Kudumbashree NHGs under the linkage banking programme at 4 per cent interest. The interest subsidy is provided for loans up to an amount of ₹ 1 lakh.

Bhavanashree

This project enabled women from the network to obtain housing loan from financial institutions. This project has benefited 41,284 members.

Management Information System–Pilot of Microfinance Modules

With the help of the Centre for Development of Advanced Computing (C-DAC) Kudumbashree has developed a digitized Management

Information System (MIS) which would enable Kudumbashree to monitor the activities from the grass root level to the Mission headquarters' level. Monitoring of Microfinance, entrepreneurship, collective farming, Ashraya, Balasabha, SJSRY and so on can be conducted through this facility. The details of an NHG once fed on to the system at the CDS level can be generated at 4 levels is the advantage of this web based MIS. This enables to track the details of any NHGs from any part of the State helping for more transparent functioning. The software development is funded by the Ministry of Information Technology, Government of India.

Micro Enterprises

Supporting and sustaining micro enterprises has always been a challenge for development administration. Problems of scale, capability, market and vulnerability and so on do not offer easy solutions. In the recent past Kudumbashree had been attempting to analyse and resolve these problems specifically and jointly, both by increasing the interface with the LSG and the entrepreneur regarding existing programmes, and by evolving new strategies and new programmes that help converge resources and address emerging issues proactively and creatively.

ME Status Study—The Directional Change

The ME Status study conducted in 2006 has helped to analyse the plethora of problems faced by the micro entrepreneurs. Issues such as lack of proper marketing, market for products, shortage of raw materials, lack of quality, unscientific methods of quality assessment, lack of modern technology and lack of funding were recognized as problem areas.

Interventions have been oriented towards addressing these problems. The various entrepreneurship support schemes of Kudumbashree are:

RME Scheme

The success of centrally sponsored enterprise programme in the urban areas prompted the Mission to come up with similar enterprise programme in rural areas. The Rural Micro Enterprises (RME) Programme was initiated to help women to set up Individual and Group enterprises. During 2006-2010, 10,333 entrepreneurships were started and ₹ 42.54 crore was granted as subsidy.

Yuvashree

Yuvashree was launched with an objective to provide opportunity to unemployed youth. Both men and women in the age group of 18-40 from family members of Kudumbashree to start enterprises. Support is provided to identify business ideas. implementation. training. loan facility and getting subsidies for the projec

Revolving Fund

Revolving fund is meant for meeting urgent requirement of working capital. Enterprises are eligible for revolving fund at 15 per cent of the total project cost subject to a maximum of INR 35.000 per group.

Crisis Management Fund

CMF is meant to meet urgent fund crisis out of a calamity, unexpected delay in release of due funds, urgent working capital to manage a spike in demand, etc.

Cluster and Networking

This fund is intended for networking enterprises of similar nature for utilizing economies of scale and for ensuring effective marketing linkage.

Innovation Fund

This fund helps enterprises with innovative ideas and technology needs. Special technology needs can be met through the technology fund.

Responsible Tourism

Inorder to tap the tourism potential of Kerala, Kudumbashree launched RT initiative. It envisaged—Increase in the scope and quantum of enterprises. Increase in local production, Local market tie up. Transformation to a responsible producer. Increase in fallow land cultivation and the development of a social institution for pricing and quality.

Special Livelihood Project

In the area of urbar employment generation, Kudumbashree has developed the Special Livelihoods Project (SLP)—an approach to ensure comprehensive livelihood planning for urban poor. The SLP is built on the premise of Local Economic Development (LED) that local production and consumption should contribute to economic development of the local population, particularly the poorer sections. Under this a linkage between the local available resources and the employment opportunities will be established to generate avenues. As a pilot project this has been implemented in Malappuram and Perinthalmanna municipalities.

Innovative Enterprises

Solid Waste Management

Kudumbashree initiated an innovative enterprise namely, 'Clean Kerala Units'. Under this enterprise, women from the poor families who are the members of the Community Based Organisations (CBOs) of Kudumbashree are engaged in door to door household waste collection and transport to the transit points fixed by the Urban Local Bodies.

Nature Fresh

Utilising the enterprise opportunity of producing and marketing fresh milk to urban consumers, Kudumbashree implemented the pilot micro enterprise project named "Nature Fresh" at Edavetti Grama Panchayat of Idukki district and then Kannady Grama Panchayath of Palakkad district. As part of the project, cows were distributed to women entrepreneurs. The milk produced is delivered to the houses within one hour in bottles by a four-member women marketing group. Traceability is ensured by numbering the cows and the same number is affixed to the bottles containing its milk. Low cost cattle sheds to ensure maximum hygiene, designed by experts have been constructed in all the homesteads. Two wheeler vehicles have been provided to the marketing group through loans. Hygienic management and fresh supply have enabled the project to charge a premium price for the milk for its freshness, and demand continues to outstrip supply. Several Panchayats are now coming forward to implement this scheme.

Amrutham Food Supplement

The AMRUTHAM unit produces a baby food supplement developed by Central Plantation Crops Research Institute (CPCRI) Kasaragod. Kudumbashree has 400 operational units. Food for 'The Take Home Ration Scheme' is provided to the anganwadi network by the Amrutham units.

IT and ITES

Much of the data entry work taken up by Government departments are being out sourced to these units which provide employment to over 2,500 poor women. In 2009-10, the IT units were taken up mostly with digitizing the BPL data and ration cards for the State Government RSBY, AABY related works. Hospital kiosks for birth registration were also taken up by various IT units.

Samagra

Samagra is a novel initiative independently developed by Kudumbashree and being implemented in the State in collaboration with the three-tier local self-governments and other agencies. It is an attempt to address the entire production supply chain holistically, by scaling up productivity both qualitatively and quantitatively and seeking viable marketing opportunities. The speciality of this project is that it ensures regular income and employment to the members of Kudumbashree. The activities delineated in the Samagra projects vary according to the nature of the project.

Cafe Kudumbashree

Started during 2009-10 with an objective to improve the existing conditions of canteen/catering units. Thrissur district mission's intervention in the canteen and catering sector has been with the formation of a management and marketing group called AIFRHM (Adebha Institute for Food Research and Hospitality Management). The team consists of hotel management professionals as well members from other fields who would provide both technical as well as marketing support to establish Kudumbashree canteens and restaurants. The restaurants were branded under a common brand called 'Cafe Kudumbashree' and standardised foods and services would be provided. The main aim of these units is to provide strong support to the units which needs help in maintaining quality, diversification of products, trying out new recipes and in adopting best practices in the industry. They had conducted training for more than 400 people in 27 batches on various activities.

TRISAT—Tribal Search and Action Team

Started in early 2009 at Wayanad district with the aim of exclusive development of tribal community by providing trainings, conducting workshops and through other means. They are achieving this mission mainly through knowledge sharing, skill development and personality development, and empowering them socially, financially and personally. 17 talented Tribals were selected as resource persons (RP). These RP's who were working with the Tribal department on an Honorarium basis, were given orientation and training about Kudumbashree and the schemes and benefits which can be availed from Kudumbashree and from other departments. 51 tribal volunteers from the community were. in turn trained by these RP.

Nedumpana Apparel Park

The Nedumpana Apparel Park is established in Nedumpana Grama Panchayat in Kollam District. The high end, semi automated tailoring facility has state-of-the-art machinery for producing high quality apparels.

Ksheerasagaram

Ksheerasagaram is an innovative project conceived for Idukki district in collaboration with Idukki District Panchayat, Nedumkandom Block Panchayat and seven Grama Panchayats of Nedumkandam Block. The three-year project was started in March 2009 and in the year 2009-2010, the project has succeeded in giving employment to 245 NHG members through cow rearing, milk marketing and value addition. Newly designed hygienic cattle sheds were constructed in all units. 490 high yielding animals were brought from outside the State which has resulted in raising the average milk production of Nedumkandum Block by 5,000 litres/day. More than 55 acres of land were brought under fodder cultivation in this project, which assisted farmers in reducing unit cost of production. In addition, 245 biogas plants were constructed so as to augment family income of these units. A unit for value addition has also been started as part of this project. Production of hygienic milk is one of the major features of the project.

Poomala Nature Fresh Project

The project is implemented in Velliyamattom Grama Panchayat of Idukki District, which has 1,500 ST families in NHGs, with the assistance of Grama Panchayat and Animal Husbandry Department. With an aim to increase general health status of children and provide a small earning for Kudumbashree women of Velliyamattam Panchayat, 1,350 backyard poultry units, have been started in Velliyamattom Panchayat. Two hatchery units have also been established in which one day old chicks from Kerala Agricultural University are raised up to 45 days and sold to backyard poultry units. The project has resulted in an additional production of 500 eggs/day.

Haritham

The project aims at cultivating vegetables required by Kochi corporation and nearby areas. Vegetables are cultivated in 48 Panchayats and the corporation are collected and then marketed. A total of 1,025 activity groups comprising of 5,125 women were formed and engaged in vegetable cultivation. Cultivation is carried out in 205 ha. Three vehicles were purchased for the purpose of marketing and started operation in the name of 'Greens'.

Thirumadhuram

The Samagra project "Thirumadhuram" formulated in the Ernakulam district is implemented jointly by Ernakulam District Panchayat, Kudumbashree Mission and Grama Panchayats. The project envisages cultivation of pineapple in a total of 500 ha. 200 ha of land was cultivated by 175 groups and 10,848 tonnes of pineapple was produced. As a part of value addition, Pineapple RTS (Ready to Serve) is marketed in the brand name of Pineshree.

Kondattom Project

Palakkad district is well-known for its Kondattom varieties. The Kondattoms are various types of crispy fries, which are originally prepared in the Brahmin Households for their domestic needs. The project aims to start 24 Common Facility Centres employing 480 women thereby producing 21 varieties of Kondattom.

Nendran Banana Project

The Nendran Project implemented in Trivandrum District aimed to bring 2,400 ha of land under Nendran cultivation by generating employment opportunities to 30,000 women beneficiaries.

Madhuram Project

The Madhuram Project started in Pathnamthitta District has the objective of providing employment to 2,000 women beneficiaries by engaging them in Bee Farming. The Rubber Plantations in Pathnamthitta provides an encouraging environment for Apiculture. Under this project, establishment of beehives, procurement and processing centres, Agmark labs and value addition of honey were implemented and executed.

Marari Mushroom

This project aims at mushroom and spawn production. Area of operation is Aryad and Kanjikuzhi Block of Alappuzha district, which has eight Panchayats. A total of 300 women from 50 units are the direct beneficiaries of this project.

Ornamental Fish Project

Ornamental fish culture is a novel micro enterprise activity taken up in Vaikkom Block Panchayat of Kottayam district, where majority of the people are depending on traditional sectors such as fisheries and coir making for their livelihood. The enterprises were started under the joint initiative of Matsyafed, Block Panchayat and Kudumbashree Mission. Market tie up with KAVIL has opened up the export market for ornamental fish.

Nivedyarm

The Nivedyam project, which aims at production of Kadali (a variety of banana) for supply to the Guruvaycor temple, is implemented in Thrissur district. The project is implemented jointly by Kodakara Block Panchayat,

Grama Panchayats and Kudumbashree mission. The bunches of Kadali banana are supplied to Guruvayur temple for daily rituals through a cooperative society for marketing. Eighty activity groups together cultivated in 40 acres of land and 8,67,292 bunches have been supplied to Devaswom so far.

Collective Farming

Collective farming was started with the sole objective of ensuring food security. It has grown beyond its objective and has become an instrument of social and economic inclusion heralding an era of new social relations by providing women a 'collective voice'. Collective farming is one of the important intervention areas of Kudumbashree in the livelihood sector.

A typical farming group was formed consisting of 4-10 members and they cultivate in one of the three types of land, viz., own, leased or Government land. Majority of the landless women groups take up land in lease for cultivation by signing a lease/rental agreement with the land owner. Out of early 75,000 hectares of fallow land in the State. 25,000 hectares of land have been brought under collective farming.

Apart from mobilizing the farming groups, the Mission provides Area incentive according to the area and crop cultivated and also production incentive according to the productivity for promoting farming, thus making the fallow land cultivable. In some cases, Training and Market support are also given.

A typical farming group formed consists of 4-10 members. These groups are now being organized as Joint Liability Groups (JLG) to make available institutional credit and also for proper monitoring. The group cultivates in one of the three types of land, viz., own, leased or Government land. Majority of women groups take up land in lease for cultivation. Eligible assistance is made available from all the converging partners. The venture is made profitable through convergence of various departments.

Saphalam Project

Saphalam Project is implemented by Kudumbashree in association with the Kasargode District Panchayat, Block Panchayat and Grama Panchayats. The Project cost is ₹ 225.31 lakhs. The project aims at collection, processing and value addition of cashew nuts. The Project aims to set up 36 cashew processing units and one cashew apple processing unit in each of 12 Grama Panchayats. 12 cashew processing centres and one cashew apple processing centre is already established thereby employing about 100 women beneficiaries. Paranky Nut is the brand developed and so far 15 tonnes of cashew nuts were processed and sold in the market for ₹45 lakhs.

Goat Village Project

A Samagra project of Kannur district, Goat Village is aimed at providing regular source of income to 5,000 Kudumbashree members in 40 Panchayats of the district, through goat rearing enterprise. The project is being implemented by Kudumbashree mission with the help of Kannur District Panchayat. The project also intends to create an organized market for goat meat. A modern slaughter house is being set up at a cost of ₹ 25 lakhs as part of this project by the District Panchayat, which will procure animals from the units. The project envisages to achieve a boost in mutton production by about 335 tonnes, milk production by 18 lakh litres annually. The project succeeded in forming 375 units which has four-goats per unit. An amount of ₹ 25 lakhs has been spent by District Panchayat for constructing slaughter house.

Manufacturing of Footwear Uppers

This Samagra Project is implemented in Cheruvannur-Nallalam Grama Panchayat in Kozhikode District is under the joint collaboration of Grama Panchayat, Kudumbashree and VKC Footwear Manufacturing Company. The local footwear industry has been beset by problems of shortage of skilled labour to work on the leather uppers. The project aims to correct this labour shortage by having a home grown skill base, that would provide support and apprenticeship till they become independent and self reliant. As part of the programme, technical skill training will be provided to 1,000 women in the area of cutting, clipping, Computer Aided Design (CAD), etc. The uppers manufactured by the Kudumbashree units will be bought back by VKC according to an MOU signed by the parties. 10 units were set up generating employment to 100 women beneficiaries.

MNREGS through Grama Panchayats

MNREGS is integrated with collective farming by providing the labour for agricultural activities like land preparation drainage facilities and irrigation. One time development of land for farming is permissible under MNREGS.

A successful case of integration of MNREGS with the Panchayat and Kudumabshree support is that of Perambra, where 140 acres of land which was lying fallow for the past 25 years was brought under cultivation by 35 farming groups. The land was previously rendered unusable because of the garbage dumping of the Perambra town. Previously clearing of the garbage dump had been tried by many others and was unsuccessful. With the determined effort of Kudumbashree women, the land could be made cultivable under the MNREGS programme, and over 100 acres of paddy was harvested for the first time in 25 years.

Monthly Markets

The monthly markets which became operational in October 2007 at district levels and later at Panchayat levels became a permanent market for the entrepreneurs which offered them regular returns. The monthly markets organized to sell the produce of entrepreneurs at a particular venue in the beginning have undergone tremendous changes, i.e., in the organization, conduct of fairs, ownership of organizing the fairs, quality and quantity of produce and so on. The platform provided entrepreneurs with an opportunity to know customer preferences, volume of sales, regular customers, their feedback, etc.

The organisation of such markets now extend to local and State level festivals and fairs like Onam, Christmas, Ramzan and so on. The State and district missions of Kudumbashree coordinate the involvement of entrepreneur units in various fairs organised by departments and agencies, both within the State and outside.

This would help fetch good returns to the entrepreneurs, and promote the products of Kudumbashree. The positioning of Kudumbashree as an eco friendly ethnic brand is also happening through this process.

Home Shop

A major marketing initiative that Kudumbashree Mission had taken up during 2009-10 was the launch of 'Home Shop' model of community marketing networks. Community marketing refers to marketing goods made by Kudumbashree enterprises and groups directly to consumers in the local community through a distribution system built with the support of Kudumbashree CBOs and managed by a professional management team. The Home Shop model emerged in Thrissur district and soon became a success with the help of a highly networked marketing team which has 500 women members, 10 MEs and a monthly turnover of over ₹ 25 lakhs. The home shop model has been established in 6 more districts.

Skill Development Training

Kudumbashree Mission organises training programmes for skill development and general orientation, EDP, PIP and performance improvement for its members.

Social Empowerment

Kerala's history of social empowerment is unparallel in the country. This has been reflected in the social index of the State especially with social welfare pension schemes, labour pensions, general health services, effective public distribution system, high enrolment and minimal dropout rates in schools, tremendous basic infrastructure development at the grass root level by the local self government bodies in housing, drinking water, cleanliness drive and so on.

Buds Special School

Buds is an innovative model developed by the Kudumbashree Mission for the development and protection of mentally challenged children to enable them access to education and training within their community. This project was formed following a survey conducted to identify the beneficiaries of Ashraya project. BUDS was formed with the support of local self government and Kudumbashree management. Today, there are 31 BUDS schools functioning all over the State. Children with autism, cerebral palsy and mental retardation are given special care in these schools.

- As of 2010, 31 Buds schools are functioning with 861 students. Seven schools are getting the special grant of the education department.
- In December 2010,11 BUDS schools were given mini buses.
- Kudumbashree Mission prepared and published a detailed guideline Handbook for Buds.
- The Mission provided training to functionaries of BUDS schools

at the Panchayat level, teachers and representatives of the parents also.

- Government of Kerala issued official orders on minimum standard of Buds. District level advisory committee and Buds school management committee were also constituted.
- Permission to utilize the NRLM funds with LSGS for supporting activities of BUDS schools was given.

Ashraya

Ashraya is a project of Kudumbashree to identify and rehabilitate destitute families under the Local Self Government Institutions. Those identified under the project were provided with livelihood necessities such as food, clothing, health coverage, pension, education, basic necessities such as house, water, sanitation facilities, development needs like vocational training, personality development trainings, care services like counselling and other training programmes.

Balasabha and Balapanchayats

The Balasabha movement has been initiated by Kudumbashree in line with the CBO network of the Mission. It aims at the capacity and confidence building of poor children through a variety of initiatives and activities, implemented for their creative, emotional, educational, intellectual and even entrepreneurial development.

- Children of the Kudumbashree network get an opportunity to learn through fun activities at camps or visits and interactions with facilitators.
- Balasabha resource persons help organise study trips for children which could help to know the nature or more about the stars, or even new models in origami.
- Presently the Balasabha has 54,411 members in the State.
- Kudumbashree initiatives of Balasabha and Bala Panchayats enabled to impart voice, face and power to children hailing from poor and vulnerable socio-economic backgrounds.
- Balasabha meets have been held at Panchayath, District and Regional levels.
- Bala Panchayat is the creation of a children's forum where

children's issues and concerns can be brought to the notice of local development planners, i.e., the LSGs.

- The focus is on providing a rights based debating space on the one hand, and opportunities for involving children in local development oriented activities either as participant or as monitor on the other. One such interface has been that of local environmental audits conducted by the children of Kudumbashree.
- Awareness programmes on various issues, residential camps, study tours, teen camps, science study classes, nature camps, Krishipaadham, holistic health programmes, co-living camps, Bala parliaments are among the activities of Balasabha.

Children from different Balasabhas from different parts of the State voluntarily came forward to actively take part in the fight against the menace of plastics. This could also be seen as the level of social awareness and responsibility among the children on issues around them.

Empowering ST & SC

The Special Tribal Project was implemented in 10 selected Panchayats of Idukki, Wayanad, Palakkad and Kasargod in the first phase. At a later stage the project was extended to all Panchayats of Wayanad district. In the second phase the project was extended to select Panchayats of 9 districts namely Trivandrum, Kollam, Patanamathitta, Kottayam, Ernakulam, Thrissur, Malapuram, Kozhikode, Kannur, Kudumbashree has been able to cover a sizable portion of Tribal families under the thrift and credit pattern of NHGs.

The skill development programme has gained steady momentum in the districts as more and more women came forward to initiate micro enterprises on their own.

- Special awareness campaign to ensure participation of ST and SC community stated in 2007-08. This has helped in improving the participation in NHGs and formation of new NHGs.
- General training and awareness classes for women and teenaged children, based on specific subjects and medical camps were also a regular feature of activities undertaken by the mission in the districts.
- Special Ashraya project in the Tribal sector was formed.

- The bylaws have been reformed in order to identify the stake holders in the ADS and CDS organizational level to ensure participation.
- Formation of special Tribal ADS in places where there are two or more Tribal NHGs are functioning.
- Under the project, the mission aims at extending support to the deprived among the Tribals by intervening in areas like housing, clothing, education, medicines and food.
- The project provides Matching grant for exclusive SC NHGs, subsidies for SC Micro entrepreneurs and financial assistance for skill training.

Women Empowerment

Gender Self Learning Programme is an educational process, formulated by Kudumbashree envisaging a platform to share debate and record both the visible and invisible representation and participation of women in social, economic, political and cultural settings. The programme tries to bring out different models to enable opportunities and operational changes in local economic development, local governance through education. The voices of women and perceptions on topics of discussion were recorded in the web portal and can be accessed at the local self government level.

The Gender Self Learning Programme implementation is carried out through Gender Resource Person Coordinators posted in all the 14 districts. The Gender RPCs were selected from among experienced social activists who were academically qualified.

The first step towards the implementation of the project State wide was to mobilize resource persons who can deliver gender sensitive strategies to make women visible in different dimensions of society. The network of resource persons have been strengthened by including more young activists who can propagate the aims of Gender Self Learning Programme at the grass root level. A hand book on '*sthreepadavi swayampatana prakriya-enthu? engane?*' (status of women—a self study, how and why?) was introduced to understand the background, aims and objectives of the education process. The introductory training sessions were held for State to ward level resource persons.

Vanita Sabha is perhaps the first step towards culling out the experiences of women at the grass root level. It is an exercise to form creative learning groups that share and understand concerns and solutions which eventually influence policy decisions.

Legal Literacy Activities

Kudumbashree has utilized the services offered by the Kerala Legal Services Society (KLSS) for its various legal literacy campaigns. A booklet, "Women and Law" on the various laws for the protection of women was prepared by Kudumbashree and distributed throughout the network.

Urban Poverty Alleviation

Kudumbashree Mission is the State Urban Development Agency of the Government of Kerala and thus plays an important role in coordinating urban poverty alleviation schemes of the Central and State governments. It is the State-level Nodal Agency for implementation of various schemes and programmes of Government of India such as: Basic Services to the Urban Poor (BSUP) and Integrated Housing and Slum Development Programme (IHSDP)—components of the Jawaharlal Nehru National Urban Renewal Mission (JNNURM) to provide housing finance for economically backward and cluster of urban poor through ISHUP (Interest Subsidy Scheme for Housing the Urban Poor). Swarna Jayanti Shahari Rozgar Yojana (SJSRY) for urban employment generation and poverty alleviation.

Integrated Housing and Slum Development Programme (IHSDP)

This is a Central Government project for the slum dwellers in the urban areas. This project has been made integrating the centrally sponsored projects VAMBAY and NSDP as Integrated Housing and Slum Development Programme (IHSDP). This project is implemented in areas where the population is up to five lakh.

Basic Services to the Urban Poor (BSUP)

The Basic Services to the Urban Poor (BSUP), a Central Government sponsored project is envisaged to provide basic infrastructural facility and urban poverty alleviation in urban areas. This project has been implemented in Thiruvananthapuram and Kochi corporations in Kerala. A complete development of the slums providing sufficient shelter and basic infrastructure is envisaged in this project.

Swarna Jayanti Shahari Rozgar Yojana (SJSRY)

SJSRY project was launched by the Central Government in 1997 with the objective to improve urban employment generation and economic empowerment through self employment. This project helps the beneficiaries to find self employment opportunities, skill development, enhancing the organizational setup and provide the required support to meet the needs of the self employed.

Interest Subsidy Scheme for Housing the Urban Poor (ISSHUP)

The ISSHUP project was implemented by the Central Government under the Jawaharlal Nehru Urban Renewal Mission (JNURM) to provide housing finance for economically backward and low income groups. This project assists the urban poor to construct or buy a new house with the help of interest subsidized loan.

Special Livelihood Project (SLP)

The Special Livelihoods Project (SLP) is a project to ensure comprehensive livelihood planning for urban poor. The project is implemented through identifying the specific needs, impart training to find and do employment and ensure regular income from the work. This project is implemented through the funds generated from and Kudumbashree urban projects.

21

Women Support Centre in Empowering Rural Women

A Case Study of Ganjam District, Odisha (India)

Sanjoy Patnaik and *Sarita Pradhan*

Background

This chapter traces the context of women in India, women and land, the women's voiced and unvoiced needs, laws and policies with regard to women and land in India and Odisha, initiation of pilot in Odisha to address women's accessibility to secured land rights, the learning from the implementation and scaling up to Women Support Centres.

No research is needed to prove that land is crucial to human living. Some of the most complicated and complex socio-economic and political conflicts in India have emerged from rural indebtedness and dispossessed peasantry, especially in the context of negligible or almost non-existent access to land. As in other countries, the causes of rural poverty in India are intimately tied to the control and use of land.

Noting the significance of direct access to land, and not just access mediated *via* male members, for the economic and social wellbeing of women and their families, and also this chapter traces women's rights to land in law and the factors impinging on women's ability to claim, control on land. Legislations, while a step forward, has yet to establish full gender equality in law.

Criticality of Land for Women

In India a rape occurs every 22 minutes, a dowry killing almost every

90 minutes and a female foeticide every 20 seconds, and with this, the country loses 10 million female births annually (Thomas, 2012). Despite its fast economic growth, women in India are vulnerable, often regarded as disposable commodities who can be raped and left to die or burnt for dowry money, whose education is not a family priority and who, given a chance, would not be allowed a birth. In a primarily patriarchal culture in which the earning potential of a man makes him an asset to the family, families reject women as liabilities. The Constitution of India proclaims women are equal to men, and India's laws give women rights over property, but is it really so?

Wide disparities in property rights are deeply rooted in tradition, and weak implementation of progressive laws are primarily responsible for multiple threats to the security of women's lives and living. Research confirms that putting more income in the control of women yields beneficial results for health, education, child nutrition and overall household income.

Around 86 per cent of women in rural India are dependent on agriculture, yet less than 10 per cent own land, which is the most important household asset to support their families and provide food, nutrition and income security (Giovarelli, 2009). Women do two-third of the world's work and produce 60-80 per cent of Africa's and Asia's food, and 40 per cent of Latin America's. Yet they earn only one tenth of the world's income and own less than 1 per cent of the world's property. They are amongst the poorest of world's poor (Barber Conable, President of World Bank, Inaugural Address at Washington, World Bank, 1986).

In rural India, the standard cultural response to a widow or a deserted woman is for her parents or in-laws to deny her access to land. This denial skilfully camouflages a very strong economic motive, which is to maintain control over property. The patriarchal forces on respective sides may allow her stay with them as long as there is no demand for her share in her husband's property, especially land. On the natal side, it is rather an easy argument for her brother to say that she should wait to get her husband's share and not claim his. The story is more or less the same for divorced women and other types of single women.

Land becomes particularly critical when a woman becomes head of the household when her husband migrates for work, abandons her, divorces her or dies. In India, studies reveal that between 20 per cent and 35 per cent of households are headed by women (UN Department of Economic and Social Affairs, 1999). The traditional system of land rights still followed in rural India gives women sustenance but hardly any ownership.

This is because women have been conditioned to prefer "security of the family" rather than independence. Generally the daughters waive their land rights in favour of their brothers, to avoid being denounced as "selfish" and for the risk of being alienated from their natal families (Pallavi, 2007).

India prides itself with a list of gender-sensitive legislation that empowers women. Increased political representation and economic independence are oft quoted examples of such empowerment. However, most of these progressive laws have yielded limited results in ensuring ownership rights over land to women. Women's rights over land in India have not gone beyond joint titling, which is limited to government land allocation schemes; inheritance rights predominantly continue to be male centric. Moreover, when women gain access to land through male relatives, as they often times do, their rights are vulnerable to breakdowns in relationships and divorce. Furthermore, women have little say over how their male relatives use or wish to use the land.

The greatest vulnerability is that women in general lack awareness of existing laws and regulations and their legal rights to own and inherit land. This lack of awareness especially in the rural areas can be attributed primarily to limited literacy. Women's restricted access to assets and a societal tradition that promotes men's control of economic resources renders rural Indian women among the poorest in the country. Without land in their names, women are not entitled to get a residence certificate that makes them eligible to access institutional credit and without this crucial residential and caste certificate, their children are denied enrolment in school.

Challenges to Secure Land Tenure for Women

It is not socially acceptable for women to talk about or assert their property rights. In a typically dominant joint family in which several related nuclear families live together, it is "not gentlewomanly" for a woman to discuss independent property rights. In a patrilocal system, in which the woman moves to her husband's village when she marries, it is not legally difficult for a woman to assert rights over land, but is considered a taboo–not conforming to traditional norms. That is why in a joint family even the son barely discusses his share of property with his father or brothers, and if he does so the family will assume that he has been ill advised by his wife. Therefore, the entire discourse on women's land rights is very strongly linked with the construction of ideal Indian woman—one who suffers, who is submissive and not assertive, and who sacrifices and does not talk about land rights. Therefore, "good women" cannot and will not wish to inherit land.

To enhance understanding about critical barriers to women's land rights in India, it is important to analyse the socio-cultural context in which such rights are advocated. In other words, we must examine the social condition that generates (or does not generate) the demand for such rights and the supply framework that determines whether such rights legally available. A woman's demand for land rights is invariably adversity based—such demands are only in the absence of her husband. The transfer of property rights from the husband to wife, especially land, is automatic and straightforward in case of a nuclear family, but rather complicated in a joint family situation[1].

In rural India, it is not normal to partition family property if the head of the family is alive. This means that while a man's father is still alive, it is uncommon for a son to own land in his own name. This has important implications for the son's wife since it means that if the son dies or abandons her, she will not be able to claim title to the son's share of the family land since all the land remains documented in her father-in-law's name, not in her husband's (the son's) name. In such cases, land administration officials find it difficult to ascertain what share of land the woman is entitled to from her in-laws, and this uncertainty very often delays indefinitely the official's handling of her claim, effectively denying her the rights that she has been legally provided.

As per the Hindu Succession Act 1956 (Amended in 2005), these single women are entitled to receive a share of land from their paternal or in-law's families but negotiating such rights in an overtly patriarchal set up such as exists in rural India becomes extremely difficult. Moreover, the laws do not require property partition (and changing the records) to occur in a time bound manner, and inheritance cases can drag on for quite some time, during which the woman will likely not be allowed to share possession of the property.

The government intends to "empower" women by allowing them co-ownership over homestead land through a joint title[2] (joint *patta*) system. But the social matrix continues to be tilted in favour of men to singularly make decisions about land transfers. In some places, women cite examples of increased domestic violence in a joint *patta* framework, as women may refuse to sign land transfer documents that are mandatory under the joint system. When there was individual ownership by men, women were hardly consulted before land transfers were considered, as it was not legally required. Therefore, domestic violence concerning land was relatively low. Although the joint *patta* has altered the legal relationships in favour of women, the societal perception of women's rights has remained almost completely unchanged, with the result that the Hindu Succession Act and other progressive laws have not actually improved women's access to land.

There are three ways that a woman can acquire rights over land: from government allocation, through inheritance and by purchase. With regard to government land allocation and purchase, a single woman will acquire the land in her individual name while a married woman will acquire the land jointly in her name and the name of her husband. Inheriting either paternal or husband's property includes a process of property division that is invariably cumbersome and complicated because family members have multiple claims. A woman who claims property by way of inheritance must fight for division of the property as it is rather uncommon for either the natal family or in-laws to initiate such property partition.

Innovative pilot to Provide Land to Single Women

In 2009 Landesa (then the Rural Development Institute) began working with the State government of Odisha to improve implementation of the State's Vasundhara homestead allocation programme by providing additional capacity to the Revenue Department (responsible for land administration) by piloting a system to train local youth, known as Community Resource Persons (CRP) to assist land administrators in implementing the State programme. While implementing the CRP pilot in Ganjam district,[3] in April 2010 district officials invited Landesa to discuss a parallel intervention to strengthen women's land rights in the district. The officials invited Landesa to design and establish an exclusive cell at the sub-district level to address women's land issues, and to undertake an assessment of women's access to land in selected villages in the district.

Landesa undertook a qualitative study in nine villages in three sub-districts to gain a deeper understanding on women's access to land in order to be able to design the centre. Key findings of the study included the following:

- A woman's land rights are highly dependent on her marital status.
- Land rights of single women were neglected.
- Women whose husbands were away are *de facto* household heads.

- Eligible women-headed households were left out of the Vasundhara homestead scheme.

Piloting the Women's Land Rights Facilitation Centre in One Sub-District

Landesa designed this exclusive cell having a unique institutional mechanism to operate within the existing land administration structure to help ensure that rural single woman can obtain homestead land. The district administration named the cell as Women's Land Rights Facilitation Centre (WLRFC) and opened it on a pilot basis at Khallikote sub-district in March 2011. The head of the sub-district supervised the centre, and a female land administration officer served as centre facilitator or nodal officer assumed primary responsibility for its operation.

The WLRFC had two broad objectives: (1) allocating land to women; and (2) building capacity and generating awareness of officials. Although a third objective—redressing land related grievances of women relating land—was originally planned, the WLRFC decided to defer this work until the team knew more about how sensitive the issues were, under the first objective, the WLRFC identified eligible women for homestead plot allocation under the Vasundhara scheme, prioritizing those women, assisting with applications for land and providing other related assistance (e.g., helping women secure assistance building a home). During the study, it was clear that to ensure land rights for women, field-level land administration officials had to be trained to the fact that women required land because the officials did not initially appreciate the idea of land rights for women. Therefore, one significant intervention was developing the capacities of the land administration officials, along with members of local self-government, field level officials of Women and Child Development Department.

This pilot was implemented in 112 villages in Khallikote sub-district with trained CRPs to identify single woman and women-headed households to be able to get a homestead plot each with support from Anganwadi workers (field level workers of Women and Child Development Department). Trained CRPs with support from the Anganwadi workers began using a structured survey format to identify women who were eligible to receive homestead land under the Vasundhara allocation programme. The cases then were registered by the WLRFC facilitator and presented to the director of the sub-district, who then forwarded the cases to subordinate land administration officials for field verification and thereafter initiated land administration processes to ensure the women obtain land rights to homestead plots.

Pilot Findings and Learning

The pilot defined an eligible single woman as somebody who is poor, who does not have a piece of land in her name, who is single (that is, who is widowed, divorced, abandoned, unmarried, differentially abled or married to man who has migrated for work), who earns less than ₹ 24,000 per annum and who does not have a government job. In this process, the WLRFC identified more than 500 single women and woman-headed households in 54 villages out of 112 villages. Based on these identified numbers, the local land administration officials initiated field verifications and came to the conclusion that 352 households were eligible to receive title to a homestead plot.

Although these women were shortlisted, it was not clear whether they would receive land. The three major hurdles in the process were as follows:

(1) The land administration officials hesitated to allocate land to single women (whether living alone or with their parents or in-laws) on the pretext that it was not clear what share of land they would later inherit from their parents or in-laws. The officials were concerned that if they allocated government land to a woman who later inherited some land from her parents or in-laws, that the officials could be the target of government proceedings.

(2) Even if a widow or an abandoned woman was on her own and did not have a title (*patta*) for her current house site, land administration officials gave the same explanation that she might inherit land in the future.

(3) The land administration officials refused to undertake field verification for the identified single women on the grounds that they had received no specific instruction or guideline from the district administration to do so.

(4) There were instances of single women getting evicted from a brother's house after the women received a plot in their name. This is the flip side of empowerment where the brother no longer has the pleasure of patronising his sister. Charity was acceptable to him, but not empowerment of his sister.[4]

However, some single women, mostly living on their own, did receive title to their current house sites. But even those widows, abandoned women and unmarried women above 30 years old whom a broad minded official identified as eligible, still faced several challenges. Three basic issues prevented women from enjoying land rights: (1) in the absence of a housing grant, women would not relocate to the vacant land; (2) it was a security threat (fear of staying alone) for such women when the land officials identified vacant government land to allocate outside the village; and (3) in many villages vacant government land (of a type that could be allocated into private ownership) was not available for allocation. These hurdles stalled the allocation process as close to 81 per cent of the women identified faced this challenge.

But perhaps the biggest lesson of the pilot was the ease with which it was possible to allocate land to large numbers of women and the fact that there were no official justifications that would deny their eligibility to receive land. Therefore, the reasons that these women had not received land in the past may have included a lack of motivation, fear of any proceedings against them and, importantly, the fact that neither the State nor the district administration had given a specific mandate to officials to identify and provide land for this category of landless. Other key lessons from the pilot were:

- Although land administration officials initially thought that it might not be worthwhile to identify such single women, during the process of field verification they realised the criticality of land (even a homestead parcel) for such women.
- It may not require legal amendments to include single women as Vasundhara beneficiaries. An example is provided by the law relating to resettlement of families displaced by development projects. While providing compensation the Resettlement and Rehabilitation Policy (2006) of Odisha included widows, abandoned women, destitute women and unmarried women above the age of 30 years as separate families without amending any specific land law. This precedence may be used to provide land to the single women without changing land laws.
- Considering the fact that some women were able to obtain land in the pilot process, the barriers to women receiving land was more about State policy rather than shortcomings in law. A separate land allocation programme focused on single women could serve as a platform on which such women's land centres could thrive and succeed.

- While designing the plan to scale up the WLRFC pilot to other parts of the district, it might be possible for existing Anganwadi workers to identify eligible women, working in place of the CRPs to do the enumeration work in the field. This would be cost effective and effective use of existing village level institutions, and could help the work to scale more quickly.
- Availability of government land inside the village cropped up as a crucial issue during the pilot. It is important to find land inside the village since providing homestead land in a secluded area outside the village is as good as not giving land at all, as hardly any of the women would relocate on grounds of security and lack of access to a government housing grant. Therefore, when it comes to giving land to single women, the policy should be to settle them inside the village and government should send necessary and clear instructions.

Scaling the Pilot throughout the District

Considering the potential of the WLRFC to address the plight of single women, in April 2012 the district administration gave a new dimension to the centre by enhancing the scope of its operations and extending its objectives to include coordinating delivery of livelihoods services and social security to which women are entitled according to different government programmes. With the aim of providing land and other livelihoods and social security benefits to single women and women-headed households, the district administration scaled WLRFC from one sub-district to the entire district with 23 sub-districts (tahsils) and rebranded the centres as *Women Support Centres (WSCs)*.

While land continues to be the major focus, the WSC has been developed as a single window delivery to enhance women's improved access to other livelihoods and social security schemes. The Anganwadi workers were trained to provide additional capacity to the local land administration officers to identify eligible single women and women-headed households. They used a pre-designed survey format to identify eligible single women within a very short period. The processed data then goes to respective sub-district land officials and rural development officials to initiate land allocation and link the women with relevant government programmes that help land owners build houses, instal sanitation facilities, etc. In each of the WSCs, a nodal officer, who is necessarily a woman land administration official, is placed to ensure that data that comes from the Anganwadi workers are entered in specific formats, compiled and provided to both the land officials and rural development officials for necessary action.

Special focus and attention is being given to data entry and developing a robust management information system (MIS). The MIS is undertaken in four steps: (1) collection of baseline information on the single women, (2) filtration of data as per the different categories of women, (3) updating the master database with the filed verification and camp court report, and (4) updating master database with information regarding the land title (*patta*). Thereafter, one copy of the data is sent to the sub-district land administration officer, identifying the women who do not have *patta* either in her name or her spouse's name for the land where she presently resides; and a second copy of the data is sent to the sub-district rural development officer, identifying whether all single women and women-headed have access to different government services.

Landesa oriented and built the capacities of all stakeholders at the district, Block and sector levels. Landesa also oriented various land administration, child development and social welfare officers at the sub-district level on the programme and WSC design. After the district-level orientation, Landesa also organised Block-level trainings to orient the local land administration officials, land surveyors and local child development officers on women and land rights along with the functioning of the WSCs. In order to collect data from the villages, Anganwadi workers were trained at the sector level. The district administration facilitated and spearheaded the entire process.

Programme monitoring takes place monthly at the sub-district (tahsil) and district level to ensure that specific deadlines are adhered to. Landesa continues to provide technical support, including support to build capacities of multiple stakeholders; to design the data management system, including monitoring of programme implementation; and to identify legal and institutional gaps for policy advocacy at the appropriate level.

In a span of three to four months the Women Support Centres have identified 57,422 single women out of 304,754 households in 1,238 villages of 11 sub-districts to avail numerous government schemes and services. A total of 46,087 women out of 57,422 will be verified for land allocation. Out of 5,384 households verified 984 households have been eligible to receive government land.

> "*Without property rights, women would continue to be considered liabilities. Dignity, self-esteem and informed*

citizenship would elude them and mother's womb would continue to be a graveyard of equality and social justice."

(Patnaik, 2013).

Notes

1. If the husband is absent from a nuclear family, it is not difficult for the wife (or widow) to assert rights to the family land, but that if the couple live with the husband's parents (a joint family), then it is hard for his wife (or widow) to assert rights.
2. The State government in 1989 made joint application both in the name of husband and wife mandatory failing which land *patta* cannot be given.
3. Ganjam, a southern district of Odisha, is primarily an agrarian district with maximum homeless as well as Vasundhara beneficiaries. Though Ganjam has a fairly good network of micro-irrigation systems, a sizeable chunk of its rural populace migrates for about 6-8 months a year for search of work in States like Gujarat. The district is also marred by high rate of liquor consumption and gambling that is invariably sustaining a land mortgage market and a vibrant rural credit operation through local *ṣahukars* (moneylenders). It is understandable that when Vasundharapatta was being distributed, in the absence of migrating men, the joint *patta* was given in the name of women.
4. Raibari, an unmarried single woman, of Lakapada village of Khallikote tahsil of Ganjam district of Odisha, was staying with her brother and his family. After she got a homestead plot from the Centre, her brother asked her to move out of his house as she has got her own land now. Raibari moved out from her brother's house and lived on her own, building a small thatched hut on her land. She is now a daily wage labour earning one dollar a day.

References

Asian NGO Coalition for Agrarian Reform and Rural Development [ANGOC]. (2009). The Prolonged Struggle for Land Rights in Asia—A Regional Overview. In *Securing the Right to Land: A CSO Overview on Access to Land in Asia* (pp. 11-34). Quezon City, Philippines: Author. Retrieved from http://landwatchasia.files.wordpress.com/2010/05/securing-the-right-to-land-full.pdf

Bumiller, E. (1991). *May You Be the Mother of a Hundred Sons*. New Delhi: Penguin Books India.

Food and Agriculture Organization (2011). *The State of Food and Agriculture*

2010-2011: Women in Agriculture–Closing the Gender Gap for Development. Rome, Italy: Author. Retrieved from http://www.fao.org/docrep/013/i2050e/i2050e00.htm

Giovarelli, R. (2009). Gender and Land Tenure Reform. In R.L. Prosterman, R. Mitchell, and T. Hanstad (Eds.), *One Billion Rising: Law, Land and the Alleviation of Global Poverty* (pp. 195-233). Amsterdam: Leiden University Press.

Pallavi, A. (2007, June 1). Land titles don't come easy for farm widows. *India Together*. Retrieved February 13, 2013, from http://www.indiatogether.org/2007/jun/wom-widowland.htm.

Patnaik, Sanjoy, *Status Report: Land Rights and Ownership in Odisha*. India: United Nations Development Programme and Ministry of Rural Development, Government of India [UNDP andMoRD]. (2008). http://www.undp.org/content/dam/india/docs/land_rights_ownership_in_orissa.pdf

Patnaik, Sanjoy (February 2013), 'Land to Women, Life for Nation', Unpublished Monograph, Landesa 2013.

Planning Commission, Government of India. (2006, July 31). *Report of the Working Group on Land Relations for Formulation of 11th Five Year Plan*.New Delhi, India: Author. Retrieved from http://planningcommission.nic.in/aboutus/committee/wrkgrp11/wg11_landrel.pdf.

Thomas, G. (2012, July 6). Disappearing Daughters: India's Female Feticide.*CBN News*. Retrieved February 13, 213, from http://www.cbn.com/cbnnews/world/2012/June/Disappearing-Daughters-Indias-Female-Feticide/

Tim Hanstad, T. and Nielsen, R. (2009). Land tenure reform in India. In R.L. Prosterman, R. Mitchell, and T. Hanstad (Eds.), *One Billion Rising: Law, Land and the Alleviation of Global Poverty* (pp. 235-276). Amsterdam: Leiden University Press.

United Nations Department of Economic and Social Affairs. (1999). *World Survey on the Role of Women in Development: Globalization, Gender and Work.*

Legislation of India and Odisha

Constitution of India (1950).
Estates Abolition Act (1951).
Hindu Succession Act (1956).
Hindu Succession Amendment Act (2005).
Land Ceiling Act (1974).
Orissa Government Land Settlement Act (1962).
Orissa Land Reforms Act (1960).
Orissa Prevention of Land Encroachment Act (1972).
Orissa Tenancy Act (1913).

22

Rural Women in Local Self Governance

State and Beyond

Monica Banerjee

Introduction

This chapter offers to investigate State's ability to alter gender relations in India. The State's omnipresent laws, policies and programmes seem not to have ushered genuine social or gender justice especially among rural societies; at best it seems to have generated only partially engendered institutions of governance or social development The author is more drawn towards the idea of seeding and nurturing inclusive and common agency of men and women in rural areas that could uphold an altering vision of micro-societies autonomously working for real empowerment of women. Contents of this chapter are based on some empirical research, however, they are also informed by almost two decades of experience of supporting grassroots civil society organizations of rural India.

Context

A study leads to the realization that mere reserving seats for women or expanding their quantitative spaces in local governance institutions might not assuage the levels of inequity and inadequacies so prevalent in the socially fragmented structures that are deeply symbolic of rural India. Merely ensuring seats in governance institutions for women without addressing the ecosystem from where she operates would mean only partial empowerment of women. Studies by scholars (Panda, 2008) reaffirm this position where such partial engendering of governance needs to be addressed by moving beyond State and exploring role of civil society in bringing a transformative and inclusive agenda to any serious attempts at engendering society.

Women in Leadership Roles of Formal Governance—Understanding What Affects Performance

In order to prefigure gender mainstreaming and justice, the Government of India, in its historic Amendment Act of 1994, made provisions for seating women in at least one-third of all leadership positions in the statutory system of governance in rural India, by way of reservations. Called Panchayati Raj Institutions, the third tier of these three levels of democratic and decentralized institutions are located in villages. India has some 2,65,000 *panchayats* and one third of them have women as their leaders, often called *Sarpanch* in many parts of India.

The researcher was engaged in empirically[1] testing the social and psychological profile of women leaders of local governance institutions only to understand how these variables affected their performances as leaders. *Inter alia*, the study revealed that despite some 44 per cent women having a considerably good perception of their leadership functions, when it came to performing these functions on ground, as high as 78 per cent of them measured either poor or average on role performance.[2]

It was obvious that many existing social, physical and psychological conditions were at play here. Role Performance was found to bear positive and significant correlation with education, annual incomes, job involvement, knowledge about panchayat activities, achievement motivation, and attitude towards roles as leaders. Significant regression coefficient values endorsed these variables to be good predictors for role performance[3] .

Yet, on measuring these attributes among women,[4] as high as 52 per cent had no formal education, 44 per cent belonged to low annual income groups, 55 per cent had low Job Involvement, 76 per cent suffered low Achievement Motivation, 56 per cent displayed less favourable attitude towards their role as leaders and 90 per cent possessed low or medium levels of knowledge about activities they needed to perform. Age had a negative and significant correlation with role performance yet high rates of fertility tied down young women to more domestic responsibilities and less public engagements. As many as 67 per cent women tested high on role conflicts. Similar findings were reported by Buch (1999), Santha (1999), Ekatra (2003) and Kaushik (1999).

Further, majority of women in 'High'[5] group of performers belonged to scheduled tribe (78.26%), had contested from open seats (69.56%), have had previous experience in politics/governance (69.56%), had associated themselves with various social organizations (65.21%) and held additional responsibilities in Panchayats (43.47%). Though for majority (78.26%) this was their first term as leaders of Panchayats, a significant 21.73 per cent in the High group were elected twice and served a second term in their respective Panchayats at the time of the survey. In contrast, majority of 'Low' group respondents belong to 'Other Backward Classes' (65.21%), had contested from seats reserved for women (100%), had contested only once or in other words were elected for the first time (100%), did not have any previous experience in politics or governance (82.60%), had no association with other social organizations (100%) and did not hold any additional responsibilities in Panchayats (95.65%). Thus, frequency distribution of *High* and *Low* groups of performers on these variables indicated that attributes like Caste, Number of terms elected, Type of seat contested, Previous experience in politics, Participation in social organizations, Holding additional responsibilities in Panchayats and Motivating factor for contesting elections might also have caused the difference between the *High* and *Low* performers.

A set of attributes ran uniformly among both the groups of performers. Majority of respondents in both *High* and *Low* groups were married and belonged to joint families with more than five members; attributes like family type, family size and marital status may not have influenced role performance of women Panchayat leaders. Though these women faced high 'Role Conflicts' in balancing Panchayat and domestic work, an insignificant correlation between Role Conflict and Role Performance implied that women leaders performed well despite high Role Conflicts. A deeper probing of correlation between dependent variables like Role Conflict and achievement motivation/attitudes/job involvement among women who ranked as high performers could have sharpened this analysis.

Challenges and Way Forward

There are several challenges and scope for doing much more for empowering women and ensuring a 'qualitative' presence in local governance institutions.

Since high Job Involvement, high Achievement Motivation, favourable Attitude towards role as Panchayat leaders and better knowledge about Panchayati Raj, *inter alia,* influences Role Performance positively, more efforts are needed to enhance these attributes in women Panchayat representatives. Both State and civil society could be a catalyst for designing mechanisms that would help strengthen these attributes. Some suggestions in this regard are as follows:

For those women, who actively associate themselves with day to day running of Panchayat activities despite various hurdles, the foremost strategy for State and civil society should be to look *beyond routine training programmes* that try to impart only the where withals of Panchayati Raj concepts and trap them only in the laws, provisions and concepts of local governance. The training programmes need to focus more on components that would help build, nurture and reinforce **self confidence** among these women to such an extent that it gets embedded or ingrained as a predominant personality trait in them. One has to consider the fact that this group of active women (and 'early adopters') is the forerunner of local governance at the grassroots level. They often know well about State and civil society interventions and look up to them for solutions. These 'ready to learn' women need to be reached early and empowered through well thought out confidence building exercises and strategies. They could then serve as examples worth emulating for other Panchayat women who are yet to gain even basic understanding of the seriousness of the position they hold in public life.

Education is universally accepted as the key to development but this is sadly in acute shortage among the women who hold key positions in rural local governance. It is only obvious that for majority of women run Panchayats, the discretion of the 'Panchayat secretaries' reign high who might not even think it important to read out or simplify the contents of a paper before taking the *sarpanch*'s signature. Understandably enough, the priority for the secretary is always to get passed or approved infrastructure development proposals like roads, culverts, wells and drinking water sources (which have more financial implications and interests along with the local contractor and 'friendly' State junior engineer at the Block development office). Though women 'Sarpanch' seemed hesitant to attend night classes run for educating adults, the government needs to take firm steps in adult education for the present incumbents. Flexible timings suiting their convenience, innovative study material which could make learning a pleasure and above all, introducing mass media for education like Community Radio are some suggestions in this direction. If women feel that social development like health, nutrition, sanitation, gender equity, education, etc. need to get a priority over physical infrastructure, then probably, education and eventually functional knowledge would help them translate this perception into adequate performance.

More and more young women should be motivated to take a leadership role in the Panchayat, if younger age is seen to influence Role Performance positively.

If participation in social organizations and holding additional responsibilities in Panchayats influences performance positively then women Panchayat leaders should be encouraged to associate themselves sufficiently with local NGOs, Mahila Mandals or self help groups and *samitis* that are often created by the locally embedded civil society organizations.

Though, it was not possible to look at the significance of association among different independent variables in this study, it could be possible that some factors have significant correlations between them. This study revealed that majority of the women panchayat leaders across the sample have high Role Conflict and less favourable Attitude towards role as Panchayat leaders, low Job Involvement, medium level of Achievement Motivation and low or medium level of Knowledge about Panchayat activities. Further studies could be done to see association among these variables for instance whether Role Conflict faced by a woman Panchayat leader influences her other traits like Job Involvement, Achievement Motivation, Attitude towards role as Panchayat leader or desire to gain knowledge about Panchayat activities.

Women as User Groups of Other Flagship Programmes of the State in Rural Areas

On a different role as a development practitioner, the researcher is engaged with a prominent philanthropic and grant making organization in India. While serving rural India for over 17 years, the researcher has stumbled upon many instrumentalities existing in other flagship programmes of the State that ostensibly provides for women's empowerment. Instances of the National Rural Employment Guarantee Act (MGNREGA), 2005 and National Rural Livelihood Mission (NRLM)[6], 2009 having got stuck in instrumentalities in the name of ensuring economic empowerment of women are common. MGNREGA's gender enabling provisions have neither succeeded in reducing wage disparities nor ensure participation of as much as 60 per cent women with children less than six years (Sudarshan, 2009, Galab, *et al.,* 2009). The trapping of Self-Help Group (SHG) movement, that the NRLM so strongly banks upon, in instrumental economic benefits, cannot be said to have empowered women, who continue to be victims of 'unpaid work' (Hirway, 2009), socially and politically.

There are two assumptions here. First, many poverty reduction programmes, laws, policies of State have failed to create gender-just institutional arrangements probably because the deeper, underlying causes of gender inequity have remained unchallenged. Instrumentality of tools like SHGs, capacity-building of women (to assume leadership roles) in isolation and without taking into account their surrounding social environment, creation and preference of non-inclusive and non-durable assets like unmetalled roads over pastures and watersheds that benefit the poor and women have failed to create common platforms where men and women, poor and marginalized, community and government line officials could come together to have a ***shared vision*** of a social and gender just society.

Where Voluntary Sector could Come in

Field experiences and empirical evidences (Sudarshan, 2008) suggest that people's agency play a critical role in allowing issues and concerns of women to be taken from the private, invisible sphere to a public space where joint action becomes possible. The second assumption is that in order to facilitate such people's agency, there needs to be a more grounded, bottom-up constructive work for transforming unequal gender relationships. And in the Indian context, it is demonstrable (Vyasulu and Vyasulu, 2000) that voluntary organizations within the civil society space are more capable of fostering and nurturing people's agency with desired outcomes. Their need based and flexible constructive work amidst a community in a reasonably small area seems to be much better placed to address democratic and gender deficits on ground than the State's top-down and inflexible approach at development with only partially engendered institutional arrangements.

Scholars world over have redeemed their faith in civil society (Parekh, 2004; Edwards, 2004; Keane, 1998; Hall, 1995), its expansive definition and inclusive usage (Hann, 1996), its ability to bring political and social transformation in different geographical and cultural contexts like Asia (Alagappa, 2004) and Africa (Comaroff and Comaroff, 1999) and also its association with family (Cohen and Arato, 1992) and gender (Howell, 2006). Many have also probed its legitimacy in competing with the State by way of parallel 'service delivery' (Pearce, 2000) and yet many (Howell and Pearce, 2001) have also expressed concerns about tendencies of outside forces to reducing civil society as *anti-state.*

Evidences suggest the suitability of civil society and voluntary sector to usher genuine gender equity and reduce instrumentalities in any programme for gender mainstreaming and equity. In so doing it obviously has to approach things differently from the State. *The long term programmes and projects in voluntary action are often guided by the hypothesis that changing community norms and men's thinking and attitudes is key to changing gender equations.* They would, therefore, focus on ***inclusive and common agency of people*** as alternate structures for probing and arriving at solutions to overcome unequal social and gender relations. They would seek to understand voluntary action's contribution and effectiveness in:

1. preparing communities towards social relationships and property relations that make women trustees of common property resources along with men,
2. in promoting dialogues among village community on regenerating the commons on which men and women depend on livelihoods,
3. their legitimacy in bringing men and women together at work sites to enhance agency to co-create more just outcomes and usher more investments in strengthening women's leadership, and
4. promoting inclusive capacity building including formation of inclusive groups of men and women for promoting awareness of gender disparities in education, health, land rights and access to resources.

There are adequate examples and analyses of voluntary organizations in rural India that offer clues into simple, practical investments that need to be made by civil society to facilitate inclusive and common agency of people for strengthening women's social positions and enhancing their performances in public domain including governance institutions. These analyses could be used to demonstrate civil society's possibly profound role in dealing not only with impact and outcomes but more significantly enduring the processes and challenges of gender based development. The significance lies in the fact that in the Indian context and contemporary times the lack of mutual trust between State and voluntary sector, showcasing the sector's contribution in ensuring effective gender based development is critical in building a complementary relationship between

State and Civil society and a sense of long-term trust in the voluntary sector's capability for deepening democracy with real empowerment of women.

Conclusion

While keenly following the institutional arrangements *vis-à-vis* empowerment of women, it occurs that it is the precise *location of institutions* that determines the *extent of empowerment* among rural women. State alone cannot create a gender just institutional arrangement as long as deeper, underlying causes of gender inequities remain unchallenged. Institutions of local self governance, an offering of the State, seem to be only partially engendered that ensure mere quantitative spaces for women. Many factors that control quality of leadership among women and hence their empowerment in fact reside outside or are external to these institutions of local governance. These factors comprise the eco-system—the social, physical and psychological—environment of the woman. It is these factors that make rural women leaders perform much below their abilities and despite being highly perceptive about their roles. Not only local self governance institutions but instrumentalities of other State rural flagship programmes too have done little to assuage the role conflicts faced by women. To generate a more profound sense of empowerment, the need is to target a rural woman's eco-system, locate and strengthen institutions that complement State policies and projects *yet probe deeper to foster more autonomous and inclusive agency of ordinary men and women.* Voluntary organizations in grassroots civil society, because of their ideal location and deeper engagement with local contexts, are frequently suited to play a critical role in delivering real empowerment for India's women in villages.

Notes

1. A research conducted in two districts of Madhya Pradesh—Betul and Raisen—with around a hundred women leaders of Local Self Governance institutions
2. In order to know the role perception and role performance, work functions were identified and a work chart containing nine functional items was developed so that respondents (here women Panchayat leaders) could be measured on them. While the work chart remained similar for judging both role perception and role performance, the five-point continuum was

modified to suit the purpose. Majority of respondents are divided between good (43.47%) and poor (40.21%) levels of role perception with very few in the average or middle level (16.30%). However, when it comes to performing these functions, majority of respondents are found to measure either poor (45.65%) or average (32.60%) on role performance. '*t*' test of significance showing significant difference in mean values for Role Perception and Role Performance ($t = 2.145$) at both 0.01 and 0.05 probability suggests gap between Role Perception and Role Performance as judged by Panchayat women themselves.

3. Role Performance of women Panchayat leaders is found to have positive and significant correlation with Education ($r = 0.304$), Total Annual Income ($r = 0.831$), Job Involvement ($r = 0.804$), Knowledge about panchayat activities ($r = 0.721$), Achievement Motivation ($r = 0.841$) and Attitude towards role as Panchayat leader ($r = 0.8361$). Age as variable is found to have negative and significant correlation with Role Performance ($r = -0.3165$). The variable Role Conflict does not have a significant correlation with Role Performance ($r = -0.057$) meaning that women Panchayat leaders could perform well even in the face of high role conflicts. To know the contribution of independent variables to the variation in dependent variable, multiple regression analysis was carried out. Out of the eight independent variables taken, the variables Age ($b = -0.262$), Education ($b = 0.355$), Total Annual Income of family ($b = 0.915$), Job Involvement, ($b = 0.907$), Achievement Motivation ($b = 0.922$), Knowledge about Panchayat activities ($b = 0.721$) and Attitude towards role as Panchayat leader ($b = 0.916$) could be termed as good predictors of Role Performance as their regression coefficient (b) values are found to be significant.The R^2 value is found to be 0.834, which, suggests that the 8 variables jointly contribute 83.4 per cent towards variation in role performance. The 'F' value is also found to be significant (F =12.48) which indicates the significant effectiveness of the eight variables in predicting the Role Performance when all the independent variables (including Role Conflict) are functioning jointly.
4. Majority of respondents are either between 35 and 45 years (43.47%) followed closely by women who are less than 35 years (39.12%), have no formal education (52.17%), are married (72.82%), belong to schedule tribes (48.91%) followed by OBC (32.60%), belong to the income group less than ₹ 30,000 annual income (44.55%), are elected for the first time in the two consecutive elections held in the State after implementation of 73rd Amendment Act (78.26%), have contested from the seats reserved for women (82.60%), have no previous experience in governance and politics (71.73%), have no association with social organizations (73.91%), do not hold any additional responsibilities in their Panchayat area (80.43%), cited 'support from community/family/social organizations' as the motivating factor for contesting elections (51.08%), have low level of

job involvement (55.43%), face high role conflict (67.39%), have medium level of achievement motivation (76.08%), have low (47.82%) and medium levels (41.30%) of knowledge about Panchayat activities and have a less favourable attitude towards their role as Panchayat leaders (56.52%).

5. On the basis of scores obtained under role performance by the respondents (women Panchayat leaders) the top 25.00 per cent and bottom 25.00 per cent were identified and put separately under 'HIGH' (high role performance) and LOW (low role performance) groups respectively. '*t*' test of significance shows significant difference between the two gorups (t=25.38) both at 0.01 and 0.05 levels of probability. Test of significance of difference in mean for various socio-economic and psychological characteristics among the HIGH and LOW groups of women Panchayat leaders through Fisher's '*t*' shows that the variables Age (t = 2.767), Education (t = 2.215), Total Annual Income of Family (t = 9.87), Job Involvement (t = 11.71), Achievement Motivation (t = 21.09), Knowledge about Panchayat activities (t = 9.19) and Attitude towards role as Panchayat leaders (t = 15.08) differs significantly in mean values for the two groups. Role Conflict is found to have no effect on Role Performance as the mean values do not differ significantly (t = 1.307 not significant at 0.01 and 0.05 levels of probability).Thus, on the basis of mean values, it is interpreted that women with higher education, high job involvement, higher annual income of their families, higher achievement motivation, higher knowledge on Panchayat activities and more favourable attitude towards role as Panchayat leaders measure high on role performance. Mean Values further suggest that women belonging to comparatively higher age measure low on role performance. (also see Banerjee:2009)
6. NREGA guarantees wage employment in every financial year to every rural household for 100 days and requires at least one-third of the workers to be women. NRLM provides a focused approach to rural poverty eradication by 2015 by bringing at least 50 per cent Below Poverty Line (BPL) households under SHG net so as to form and strengthen people owned organizations.

Bibliography

Alagappa, M. (2004). *Civil Society and Political Change in Asia* (Stanford, California: Stanford University Press).

Banerjee, M. (2009). Variables Influencing Role Performance of Women in Panchayats, *Productivity,* April-June, Vol. 50 (1), pp. 50-55.

Buch, Nirmala, (1999). *From Oppression to Assertion: A Study of Panchayats and Women in M.P., Rajasthan and U.P* (Centre for Women's Development Studies, New Delhi).

Comaroff, J.L. and Comaroff, J. (1999) *Civil Society and Political Imagination in Africa-Critical Perspectives* (USA: University of Chicago Press).

Edwards, M. (2004). *Civil Society,* (Cambridge, UK: Polity Press).

EKATRA (2003). *Women and Governance; Reimagining the State* (Ekatra, Society for Development Alternatives for Women: New Delhi).

Galab, S.; E. Revathi; P.P. Reddy and C. Ravi (2009). NREGS and Women's Economic Empowerment. Paper presented at UNIFEM National Workshop on 'NREGA and Women's Empowerment,' New Delhi: India, August 31.

Hall, J.A. (1995). In search of civil society, in: J.A. Hall (Ed) *Civil Society, Theory, History Comparison* (UK: Polity).

Hann, C. (1996). 'Introduction, Political society and civil anthropology', in Chriss Hann and Elizabeth Dunn (eds.) *Civil Society–Challenging Western Models* (London:Routledge).

Howell, Jude and Pearce, Jenny (2001). *Civil Society and Development—A Critical Exploration*, (London, Colorado:Lynne Reinner Publishers).

Howell, J. (2006). Gender and Civil Society, in: M. Glasius, M. Kaldor and H. Anheier (Eds), *Global Civil Society 2005/6* (London, Los Angeles: Sage, LSE, UCLA).

Kaushik, S. (1998). *Participation of Women in Panchayati Raj in India : A Stock Taking". A Study of Six States : Haryana, Madhya Pradesh, Orissa, Rajasthan, Tamil Nadu and Uttar Pradesh.* (Centre for Development Studies and Action, New Delhi).

Keane, J. (1998) *Civil Society: Old Images, New Visions* (Cambridge: Polity).

Khetan, N. and Mehta, A.S. (2007). Building a more gender just and equitable society; Overcoming the internal contradictions to self governance. Paper presented at the IFPRI International Conference on *Taking Action for the World's Poor and Hungry People*, Beijing, October 17-19.

Panda, S.M. (2008). *Engendering Governance Institutions: State, Market and Civil Society* (New Delhi: Sage).

Parekh, B. (2004), 'Putting Civil Society in Place', in Marlies Glasius, David Lewis and Hakan Seckinelgin (eds), *Exploring Civil Society—Political and Cultural Context* (Oxon, New York: Routledge).

Pearce, J. (2000). 'Development, NGOs, and Civil Society: The Debate and Its Future, in Jenny Pearce (introduced) *Development, NGOs and Civil Society* (Oxford: Oxfam GB).

Santha, E.K. (1999). Political Participation of Women in Panchayati Raj; Haryana, Kerala and Tamil Nadu. *ISS Occasional Paper Series* 24 (Institute of Social Sciences: New Delhi).

Sudarshan, R. (2008). Engendering Governance: A Preliminary Enquiry into Formal and Informal Institutions, in S.M. Panda (Ed) *Engendering Governance Institutions: State, Market and Civil Society* (New Delhi: Sage).

Sudarshan, R. (2009) NREGA in Palakkad, Kerala. Paper presented at UNIFEM National Workshop on *'NREGA and Women's Empowerment,'* New Delhi, August 31.

23
Women's Empowerment in Panchayats (India)

Can they Break the Glass Ceiling?

Bidyut Mohanty

Introduction

In a patriarchal and tradition bound society like India, the dominant ideology has been to devalue women's role in economic, social and political institutions. The normative value systems give sanctions to such guiding principles through socialization, rituals, and narration of epics, etc. Further, the subordinate position of women become quite evident in terms of access to food, health care facilities, etc. As a result, the human development indicators such as maternal mortality and female infant mortality rates remain unacceptably high and literacy rate low. Even though they spend 95 per cent of their time in doing domestic chores, and are in charge of care economy, their contributions are not recognized as economically gainful activities. Hence, they remain devalued and their daughters become unwanted.

In order to rectify the above structural constraints, women have been given representation in political system, since 1993, particularly at the local level to begin with, so that they take active part in the political decision making process particularly in the matter of village development. Two decades have passed. Four terms of Panchayat elections have taken place all over the country resulting in generation of at least four million women leaders and creating an awareness among eight million women about the political process. This unique experiment in turn has generated a kind of social mobilization of an unprecedented scale. One was hoping that the presence of such large number of women in public space and given so many functions such as food security including nutrition, health, livelihood, sanitation, safe drinking water, etc., to Panchayats, the villages would be getting some of the basic needs fulfilled. But one still comes across deaths in mid-day meals centres, high maternal and infant death rates, sporadic breakout of dysentery, lack of safe drinking water and so on and so forth. On the top of it, the level of malnutrition is still very high. Thus one finds a number of contradictions such as high growth rate, a million plus women grassroots leaders, around one million women self help groups operating in the public place but still marginalized community including women are devoid of basic services and the girl child still gets a very raw deal.

In order to explain the anomalous situation one may suggest the following hypothesis. Most of the women leaders are not performing in a desired manner because of constraints at the institutional level of the local government system as well as at the societal level. The general societal attitude prevails in the functioning of local government as well. But wherever, they are benefiting from the welfare schemes that is primarily due to the political will, handholding of members of civil society and the presence of women's collective.

This chapter analyses the above issues in threadbare to test the hypothesis by using primary and secondary data.

Evolution of Panchayati Raj System from Women's Perspective in India

In India the concept of Panchayat is not new. But earlier times it was dominated by the five influential male elders of the village. Those elders used to settle social disputes of the villages. In other words, women's voice was never heard in those space. During the freedom struggle the revival of Panchayati Raj system became very popular. Authors like Premchand (1997 r.) wrote stories like *Panch Paremeswar,* and Chatursen Shastri (2010, r.) wrote *Vaishali ki Nagarvadhu.* Premchand for example showed as to how the Panchayat chief could be justice provider even to his adversaries. Similarly Chatursen pointed out that even during the Buddhist era women participated in decision making process. He cited the case of Amrapalli. Of course, both of these belong to the realm of literature. But it can be pointed out that literature is recognized as a source material in the present day social science research since the literature reflect the reality of the contemporary society though sometimes in an exaggerated form. During the colonial period also the rulers tried to implement various forms of Panchayti Raj system (Buch, 2013).

For the first time after the independence, however, Balvantray G. Mehta Committee recommended cooption of two women members—one from Scheduled Caste community and the other one is from Scheduled Tribe community (Mehta, 1957).

The *Towards Equality Report–1975*[1], which was set up to evaluate the social and economic conditions of Indian women presented a very bleak picture namely, low literacy rate, low work participation rate, high maternal mortality rate, etc., but still it did not recommend the seat reservation in the political space. It was perhaps due to the fact that the members were still under the illusion that women would be able to come up as able leaders on their own rights. They, however, recommended all women Panchayats to look after the welfare activities of women. At the same time it might be pointed out that there was a note of dissent within the committee and two important members of the committee recommended seat reservation for women in the political institutions. The National Perspective Plan in 1988-2000 for women on the other hand recommended 30 per cent reservation of women in the Panchayat level. But it was not taken up till 1987, when Karnataka Panchayat act reserved only 25 per cent seats for women at the Zilla Parishad level (Mathew, 1994, reprint—2002). Finally the historic act namely, Seventy-third Constitution Amendment Act 1993 was passed and as per the Article 243(D) of the Act 1993, not less than one-third seats has been reserved for women including the women from Scheduled Caste and Scheduled Tribe communities in all three tiers of Panchayats both at the membership and presidentship levels. The clause of 'not less than one-third' has been interpreted differently by different States, and some States have given more than one-third seat reservation. Recently some States, however, have reserved 50 per cent seats for women in the local bodies. Total number elected women representatives in all three-tiers of Panchayats is approximately 10,38, 045 or 1.2 million. The percentages varied from 30 per cent in Kerala to 54 per cent in Bihar (NIRD, 2008). By 2008 Bihar had already given 50 per cent reservation to women. On the other hand, Kerala's figure looks like an underestimate. Altogether about 37 per cent women have been elected throughout India.

The Structure of Panchayati Raj Institutions

The Panchayats have a three-tier system such as Gram Panchayats, Block

Panchayats and District Panchayats to which about three million persons are elected every five years, out of which one-third/fifty per cent are women as noted above. There are about 532 District Panchayats, 5,912 intermediate Panchayats and 2.3 lakh village Panchayats all over India. It is interesting to note that women are heading in 175 District Panchayats, 1970 Block Panchayats, and more than 77 thousand village Panchayats all over India. Altogether there are three million elected representatives of which 6.60 thousand are SC and ST members (Mathew, 2013).

As per the Seventy-third Constitution Act 1993, the Panchayats have their own Election Commission and Finance Commission to look after the election matters and that of finance. Regular elections take place in all the States. It is also important that women of SC and ST as well as those of other category have been represented in the local government system. From time to time, the Finance Commission is constituted and the Commission decides the amount to be allocated to the Panchayats.

So far as the power and authority of the local government system is concerned it is mentioned that the Legislature of a State by law, will endow them with "such power and authority as may be necessary to enable them function as institutions of self-government and such law may contain provisions for the devolution of powers and responsibilities upon Panchayats at the appropriate level with respect to 243-E". In particular, the Panchayats are supposed to prepare the economic development plan and that of social justice which is included under Eleventh Schedule. Incidentally, under the Eleventh Schedule 29 developmental subjects have been assigned to the Panchayats for preparing the development plan and implement schemes as deemed necessary. Those developmental subjects consist of agriculture, food security, sanitation, safe drinking water, etc. In evaluating the devolution of power in letter and spirit to Panchayati Raj Institutions Mathew (2013) wrote that several Round Tables of the State Ministers in charge of the Panchayati Raj have met up to suggest several important aspects to empower the Panchayats. The points of discussion ranged from activities mapping, to formation of District Planning, etc., but nothing in terms of action has been taken up.

As is evident from above description, Panchayats do not have any power to raise their resources they could only implement and monitor schemes, whenever it is necessary. In turn, they depend on the financial support of the Central and to some extent State governments. As for example the Twelfth Finance Commission has allocated ₹ 200 million to implement need based development programmes. (NIRD, 2008).The activities are determined at the Central and State level leaving no say for the local government system. Mathew (2013) has also documented various constraints which hampering the effective functioning of Panchayats.

However, since 2006 the Gram Panchayats are getting huge sum of money under right based scheme called Mahatma Gandhi National Rural Employment Guarantee Scheme (MGNREGS). Starting from 2006, ₹ 290 million have been utilized to pay to the labour only. (Ministry of Rural Development, Government of India, Annual Report 2012-13). Under the MGRNEGS some of the male sarpanches have ability to identify the beneficiaries who are entitled to get job card. It is mandatory for them/her to call Gram Sabha to discuss the list of beneficiaries for the scheme, though in many places it does not happen. The role of Panchayats stops at that point. The lines department officials, junior engineers and *rozgar sevaks* (helpers to implement the schemes) not only choose the kind of construction work to be done but also where it is to be done. Similarly for the provisions of sanitation, safe drinking water, food distribution, agriculture, etc., the lines departments take over and the Panchayats are sidelined. Only one or two Panchayat members represent the whole of Panchayats in different committees which have been constituted to monitor or plan the activities. Many a time women Ward members have been chosen who do not any knowledge regarding the functions of health or sanitation committee and hence they do not carry the message to the Panchayats.They just go and attend the meetings which often do not take place and just let it go. In other words, the Panchayats are not at all aware of the developmental activities except construction of roads, Indira Awaas Yojana and ASHA, the health worker who helps women to go to the hospital in case they are pregnant. In some Panchayats, the chiefs try to monitor the activities of the sanitation work, health related work, food distribution, but the executing functionaries are not at all responsible to them.

In other words, the three-tier panchayats have been constituted but those institutions are devoid of power, funds and last but not the functionaries. Of course, there are State level variations. For example, Kerala has given 40 per cent of total budget money to the Panchayats/ Nagar Palikas to spend on whatever, they want (Mathew, 2013).In all the other cases, the funds are tied funds. The Panchayats do not have any choice to spend it. On the whole, however, the Panchayati Raj institutions lack any power because there is no power with them to raise their own resources, they do not have any autonomy to plan and execute the development plans nor they can implement the centrally sponsored schemes without taking the help of executive functionaries. Further, the social structure has not changed much since the agriculture supports more than sixty per cent of the work force. So the agricultural labourers are dependent on the cultivators Hence, as Panchayat leaders of SC and ST communities have no independent say. Coupled with that the caste, class and ethnicity and patriarchy keep women leaders doubly shackled. Most of them are least aware about the modern institutions like Panchayats. Thus at least half of the women are not allowed for taking up the mantle of decision making task as one will see in the next section.

The Socio-Economic Conditions of the Elected Women

Several micro studies have shown the socio-economic conditions of the elected women representatives. See for example, (Mohanty, 1999), Mathew (1994), Kaushik (1996), Government of India, Ministry of Panchayati Raj, 2007), etc.

An all-India survey was conducted in 2007 taking large sample to find out as to how the women are doing in the Panchayats. It is noticed that the mean age of a Sarpanch is 32 and that of a Ward member is 34. (Government of India, Ministry of Panchayati Raj, 2007). In fact, the elected women representatives of the south and east are relatively of younger age group compared to those elected in northern States. Unfortunately, the all-India figures focused only on the Gram Panchayat members and Sarpances. The members of higher tiers were omitted.

Coming to social background of the women Panchayat members, at the all-India level, the percentage of SC women constituted 18 per cent and that of ST is 11.0 per cent. (NIRD, 2008). The all India studies showed that more than 87 per cent women Panchayats are married. The Institute's micro study (1997-2001) tried to get the occupational distributions of the women in local government system, and it was noticed that at least 90 per cent of them described themselves as housewives. However, some women belonging to service castes or that of *dalits* described themselves as weavers, fish sellers or daily labourers. Further only a few called themselves as cultivators.A couple of them from the general castes wrote their occupation as service or business. But the fact that 90 per cent of them perceive themselves as housewives reflected the view that they themselves were not aware of their own worth (ISS-Monitoring and Evaluating elected women representatives in three districts of Odisha, 1997 to 2001)[2].

The Institute's started its capacity enhancement programme when the first batch of women got elected. Hence all the women of the project area were first timers. But it was heartening to note that in 2007, the percentage has come down to 87 per cent slightly lower than that of all-India figure. We are yet to get the recent data but one hopes that the percentage would be even lower. At the same time one must note that some women who contested during the first election tried to contest in the recent Panchayat election of Odisha and were seen campaigning for themselves along with women's groups.

Finally we also looked into the persons responsible for sending women to politics. In 2007, the all-India survey showed that only 14 per cent elected women representatives, chose to contest the election, on their own leaving 86 per cent women to be encouraged by the family, community and political parties. Given the low female literacy rate in India in general and those of SC and ST in particular, it is obvious that majority of the elected women representatives of the Gram Panchayats would be illiterate. But the level of literacy would be relatively higher in the higher levels that is Block Panchayats and District Panchayats.

Given the present scenario it is obvious that majority women are yet to decide on their own to opt for political carrier. Coupled with that most of them are still overburdened with the domestic chores and have no access to information flow except perhaps some sporadic trainings which is conducted by the government officers or NGOs. It has tremendous implications for their efficiency while working in the Panchayats as we will see a little later. Thus their socio economic conditions are not at all conducive of playing effective leadership role. The above kind of background of of women is due to the social barriers in which they operate.

How are the Women in Panchayats Performing ?

First of all it was noticed above that in the present form Panchayats are given two tasks such as preparing the development plans and implementing as well as monitoring certain government schemes. It is also noticed that most of the women are first timers and most of them are supported by their male family members and do not have much knowledge about the role of Panchayats. Besides most of the Ward members of the Gram Panchayats particularly from SC and ST are illiterate. Even the woman Sarpanch or the chief of Gram Panchayats is not highly qualified. Given this kind of background, most of the women Panchayat members particularly at the Gram Panchayat level are unable to prepare the development plan. Not only that most of them are not aware of what kind of development schemes are coming to the Panchayats nor they have any knowledge regarding amount of money coming to their Panchayats. Similarly, they do not know as to which ministry' s schemes are coming to be implemented at the village level. Sometimes they also do not know the difference between the Gram Sabha which is the assembly of adult villagers and Gram Panchayats which is village council.

Some Positive Results

In the above cases women in Panchayats have been treated as a homogeneous category and it looks as if almost all the elected women members are not performing at all.

But some women in Panchayats work as active leaders under certain conditions. Those are:

(a) NGO Support.
(b) Active Women's Collective.
(c) Political Will.

First of all the list is not exhaustive. Political party and the family members may play a positive role. For that reason we have dealt with the most common factors whose role is relatively more prominent.

Further all the enabling factors are not mutually exclusive. For example, the NGOs do hand holding and try to encourage the women leaders to form collectives. Because by doing so, women strengthen their lobbying power. Sometimes the women's collective try to strengthen the Gram Sabha and in other cases they work through the members of Panchayats. But in other cases the members of women movement form the collective and try to get things done. One has Self Employed Women's Association (SEWA) in mind. Besides the NGOs sometimes the government also tries to facilitate the formation of women's collective for the micro finance programme. Kerala model of Kudumbashree is a case in point. Some of the members of the programme also have become Panchayat members and are working for strengthening the role of Gram Sabha.In other words the women's collective is combination of various other factors. Besides facilitating the women's collective the government functionaries also work through the Gram Panchayats for delivering the basic services. Certain schemes are routed through Panchayats and are implemented well by the government functionaries benefit women more.

In next section we will try to discuss each specific case to show the achievements.

NGO Supported Elected Women Representatives

One of the earlier efforts of the Institute of Social Sciences, (1997-2001) mentioned above, showed that after the intensive training period, women's own perception changed which is most important point to note. A few of them got bathing steps constructed for facilitating women's use of ponds. It was also noticed that women in the tribal District like Rayagada came to Palli Sabha in the hope of getting widow pension and old age pension, etc.

Further the awardees of the programme of Women's Political Empowerment Day Celebrations[3] organized by the Institute of Social Sciences, showed that the successful elected women representatives take up development activities as well as social issues such as domestic violence, promotion of the status of girl child, widow remarriage, etc. They generally work with an NGO. Jafri and Singh (2006) who have done a lot of work through their NGO known as Samavesh have noticed a similar kind of result as above in case of Dewas District in Madhya Pradesh.

Women's Collective

Similarly the Institute of Social Sciences, New Delhi, had evaluated the activities of a project of UNDP which showed the active role of women in Gram Sabha as well as in Gram Panchayats after being a part of women's collective. Here also the NGOs have helped them in forming the women's collective. Incidentally, the above project started in 2003 and ended in 2008[4]. It covered one district and two Blocks in each State. Altogether ten States were taken up. It was noticed that women Panchayat members backed by the self help groups, have tried to air women's concerns in the Gram Sabha, working as an advocacy groups to implement drinking water facilities on a priority basis, ensuring uninterrupted power supply in the Panchayats, spending Panchayat's own revenue in improving the drainage system, supply of electricity, encouraging women to avail the facilities of Janani Surakshya Yojana (JSY), etc. (UNDP, n.d.). In other words, women Panchayat members are becoming effective leaders backed by the women's groups cutting across caste and class. Because they were addressing the issues of basic services which touch everybody's life irrespective of caste and class position. Further the same type of women's collective is also noticed by Lindberg *et al.* in Tamil Nadu while conducting a study in 2011. Again, Devika (2007) noticed that the women in Kudumbashree programme not only formed women's collective, but some of them contested for election at the Panchayat level and others are getting things done such as leasing in the land for ensuring livelihood and working for reforestation, etc., through Panchayats. They also have been appointed as social audits in case of MGNREGS.

Political Will

It is interesting to note that whenever, the political will is positive, the women benefit more. Implementation of MNREGS which started in 2005 is one such point. The Central Government has been very keen to push the implementation of the scheme. Various measures have been taken up to see to it that it is implemented Hence the panchayats are pumped with a lot of money and the sarpanch takes part in selecting the beneficiaries. Thirty per cent of the total work load is reserved for women in this scheme. As a result, women are reaping benefits of such reservation. In many southern States the percentage of women workers is more than sixty per cent (Ashok Pankaj, ed. 2012). Ashok Pankaj for example points out that because of the positive attitude of the civil servants women are getting more benefits.

Finally, in 2008 Beaman, Duflo, Pande and Topalova tried to find out if women in Panchayats are really making a difference or not. They of course, did not cite any enabling factor for such success. The authors analysed the data for eleven major States. Data was collected on the basis of reservation status of 1995-2000. It was noticed by them that women headed Panchayats did much better in terms of children's immunization, monitoring the health programmes and increased investment in drinking water. Besides more women attended the Gram Sabha meetings wherever, women happened to be the Pradhans (*ibid).*

The all-India study on elected women representatives which was conducted by the ministry of Panchayati Raj, Government of India, also tried to find out the quality of participation of women leaders in different space such as Gram Sabha, Panchayats, community mobilization, etc. It was noticed that at the all-India level as high as 86 per cent female Pradhans organized and attended the Gram Sabha meetings in contrast to 93 per cent males who attended the same. On the other hand, only 60 per cent Ward members did the same which was lower than that of male

Ward members. Unfortunately, the study did not give the State level data. A question was asked on taking initiative for the enrolment of the school children. In case of Odisha 41 per cent female Pradhans and 44 per cent female Ward members said in positive. Both the percentages are below the national average. Finally, the study tried to assess if any positive impact has taken place after women's entry to the Panchayati Raj system. It came to the conclusion that a sizeable proportion of women namely, 79 per cent have an enhanced self perception, followed by 81 per cent being confident and 74 per cent have attained decision making ability.

Thus it is seen that women are becoming effective leaders in the local government system whenever, the above conditions such as the hand holding of NGOs, Women' s Collective and Political will are fulfilled.

Social Constraints faced only by Women Leaders

Along with the above institutional constraints women leaders also face women specific constraints as well. In spite of the women's reservation in Panchayats, participation in self help groups and NREGS, the women still face violation of human rights such as discriminating access to food, health services and education. Further the girl child also does not have right to live as the incidence of female feticide is increasing. Sometimes, women leaders face inter-caste and intra-caste violence because of their presence in the Panchayats or taking part in the self help groups. As for example the child sex ratio at the all-India level has declined from 927 to 914 between 2001 and 2011. It was reported by the Census Commissioner C. Chandramouli (ETarticles.economic times.indiatimes.com/2011-03-31/news/29365989_I_ratio-males–girl-child). This phenomenon is prevalent in almost all the States. This is most cruel form of violence. Secondly women suffer from other types of violence. As for example the National Family Health Survey 2005-06 reported that a substantial proportion of married women have been subjected to physical and mental form of violence. Incidentally, out of all States, Bihar seemed to be most abusive, the percentage being 59. It is followed by Madhya Pradesh, 45.8 per cent, Rajasthan, 46.3 per cent, West Bengal 40.3 per cent. (NFHS-111-2005-6). According to the India's National Crime Records Bureau, on an average about 125 women faced domestic violence in 2000 which increased to 160 in 2005 (NCRB). Recently some scholars have documented the incidence of violence against women since 1985-2007. It included the period of women's representation in local government. They noticed that across all categories, the violence against women has increased by 44 per cent. The rape cases per capita rose by 14 per cent and that of abduction by 13 per cent. But the authors are of the opinion that it is partly due to women's presence in Panchayats. Because women themselves are becoming conscious of their own rights (Ghosh, 2011).

Intra-Caste and Inter-Caste Violence

Unlike the women of high caste community, women from *dalit* community face violence from caste and class patriarchies. A survey conducted among 500 *dalit* women in four States between 1999 and 2004. According to them, among many factors political representations in local government has increased the violence against them (Irudayam *et al.*, 2006).

Of course the increase in violence could partly due to women's assertions and defiance of the caste domination. In other cases the economic dependence plays a role in keeping *dalit* women subdued. Thus one sees that in spite of the political representation the dignity of women in the community has not been restored.

Conclusions

The women were given not less than one-third seats in the local government system in the historic Act 1993 with a view that it would create an enabling situation in which grassroots women leaders would be taking decisions affecting millions of people in the rural areas. The enabling provision has generated a large number of grassroots women leaders throughout India. That in turn, has created a social mobilization by bringing a million plus women to the public forum. However, women are unable to function properly in the Panchayati Raj Institutions because those institutions are devoid of real power and depend for financial resources on the Central Government as well as on the State government. Besides even in the rudimentary set-up those institutions require detailed budgeting planning and keeping records which women are unable to take up. Because the socio-economic conditions of those leaders show that most of them are semi-literate, and get elected not due their own choice but because of family or the community. In other words most of them are ill-prepared.

However, many studies show that some of the women leaders have become effective in the Panchayats backed by the NGOs, women's collective, or political will. Yet the percentage of proxy women is very large.

Along with their household responsibilities, the participation in Panchayats become quite difficult. Of course, in some cases they do get the family support, but women leaders being in the reproductive age groups become busy in family raising activities. As a result, they lag behind their male counterparts in certain cases.

The end result is even though the seat reservation in the local government system has fulfilled the necessary condition towards materializing the objective of making women visible in public place and thereby influencing the cultural attitude of the society, that step alone has not been sufficient. Otherwise, the value of the girl child would not have been diminished in the prosperous regions. Or the violence against women would not have increased at all. One needs a series of other enabling measures along with active campaign to change the societal values towards the women in general and girl child in particular.

Notes

1. In fact the question of seat reservation particularly at the level of higher political institutions was summarily rejected by the main body of the report, though three important members of the Committee namely, Neera Dogra, Vina Majumdar and Latika Sarkar had given note of dissent. How ever, the Committee conceded to set up Statutory Women's Panchayats at the village level, to ensure greater involvement by women in the process of political participation. This was backed up on the ground of invisibility of women in the Parliament and State Assemblies along with other social factors. (Towards, Equality, 1975).
   For the first time the *National Perspective Plan for Women 1988-2000* recommended 30 per cent seat reservation at the local government level only.
2. The Institute of Social Sciences, New Delhi had engaged in a three year project in which the project stuff wanted to assess results of the capacity building of elected women representatives of three districts of Odisha. The study area consisted of one coastal district, one land locked district and the third one is a tribal district. We conducted a series of intensive activities taking 234 Panchayats women members most of whom belonged to the Gram Panchayat level. In terms of area-wise, it constituted 20 Panchayats six Blocks.
3. Since 1994 the Institute of Social Sciences, New Delhi organizes the programme with an aim to mark the occasion of the passage of Seventy-third Constitution Amendment Act 1992 in which women got seat reservation. Every year, five to six hundred women elected representatives come together to Delhi to gain confidence from each other's experience,

build group solidarity, etc. On that occasion, a couple of elected women are chosen to be given awards for their achievements.

4. The UNDP started a project with view to enhance the capacity of women Panchayat members in ten States by monitoring and evaluating them from the beginning to the end. This included working with them before the election till end of the term. The NGO partners started giving training before the election and conducted various activities to increase their information inventory on different schemes, relevance of Gram Sabha and Panchayat meetings. The project continued for four to five years after which the activities were evaluated by the independent organizations. The NGO partners included self help groups and elected women representatives.

References

Acharya Chatursen. (2010 r.). *Vaishali ki Nagarvadhu*, (Nai Dilli: Rajpal & Sons.).

Ashok Pankaj (ed.) (2012). *Right to Work and Rural India: Working of the Mahatma Gandhi National Rural Employment Guarantee Scheme* (New Delhi, Sage).

Beaman Lori, Esther Duflo, Rohini Pande, Petia Topalova (2008). 'Women Politicians Gender Bias, and Policy-making in Rural India' in UNICEF *The State of the World's Children*. pp. 1-36.

Buch Nirmala (2013). 'Panchayats and Women' in Mathew (ed.) *Status of Panchayati Raj in the States and Union Territories of India 2013*. (New Delhi, Concept), pp. 50-65.

Devika, J. (2007). "Between 'Empowerment' and 'Liberation' The Koodumbasree Initiative in Kerala." *The Indian Journal of Gender Studies*, Vol.14, Number 1, pp. 33-60.

Government of India (1974). *Towards Equality: Report of the Committee on the Status of Women in India.* (Ministry of Education and Social Welfare, Department of Social Welfare).

Government of India (1988). *National Perspective Plan for Women–1988-2000.* (Department of Women and Child Development, Ministry of Human Resources Development).

Government of India (2008). *Study on Elected Women Representatives in Panchayati Raj Institutions*, Ministry of Panchayati Raj, New Delhi, Government of India (2011).

Ghosh Subir (2011). 'Panchayati Raj has helped in reporting of crime against women' *Asian Correspondent* (October, 2) www.write2kill.in/columns/deadline-delhi/panchayti-raj-has-helped-reporting-of-crimes-against-women.html.

Institute of Social Sciences, New Delhi (1997-2001). 'Monitoring and evaluating the Performance of the elected women representatives' in three districts of Odisha. (Unpublished Manuscript).

Irudayam, Aloysius, S.J. Jayashree, P. Mangubhai, Joel G. Lee (2006). 'Dalit Women Speak Out Violence against Dalit Women in India: Overview Report of Study In Andhra Pradesh, Bihar, Tamil Nadu/Pondicherry and Uttar Pradesh' *National Campaign on Dalit Human Rights* (New Delhi) idsn.org/uploads/media/Violence _against _Dalit_women.pdf

Jafri, Anwar and Vikas Singh (2006). "Gender Mainstreaming in District Plans in Madhya Pradesh" in Jayal, Niraja Gopal *et al.* (eds.) *Local Governance in India; Decentralization and Beyond*. New Delhi, OUP. pp. 324-354.

Kaushik Susheela (1996) *Panchayati Raj in Action: Challenges to Women's Role* (New Delhi, Friedrich Ebert Stiftung).

Mathew George (2002, r.) *Panchayati Raj: From Legislation to Movement* (New Delhi, Concept).

Mathew, George (2013). 'Panchayati Raj in India—An Overview' in Mathew George (ed.) *Status of Panchayati Raj in India* (New Delhi, Institute of Social Sciences, and Concept Publishing House), p. 11.

Ministry of Health and Family Welfare, Government of India (2005-6). 'Fact Sheet: National Family Survey NFHS-111.

National Crime Record Bureau (2007). http://HYPERLINK http://www.asianews www.asianews.it. 'Rising domestic violence.'

UNDP (n.d.) *From Reservation to Participation: Capacity Building of Elected Women Representatives and Functionaries of Panchayati Raj Institutions.* (New Delhi, UNDP).

24

Ensuring Women Benefit from Inclusive Business Models

A Case of the Oil Palm Project in Uganda

Connie Magomu Masaba, Ann Turinayo and *Steven Jonckheere*

Introduction

Agriculture is the main stay of the rural population in Uganda. The rural population accounts for 73 per cent of the total population, of the estimated 34 million people. The agricultural sector in Uganda contributes 31.8 per cent of the GDP. (UBOS, 2010). In the rural areas, the sector employs 80 per cent of the rural dwellers. The sector provides raw material for the factories in the country.

Rural women form the majority of the population that is actively involved in the agricultural sector with 90 per cent deriving livelihood from agriculture as compared to 53 per cent of rural men (FAWODE, 2012). The rural women till the land to ensure there is enough food for their families and some to spare for the market, to bring in income to meet non-farm produced requirements. Rural farmers still depend on the hand hoe and other rudimentary equipment for tilling their lands to grow food and other crops, making it unattractive to the young and able bodied men.

In terms of land ownership and control of production resources, women have remained as users of factors of production that belong to men. While access is possible to them as providers of labour, control has been elusive as many women do not own land. The men undertake the marketing function of the produce and solely decide on how to use the income without the input of the women. It is reported that 70 per cent of marketing decisions are made by men while 15 per cent are made jointly, leaving only 15 per cent of marketing decisions made by women (FAWODE, 2012). This has discouraged women from giving their all since there is no incentive for doing so.

The Government of Uganda (GoU) has shown commitment in improving the plight of women and overcoming gender inequality as exemplified from the Constitution, National Gender Policy, and National Development Plan that all recognise the central role of women in development. These, at least on paper, provide avenues for policies and programmes that aim at the elimination of discrimination, inequality, and the subjugation of women by men and society.

The President of Uganda is quoted as having said, "Our policy aims at strengthening the position of women in the economy by raising the value and productivity of their labour and by giving them access to, and control over productive resources. By productive resources, I mean land, capital, credit, seeds, fertilizers, tools, water, energy, education, information" (The President, MuseveniYoweri Kaguta, 1998).

There is, therefore, commitment from the highest office to overcome inequality and strengthen women participation and control of resources and outputs in agriculture.

In this chapter, the experiences of rural farmers, especially women, in taking part in agriculture as a business are shared. The experimentation with inclusive business models and how the rural farmers including women farmers are involved in activities and decision making processes are presented. The chapter shares lessons learned from experiences of farmers that have benefited from the IFAD supported Vegetable Oil Development Project (VODP) in Uganda, on the islands of Kalangala. The chapter shares the efforts made in addressing constraints faced by rural women households in the agricultural sector. Through the inclusive business model, women farmers have been supported to ensure they benefit from the project just like their counterpart men farmers.

Background

It is recognised that poverty is more rampant in rural areas where agriculture is the main activity, and where the biggest populations of countries like Uganda is. It is also recognised that in order to develop, countries like Uganda need to improve the agricultural sector which currently employs majority of the population. Women being more than half of the population, need to be effectively engaged in the efforts to improve agriculture. Access to and control of factors of production is a major part of the efforts to increase agricultural production and hence increase rural incomes.

Socially, Uganda is a patrilineal society where men have always had control over production resources especially land. Men have had opportunities for gainful employment because they have gone to school and acquired skills as opposed to the women. The women have been left behind to fend for the men as the men go out to find money to supposedly support the family. Although there are efforts towards gender equality, a lot remains to be done. While the women contribute a lot to agriculture in terms of labour, their benefits from the sector are meagre because they do not have control over the agricultural produce. There is need to appreciate the role of the Ugandan woman in the agriculture sector. What role does the woman play? What benefits accrue to women from agriculture? How can women, especially rural women benefit more meaningfully from their involvement in agriculture?

According to FAWODE in the Gender Policy Brief for Uganda's Agriculture Sector (2012), the constraints to gender responsiveness in the agriculture sector include the following:

Constraints to Gender Responsiveness in the Agriculture Sector in Uganda

(i) Lack of Ownership and Control of Land

Land being a major factor of agricultural production, if not accessed and controlled by the main users for production, is a disincentive to agricultural production. It is also a major limitation given that the women who are the major users of the land cannot make decisions concerning which crops to grow, when to grow them and what investment to make on the land. This has limited women efforts to improve production and productivity and has affected willingness to invest in the land.

Access to land and other natural resources for women is marred by issues of inheritance, where for a long time, women have been excluded from inheriting property, whether from their spouses or their parents; polygamy–where a number of women are married to one man and there is no security of tenure for any of them should the man die; as well as extreme poverty which makes it impossible for most women to acquire their own land. The other is the current effects of climate change on agriculture and agricultural production generally.

(ii) Limited Markets and Market Access

Traditionally, women are predominantly involved in food production for family food requirements with limited amounts for the market. As soon as a crop becomes commercially viable, the men take over that crop, leaving the women out. This has affected women efforts to increase their incomes. Women are involved in cash crops mainly as employees providing labour for the men. Market decisions are by and large made by men on when to sell, at how much and what to use the proceeds for, leaving out the major producers—the women.

(iii) High Cost and Limited Access to Improved Farm Inputs and Production Technology

Lack of access to improved agricultural technologies and inputs has limited farmer performance especially women who are majority in the sector. Many of the women farmers cannot access the inputs due to lack of funds to purchase them. In some cases, it is due to lack of information about where to find the inputs.

(iv) Lack of Access to Agricultural Credit Facilities

Women farmers cannot easily access credit because of lack of collateral to secure the loans. In some cases, they do not have information about what credit facilities are available. In other cases the interest rates are high, discouraging the farmers from accessing the funds. This has limited investment in farm inputs which has resulted in low production and productivity.

(v) Inadequate Agricultural Extension Services

Without access to agricultural extension, the farmers cannot know how to employ new technologies leave alone where to access improved inputs and why they should apply the new technologies. While this is a challenge to all farmers, the women farmers are even more disadvantaged in that even the few times when farmer trainings take place, the women farmers will most likely be at home undertaking other chores. When the messages are written on brochures and pamphlets, the women farmers may not be able to read because many did not go to school and, therefore, cannot read and write.

(vi) Lack of Gender Analysis to Inform Policy Formulation, Planning and Budgeting in the Agriculture Sector

Without gender analysis, policy formulation may not address the real issues faced by women, and the interventions designed might leave out important considerations that would benefit the women farmers. For instance, while the interventions may be designed with women as the targeted beneficiaries, if the investment targets cashcrops without addressing who controls cashcrops, the women may not benefit.

(vii) Decline in the Agriculture Sector Growth

Decline in the returns from the agriculture sector has affected incomes of smallholder farmers especially the women. This has been due to fluctuating and low prices and limited public sector investment in the sector. Low prices during harvesting periods have discouraged farmers from investing in the sector. These developments have left poor rural women and old men as the main players in the agricultural sector, as the able bodied and youth go to urban areas in search of better opportunities.

(viii) Increasing Food Prices Globally

Increasing food prices has presented both a challenge and an opportunity if handled properly. The opportunity is that the increasing prices have drawn interest from both the public and private sector to invest more in the agricultural sector to take advantage of the opportunities of the increased prices and also to ensure the world population has access to food. The challenge is that with increased prices and food crops become commercially viable, men are getting interested in crops that are otherwise a women domain, which could disenfranchise women from the already limited space they have been enjoying. With increased interest by conglomerates in the agricultural sector, land acquisition for commercial agriculture could affect the poor farmers that depend on these lands for their livelihood, especially poor rural women.

Whereas it is prudent to acknowledge that credible steps have been made in addressing issues to do with women's access to land, security of tenure and division of labour at the small family level, it is worthwhile to note that the successes are still limited compared to the overwhelming numbers of women faced with no access to land for especially commercial agriculture. This is coupled with exclusion of women from the decision making process concerning many issues that affect them like marketing of the produce; how to use the funds from the sale of the farm produce; access to agricultural credit; inputs for improving production and productivity; and extension advice, which in many cases is gender blind, with no direct target to the women who are the major players in the agricultural sector.

INCLUSIVE BUSINESS MODELS (IBMs)

Definition and Characteristics of Inclusive Business

Inclusive business is a business initiative that, keeping its profit nature, contributes to poverty reduction through the inclusion of low income communities in its value chain. It is all about including the poor in the business process either as producers or consumers or both. In IBMs, businesses do well by doing good. Inclusive business models try to find synergies between development goals and the company's core business operations.

According to IFCF/World Bank, Inclusive business models expand access to goods, services, and livelihood opportunities for those at the base of the global economic pyramid in commercially viable, scalable ways. IBMs take the base of the economic pyramid as valuable economic partners for business, as both talented and resilient business entrepreneurs, and value conscious consumers. Private business should view inclusive business models as opportunities for market growth and competitive advantage. For development agencies, inclusive business represents a powerful approach to achieving the goal of inclusive growth and development.

Inclusive models are able to achieve higher socio-economic value for communities. IBMs also present an exciting opportunity for the private sector because they are good for business. Commercially viable business linkages between large corporations and micro, small, and medium enterprises in developing countries can play a vital role in creating local jobs, improving livelihoods, supporting gender diversity and enhancing economic options. In addition, they also facilitate transferring skills, technologies, quality management and sound business standards along value chains.

Box 24.1: Key Concepts

A *business model* is the way in which a company structures its resources, partnerships and customer relationships in order to create and capture value, in other words, a business model is what enables a company to make money. Business models are considered as more *inclusive* if they involve close working partnerships with local landholders and operators, and if they share value among the partners.

Inclusive business models are designed to deliver mutual benefits for business by generating sales and profit growth and for low-income communities by creating jobs and increasing incomes.

In the agriculture sector, IBMs call for involvement of smallholder farmers as effective business partners in the production process and the business; and not just as beneficiaries.IBMs in agriculture call for involvement of the communities in decisions concerning their land, what to be produced and how they participate as partners. They call for effective consultations with the communities, ensuring the voice of the smallholders is heard and encouraged to bring out the concerns of the communities, ensuring ownership of the factors of production by the smallholders, sharing of the risks involved in the business by all the partners and ensuring that the rewards accruing from the business are proportionately shared by the big investors and smallholder partners.

Because the agricultural sector is faced with lots of challenges, partnerships are important in addressing the challenges so that there is agricultural growth. Public Private Partnerships (PPPs); if inclusive of the communities can be one positive way in attracting investment to the agricultural sector and at the same time ensuring that smallholder farmers continue to contribute to the sector and benefit from the partnerships. Inclusiveness improves these partnerships by securing the interests of the smallholders. As well stated by IFAD, Rural people as part of the solution for global food security must be a priority for governments, the international development community and any other investors. Women form half of the world population and a higher percentage of women is involved in agricultural production hence the need to incorporate them in addressing agricultural development challenges and efforts.

Challenges Faced in Agricultural Sector in Uganda

- Low levels of investment about 4 per cent of Budget of most SS countries as opposed to 10 per cent CAADP recommendation and 14 per cent in Asia.

- Use of rudimentary equipment—the hand hoe.
- Lack of improved technology in the sector.
- Unattractive to young population because of being laborious characterized with drudgery.
- Low contribution share to GDP (24% in Uganda).
- Undependable markets and fluctuating prices.
- Characterized by sale of primary products with no value addition in the sector.
- Low Private sector funding in the sector.

Requirements by Smallholders in order to Contribute to Agricultural Sector Growth

To perform to their potential, smallholder farmers and rural communities need:

- secure land and natural resource rights,
- better access to inputs,
- technical expertise,
- agro-processing and other off-farm opportunities,
- finance, and
- markets.

Inclusive business models are better placed to address many of these challenges and meet smallholder farmer needs as outlined above.

EXPERIENCES OF THE VEGETABLE OIL DEVELOPMENT PROJECT IN ENSURING WOMEN BENEFIT FROM INCLUSIVE BUSINESS MODELS

Overview of the Vegetable Oil Development Project

Vegetable Oil Development Project (VODP) is a Government of Uganda project, implemented with support of loan funds from the International Fund for agricultural Development (IFAD). The project follows a Public Private Partnership model. The Government of Uganda supports small scale farmers to grow oil palm and the Private sector, Bidco Uganda Limited (BUL) establishes a nucleus estate, a mill that also serves as market for farmers' fresh fruit bunches, as well as providing technical backstopping to the farmers. The farmers are represented by a Trust—

the Kalangala Oil Palm Growers' Trust. The PPP has been made possible by the ability of government to attract a suitable and willing private sector investor, and by IFAD's recognition that smallholder farmers are often private sector entrepreneurs. Indeed, in the Kalangala islands where oil palm is grown, it is evident that small scale farmers are the main investors in land and agriculture and should be at the centre of agricultural development, food security and poverty reduction strategies, policies and programmes. The inclusive business models in this case are exemplified by the fact that smallholder farmers have been enabled to secure land and other natural resource rights. Four criteria have been used to assess value sharing, namely, ownership, voice, risk and reward.

VODP was launched in 1998. It was envisaged that the project would reduce Uganda's reliance on imported vegetable oils and address the country's low per capita vegetable oil consumption. By revitalizing national vegetable oil production, the project would also increase the income of small-scale farmers. The first phase of the project ended in 2012 and second phase will be completed in 2018.

From the onset, the oil palm sub-project of VODP was conceived as a PPP, the first of its kind in Uganda—for oil palm development. While the Government committed to developing the infrastructure in the area, a private sector partner brought technical expertise for the development of the plantation, as well as modern and environmentally sound processing methods that produce a high quality product compliant with food safety standards. The partnership also implements an inclusive business model, combining small-scale production with large-scale processing and integrating small-scale producers into the wider economy.

Despite significant setbacks, early results indicate that the project is having a positive impact on Bugalaisland. Some of the impacts include improved tenure security for smallholders including for women farmers, increased employment and incomes, and improved infrastructure for smallholder farmers with active involvement of women farmers.

In order to meet the domestic demand for palm oil, Uganda has relied heavily on imports. Expenditure on palm oil imports in 2010 was greater than that on any other agricultural commodity, amounting to more than USD 177 million for 203,096 tonnes (FAOSTAT, 2012). It was envisaged, in the 1990s, that the VODP would help reduce the reliance on imports, and address the low per capita intake of vegetable oils.

Establishing the Partnership

Following IFAD's agreement to support the VODP in 1997, a competitive bidding process was launched to contract a private sector company to develop the oil palm plantations and processing facilities. After two years of inconclusive negotiations with a local company, the Government of Uganda entered negotiations with Bidco Oil Refineries Limited of Kenya. Bidco's proposal, with which the Government ultimately agreed, was that 40,000 ha of oil palm plantations would be developed, as well as a 300 tonnes/day refinery at Jinja to produce the crude palm oil. The first phase of the project involved the development of 10,000 ha of oil palm plantations on Bugala Island in Kalangala District of which 6,500 ha would comprise the nucleus estate and 3,500 ha of smallholder plantations.

Box 24.2: Oil Palm

Oil Palm (Elaeisguineensis) is native to the tropical rainforests of West Africa, and the processing of oil palm fruits for edible oil has been practiced in Africa for thousands of years. Indeed, palm oil, which is rich in carotenoids that produce a deep red colour, is a core ingredient of much of West African cuisine and is important in human diets. In particular, red palm oil is important for the high amount of vitamin A and it contains (FAO, 1997). Palm oil has a high potential productivity, with the highest yield of oil per unit area compared to any other crop (FAO, 2002) and its cultivation can, therefore, derive significant economic benefits in addition to its nutritional benefits. The fact that it bears fruit all year round and harvesting is undertaken atleast twice every month for a period of twenty five years, makes it a good candidate for a stable sustained source of income for smallholders. There are environmental risks inherent to palm oil cultivation and processing, such as potential damage resultant from untreated aqueous effluent (FAO, 2002) and careful consideration must be given to the mitigation of such risks.

The government committed to ensuring the acquisition and leasing of the necessary land to Bidco for the nucleus estate, ensuring compliance with the environmental safeguards set out by the National Environmental Management Authority (NEMA), and ensuring the formation 'of a farmers' organisation, the Kalangala Oil Palm Growers Trust (KOPGT). Additionally, the government committed to developing the required infrastructure, including upgrading the Kalangala district road network and establishing a ferry service to and from the island. The Government obtained financial and technical support from IFAD in order to fulfil its obligations.

To implement the agreement, Bidco formed an international corporate partnership, Bidco Uganda Limited (BUL) and Oil Palm Uganda Limited (OPUL), with Wilmar International, Josovina and ADM (previously Archer Daniels Midland). The establishment of OPUL represented the convening of significant expertise in oil palm development and marketing.

Main Stakeholders and their Roles

Box 24.3: Main Stakeholders and Their Roles

- *Smallholder farmers:* Smallholders are both first inhabitants and earlier migrants to the island. Many are tenants of, or even occupants on, large areas of land owned mostly by absentee landlords. Current smallholders have typically established about 2-4 ha of oil palm (although in some cases it may be as much as 10 ha). Some have already started harvesting oil palm fresh fruit bunches (FFB) which they sell to the palm oil mill set up by OPUL on the nucleus estate. A total of 3,756 hectares have been planted by farmers of which 1,451 hectares have reached maturity and are under harvesting. A total of 1,610 farmers are participating in the project of which 578 are women.
- *KOPGT:* The Kalangala Oil Palm Growers Trust (KOPGT) was established in 2006 by the Government of Uganda using IFAD funds in order to represent the interests of smallholder farmers within the public-private partnership. Its main functions include acting as an intermediary between the farmers and OPUL, smallholder mobilisation, provision of extension services (e.g., on-farm technical guidance for land preparation, lining, holing and planting, maintenance, and eventually harvesting), financial management (including the oil palm development loan programme) and marketing of oil palm fresh fruit bunches. KOPGT is composed of three smallholder farmers, civil society, district local government and central government ministries of Agriculture, Finance and Justice.
- *KOPGA:* The Kalangala Oil Palm Growers Association (KOPGA) was established on the basis of a decision made by farmers in 2007, as they believed that the establishment of their own association would enable them to present their voice more effectively. KOPGA offers farmers a platform on which to participate in discussions and to formulate proposals and requests that can then be negotiated within KOPGT.
- *Government of Uganda:* The Government was responsible for ensuring the acquisition and leasing of land to Bidco for the nucleus estate, providing the legislative environment to ensure the successful take-off of the project, ensuring compliance with the environmental safeguards, establishing KOPGT, and putting in place the required transportation infrastructure.
- *BUL:* Bidco Oil Refineries Ltd of Kenya, founded in 1970, began focusing on the manufacturing and marketing of edible oil, fats and soaps in the 1990s. It has since become a market leader in soap and cooking oil brands in East and Central Africa. It is part of OPUL. Bidco Oil Refineries in partnership with others formed Bidco Uganda Limited (BUL) to implement the project activities in Uganda.

- *OPUL:* Oil Palm Uganda Limited (OPUL) is an international partnership of private companies formed by BUL to initiate and implement the investment in Bugala, Kalangala. BUL holds a 90 per cent share in OPUL, with the remaining 10 per cent held by KOPGT on behalf of the participating smallholders. OPUL's main activities include the establishment of oil palm nurseries for the nucleus and smallholders, establishing the nucleus estate and palm oil mill, managing land under the out-grower scheme for the initial three years of plantation establishment, and providing services and inputs to KOPGT to support the cultivation of oil palm by smallholders. BUL is OPUL's sole buyer.
- *IFAD:* IFAD has provided loan funding to the Government of Uganda to implement VODP. It carries out a facilitator role and provides support to KOPGT.

VODP's oil palm sub-project can be classified as a nucleus estate model, where the agribusiness company (OPUL) combines contract farming ("out growers") with direct involvement in production through a plantation estate. Smallholder farmers grow and deliver fresh palm fruit bunches to KOPGT on a daily basis at an agreed price. OPUL, through KOPGT, provides upfront inputs, supports with land preparation, seedlings, and technical advice. This is charged by KOPGT as part of the farmers' loan which is paid by KOPGT to OPUL using IFAD funds. KOPGT organises transport for farmer inputs and harvests from and to the nucleus estate respectively.

VODP is also an example of a joint venture, as it entail co-ownership of OPUL, the business venture, by two independent market actors, Bidco (the agribusiness) and KOPGT (the farmers' organisation). The joint venture involves sharing of financial risks and benefits and decision-making authority in proportion to the equity share.

The partnership agreement foresaw OPUL establishing a nucleus estate and a crude palm oil mill on Bugala Island in Kalangala District. In addition, OPUL provided an implementation plan that included the importation of oil palm seedlings, nursery facilities and a complete support package for participating growers. The support package included land surveying and preparation, digging of holes, planting, provision of inputs at cost, advice, transport and other services.

With financial support from IFAD through the Government, KOPGT was established in 2006 as an intermediary between OPUL and the smallholder farmers. Farmers must register with KOPGT in order to participate in the project, and to access financing under the oil palm development loan programme.While farmers pledge to follow the recommended agronomic practices for oil palm production through an agreement signed between the farmers and KOPG, the Trust performs a range of functions on their behalf. It administers the loan programme. Repayments are carried out through KOPGT, which deducts a pre-agreed percentage from the payment for the farmers' ffbs (fresh fruit bunches) to be lodged in an Oil Palm Development Account held by KOPGT. The Trust has furthermore implemented a voucher system to manage the transactions around the inputs and services required by farmers. KOPGT also collects the fresh fruit bunches from farmers and delivers them to OPUL. Participating farmers agree to sell all fresh-fruit bunches to OPUL, (at a price determined through a pricing formula that was prenegotiated by government and incorporated in the cooperating agreement between Government and BUL which, in turn, sells all crude palm oil to BUL, which is responsible for processing and marketing the refined products.

Box 24.4: Organogram of VODP's Oil Palm Sub-project

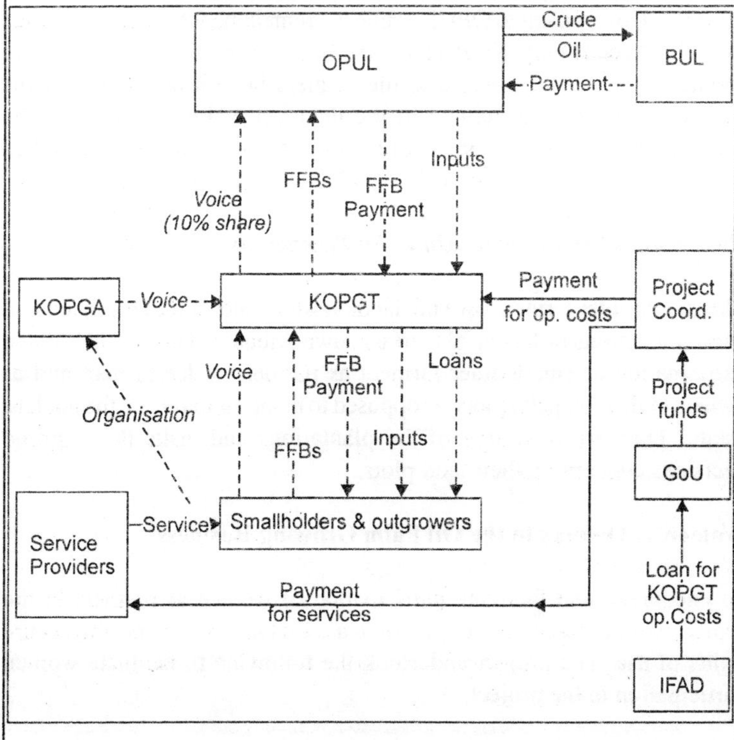

How Women have Participated in and Benefited from the VODP IBM

The project has been classified as an inclusive business model because of the central role the smallholder farmers have in the production process. The project has endeavoured to address the constraints that smallholder farmers encounter in agriculture, particularly women farmers. The project has included smallholder farmers in decision-making, and views the farmers as partners in the investment.

Ownership

Shareholding in the Company—OPUL

BUL (the agribusiness) and KOPGT (the smallholders) co-own the business: KOPGT acquired a 10 per cent minority share in OPUL in 2006, using funds provided to the Government by IFAD and the land leased by Government to OPUL, while the remaining 90 per cent is owned by BUL. Accordingly, KOPGT retains two seats on the OPUL board of management. This ensures that the farmers benefit as owners of the company but also participate in the decision making process of the company. It also builds a sense of belonging among the farmers. When the company starts making profit, KOPGT will receive dividends.

Ownership of Smallholder Oil Palm Plantations

The smallholder farmers own the land on which they have established oil palm plantations or have rights of use own Kibanja. This has facilitated participation of smallholder farmers as partners in the project and as owners of their oil palm plots, as opposed to being labourers on the nucleus estate. They are in charge of the plantations and make the required decisions concerning their land plots.

Women as Owners in the Oil Palm Growing Business

To encourage and facilitate participation of women as partners in the project, women had to be supported to access land as owners or to secure rights of use. The project undertook the following to facilitate women participation in the project.

Facilitating Access to and Control of Land by Women Farmers

(i) Established a land fund from which it provided a loan facility to assist women to purchase 'kibanja' to grow oil palm;

(ii) Put a limit on the maximum size of land the project would support per individual farmer. In order to increase the size of land per household, husbands were forced to let their wives participate in the project in their own right as farmers;

(iii) Removed the minimum size of the land the farmer would commit in order to participate in the project, which encouraged women farmers who normally have very small parcels as allowed by their husbands or male relatives;

(iv) Encouraged men to give user rights to their wives so they could participate as farmers in their own right;

(v) Approached the District to provide public land available for the benefit of poor women to facilitate their participation in the project;

(vi) The project brokered share cropping arrangements with landlords so that women farmers could access land for participation in the project;

(vii) A total of 1,023 ha of public land that was originally acquired for the nucleus estate was handed back over to the communities and used for several purposes, such as settlement, oil palm production, food crop production or livestock keeping. Through the project about 460 farmers were granted access to public land. Mailo landowners were financially compensated on a willing seller-willing buyer basis. Some of the land that was purchased could not be used for the nucleus estate as it was too scattered. This land was allocated to the poorer farmers, especially women and youth.

Facilitating Access to Production Credit by Women Farmers

(viii) The project waived the requirement of a certificate of title as collateral for accessing production credit and instead encouraged group collateral and use of the plantation as security for the loan funds.

(ix) A simple letter from the local leaders would suffice as proof that one had right of use kibanja and would therefore be supported with loan funds, following inspection of the plot of land to be used for planting oil palm.

(x) In terms of collateral, the project introduced co-guaranteeing/group guaranteeing as an alternative to provision of a land title. In addition, treating the oil palm crop as collateral in itself, helped women farmers relax about the fear of loss of their small pieces of land.

Control and Decision-making Concerning the Women Oil Palm Plots

(xi) Women farmers registered with the farmer organisation as individual farmers as opposed to being just part of the household;

(xii) Women signed agreements with the farmer organisation as participating farmers; and

(xiii) Women opened individual bank accounts with the commercial bank, through which the project provided financial support in the form of production credit. The women farmers run their own bank accounts.

Marketing of Oil Palm Fresh Fruit Bunches from Women Owned Plots

- Women farmers, just like the men, participate in marketing their ffbs.
- They harvest, weigh and record their crop weight.
- Where the woman farmer needs support, the project organises labour gangs to undertake activities in the women' plots and the gangs are paid using loan funds.
- The payment is made to the women bank accounts.
- With control of the sales, the women decide what to send their money on.
- Where there are challenges, the project participates in holding discussions with the household to ensure harmony.
- Training and sensitization of farmers on gender issues, women rights and the need for respect for both men and women is part of the activities of the project.

All these efforts resulted into 578 (36%) women farmers (out of 1,610 registered farmers), participating in the project in their own right as farmers with decision making powers on their plots, including marketing of their produce and access to the sales which are deposited on their bank accounts.

Efforts to Strengthen Tenure Security

Plans are underway to grant farmers who are tenants on public land with either lease or freehold title deeds, and to work with landlords to let the farmers buy out the lands they are using so that they can secure their land ownership hence improving tenure security.

Strengthening the tenure security of tenants on mailo land–who typically do not have documented land rights–is more challenging. It is estimated that only about 5 per cent of members are the original mailo land owners. Most of the remaining members who are landowners acquired their land from the original mailo landowners, including women and youth who were able to purchase land with the support of the project.

A growing number of mailo land owners have or are willing to sell the land to tenants/occupants and the latter are now better able to buy the land they are using given their increased income from oil palm production. Additionally, some KOPGA members used the production loans provided by KOPGT to buy land. This approach has been particularly useful for women and youth.

Voice

Consultations with the Communities

In the appraisal stages of VODP, between 1990 and 1996, wide consultations were undertaken, involving farmers, church leaders, central government, district officials, donors and some private investors. Though stakeholder analysis was not performed (it was not a common practice at that time), smallholders, including women both on Bugalaisland and in the north-east, were enthusiastic about the project.

Decision-Making in Relation to the Investment

Business decisions are taken by the company. The smallholders involved in VODP are able to influence those decisions to a certain degree. In the planning stages, significant consideration was given to devising means of ensuring that farmers would be able to represent their interests within the partnership. Through their membership in KOPGT, and given its share in OPUL and its role on the pricing committee and services cost panel, farmers have a say in decision-making around prices paid for fresh fruit bunches, transport costs and input costs. The 10 per cent share secures two seats for the farmers on the OPUL Board which gives farmers an opportunity to influence the OPUL Board decisions concerning the business especially those that affect farmers.

Farmers Organisation as a Farmers' Voice

Farmers are organised in KOPGA and represented on the farmers' trust—KOPGT whose mandate to protect and pioneer the interests of smallholder farmers. Representatives are designated by farmers from each of the six production blocks to act as spoke persons on their behalf at KOPGT. The three seats held by farmers on the KOPGT Board of Trustees are filled through an election process.

KOPGA offers farmers their own platform, on which they can participate in discussions and formulate proposals and requests that can then be negotiated within KOPGT. The Association is democratic, with an Executive Committee and representatives to KOPGT being elected every three years, with an annual general meeting. KOPGA is organised at lower levels in Blocks (parish level) which are further organised in units at village level. At these two lower level farmer governance structures are in place with an executive elected by all farmers in the Block or unit as is applicable, every two years.

Women's Voice in the Farmers' Organisation

To ensure that women voices are heard within the farmer management structures, it is enshrined in the KOPGT and KOPGA constitution that at least 30 per cent of the leadership positions are held by women. This ensures that women are part of the management of the farmer organisation up to the highest level. They participate in the Annual General Meeting and have the same vote as their male counterparts. Currently, the Vice Chairperson of the farmer organisation is a woman. A total of 92 women are involved as leaders at different levels of the farmer structures, which 50 per cent of the leadership positions.

Risks

The risks are shared among the partners in the project. This helps the smallholders not to bear all the risks of production and marketing since all partners have their shares and have together developed mitigation measures.

Crop Production Risk

The smallholders bear crop production risks linked to weather, pests and other factors affecting harvest which could affect the farmers' income.

OPUL also bears the risk associated with crop production because they have a nucleus estate with oil palm plantations.

Government bears crop production risk which could affect the repayment of the loan funds since repayment is tagged to the sale of ffb by farmers.

The crop production risks are mitigated by involving OPUL that has experienced partners in oil palm production and, therefore, have the knowledge on how to grow and manage the oil palm plantations. Farmers use the same source of seedlings, fertilizers and other inputs as OPUL. They also follow the agronomic practices employed by OPUL.

Market Risk

Clear commitments for OPUL to purchase all farmers produce (subject to agreed quality standards) as enshrined in the cooperating agreement, at guaranteed prices shift market risk from small holders to the company.

Smallholders bear the risk fluctuating prices because the price paid for ffb is determined through a pricing formula that is tagged to the international price for crude palm oil which fluctuates.

While the pricing formula exposes farmers to fluctuating international prices, the farmers are secure from effects of price control as a result of one buyer-monopolistic situation because the price is determined through predetermined and agreed pricing formula.

To protect farmers from risks of having fresh fruit bunches unduly rejected by OPUL, the KOPGT fresh fruit bunch Inspection Officer regularly inspect the grading of fresh fruit bunches at the points of purchase (outgrowers' fields or collection points). The Inspection Officer also inspects the weighing operations at the mill and OPUL's bookkeeping and payment operations on a regular basis. The farmers are in addition regularly trained on the harvesting and grading standards.

OPUL bears the risk of marketing the palm oil although this is mitigated by the fact that the demand for palm oil in Uganda and the region is high and currently being met by imports from Malaysia and Indonesia.

OPUL also bears the risk of investing in the mill and other heavy equipment fro value addition, which farmer does not have to face.

Loan Associated Risk

The risks associated with the loans administered by KOPGT are mitigated against using the co-guaranteeing approach, whereby each loan agreement is signed jointly by a group of 5-7 farmers who mutually agree to the repayment of the financing. In the event that a group member fails to repay the minimum payment due to mismanagement of the oil plot, failure to follow the recommended practices or engagement in side selling, the co-guarantors are obliged to jointly repay the amount owed by that member.

The system encourages farmers to ensure that good crop husbandry is practiced by all group members and that the crop is sold fully to OPUL. Part of the profits made by selling the ffbs to OPUL is used to repay the loan. Farmers therefore do not use other sources of income or land/land rights to repay the loan. Farmers use 33 per cent of their sales to repay the loan until the loan is fully repaid. This enables farmers receive substantial amounts as take home income.

In addition to the co-guaranteeing approach, the oil palm crop on the land is security in itself in that if it does not bear the required fruit due to negligence by the farmer, KOPGT can take it over, manage it and recover the loan funds through sale of the harvested ffb from a given plot, then return the land and the crop to the farmer after the loan is fully recovered. This has enabled farmers participate in the project without fear that they would lose their land if they did not repay the loan funds.

In order to register, farmers are required to demonstrate their legitimate status on land and sign the Agreement of KOPGT Association. At the onset, a land title or Certificate of Occupancy was required for each plot. This gave rise to difficulties for farmers in accessing the project, since they were often tenants on their land without formal documentation, and landowners were often reluctant to negotiate and for Certificates of Occupancy to be issued. KOPGT, therefore, later relaxed the requirements so that farmers could register with a letter from the local council and the support of five witnesses where the original landowners had not reclaimed the land.Requiring farmers to demonstrate their legitimate access to the land on which they wish to cultivate oil palm, and to pledge the land for 25 years means that they maintain the use-rights of the investment, and that it can be used as collateral in accessing financing from KOPGT.

The women farmers have benefited from relaxing the requirements for access to credit and participation in the project since many of them do not land titles to present as security. They are also not scared of committing their limited land for fear of the land being taken over in case of failure to repay the loan.

They also do not have to bear the risk of over production because the company has committed to purchase all the oil palm fresh fruit bunches at a price determined using an agreed pricing formula and tagged to the international palm oil price.

Reward

The smallholder farmers including the women farmers and the private sector partner and the government all share in the rewards associated with participation in the project.

Rewards to the Smallholder Farmers

- OPUL provides a complete support package for participating growers, which includes land surveying and preparation, digging of holes, planting, provision of inputs at cost, advice, transport and other services.
- Through their membership in KOPGT, and given its share in OPUL and its role on the pricing committee, farmers have a say in decision-making around prices paid for fresh fruit bunches, transport costs and input costs.
- The pricing formula assures that the farmer gets a fair price, based on the international crude palm oil price and the oil extraction rate, and is not determined by the buyer, i.e., OPUL.
- The participating growers furthermore benefit from KOPGT's loan programme, which provides credit to smallholders for land preparation, seedlings, inputs and working capital, but also to purchase land.
- Farmers have an assured market for their produce which is normally a big challenge for smallholders.
- The 10 per cent shareholding will in future bear dividends for KOPGT members.
- The farmers have benefited from improved access to extension services from KOPGT. The staff visit farmers in their gardens and provide advice on planting, fertilizer application, harvesting, grading, to mention some.

- Farmers have an alternative source of income to fishing and timber harvesting.
- Farmers have a steady income paid monthly which will last for 25 years.
- smallholders benefit from the formal legal recognition of their tenure through official recognition by land owners. In the case of private land this is done either through the purchase of user rights using the income generated through their participation in the project or through officially recognised sharecropping agreements.

Specific Rewards to Women Farmers

- Because the extension services are given within the plantations, the women farmers have befitted from the trainings and are in some cases getting better yields. Targeted extension advice has benefited many of the women farmers that sometimes do not participate in training meetings outside their gardens because of other family chores. In this case the training is given as the farmer takes care of her garden.
- The women farmers particularly benefit by being able to participate in a commercial venture in their own right as farmers.
- They have access to their income from sale of ffbs to the mill.
- They also have improved security of tenure give that they are growing a tree crop that will last not less than 25 years.
- They are receiving an income from the sale of ffbs and are now able to purchase more land for themselves hence improving tenure security.
- Access to the land fund facilitated some of the women to purchase land for oil palm production and have now started repayment of the loan.
- Given that the loan is tagged to ffb sales, they do not have to worry about where to get funds to repay the loan and all they have to do is to manage their plantations well, which is not a big challenge since they are experienced in farming.
- They are assured of a steady income that helps them meet the household needs including educating their children and building better houses for themselves.

Rewards to the General Community

- The community benefits from a new opportunity for income generation that offers a relatively high return as a result of fresh fruit bunch prices being linked to the world crude palm oil price; and steady income due to harvesting atleast twice every month for a period 25 years.
- The nucleus estate provides employment for a number of staff. A total of 2,000 people are employed on the nucleus estate and an estimated 500 work on the fields as labourers.
- The increased investment in the region and the associated increases in incomes has had a multiplier effect whereby economic activity has expanded more broadly and the wider community is benefiting with new businesses sprouting.
- Improvements have already been seen in business and tourism in the region.
- The local community also benefits from the improved infrastructure (e.g., roads, ferry service) and services (e.g., financial, public) in the region.
- OPUL employees on the nucleus estate also benefit from free access to a health clinic maintained by OPUL.

Rewards to Government

- Employment has been generated for the population.
- Taxes are paid by the company and the workers.
- Infrastructure improvement in the area hence meeting some of the would be requirements for Government to meet.
- Increased investments in agricultural sector with value addition
- Opening up the Island to the outside world which has resulted in increasing tourism.
- Import substitution hence saving of foreign exchange.

Rewards to OPUL

- Establishment of a new business by partners in Uganda.
- Access to ffbs from smallholder farmers' gardens.
- Profits from the business.
- Market for their products.

EARLY RESULTS AND IMPACTS

Inclusive Business Models Improve Land Rights for Smallholders particularly Women Farmers

Early results suggest that the project has been successful in improving land rights as mentioned above. While challenges remain in regard to the issuance of Certificates of Occupancy, the tenure security of mailo landowners and tenants has improved. The project has provided some solutions to the impasse between mailo land owners (who have *de jure* rights but are unable to use their lands) and tenants (who have *de facto* and *de jure* rights but are unable to register their rights). The support the project provided in surveying the individual plots and developing land use plans has allowed for farmers to be located on a map with their piece of land '*kibanja*' clearly identified.

By encouraging women farmers to participate and supporting them to access land for growing oil palm, the tenure security for the women farmers has improved. Mailo landowners are reluctant to grant Certificates of Occupancy to tenants/occupants but at least some owners are willing to sell the land to tenants/occupants and the latter are now better able to buy the land they are using given their increased income from oil palm production. In some cases occupants have already purchased or are planning to approach owners to buy the land they are using. In some cases KOPGA members have used the production loans provided by KOPGT to buy land. This has particularly enabled women and youth to access land.

Rural Women Empowerment

The project has helped address gender disparity in the community, by challenging the traditional gender division of labour, increasing women's access to farm assets and income-generating activities, and promoting their participation in, and leadership of farmer groups.

Improving women decision making on the oil palm plots including access to the income from the sale of ffbs is a sign of empowerment. Women are further empowered through running of their own bank accounts where the loan funds and sales funds are deposited and accessed. Women have access to and control of land.

With increased and steady income from oil palm sales, the woman farmer has reported to be able to send her children to better schools, meet household costs, in some instances, build better houses and establish other businesses to further enhance their incomes.

Other significant impacts include higher land values, improved access to financial and government services, transport, and utilities (mobile phone services). Additionally, business, tourism and trade have improved, while increases in farmers' income have led to increased investment in housing and education.

Employment has been created for about 4,000 people; with 2,000 employed at the nucleus estate and palm oil mill, 500 field labourers on smallholder plantations and a further 1,523 directly involved as smallholder farmers. OPUL employees have benefited from wages, housing, subsidized food, free health care and social security. Employment conditions on the estate compare very favourably with similar types of work elsewhere (e.g., sugar plantations) and many are able to remit savings to their families of origin. The project also successfully empowered farmers, particularly through their membership in KOPGT and KOPGA.

Infrastructure facilities and services have improved dramatically, and production in other crops, livestock and complementary agricultural activities, tourism and other non-agricultural enterprises is expanding. Forest reserves are now clearly demarcated and illegal logging is down. There is less reliance on dwindling fish stocks.

Kalangala District benefits from funds contribution from OPUL, while the Government has benefited from taxes paid by BUL annually. Ultimately, the project has had a significant positive impact on the island. Kalangala District's ranking on the UNDP Human Development Index for Uganda is telling; while, in 2000, Kalangala District was ranked as the fifth poorest district of 76, its position had improved to 69th by 2007.

LESSONS LEARNED

The project has illustrated that an effective partnership can be developed between rural smallholders and the private sector, and that such partnerships can produce positive development outcomes for rural communities.

The project has also demonstrated that women can effectively participate in commercial ventures if supported to access land.

Furthermore, the project has shown that governments can play a positive role in agricultural investment projects, particularly in terms of creating the appropriate policy environment, mobilising smallholders to organise, support and make it possible for women farmers to participate and ensuring that the required infrastructure is made available and building trust amongst the various partners.

Flexibility in the requirements for project implementation is important if the targeted group is to be reached. Understanding the gender dynamics in the project area is important in designing interventions to support the rural poor particularly women. Without access to land, the poor rural women may continue in their poverty.

While the household approach is commendable, it may not necessarily meet the requirements of women in the household since they normally will not have a say on the use of the income. It may be worthwhile considering individuals in the household and encouraging their participation for the good of the household.

Choice of the kind of partner to participate in the inclusive business models is important, requiring flexibility and accommodation of different requirements of communities, like giving up the need to have one contiguous nucleus estate for a fairly scattered one due to the realities on ground. These kinds of partnerships take long and require involvement of many players including government, civil society and development partners.

Of particular value in terms of the project's success in improving the livelihoods of the local community was the inclusion of smallholders particularly women in all decision-making processes, beginning with the community consultations in the appraisal stages, and ensuring that, through KOPGT, they could continue to represent their interests as the partnership matures.

The establishment of KOPGA illustrates that farmers are empowered when they are organised and women are important players in the farmer organisation structures, but efforts to ensure that they are part of the leadership structure are vital.

Efforts to empower rural women in this project have illustrated that there is still need for strategic intervention to enable women participate in investments that target the rural areas, especially access to and control of factors of production, especially land.

Government has a central role in building confidence and trust among the partners and also in ensuring that both men and women participate in these interventions

That the partnership has been successfully established despite the long delays and the inexperience of the government and local communities in engaging with the private sector in such an agreement demonstrates that building partnerships takes time and that it can be worth persevering.

Conclusion

Where outside investment is needed to sustain agriculture and improve productivity and livelihoods, business models that support local farmers are more promising and involvement of smallholders as effective partners results in better development efforts and also makes business sense.

Women farmers are commercial oriented and require special support to access land so they can participate in production ventures.

To enable participation of women in such commercial ventures, deliberate efforts by the powers that be, is necessary to meet the needs of the women farmers. Small efforts like negotiation with household leaders that control factors of production can go a long way in ensuring that women who are the major providers of labour in agriculture are facilitated to be more productive and benefit from their sweat.

The success of such partnerships and the real benefits to smallholder farmers and rural communities more generally, depends on the level of ownership, voice (governance), risk-sharing and benefit-sharing between partners. Some serious investors in agriculture are increasingly looking towards mutually beneficial and sustainable partnerships as it makes good business sense. And many smallholder farmers are prepared to negotiate if they are properly consulted, well informed of the implications and potential risks, and see a real benefit.

References

FAWODE (2012), Gender Policy Brief for Uganda's Agriculture Sector.

FAOSTAT (2012). http://faostat.fao.org/CountryProfiles/Country_Profile/Direct.aspx?lang =en&area=226

Food and Agriculture Organization (2002) Small-scale oil palm processing in Africa, http://www.fao.org/docrep/005/Y4355E/y4355e03.htmFood and Agriculture Organization, Rome.

Annexure–A

Case Studies of Women Farmers in the Oil Palm inclusive Business Model

Women Benefiting from Oil Palm Growing on Bugala Island, Kalangala Distirct

In Uganda Women tend to be denied or have weaker rights on land access and use for growing commercial and perennial crops. For a long period of time cash crops growing was considered a man's domain, Vegetable oil development project changed that by engaging in gender mainstreaming in the project. The project is addressing gender equity by providing equal opportunity for men and women participation. Women have been registered in their own right as farmers. From a total of 1318 farmers 579 are females.

Cases of Women Beneficiaries

1. Zalwango Betty

Zalwango Betty is 42 years old farmer in Bbeta west Block; married with 4 children

Acreage: 6.07 ha
Previous occupation: house wife.
Land ownership: kibanja owner on public land.
FFB Harvested since 2010 to date: 128,519 kgs.
Amount received in gross: UGX 49,752,260.

Achievements

- Her children study in private boarding school in Masaka town,
- She is constructing a 3 bed roomed permanent house (in completion stages),
- She has also bought a personal car, and
- Has opened a shop which is selling merchandise on the island.

2. Nabosa Euralia

Farmer: Nabosa Euralia
Block: Bbeta west
Acreage: 3.24 ha
Previous occupation: House wife
Land ownership: Kibanja owner on public land
FFB Harvested since 2010 to date: 67,794 kgs
Amount received in gross: UGX: 26,358,990

Achievements

- Has a 2 bed roomed permanent house,
- Her children are in private boarding school,
- Bought good furniture in her house, and
- Bought Commercial plot on the main land in Masaka.

3. Namuyozi Berna

Farmer: NamuyoziBerna
Block: Bbeta west
Acreage: 4.05
Previous occupation: Brewing local drinks
Land ownership: Kibanja owner

Her palms trees have not started fruiting yet but she managed to save from paying herself for family labour instead of hiring labour and used the money to invest.

Achievements

- Has constructed a bedroomed permanent,
- Has bought commercial plot in Kampala,
- Has constructed commercial house for business in Kasekulo, and
- Has taken her children to good school.

4. Akirapa Tabitha

Akirapa Tabitha is a farmer 59 years old and widowed. She is looking after 8 children, 2 are her grand-children and 5 are orphans under her care.

Block: KayungaKizira
Acreage: 2.43 ha
Previous occupation: Burning charcoal, and subsistence farming
Land ownership: Kibanja owner
FFB Harvested since 2010 to date: 63,720 kgs
Amount received: UGX 25,292,811

Achievements

- Taking care of orphans and has taken them to good schools,
- Has constructed 2 bed roomed permanent house,
- Has bought better household items like utensils,
- Bought a mobile phone, and
- Has installed a solar panel in her house for lighting and charging her phone.

Tabitha's first house. She calls it the Charcoal house. On the left is her new house under construction which calls Binazi house meaning oil palm house. Tabitha who is in the middle of the picture was visited by the President of IFAD and Government of Uganda Officials including the Minister for Agriculture, when the picture was taken.

5. Namugalura Rose

Farmer: Namugalura rose
Block: Bujumbablock Mulabana
Acreage: 2.02 ha
Previous occupation: House wife
Land ownership: Kibanja owner
FFB Harvested since 2010 to date: 137,604 kgs
Amount received UGX: 54,182,420

Achievements

- Her family is more stable financially and they are able to manage their domestic expenditure in a much easier manner.
- Her children study in good schools in Masaka and Kampala.

- She is helping her husband to construct their permanent house.
- She is able to take care of some relatives who need assistance.

In their Own Words

The Story of Euralia Nabbosa

> "Before the Oil Palm project I was just a house wife. My husband was a fisher man and I cultivated a small plot of land for some food. If my husband did not give me money, then I could not buy salt or soap.
> When the LCs came to teach us about growing oil palm, my husband said he would continue fishing and he did not want to be a farmer. So I registered and decided to become a farmer. I now have a garden of 10 acres for myself and 3 acres for my children.
> I have been able to move from the wooden house in which we used to live and now I have built this house here. You can see I have put a garage because I also want to buy a car. I am also trying to buy a plot on the mainland in Masaka, so that I can give the houses on rent constructed over that plot. So far, I have bought one plot in the trading centre in Kalangala. I also want to get more farm land. I want to be a landlord and be able to give my children school fees to go to the best schools.
> I would still be just a housewife who sits at home waiting for my husband to come back from the lake and buy salt, food, clothes, soap, and other household things. Now, I feel I am a useful woman, I have built the house in which we live, and I am so happy that I am a farmer of oil palm."

The Story of Enid Nadunga

Enid Nadunga is a widow aged about 75 years. Before joining the oil palm project, she depended on her children for handouts and financial support which was not regular given that the children also had their own family demands. She needed money for food, medication, dressing and supporting education for her grandchildren who are orphans. One of her daughters decoded to help her join the project by buying for her about 4.8 ha of land which she planted with oil palm. Enid is now harvesting and has a monthly income of about USD350. With this money, she meets the cost of food, medication and supports her grandchildren with education requirements. She supports her village mates with food when they do not have. She is happy and does not have to depend on her children for income any more. Her children are very relieved that their mother will not lack money because she gets a monthly income that goes to her own bank account. Enid now jokes that she is a rich old woman in her village. She now employs a young man who is an orphan and is working to get tuition fees for college. This young man takes care of the oil palm garden and ensures that harvesting is done on time and fruits properly measured and delivered to the mill. In return, he gets a salary paid by Enid. He is also happy and has hope that he will be able to go to college and finalise his education. He has secured admission in a university nearby and has registered for weekend programme so he can continue with his farm work during week days and, therefore, continue earning a salary form Enid.

The Story of Nabukera and Musimenta who are oil palm farmers, adopted from the Saturday Monitor of August 10, 2013.

www.monitor.co.ug by Batte Edgar.batte@ug.nationmedia.com

"Couple Finds Gold Mine in Palm Oil"

In 2005, Edison Musimenta met partner, Rosemary Nabukeera. The two were fishing on Lake Victoria. Musimenta was also a lumber jack while Nabukeera had come from Masaka to earn to start a new life after her parents failed to support her in school. She says at home her parents only took boys to school as girls did chores in the home waiting to get married. "I needed to fulfil my own needs so I asked my parents to let me come here and start a new life," she says. There, while she carried out her fish trade, Musimenta admired her and the two started dating. "There were frequent raids on the lake by marine police and law enforcers who chased and arrested us for fishing immature fish. We got locked up too, a couple of times. We decided to find a new source of livelihood," Musimenta explains as he bends over to pick a bunch of palm oil fruits. He goes on to put more bunches into a basket which he passes on to his partner to take and heap at a central place. Musimenta and Nabukeera work together and share common goals. Working together has enabled us to get the most out of growing palm fruits," she says before she goes on to disclose that they made two million shillings the last season.

Business Partners

"She is my accountant and together we have developed. Over there is our new house," Musimenta shows me his new house. Just adjacent to this house is a wooden house where the couple and their six children stay. The development will be more fulfilling when they move into their bigger house. "We have invested some Shs 20 million in it so far," Nabukeera adds. Musimenta says that he was inspired to start growing palm oil trees when he realised that Government was supporting farmers by giving them seedlings and loans. "From cutting timber, I had earned some money and used about Shs 200,000 of this money to acquire four acres of land," Musimenta says. He used the land to grow palm trees. "We underwent some training on the best farming methods. I was taught how to line the trees and how to dig the holes. I started planting on four acres of land". This was in 2007 and a year later my wife also joined me," the father of six explains. Nabukeera believes palm trees are the way to go. "If you look after the palm tree well, you can harvest after four years which is the standard time for the trees to grow," she says. "My first harvest earned me only Shs 45,000. I did not give up. Today I can earn up to 2.5 million shillings. I now grow trees on 10 acres of land. I can earn a low of 1.3 million shillings," Musimenta explains. He adds that in a month he can harvest thrice. Explaining, "I have six children for whom I pay fees. The one in Senior Four (S.4) I pay Shs 300,000, another in S.2 I pay Shs 300,000 and then another in S.1 I pay Shs 250, 000. I have three in Primary School for whom I pay Shs 600,000 in total," Musimenta explains. For Nabukeera earning well has earned her respect at home. "I am respected at home yet I have never gone to school. When I go home my contemporaries say Miss Nabukeera has arrived," she proudly says.

25

Reducing Gender Disparity through Empowerment of Grassroots Rural Women in Bangladesh

Issues and Strategies

Abul Hossain

Introduction

Bangladesh is an agrarian country with an area of 1,47,570 sq. km where live 153.6 million people (2012) with population density 1015 persons/ sq. km (2011). The annual per capita national income is US$ 923 (FY 2012-13) and 31.50 per cent people live under poverty line I with 17.60 per cent below poverty line II. Total labour force (15+ years) is 5.41 crore (male: 3.79 and female: 1.62) of which 47.0 per cent engaged in agriculture sector followed by industrial sector (17.64%) and others (35.06%)[1]. Moreover, Bangladesh achieved gender parity at primary and secondary level of education and reduces the maternal and child mortality significantly. Around 70 per cent people live in rural areas where the main source of income is agriculture. There exists a significant disparity of the women community between the rural and urban settings. The comprehensive efforts of the Government machineries and Non-Governmental organizations (NGOs) for exploiting the potentiality of rural women create an opportunity for their socio-economic empowerment in various sectors.

The Constitution of Bangladesh provides the provisions for rural empowerment as follows:

> *The State shall adopt effective measures to bring about a radical*

> *transformation in the rural areas through the promotion of an agricultural revolution, the provision of rural electrification, the development of cottage and industries, and improvement of education, communications and public health, in those areas, so as to progressively remove the disparity in the standards of living between the urban and the rural areas.*[2]

The National Women Development Policy 2011 for economic empowerment of women emphasizes to give full and equal opportunity to women in health, education, training, lifelong education, technical education, income generation training, information and technology, etc. It also reiterates to give women the rights to wealth and resources earned through income, succession, loan, land, and market management[3].

The Fourth World Congress of Rural Women held in South Africa in 2007 reiterated the need to provide full and equal access for rural women to productive resources, including the right to inheritance and ownership of land and other property, credit/capital, appropriate technologies, markets and information.

The Dhaka Declaration of the Tenth Women Affair's Ministers Meeting of the Commonwealth Countries held in Dhaka during 17-19 June, 2013 acknowledged the progress made so far in empowering women entrepreneurs and noted that strengthening women's economic opportunities including enterprise development, will enable them to take up leadership roles. It also called for the creation of an enabling environment for everyone, both in the formal and informal sectors, and including those who may want to start up or grow their business.

The United Nations Population Information Networks (POPIN) indicates that women's empowerment consists of five dimensions: (i) women's sense of self-worth; (ii) choices; (iii) access to opportunities and resources; (iv) the power to control their own lives; and (v) ability to influence the direction of social change. The social status of women in Bangladesh has continued to remain quite low, particularly in rural areas. As a result, they face adverse conditions of economic inequality and social oppression. They are one of the most deprived groups of the society[4].

Bangladesh has made remarkable progress in the areas of poverty alleviation, reducing the prevalence of underweight children, increasing enrolment at primary schools, lowering the infant mortality rate and maternal mortality ratio, improving immunization coverage and reducing the incidence of communicable diseases[5].

Bangladesh's Progress on the MDGs

Bangladesh has already met several targets of the Millennium Development Goals (MDGs) like reducing poverty gap ratio, attaining gender parity at primary and secondary education, under-five mortality reduction, and others. The inclusive growth has contributed to poverty reduction from 56.7 per cent in 1991-92 to 31.5 per cent in 2010. But challenges of reducing income inequality and low participation of women remain a major concerns. Promoting equitable access to education, reduction of dropouts, improvement in completion of the cycle, and specific public interventions on focusing girl's education help to achieve gender parity (girls: 99.4% and boys: 97.2%). The successful programmes for immunization, control of diarrhoeal diseases and vitamin A supplementation contributed to reduce the under-five mortality rate (from 146/1000 live births in 1990-91 to 53/1000 in 2011) and infant mortality rate (from 92/1000 live births in 1990-91 to 43/1000 in 2011) significantly. Maternal mortality rate has been declined from 574/100,000 live births in 1999-91 to 194/100,000 live births in 2010[6].

Microcredit Programme for Self-employment of Women

The main objective of this programme is to improve the socio-economic status of women through poverty reduction and generation of self-employment opportunities by providing microcredit to the poor and distressed women[7]. The NGOs have created huge job opportunities for the poor women by their microcredit programmes. It is noted that 30 organizations (excluding Grameen Bank) disbursed Tk. 24,096.95 crore in 2011. The outstanding loan stands at Tk. 20,785 crore among 188.9 lakh poor people and total savings stand as Tk.7,352 crore in FY 2011-12 and over 95 per cent of the savers are women[8]. The Grameen Bank, up to June 2012, disbursement Tk.76,488.90 among 83.79 lakh people of which 80.54 lakh were females. It delivers products like home loan, education loan and credit to street beggars[9]. In addition, State Owned Commercial Banks (SOCB) disbursed Tk. 22110.89 crore and cumulative beneficiaries are 1.29 crore (approximately) with recovery rate 97.44 per cent[10]. Moreover, 12 administrative ministries disbursed Tk. 100,181.63 up to June 2012. To discipline microcredit operations of NGOs, a Microcredit

Regulatory Authority Act came into force in 2006 and a Microcredit Regulatory Authority (MRA) was established In order to sustain the microcredit programmes for poverty reduction, the Government emphasizes on developing small entrepreneurs[11].

Migration (both Internal and External)

It is estimated that around one crore Bangladeshi citizens are working around the world, majority of whom are in Middle Eastern countries. These migrant workers sent US$ 14.17 billion in 2012 which is 11 per cent of GDP, six times of foreign aid and 13 times of foreign investment[12]. Moreover, due to river erosion in coastal areas of the south and desertification on the north, other natural disasters, and seasonal unemployment people migrate from rural areas to the urban areas (particularly, the capital and other major cities). Most of these overseas workers and internally migrated people send the major portion of their earnings to their families in the rural areas. This financial support provides the opportunity to their inmates for doing micro business, purchasing property, educating children and renovating households. It also contributes to raise their social status. The cumulative impact of such support is manifolds.

Development of Women Entrepreneurship

The cooperative movement in the 1960s and the microcredit support in 1980s mobilized the poor women community in the rural area for developing various entrepreneurships. The group formation of the women for collateral free credit, participation in the community and courtyard meeting during disbursement, recovery, and life skill training make them aware about the changed perspective of the society. This social engagement of the rural women learned to start the micro business, go for marketing in their locality, take their product to a better growth centres and sometimes link with chain marketing facilities. The potential entrepreneurs even participate in national and international fairs and export their products to other countries. The inclusion of such women entrepreneurs into various chambers of commerce and industries and creation of Women Chamber of Commerce and Industries provides incentives for their further empowerment. A study conducted recently made following recommendations for improving women's access to productive resources as well as their status in the rural community:

(i) enhancing rural women's income generating activities by providing literacy, technical information and skills, inputs and credit (in kind of cash) for agricultural and non-agricultural production; (ii) transferring cost-effective and suitable technologies for women through extension agencies; (iii) establishing formal and non-formal institutions for technical assistance and capacity building for women; (iv) ensuring women's participation in rural development schemes and community decision-making;(v) ensuring women's rights to land and property by the government including local authorities; and (vi) implementing awareness raising programmes on different aspects of gender at the village level[13].

Social Safety Net Programmes (SSNPs)

In 2010-2011 fiscal year there were 99 social safety net programmes under 21 ministries/divisions and total allocation was Tk.19,310 crore. Major activities included cash transfer for allowance of old citizens, destitute women, insolvent freedom fighters, climate change fund, welfare fund for poor lactating mother and national services, physically handicapped and orphans. The major ongoing social safety net programmes include: food for works programme (FFW), vulnerable group development programme (VGD), vulnerable group feeding (VGF), food and livelihood security programme (FLS), rural infrastructure maintenance programme (test relief). Special ongoing programmes include employment generation for the ultra-poor, *ashrayan* (poverty alleviation and rehabilitation) project, and *ektibari ekti khamar* (one house, one farm).

Allocation Pattern of Social Safety Net Programmes[14]

Programmes	*Budget 2011-12*	*Budget (2012-13)*
Cash Transfer (various allowances)	7069.70	7645.58
Cash Transfer (special)	56.10	59.12
Food Security Programmes: Social Protection	7102.57	7072.55
Microcredit Programmes	323.00	342.70
Miscellaneous fund	3635.53	2813.29

Source: Finance Division, Ministry of Finance

Cash transfer programmes include: (i) old-age allowance, (ii) rehabilitation of acid-burnt women and physically handicapped,

(iii) allowance for physically challenged insolvent citizens, (iv) allowance for widowed, deserted and destitute women, (v) maternity allowance for poor women, (vi) honorarium programme for insolvent freedom fighters and their dependents, (vii) training and self-employment programmes for insolvent freedom fighters and their dependents.

Impact of Social Safety Net Programmes

Vulnerable Group Development (VGD) Programme

The Vulnerable Group Development Programme has been developed for food security and empowerment of the ultra-poor women of the rural areas. Under this programme, training on awareness building, self-employment and income generation activities are being provided. Throughout Bangladesh 7,50,000 beneficiary women are receiving 30 kg of rice or 25 kg of nutritional flour every month for a period of 2 years cycle. The beneficiaries include landless and assetless women who are widowed, divorced, deserted by husband, mother of malnourished child, lactating mother, and whose husbands are sick or disabled. A recent study conducted by Bangladesh Academy for Rural Development (BARD) reveals the impact of VGD programme on family income and food security as follows:

Change of Status of the beneficiaries	*Before participation (%)*	*After participation (%)*
Food security for the whole of year	1	24
Food deficit throughout the year	82	30
Take 3 meals a day	17	50

There are some impact of VGD programme and these are as follows: (a) it changes the food habit, (b) price of rice and wheat does not increase in the market if there is VGD programme area, (c) daily food is assured, (d) beneficiaries can meet their other needs, (e) creates social awareness, (f) family income raised, (g) number of beggars could not raise in programme areas, and (h) after the ending of cycle, beneficiaries can become self-reliant.

Lactating Mother Programme

Under this programme, 77,625 working lactating mothers of city corporations, districts and other municipal areas are given a monthly allowance of Tk. 350 for 2 years. In 2013-14 fiscal year the rate of allowance has been increased by Tk. 50 and the number of beneficiaries by 10 per cent. The main objective of this programme is to bring overall change in health, birth control, nutrition and livelihood. Sixty four NGOs, BGMEA and BKMEA are providing training to these beneficiaries[15]. A recent study conducted by Rural Development Academy (RDA) reveals the impact of this programme on family income and food security as follows:

Change in socio-economic condition	*Before participation (%)*	*After participation (%)*
Family income	Tk. 2710	Tk. 3971
Number of family with food availability throughout the year	1	28
Family with at least food arrangement for 6 months	63	88
Take 3 meals a day	15	68

The impacts of the this programme include: (i) health, nutrition status as well as child's physical condition have been improved than others; (ii) beneficiaries eagerly provide exclusive breast-feeding to their children; (iii) consume nutritious food during pregnancy; (iv) suffered less from severe complicacy during pregnancy and post-natal period; (v) beneficiaries enjoyed better social status than others; (vi) demand for dowry and torture by husband reduced; and (vii) prevalence of adoption of family planning methods increased.

However, the challenges of SSNPs include (i) due to absence of data base of poor population there is a difficulty in selecting areas of ultra-poor population; (ii) difficulties and expansion coordination activities due to excess amount of extension and implementation of activities; and (iii) absence of skills of local government organizations, especially union parishad in implementation of activities. An initiative has been made by the government to create a national population register through collecting geometric information of ultra-poor population to prepare database of poor population and distribute smart card. A central monitoring committee has also formed for overall monitoring, supervision, and coordination of SSNPs and to enhance the capacity to women machinery for effective implementation of the programmes.

Promoting Victorious Women (Joyeeta)

The poor women in the rural areas are mobilized to form cooperative society being registered under the Department of Women Affairs (DWA) of the Ministry of Women and Children Affairs. The number of the members vary from 50 to 200. There are 16,000 such societies already registered under the DWA as on December 2012. The members of these societies are given income generation training on various trades at the Women Training Centres (WTC) in the offices of 64 District Women Affairs Officers and 192 Upazila Women Affairs Officers. The women after receiving such training become confident about their potentiality to start new business. Ministry of Women and Children Affairs give a grant of Tk. 20-30 thousand to promising societies as grants. The various government departments, non-government organizations, State owned commercial banks, specialized commercial banks, and other non-conventional financial institutions provide microcredit for small business. They utilize the grant as seed money and multiply it by providing loan to their members. The new entrepreneurs have to face three major challenges as follows: (i) scope of marketing of the products in the local area is very limited; (ii) competition with professional designers and business community; and (iii) lack of resources for graduation towards higher level of production.

To overcome these problems the government established one market place Joyeeta (victorious women) at the Rapa Plaza of the Dhanmandi, in the heart of the Dhaka City. A total of 140 shops are allotted to the successful women societies in the shopping complex. Moreover, the women who run the shops are given free accommodation by the government to reduce their burden of staying in Dhaka. The grassroots women entrepreneurs have direct access to the market in the capital. As there is no middlemen in the business they can maximize their profit. The entrepreneurs are given special training on marketing techniques. The Department of Women Affairs has also taken initiatives to organize special training programmes for them on latest designs and techniques so that they can compete other business professionals.

Conclusion

It is evident that without addressing gender inequality, the desired development may not be achievable. Traditional attitudes and gender-stereotyped roles towards women often prevent society as a whole to recognize women's equal rights in both private and public sphere. The comprehensive efforts by the Government machineries and non-government organizations help to improve the livelihood, decrease the prevalence of poverty, and reduce maternal and child mortality significantly. The attainments of gender parity in primary and secondary levels, increased access of the women community to various sectors, and supports under social security and safety net programmes will contribute towards further development in future. Moreover, the efforts of mobilizing the poor rural women, given them training and credit, encouraging them to start new entrepreneurships and linking them to the marketing chains in the urban areas create an enormous opportunity for employment generation. It is expected that continuation and expansion of these efforts may help revolutionize the rural economy.

Notes

1. *Bangladesh Economic Review 2013*, p. xvii.
2. *Constitution of the People's Republic of Bangladesh,* October 2011, Article 16.
3. *National Women Development Policy 2011*, Ministry of Women and Children Affairs, GoB, March 2011.
4. *Rural Women's Empowerment through Self-income Generating Activities: A Study on NGOs Credit Programs in Bangladesh* by Md. Rafiqul Islam. wwwjournals.sfu.ca/jgcee/index.php/jgcee/article.
5. Millennium Development Goals (MDGs): Bangladesh Progress Report 2012. General Economic Division (GED), Bangladesh Planning Commission, June 2013.
6. *Bangladesh Economic Review 2012*, p. 234.
7. *Ibid.*, p. 234
8. *Ibid.*, p. 242.
9. *Ibid.*, p. 245.
10. *Ibid.*, p. 246.
11. *Ibid.*, p. 248.
12. *Budget Speech (2013-14)*, Ministry of Finance, 6th June 2013, p. 63.
13. Shahnaj Perveen, "Access of Rural Women to Productive Resources in Bangladesh: A Pillar for Promoting their Employment", *International Journal of Rural Studies*, Vol. 15(1), April 2008.
14. *Bangladesh Economic Review 2013*, p. 246.
15. BGMEA stands for Bangladesh Garments Manufacturing and Exporting Association and BKMEA Stands for Bangladesh Knitwear Manufacturing and Exporting Association.

26

Strategising Livelihood Approaches through Organisations

A Case Study of Chhattisgarh (India)

Sonali Mukherjee

Introduction

There has been considerable debate surrounding the impact of Self-Help Groups (SHGs) on poverty alleviation and women's empowerment since the last three decades. Survival in impoverished conditions is a huge challenge which the poor all over the world brave through. Situation is worsened by failing State machinery and unplanned development policies. Further, poor women live life on a double-edged sword as they are physically weak and socially abused and excluded. Situation examined in this chapter is that of two villages in Raigarh district in Chhattisgarh State in India. Since the 1980s, microfinance has been popularly upheld as the vehicle for poverty alleviation and women's empowerment, especially through group loans. Women's participation was suddenly pushed forth vigorously in the development plans. Grameen Bank model has pioneered the concept of addressing the serious issue of poverty through microcredit to rural women (Yunus, 2004). Access to immediate credit has helped the cause of the rural poor to some extent but certainly it has not benefited women in gaining economic, political or social agency in the wider societal context (Kannabiran, 2005; Muhammad, 2009; Sharma, 2011; Kumar, 2013). Some of the studies (Galab and Rao, 2003; Kabeer, 2005) do report enhancement in women's confidence, knowledge, ability to negotiate, etc., but most scholars have agreed upon the fact that microfinance cannot be used as a tool for women's empowerment.

As observed by other studies as well (Kumar, 2013), one of the major problems in the microcredit enterprise is that a huge number of petty traders or micro enterprises have emerged without linkages to the bigger markets. This has created huge gaps between their aspirations and actual achievements resulting in sheer frustration. This trend is a potential threat to the entire enterprise. Also creation of other sources of livelihood has further taken the rural population away from agriculture. This is not to argue that the rural poor should not be exposed to other sources of livelihood but to say that backbone of rural economy is agriculture and efforts should be made to consolidate this by providing the poor not only with material resources but also knowledge resources in terms of training and better skills to help the dwindling agricultural scenario. Rural women especially the *dalits*, are anyway involved with almost all the agricultural and other allied activities. To harness their skills further and help them in joint leasing of land would help them in their economic productivity and overall economy would also get a boost. Microcredit enterprises operate through the formation of Self-help groups.

About Self-Help Groups

A SHG is typically an association of 10 to 15 marginalised women who have realized the importance of saving and have joined hands in improving their impoverished State. These groups have helped to create an identity for its individual members and also provided a platform for redistribution of knowledge base regarding various government plans and policies. When the SHG stabilizes in form and activity, then only it moves to the next level, i.e., of the cluster. SHGs of adjacent villages which are within a radius of 2-3 kms are combined together to form clusters. These clusters then together take up the issues which are extremely pertinent like basic infrastructure facilities and sometimes locally relevant, like cases of alcoholism, domestic violence, etc. Since their strength is more, therefore, they are able to put pressure on the Panchayat to get work done. Cluster also helps in maintaining discipline in the individual SHGs. Further, these clusters together form a bigger body, i.e., a federation. A federation is responsible for improving access to entitlements and public services; and for saving and credit function by providing systematic services and support. All members from each cluster elect one among themselves as representatives who make up the governing body of the federation and attend its monthly meetings. They are responsible for planning activities, monitoring and evaluation, and giving direction to the staff of the federation. Though this work is primarily based on the SHGs formed by PRADAN[1], there are 3,247 SHGs in Raigarh district which are formed by Government[2]. They have been formed under the microfinance scheme. But unfortunately, the presence of these SHGs is just not felt in Raigarh. Most of these groups have simply disappeared. It would be worthwhile to analyse the success story of PRADAN. It has helped 8,652 rural women to organize in 721 SHGs.

To begin the discussion, some of the questions addressed in this chapter are:

1. What were the factors of change? How resistant or amenable were they as individuals or as a community with the advent of the concept?
2. What are the strategies that facilitate the organisation of poor women into such SHGs? In other words, what are the various negotiation strategies of these women *vis-à-vis* their men which enables their participation in a group activity like that of an SHG?
3. What did they really seek when they first joined a SHG? Has that been fulfilled? How enabling or disenabling has been their journey as part of a SHG? Society being highly patriarchal, where are the men of these households located?
4. Where do they see themselves now? What are their future ambitions?
5. Ambiguities or problems on the way to their empowerment? Do they feel empowered? What are the real challenges to the empowerment and liberation of women? Some suggestions for future or way forward.

Methodology

The present study is focused on women located in Raigarh district of Chhattisgarh State in India. Intensive study was conducted in two different villages namely, Bhagwanpur and Amapal in Tamnar Block. In Bhagwanpur, eight SHGs and in Amapal, five SHGs have been formed by PRADAN. It can be pointed out that since PRADAN was approached for examining the role of SHGs in poverty alleviation, it is possible that PRADAN mentioned only about those areas where the SHG created by them have been functioning reasonably well and have been able to create visible impact. Methodologically it would have been incorrect if this study was a comparative impact assessment of all the SHGs created by

PRADAN but this study is only trying to assay a path towards poverty alleviation through SHGs. So it is only reasonable that successful case studies are quoted in this chapter to uphold the strategy of creating SHGs and also locate the 'empowerment strategy' within a certain context, that is, of creating an environment for the women to make a sustained effort towards their personal and community growth.

Fifty SHG members from Bhagwanpur and thirty SHG members from Amapal were interviewed through semi-structured interview schedules. Observation method and focused group discussions (FGDs) were used to substantiate the narratives and interviews. Some of the questions in the interview schedule were answered by recall method by the informants. These SHG members were indebted to PRADAN for what they believed was a significant contribution of PRADAN as they showed the path out of poverty. There was a possibility of their distorting their answers regarding the organisation as they could fear they would be excluded from their future interventions, therefore, repetitive questioning was done to cross check the answers and recognise further issues for analysis. Other women, thirty of them, who were not SHG members were called for focused group discussions so as to derive a comparative perspective.

Further, FGDs were held with both members as well as non-members. Through FGDs, an effort was made to ascertain their needs and aspirations and also the quotient of their empowerment due to the membership of a SHG. Also a sense of the prevailing perceptions regarding the functioning of these groups; and ways and means of improving the situation further could be derived through these FGDs. Men dominate the social, economic as well as political life of rural women. Therefore, their views were also taken. Five men from each village were included in group discussions.

Findings

Raigarh district in Chhattisgarh where this work is located is known for its expanding industries like sponge iron industries, coal mining, etc., but lack of a strong organizational base does not let the local rural population reap the benefits. Women are in a worse situation as they are usually part of unorganized labour force recruited through contractual agencies that run the entire business on their whims and fancies. So the women, who are battling with the patriarchal mindsets of their men, are also a victim of the restrictive occupational structures. In such a state, livelihoods of the major chunk of the communities are dependent on meagre resources. Some of the men in Bhagwanpur village work in Jindal

Steel Plant Limited in the semi-skilled and skilled sector. They got these jobs in lieu of their agricultural land which by their own admission was not very fertile. Some of the women work as part-time helps in the houses of the officers working in the steel plant. Some have rented a section of their house to outsiders working in the plant, thus adding to the income. Women collect fuel wood from the forest and sell. This income has gone down because of increasing deforestation. In Amapal, the primary occupation is agriculture on self-owned small lands or leased in land. They sell their vegetables produced from the kitchen garden and also the fuel wood collected from the forest.

To generate awareness about livelihood sources a lot of persuasion by PRADAN was required to bring together people from all communities. Poverty and landlessness brought together backward castes like Yadav, Rawat, Chauhan, Channahu, etc.; Scheduled Tribes like Tikri, Oraon, Munda, etc.; and general caste Hindus. All came in unison to voice their problems and issues. It has been projected in other studies that the collective identity people put forth to make public claims is derived from common interests, experiences and solidarity (Taylor, 1999). This collective strength had initially kick started the momentum.

Table 26.1: List of Names of SHGs in Bhagwanpur

S. No.	*Name of the SHG*	*No of years of establishment*	*Present Status*
1.	Chandrahasini	5 years	Running
2.	Gulab	7 years	Running
3.	Suryamukhi	5 years	Running
4.	Sharda	8 years	Running
5.	Jyoti	11 years	Running
6.	Saraswati	5 years	Running
7.	Lakshmi	11 years	Almost non-functioning
8.	Gayatri	5 years	Running

In Bhagwanpur, except Lakshmi SHG, all the others are doing fine. When comparison was made with other SHGs, it was realized that in Lakshmi, leadership is not strong enough to hold the reins and enforce discipline on the other members. Also new members have not joined that group since a long time. A loan amount of ₹ 26,000 is due to the bank. Members are not willing to return that amount. Pressure is being built on the members in the cluster meetings to repay the loan amount

There are some guidelines which need to be strictly adhered to maintain a SHG. All SHG members must meet their respective groups on a designated day of every week. Also there is a fixed time for the meeting which is usually in the afternoon. At the beginning of the meeting, an incense stick is lit and till the time it is burning people are allowed to enter otherwise the member has to pay the fine of an absentee. If somebody does not have a valid reason and remains absent then she has to pay a minimal fine. A member has to deposit some saving and the fixed amount of money towards the loan (if she has taken any) every Sunday. If the person does not get the fixed amount of money (towards the loan amount) any week then that member has to pay double amount next time. Fearing the doubling of the amount the member does not default. These rules are strictly followed by Jyoti SHG as reiterated by its chief and, therefore, this SHG has survived 12 years. There are three important assets of an SHG; register, treasury box and the key to the box. These three items are kept with three different members by rotation. All the decisions like loan amount, interest rate, repayment strategy, dealing with defaulters, etc., are all taken collectively in the group.

Table 26.2: List of SHGs in Amapal

S. No.	*Name of the SHG*	*No of years of establishment*	*Present Status*
1.	Jyoti Jwala	12 years	Running
2.	Arti	5 years	Running
3.	Shanti	8 years	Running
4.	Purnima	4 years	Running
5.	Shruti	5 years	Running

The mean age of members from both villages was found to be 37 years. In fact, mean age of members of SHG which were comparatively new and were running for five years, were found to be 28 years. It can be estimated that younger women have been more enthusiastic about joining SHGs. It is probably their stamina and will power which has sustained their membership. Also they have lapped up the opportunity owning to their courage to take up new challenges. FGD on this particular aspect revealed that in many cases, it has been the support of their mother-in-law which has helped them in their participation.

Saving was introduced which led the poor people to realize the importance of saving at the time of crisis. Except one 79 members felt this to be the primary reason for them to join SHG. They could take loan at an annual interest of 2 per cent whereas earlier they were taking loan from moneylenders at a monthly interest of 3 to 5 per cent. Many a time they deposited their gold, silver and even utensils to get some money.

Since the interest was huge, therefore, they could afford to take loan only at times of acute crises. Now they save and are in a position to take lcan from Raigarh Grameen Bank where all these SHGs have an account except Jyoti SHG (in Bhagwanpur) which has an account with Allahabad Bank. All the members feel happy to have come out of the grip of the moneylenders. This was the enabling factor for men of 54 per cent of the respondents' household to let them join a SHG.

40 per cent of the members informed that their mobility outside the village has increased in the post-membership period. Hence, they have become more worldly-wise. They regretted being illiterate or lowly educated, partly for want of opportunity and partly for being oblivious of the world outside. All these members are trying to ensure that their children are able to access education. 21 per cent of the members are sending their children beyond matriculation. Most members felt that they have slowly and steadily realized some of their dreams. 15 per cent have built a *pucca* (cemented) house with a toilet within the compound of their house; 20 per cent have bought television sets and 8 per cent have bought motorbikes.

A great sense of achievement is reflected by the members during FGDs. The fact that they have better purchasing power than earlier times keeps them pushing forward. Over the years their confidence level and self esteem has gone up. They felt that they have more control and agency over their own and their husbands' earnings. Many of them have bought small pieces of gold and silver jewellery with or without the permission of the male members of the household. Some of the women expressed extreme relief for being economically independent and not at the mercy of their husbands and sons. Non-members who were present in the FGDs felt at a loss. Most of them said that their husbands were against group solidarity. Probably they felt threatened that they would no longer be able to subjugate their women as they might get more assertive. Therefore, to dissuade these women, their husbands always found some or the other fault with SHG members. They alleged that the members neglected their homes and their families especially their children. To make matters worse, these men sometimes tried insinuating the male members of the households of the members.

Most of the men who were present in these meetings shied away from commenting, but one of them emphatically said that if women are not kept in control, there is a breakdown of society. Nonetheless most people agreed upon the generation of awareness of better social values. There is a significant rise in the age at marriage. It has gone up from

11-12 years to 20-21 years for girls and from 14-15 years to 22-24 years for boys. This has prevented girls from getting bogged down by pregnancy at an early age. This leaves them with an opportunity of acquiring education and other technical knowledge. They can also learn some craft which could help them to earn some extra money in the future.

A Narrative Summing up a Member's View on SHG

Latadidi is an ordinary village woman, aged 42 years, had no education, and is today a woman who not only solves her own problems but others as well. She is well aware of all the government schemes running in the village. She seemed unhappy with the fact that there is lot more policies available for the rural poor but it is not reaching them because of lack of propaganda and non-cooperation of the government officials. She planned to raise her voice along with others on the Federation meet. She sums up thus,

> *"Earlier when there was no SHG, we were scared of coming out Now we can run the household as per our choice. We discuss and do as we think is right. Earlier we could not save five rupees also. From the time I have joined SHG, I am in touch with others. Every Sunday, we meet at 2 pm for an hour. Every Sunday we deposit at least ten rupees and a tally is kept in the collection register. When any need for education, health or agriculture arises we can take out money. Some people keep poultry, animal husbandry, and earning some money as well. I am very proud of the fact that our SHGs are doing so well. Since the group meets every Sunday we are able to share our joys and sorrows. In case there is a problem in any of the household we solve it through the SHG. We are in touch with the Panchayat. In the Gram Sabha meeting we women make our presence felt. Wherever there is a need for a repair of the road or boring then we put it across to the Gram Sabha. All of us have got rid of our fear and shame. We speak up openly. We discuss health issues as well. If someone is not well then we send the person to the hospital or get a nurse or a mitanin to sort out the health problem. Hygiene is also taken care of. We keep a check on the mid-day meal provided in the school and also on the food provided at the anganwadi. We also discuss about issues regarding bank loan. We also discuss in the cluster meetings*

> *about our problems. Now there is a representative from each village in the Raigarh Mahila Sangh. We are planning to demand a* bhavan *for holding our meetings. We will put it up with the collector. We are together, therefore, we do not feel lonely. A widow also does not feel that her husband is not there. Earlier no one (women) used to go to the market. Now our respect has gone up. Even a drunkard wishes me on the road and enquires about my whereabouts. We do not want to cease being members of SHG, we only hope to take it forward and flourish. Now we do not have to beg from others. Earlier we would pledge our jewellery, even our utensils and take loan. We pay our interest on time and we do not feel bad as we can take loan anytime, our bank is always there for us. Earlier we had to give huge interest and, therefore, we could not take loan, now we can dream of big things and fulfil our wish as well."*

Analysis and Conclusion

Within the cultural matrix of a rural setting, women are inheritantly in a subjugated position. Impoverished state and rigid patriarchal structures limit any form of social, economic and political movement of women. In such a restrictive gendered space, women need that extra 'push' to take measured steps out of poverty. This chapter would like to point that providing microcredit to women through self-help groups can help them move out of poverty provided a focused and sustained effort is made.

There is a distinct difference between the two village settings. Bhagwanpur is slowly turning into a small town with better infrastructural facilities including healthcare, education and anganwadi services. Women in Bhagwanpur are more proactively involved in SHGs compared to Amapal. Depending on the success of the SHG, different women showed different levels of economic agency. Members of SHG of Bhagwanpur showed higher levels of economic agency compared to SHG of Amapal. Cohesiveness among the group members seemed to be their general strength.

Their empowerment is not in gaining individual agency but in dealing with the stress and bringing the family above the impoverished state. So their accomplishment in terms of developing resources (borrowing from Kabeer, 2005) is most prominently put forth by most individuals as evidence of success. Achievements for the family are considered more valuable than self achievement. Their self esteem gets boosted with this. Taking this argument further then one could probably derive that with access to resources or opportunities of work or training women in Bhagwanpur and Amapal village have come this far.

It can be assumed to an extent that with garnering of resources, their contribution to household economy is noted (may not be appreciated openly given the patriarchal mindset). This gives them a kind of agency in terms of physical mobility as participation in many of the activities involves movement outside home. Vocal expressions by the women in gendered spaces like public meetings, market areas, Panchayat Ghar, etc., may not have found so much of place, but their visibility in these places has gone up. Also, intra-women conversations across villages have broadened their world view. This further involves the suppressed voices in legitimizing their needs and confronting their men folk at least within the household.

Earlier, even if some of the women were interested in taking up work in the labour market, they were unable to do so in the absence of their husbands' permission. Patriarchal mode of dominance did not allow the women to have any kind of autonomy in the choice of work. She had to look after household chores which did not give her much time to work outside home. Also, there were no facilities for looking after small children. Now, there are anganwadis successfully run by the government. Further, being (mostly) illiterate, she had no access to any kind of formal training which would help her to decide the kind of wage she could earn through her skills. Presently, there is a significant rise in the number of girls going to school. The avenues of occupation which were unexplored have been opened. They have learnt to manage household work with other income generating work. Silk reeling craft has been learnt by many young women and girls. All these activities have helped in capacity building. It is extremely essential to take this course of capacity building to the next stage by providing them with resources to augment their production capacity; whether in silk reeling craft or handloom or agriculture or any other. Also linkages to the market should be provided. Unless this is done, poor with their meagre resource base would always be on a shaky ground.

Currently it is observed that the money that is so earned is spent in meeting the household expenses and also small saving. Since the men are in the habit of quarrelling and snatching their income after drinking, women have learnt to deal with this problem in a better way. SHGs of Bhagwanpur and Amapal have even closed down the local liquor shops in the villages. Many a time women save a little of their earning and spend it on themselves, by buying sarees, and even jewellery.

An incident was narrated during a FGD, where the members could show courage in taking a stand in favour of a girl who was molested in

Bhagwanpur. They not only caught the offender but were also able to hand him to the police. Joint expression of revulsion over sexual violence is an indicator of strength. They are no longer willing to suffer violation of their dignity at the hands of men (at least from men outside their household). While narrating the incident, a sense of pride and achievement was palpable in their voices. These forms of resistance are positive indicators of empowerment which they themselves endorse by comparing their present strength with their earlier subjugated form.

The contributions made by women towards sustenance of family have long been recognized since the work of Boserup (1970). Despite this recognition, there is a constant negation of their existence in the social sphere. Most of these SHGs comprise women and they are the ones given training for various skill development. If they succeed to hone their skills and develop a successful economic enterprise they are further pushed into another circle of workload and if they fail then they are burdened with guilt and ridiculed for their efforts. Therefore, it is extremely essential to address this gendered aspect by including men in all training workshops and skill development programmes (Kannabiran, 2005). Most of the communities are patriarchal. Male exclusive growth policies meant for women's empowerment would not go down well with the men as pointed by Galab and Rao, (2003). Their study reported that men did not cooperate and sometimes they deliberately sabotaged the efforts of women.

In the case of PRADAN, there was constant motivation from them along with encouraging participation by the people; then intervention at all levels and finally there was follow-up, which led to their success. In the case of SHGs formed under the government scheme, there is simply no follow up. One important thing that was felt time and again while interviewing the members is that they were too used to the help provided by PRADAN. The members are resentful of the fact that PRADAN is slowly withdrawing its support. In that case, there is always a chance that these SHGs might slowly fade away. Therefore, there is need for regular training classes by experts who can wean them away from external support in a more effective manner. While it is possible to emulate the success of PRADAN in the formation of SHGs but it is important to learn from their mistakes as well. Relevant and logical changes need to be made in the implementation process to make the SHGs more sustainable. While concluding it is worth quoting Kabeer (2005, p. 4709) that it is ultimately "the calibre and commitment of the people who are responsible for delivery. The design of financial services to the poor should be based on an empirically based understanding of the relationship between context, approach and impact".

Notes

1. Professional Assistance for Development Action.
2. Data provided by Ministry of Women and Child Development.

References

Boserup, E. (1970, reprinted 1997). *Women's Role in Economic Development*. London: Earthscan.

Galab, S. and N. Chadrasekhara Rao. (2003). Women's Self-Help Groups: Poverty alleviation and empowerment. *Economic and Political Weekly*. 38(12/13): 1274-1283.

Kabeer, Naila. (2005). Is Microfinance a 'Magic Bullet' for Women's Empowerment?: Analysis of Findings from South Asia. *Economic and Political Weekly*. October 29, 2005: 4709-4718.

Kabeer, Naila and Helzi Naponen. (2005). Social and Economic Impacts of PRADAN's Self-Help Group Microfinance and Livelihoods Promotion Programme. Working Paper No. 11. Improving the Impact of Microfinance on Poverty. Imp-Act. Sussex: The Institute of Development Studies.

Kannabiran, Vasanth. (2005). Marketing Self-Help, Managing Poverty. *Economic and Political Weekly*. 40(34): 3716-3717-3719.

Kumar, Lakshmi. (2013). Illusion of Women Empowerment in Microfinance: A Case Study. *Economic and Political Weekly*. 48(15): 70-76.

Leach, Fiona and Shashikala Sitaram. (2002). Microfinance and Women's Empowerment: A Lesson from India. *Development in Practice*. 12(50): 575-588.

Muhammad, Anu. (2009). Muhammad Grameen and Microcredit: A Tale of Corporate Success. *Economic and Political Weekly*. 44(35): 35-42.

Sharma, Kumud. (2011). Small Loans, Big Dreams: Women and Microcredit in a Globalising Economy. *Economic and Political Weekly*. 46(43): 58-63.

Taylor, Verta. (1999). Gender and Social Movements: Gender Processes in Women's Self-help Movements. *Gender and Society*. 13(1): 8-33.

Yunus, Muhammad. (2004). Grameen Bank, Microcredit and Millennium Development Goals. *Economic and Political Weekly*. September 4, 2004: 4077-4080.

Index